KEY CONCEPTS IN ROMANTIC LITERATURE

Palgrave Key Concepts

Palgrave Key Concepts provide an accessible and comprehensive range of subject glossaries at undergraduate level. They are the ideal companion to a standard textbook making them invaluable reading to students throughout their course of study and especially useful as a revision aid.

Key Concepts in Accounting and Finance
Key Concepts in Business Practice
Key Concepts in Criminal Justice and Criminology
Key Concepts in Cultural Studies
Key Concepts in Drama and Performance (second edition)
Key Concepts in e-Commerce
Key Concepts in Human Resource Management
Key Concepts in Information and Communication Technology
Key Concepts in International Business
Key Concepts in Innovation
Key Concepts in Language and Linguistics (second edition)
Key Concepts in Law (second edition)
Key Concepts in Leisure
Key Concepts in Management
Key Concepts in Marketing
Key Concepts in Operations Management
Key Concepts in Philosophy
Key Concepts in Politics
Key Concepts in Public Relations
Key Concepts in Psychology
Key Concepts in Social Research Methods
Key Concepts in Sociology
Key Concepts in Strategic Management
Key Concepts in Tourism

Palgrave Key Concepts: Literature
General Editors: John Peck and Martin Coyle

Key Concepts in Contemporary Literature
Key Concepts in Creative Writing
Key Concepts in Crime Fiction
Key Concepts in Medieval Literature
Key Concepts in Modernist Literature
Key Concepts in Postcolonial Literature
Key Concepts in Renaissance Literature
Key Concepts in Romantic Literature
Key Concepts in Victorian Literature
Literary Terms and Criticism (third edition)

Further titles are in preparation
www.palgravekeyconcepts.com

**Palgrave Key Concepts
Series Standing Order
ISBN 1–4039–3210–7**
(outside North America only)

You can receive future titles in this series as they are published by placing a standing order. Please contact your bookseller or, in the case of difficulty, write to us at the address below with your name and address, the title of the series and the ISBN quoted above.

Customer Services Department, Macmillan Distribution Ltd
Houndmills, Basingstoke, Hampshire RG21 6XS, England

Key Concepts in Romantic Literature

Jane Moore and John Strachan

First published 2010 by
PALGRAVE MACMILLAN

Palgrave Macmillan in the UK is an imprint of Macmillan Publishers Limited,
registered in England, company number 785998, of Houndmills, Basingstoke,
Hampshire RG21 6XS.

Palgrave Macmillan in the US is a division of St Martin's Press LLC,
175 Fifth Avenue, New York, NY 10010.

Palgrave Macmillan is the global academic imprint of the above companies
and has companies and representatives throughout the world.

Palgrave® and Macmillan® are registered trademarks in the United States,
the United Kingdom, Europe and other countries

ISBN 978–1–4039–4889–2

This book is printed on paper suitable for recycling and made from fully
managed and sustained forest sources. Logging, pulping and manufacturing
processes are expected to conform to the environmental regulations of the
country of origin.

A catalogue record for this book is available from the British Library.
A catalog record for this book is available from the Library of Congress.

10   9   8   7   6   5   4   3   2   1
19 18 17 16 15 14 13 12 11 10

Printed and bound in Great Britain by
CPI Antony Rowe, Chippenham and Eastbourne

Contents

List of Illustrations

General Editors' Preface

The purpose of Palgrave Key Concepts in Literature is to provide students with key critical and historical ideas about the texts they are studying as part of their literature courses. These ideas include information about the historical and cultural contexts of literature as well as the theoretical approaches current in the subject today. Behind the series lies a recognition of the need nowadays for students to be familiar with a range of concepts and contextual material to inform their reading and writing about literature.

This series is also based on a recognition of the changes that have transformed degree courses in Literature in recent years. Central to these changes has been the impact of critical theory together with a renewed interest in the way in which texts intersect with their immediate context and historical circumstances. The result has been an opening up of new ways of reading texts and a new understanding of what the study of literature involves together with the introduction of a wide set of new critical issues that demand our attention. An important aim of Palgrave Key Concepts in Literature is to provide accessible introductions to these new ways of reading and new issues.

Each volume in Palgrave Key Concepts in Literature follows the same structure. An initial overview essay is followed by three sections – Contexts, Texts and Criticism – each containing a sequence of alphabetically arranged entries on a sequence of topics. 'Contexts' essays provide an impression of the historical, social and cultural environment in which literary texts were produced. 'Texts' essays, as might be expected, focus more directly on the works themselves. 'Criticism' essays then outline the manner in which changes and developments in criticism have affected the ways in which we discuss the texts featured in the volume. The informing intention throughout is to help the reader create something new in the process of combining context, text and criticism.

John Peck
Martin Coyle

Cardiff University

General Introduction

This book offers a guide to the extraordinary efflorescence of English literature in the 'Romantic period', as the era between the outbreak of the
French Revolution in 1789 and the passing of the Reform Act in 1832 is
commonly denominated in conventional accounts of literary history. This
relatively short period of time is rich in great literature, boasting as it does
what are generally labelled the first (Blake, Coleridge and Wordsworth) and
second (Byron, Keats and Shelley) generations of Romantic poets, several
remarkable novelists (Jane Austen, Maria Edgeworth, James Hogg, Walter
Scott and others), and potent and gifted essayists (Thomas De Quincey,
William Hazlitt, Leigh Hunt, Charles Lamb amongst them). Literary historians have also reminded us that there were many important and highly
significant women poets active in the age, from Mary Robinson and
Charlotte Smith in the 1780s and 1790s through to Felicia Hemans and
Letitia Elizabeth Landon in the 1820s and 1830s, figures who, though critically respected and highly successful in their day, have been – until recently
– omitted from the Romantic canon.

Key Concepts in Romantic Literature is divided into three parts. The first,
'Contexts: History, Politics, Culture', examines the external forces which
shaped the writers of the Romantic period, exploring the social, historical
and philosophical contexts in which those authors worked. Poets and
novelists do not write in a vacuum untouched by the world around them,
and it is important that students of English literature have a sense of the
society which fashioned the works that they discuss and critically dissect.
This part of the book surveys British politics in the period after the cataclysmic French Revolution, which the poet Shelley rightly described as 'the
master theme of the epoch', as well as showing how the contemporaneous
Industrial Revolution indelibly changed the economic landscape of Great
Britain. The Romantic poets emerged from the maelstrom of late Georgian
British politics ('late Georgian' refers to the final third of the period between
the accession of George I in 1714 and the death of George IV in 1830). This
was by no means an age of political serenity: the first half of the Romantic
age was dominated by European war and the second part, after the fall of
Napoleon in 1815, was characterised by financial turmoil, political unrest
and abortive revolution. Abroad, alongside its being embroiled in the
Revolutionary and Napoleonic Wars, this was the period in which
the British Empire was growing apace and attempting to recover from the

recent, shattering loss of the American colonies in the 1770s. Great political issues such as these permeated through the literary consciousness of the age, alongside equally resonant matters such as the abolition of slavery, the position of women, and the future of Ireland and the so-called 'Catholic question'. We also examine the intellectual context which shaped British Romanticism, considering contemporary philosophy, religion (and athe-ism), science, and medicine.

The second part of the book, 'Texts: Themes, Issues, Concepts', exam-ines the literature of the Romantic period in detail, addressing the Lake Poets Wordsworth and Coleridge alongside the other important poetic voices of the age: the iconoclast William Blake, the extraordinary cultural phenomenon that was Lord Byron and 'Byronism', the philosophical and poetical radical P. B. Shelley, the peerless prodigy John Keats and the remarkable women poets such as Smith, Hemans and Landon, who flour-ished in their day and are only now beginning to be read with assiduity once again, together with the no less noteworthy body of labouring-class poets, as we now call them (contemporaries preferred the term 'peasant poets'), figures such as Robert Burns and John Clare, who rose from relatively humble backgrounds to poetic eminence.

We should not see the Romantic period as notable in literary terms purely because of its poetry, and this part of the book also covers the other key literary genres in the literature of the day: the drama (Romantic-era theatre, like its women's writing, has been the recipient of much recent crit-ical attention), the novel, the national tale and the Gothic romance. This section also discusses British poetry from outside England, from Scotland, Wales and Ireland – from 1801 a part of the United Kingdom – and examines some of the most crucial literary preoccupations of the writing of the age: nature, medievalism, the periodical essay, and discusses the frequently ferocious satire evident throughout the age.

The third and final part of this volume, 'Criticism: Approaches, Theory, Practice', examines the way in which Romanticism has been received from its earliest inception to the criticism of the present day. From the first, Romantic verse prompted debate and discussion; though we now think of them as 'canonical' writers of great importance, many of these poets were contentious in their day. William Wordsworth, for instance, was derided by some as a namby-pamby simpleton and John Keats by others as a vulgar 'Cockney'. From contemporaneous criticism, whether laudatory or vituper-ative, to Victorian idealisation of the Romantics, and after that to the late nineteenth- and early twentieth-century institutionalisation of the poets in early university syllabi, the repudiation of Romanticism by T. S. Eliot and the modernists, and on to the modern-day controversies attendant to decon-struction, the Yale School, psychoanalysis, feminism and the New

Historicism, this book surveys the way in which Romanticism has possessed an enduring appeal for literary criticism of all casts.

A note to the reader

This volume has something of the work of reference about it, and is not necessarily to be read from start to finish as if it were a novel, play or poem. Given that many readers will dip into the book where it suits their current need for information rather than reading the whole as continuous prose, some information is repeated occasionally, though, of course, written differently. An entry on 'What is Romanticism?', for instance, and an entry on the 'Literary and Philosophical Key Concepts' of the first generation of Romantic poets will both need to cover such issues as the creative imagination and nature. However, this overlap is kept to a minimum, and each essay is accompanied by cross-referencing as required.

Introduction

What is Romanticism?

'Romanticism', declared the critic Thomas McFarland in 1987, 'is the true beginning of our modern world.' Though such bold idealism regarding the importance of the Romantic era has come under fire in recent years, notably from the New Historicist critics discussed below, the sense that there was something epoch-making about the literature of the period around the turn of the nineteenth century is difficult to shift, and perhaps with good reason. For better or worse, the work of Wordsworth, Blake and Coleridge, and that of Byron, Shelley and Keats after them, changed the face of English poetry. For well over a century, whether admiring the Romantics and learning from them (Tennyson, Arnold and much of Victorian poetry) or, indeed, consciously repudiating their values (T. S. Eliot, Ezra Pound and much of modernist poetry), Romanticism shaped the nature of English verse from the late eighteenth century to the 1920s, and it continues to cast a long shadow to this day.

Despite its contemporary resonance and posthumous influence, the idea of 'Romanticism' is a hotly contested notion. Beyond stating that in terms of English literature it is generally seen as the writing of the period between 1789, the date of the French Revolution, and 1832, the year which saw the passing of the Great Reform Act, and pointing out that it has not much to do with 'romantic' in the St Valentine's Day sense of the term, defining Romanticism is not easy. As E. B. Burgum wrote in 1941, a critic 'who seeks to define Romanticism is entering a hazardous occupation which has claimed many victims'. Nonetheless, many have tried. Perhaps Arthur O. Lovejoy's famous 1924 notion of a 'plurality' of 'Romanticisms' lacking in a single unifying definition is more relevant than ever today when women poets and dramatists have somewhat belatedly been admitted to the Romantic canon. Indeed, part of Romanticism's appeal is the very plurality of its taxonomy. The leading New Historicist critic Jerome J. McGann optimistically contrives to see this very vagueness as a positive, writing in 1999 that 'it is the very looseness of the term that can promote helpful critical discussion. For the phenomena associated with Romanticism and Romantic poetry are volatile even to this day.' The present authors, studying Romantic poetry as undergraduates in the 1980s, were presented with courses entirely devoted to the so-called 'Big Six' male poets (Wordsworth, Coleridge, Blake, Byron, Shelley and Keats) in a manner unthinkable twenty

critics argue

years later, when survey courses on Romantic poetry included the likes of Mary Robinson, Charlotte Smith, Felicia Hemans and Letitia Elizabeth Landon as a matter of course. The nature of Romanticism is indeed volatile and has been so from the start of the nineteenth century.

Whatever its fruitful instability, certainly 'Romanticism' is a critical label that it is very difficult to do without, and it is indeed possible to make generalisations about the nature of that extraordinary cultural movement. Thomas McFarland's argument quoted above that Romanticism marks the origin of 'our modern world' might have an element of special pleading or exaggeration about it, but in terms of the history of British and European poetry, it has the ring of truth. Historically, critics have argued that there was a 'shift in sensibility' in the Romantic era, a move from the eighteenth-century neoclassical poetic paradigms of 'mimesis' (imitation), the following of ancient precedent, and didacticism, and a simultaneous departure from the Enlightenment philosophical values of rationalism and empiricism towards an expressive literary model, that is, towards the sense of poetry as proceeding from the individual poetic genius and imagination of the poet together with a philosophical cast of mind more attuned to the sublime, the transcendental and the supernatural. Indeed, Romanticism and the supposed change in poetic values which it represented in many ways still condition the way in which most people – though not necessarily most poets – think about the nature of poetry today. Take the notion of what makes a good poem; though not all contemporary versifiers would agree with the idea, many people would see this as poetry which is 'self-expressive', 'original', or 'imaginative'. All of these concepts are high Romantic notions. And, though it might seem odd to us today, none of them was particularly important to neoclassical poetics in the period before the Romantics, in the so-called 'Augustan' period of the earlier eighteenth century, the age of Alexander Pope and Jonathan Swift.

In Romantic literature, we see the clear emergence of a central emphasis upon the 'imaginative genius' of the poet. Though praising imaginative originality might seem an eminently natural thing to the modern eye, this expressive model of creation is rather remarkable in eighteenth-century thought. According to the neoclassical literary paradigm, the poet such as Pope or Dr Johnson derives his raw material from the perception of the world around him (and occasionally her). To the Romantic poet, however, more emphasis is placed on the work of art coming from within, on the internal being made external and upon the 'wondrous interchange' – to use Wordsworth's phrase – between poetic selfhood and the external world. Instead of imitating the external world, poetry – for the Romantic – often comes about as the result of an impulse within the poet. And the key term for this impulse is the 'creative imagination'. In the Romantic period, the emphasis shifts, that is, from the neoclassical priorities of learning, imitation, judgement and decorum to a particular stress on the poet's natural spontaneity and genius.

Politically, Romanticism is permeated to the core by the French Revolution and France and the British reaction to it. *Intellectually*, it takes issue with the rationalist emphasis evident in much eighteenth-century Enlightenment thought. In the work of Wordsworth, Coleridge and Blake, and after them Keats and Shelley, there is a sense that there is something within the human individual for which empiricist thought fails to account, 'a sense sublime', to borrow another phrase from Wordsworth, 'of something far more deeply interfused'. And the Romantics have various names for that other: the sublime, the imaginative, the visionary, the poetic. *Thematically*, there is a concentration on 'nature'; but on the elemental side of nature rather than the carefully landscaped nature evident in neoclassical poetic imagery. Wordsworth, Coleridge and Shelley offer a vision of the wild and sublime power of the landscape and the centrality of humanity's relationship with nature. *Emotionally*, British Romanticism often expresses an extreme assertion of individual experience. *Poetically*, Romanticism took issue with the theoretical concerns and poetic practices of the neoclassical tradition: Wordsworth's literary criticism berates what he sees as the moribund formalism and laboured decorativeness of the 'poetic diction' of eighteenth-century poetry. Romanticism was also an acutely self-conscious literary form, whether in Coleridge and Wordsworth's autobiographical verse (the latter jocularly pointed out that 'it was a thing unprecedented in literary history for a man to talk so much about himself'), or in Keats's career-long tendency to write poems about poetry – 'meta-poetical' poetry – and the creative urge ('Romantic poems tend to be about romantic imagination' wrote W. K. Wimsatt and Cleanth Brooks in 1970).

Above all, perhaps, *selfhood* has generally been seen as the central occupation of Romantic poetry. The critic Harold Bloom once wrote that [...]e of ferocious selfhood', and he was only half joking. After [...]770–1850), the poetic consciousness moves to the heart of [...]s. Certainly Romanticism stresses individual experience and, in particular, the individual experience of the poet, who is often characterised as a seer, a figure in receipt of intuitive truth who has a sense, sometimes strongly, sometimes tentatively, of the infinite and the transcendental. Romantic poetry manifests a stress on the poetic subject, whether in moments of exhilaration and inspiration or in periods of doubt and anxiety, as in the Romantic crisis lyric – Coleridge's 'Dejection. An Ode' (1802) or Wordsworth's 'Immortality Ode' (published 1807) – where the poet feels a sense of poetic and personal loss, which may – as in Wordsworth's poem – or may not – as in Coleridge's poem – be resolved by what the latter calls the 'shaping spirit of imagination'.

So, what did this all-important word 'poetry' mean to the Romantic poets? In what is conventionally seen as one of the foundational documents of British Romanticism, William Wordsworth's combative 'Preface' to the *Lyrical Ballads* (1800), one of the most notable critical polemics in English literary history, the poet declares that 'I here use the word "Poetry" ... as opposed to the word Prose, as synonymous with metrical composition.' This plain-speaking characterisation is uncontentious in contemporary terms, conforming as it does to Dr Johnson's definition of poetry in his 1755 *Dictionary of the English Language*: 'Metrical composition; the art or practice of writing poems'. However, after beginning with the bald Johnsonian usage, Wordsworth goes on to insist that metrical composition must be used in a particular manner, a manner which epitomises imaginative activity. 'Poetry is the spontaneous overflow of powerful feelings', he declares, in the most notable short definition of the expressive literary model (though this is not to say that poetry has absolutely no connection with reason or thought; Wordsworth also insists that a poet is 'a man ... being possessed of more than usual organic sensibility, [who] had also thought long and deeply'). The simple notion of poetry as metrical composition is insufficient; for Wordsworth, metre must be employed in verse which speaks from the heart and the imagination.

Wordsworth returned to this idea subsequently, refining it in even more elevated fashion in his 1816 'Essay, Supplementary to the "Preface"' (i.e. to the *Lyrical Ballads*): 'Poetry proceeds ... from the soul of man, communicating its creative energies to the images of the external world.' In this and in several of the most notable conceptualisations of poetry offered by Romantic-era poet-critics, from Wordsworth and Coleridge to Shelley and Keats, what we are actually dealing with is what a given poet or critic would *like* poetry to be rather what it actually *is*. When we write of a poet's 'definition' of poetry – Wordsworth's 'emotion recollected in tranquillity' or Coleridge's notion of poetry (in the *Biographia Literaria* (1817)) as an art which 'brings the whole soul of man into activity' – what we are usually examining are idealist formulations, often made in some kind of poetical manifesto, rather than scholarly attempts to define poetry in a cool or dispassionate manner. Indeed, such declarations are frequently prompted by an awareness that poetry as it is currently manifested is nothing like what the poet-critic is declaring it to be. Thus Wordsworth, faced with a residual fondness amongst the reading public for the Popean couplet and 'poetic diction', is simultaneously offering a call to arms and repudiating the inheritance of early eighteenth-century poetry. He is describing the best form of poetry, celebrating what poetry should be rather than describing what it is. In the preface to his 1815 *Works*, Wordsworth quoted a dictum of Coleridge's approvingly: 'every great and original writer, in proportion as he is great or original, must create the taste by which he is to be relished'. Wordsworth's poetry did not sell well in its early years and his work was also critically contentious, notably in the stinging attacks by the editor of the *Edinburgh Review*, Francis Jeffrey. However, after an initially mixed reception, attacked by Jeffrey but championed by the poetic avant garde, Wordsworth did create a taste for his work and, indeed, achieved the status of a classic during his long lifetime, his verse heavily influencing the poetry of the next hundred years and beyond. As Thomas De Quincey wrote in 1835, 'up to 1820 the name of Wordsworth was trampled underfoot; from 1820 to 1830 it was militant; from 1830 to 1835 it has been triumphant.'

Wordsworth's expressive model of poetry, with its emphasis on the emotional power of poetry, influenced the so-called 'second generation' of Romantic poets in Byron's 1813 conceptualisation of poetry as 'the lava of the imagination, whose eruption prevents an earthquake', Shelley's contention in the 'Defence of Poetry' (1821) that poetry, 'in a general sense' was 'the expression of the imagination', and in Keats's declaration in a letter of November 1817 that 'I am certain of nothing but of the holiness of the Heart's affections and the truth of the Imagination.' This second generation of Romantic poets veered between adoration of Wordsworth to frequent expressions of a kind of patricidal venom towards the poet. However, though Keats defined his verse against Wordsworth's in negative terms, characterising his own work as lacking in Wordsworth's 'egotistical sublime', though Shelley satirised the poet in his *Alastor; or, the Spirit of Solitude* (1816), on account of his political apostasy in turning from Radical to Tory, as one of those whose 'hearts are dry as summer dust', and though Byron mocked the Lake poet in his satires, from *English Bards and Scotch Reviewers* (1809) to *Don Juan* (1819–24), all of them were shaped and formed by Wordsworth. Indeed, Byron, whose third canto of *Childe Harold's Pilgrimage* (1816) is so infused by the Wordsworthian sublime and sense of the imagination, jestingly described the poet's work as a kind of inescapable contagion, writing in January 1817 that 'Shelley, when I was in Switzerland, used to dose me with Wordsworth physic even to nausea. ... I should, many a good day, have blown my brains out, but for the recollection that it would have given pleasure to my mother-in-law.'

Quite apart from his complex influence on the second generation of the Romantic poets, it is fair to say that Wordsworth shaped the poetic consciousness of the whole of the nineteenth century. Certainly, the Romantic vision prompted a significant number of later, Victorian conceptualisations of poetry, the most concise formulation of which is Thomas Hardy's declaration that poetry is 'emotion put into measure', a definition which manages to combine in four words both the functional ('measure') and the idealist ('emotion') definition of the term. John Ruskin's *Lectures on*

Art (1870) poses a rhetorical question and answers thus: 'What is poetry? The suggestion, by the imagination, of noble grounds for the noble emotions.' It is in the face of such brazen post-Romantic idealism that modernist attacks on Romantic ideas of poetry were aimed, a fact best demonstrated in T. S. Eliot's declaration in 'Tradition and the Individual Talent' (1919) that 'Poetry is not a turning loose of emotion, but an escape from emotion; it is not the expression of personality, but an escape from personality.' Literary movements are fond of issuing manifestos and calls-to-arms, and here Eliot repudiates his immediate poetic inheritance just as Romantic – at least Wordsworthian Romantic – notions of poetry were themselves reactions against earlier, neoclassical notions of poetry.

Two important caveats should be made here. As we will see in the 'Texts' and 'Criticism' sections of this book, such representations of the nature of Romantic poetry, which stress the importance of the creative imagination and emphasise the centrality of the first and second generation of Romantic poets, have been put under great critical pressure in recent years, from two main sources. First, in the last two decades, feminist critics have pointed out that the standard narration of ('Big Six') Romantic poetry is solely confined to male poets, and ignores the fact that the Romantic era possessed a significant number of female poets who were both critically esteemed and highly successful in their day. Secondly, the revisionist criticism prompted by the work of Marilyn Butler in Great Britain and the New Historicist school inspired by Jerome McGann in North America has argued that Romantic criticism has generally been a criticism in thrall to Romanticism's own self-representations, a sense, in Butler's terminology, that critics 'of English Romanticism have tended to seem dazzled by the brilliance of the theoreticians of that movement', and consequently have been unwilling to offer a dispassionate critical analysis of their work. Such criticism also argued that, historically, Romantic criticism, as well as being preoccupied with such issues as the creative imagination, the sublime and so on, has also tended to concentrate on the formal properties of the works under discussion and is inattentive to the socio-historical contexts in which it was written. There has undeniably been a 'turn to history' in Romantic Studies since the late 1970s, away from the single attention to the text alone evident in the New Criticism of previous decades.

In conclusion, it should also be pointed out in any general discussion of the nature of Romanticism that the 'Romantic poets' did not see themselves as such. In Britain the word had several meanings, none of which pertain to our modern sense of the term. Dr Johnson's *Dictionary* defines 'romantick' as 'resembling the tales of romances, wild', 'improbable, false', and 'fanciful; full of wild scenery'. As Ian Jack amusingly puts it, 'Wordsworth, Byron, Shelley and Keats did not regard themselves as writing "romantic" poems and would not – in fact – have been particularly flattered if they had been told that was what they were doing.' The word did not carry the connotations it does today. This is not to say that there was not a sense that something new was happening in the poetry of the early nineteenth century. From the 1790s onwards there was a perception that a 'new school' of poetry was at work, a notion, characterised by Shelley, of the 'spirit of the age acting through us all'. The notion of a 'Romantic School' of poetry was posthumously applied by Victorian critics seeking to make sense of the poetry of the opening decades of their century. The actual term 'Romantic' began to be applied only later (George Whalley dates the first appearance of the term 'English Romantic School' to Hippolyte Taine's *Histoire de la Littérature Anglaise* (1862–7; English version 1871–2)), particularly amongst literary historians of the last quarter of the nineteenth century.

The eighteenth-century word 'romantick', Johnson tells us, derives from the word 'romance', 'a tale of wild adventure'. In Britain in the eighteenth and early nineteenth centuries, it was understood in literary terms in the twin senses used by Horace Walpole in the preface to his Gothic novel *The Castle of Otranto* (1764), where he speaks of the 'ancient romance' – medieval tales of chivalry such as Chaucer's 'Knight's Tale' – and of the 'modern romance', the English novel in the manner of Defoe, Richardson and Fielding. So, how did the term change in meaning? The antecedents of the modern literary sense of 'Romantic' lie, in fact, in German literature and the modern sense was borrowed in the Victorian era from debates which had resonated through European – and in particular German and French – culture from the turn of the nineteenth century. When Wordsworth and Coleridge were in Germany in the winter of 1798–9, a controversy was beginning which would eventually change the nature of the word 'Romantic' in Britain. In 1798, August Wilhelm von Schlegel (1767–1845), the critic, philosopher and translator of Shakespeare, and his younger brother, the essayist and critic Friedrich von Schlegel (1772–1829), published a polemical magazine *Das Athenäum* (1798–1800) which noisily proselytised for what it called 'romantisch' poetry. In 1798 Friedrich declared that 'Romantic poetry is a progressive, universal poetry,' and between 1801 and 1804, August subsequently formulated the tenets of the new school in a series of lectures. The Schlegels, who saw themselves as twin volcanoes of literary-philosophical subversion, celebrated the Romantic, in contradistinction to the classical, which they characterised as dry and arid when compared with Romanticism, which was 'forever striving after new and wonderful births'. The quarrels over Romanticism made little impact in the United Kingdom; as late as 1831, Thomas Carlyle, writing on the German poet Schiller, declared that 'we are troubled with no controversies on Romanticism and Classicism'. However, within fifty years of Carlyle's blithe pronouncement, Victorian critics began to view matters rather differently, seeing Wordsworth and Coleridge's 1798 *Lyrical Ballads* as the founding document of what was now claimed as a British form of 'Romanticism' (with Wordsworth's attacks on neoclassical poetry and Enlightenment empirical philosophy in the 1800 'Preface' recast as the British equivalent of *Das Athenäum*). The 'Lake Poets' and their successors were thence christened once more, this time as the British 'Romantic Poets'.

See also   Literary and Philosophical Key Concepts I; Literary and Philosophical Key Concepts II.

Further Reading

M. H. Abrams, *The Mirror and the Lamp* (1953).
Harold Bloom, *The Visionary Company* (1961).
E. B. Burgum, 'Romanticism', *Kenyon Review*, III (1941), 479–90.
Marilyn Butler, *Romantics, Rebels and Reactionaries* (1981).
Ian Jack, *English Literature 1815–32* (1963).
Arthur O. Lovejoy, 'On the Discrimination of Romanticisms', *PMLA*, 39 (1924), 229–53.
Iain McCalman (gen. ed), *An Oxford Companion to the Romantic Age* (1999).
Thomas McFarland, *Romantic Cruxes: The English Essayists and the Spirit of the Age* (1987).
Jerome J. McGann, *The Romantic Ideology* (1985).
George Whalley, 'England/Romantic–Romanticism', in Hans Eicher (ed.), *'Romantic' and its Cognates: The European History of a Word* (1972), 157–262.
W. K. Wimsatt and Cleanth Brooks, *Literary Criticism: A Short History* (1970).

Historical Definitions and Conceptualisations of Romanticism

> Although the word 'romanticism' refers to any number of things, it has two primary referents: (1) a general and permanent characteristic of mind, art, and personality, found in all periods and all cultures; (2) a specific historical movement in art and ideas which occurred in Europe and America in the late eighteenth and early nineteenth centuries. I am concerned only with the second of these two meanings.   (Morse Peckham, 1951)

A notable contribution to Romantic Studies between the two world wars came in the form of Ernest Bernbaum's five-volume *Anthology of Romanticism and Guide through the Romantic Movement* (1929–30). In the first volume of this collection, the promisingly titled *Guide through the Romantic Movement*, Bernbaum (1879–1958), then Professor of English at the University of Illinois, had the fine idea of letting the critics, poets and philosophers who had written on Romanticism – since the brothers Schlegel at the turn of the nineteenth century – speak for themselves. Bernbaum's catalogue of quotations is reproduced (and expanded and dated) below as testimony to Arthur Lovejoy's 1924 notion, discussed above, of the 'plurality' of 'Romanticisms'.

Bernbaum's quotations, drawn from thirteen decades of polemical thought, show that Romanticism did not rise untroubled like some literary loaf of bread. From its first appearance Romanticism was not to all tastes: what some relished, others spat out. The reader will also note a willingness to indulge in high idealism, elevated rhetoric and sweeping generalisation here, alongside a tendency towards either blanket approval or condemnation, as attacks on the classical consensus of eighteenth-century traditions of thought caused some literary feathers to ruffle. The taxonomic difficulties attendant to the very concept of Romanticism discussed in 'What is Romanticism?' above are also much in evidence; this is a literary form which has been defined in a diverse number of ways since its first beginnings. Also apparent in the early quarrels about Romanticism is the predominance therein of poets and philosophers; only towards the end of the period were these debates institutionalised and starting to become the province of scholars based in universities (and even then not uniformly; T. E. Hulme, modernist polemicist, and Theodore Watts-Dunton, mentor of Swinburne and periodical critic, were not based in the academy).

1798–1928

Romantic poetry is a progressive, universal poetry ... Other kinds of poetry are now finished ... The Romantic poetry is still in the state of becoming; that, in fact, is its real essence, that it should forever be becoming and never be perfected. It can be exhausted by no theory.   Friedrich von Schlegel (1798)

Romantic art and poetry delight in indissoluble mixtures; all contrarieties, nature and art, poetry and prose ... the secular and the divine, art and death are all blended by it ... The Romantic [is] forever striving after new and wonderful births. August Wilhelm von Schlegel (1801–4)

The poetry of the ancients was that of possession, ours is that of yearning [and] hovers between recollection of the past and presentiment of the future.   August Wilhelm von Schlegel (1801–4)

Classicism is health; Romanticism is disease.   Johann Wolfgang Von Goethe (1829)

Romanticism is, at any time, the art of the day; classicism, the art of the day before. Stendhal (Marie-Henri Beyle) (1830)

Classic art had only to portray the finite ... Romantic art had to represent, or suggest, the infinite.   Heinrich Heine (1833)

Nothing other than the revival of the poetry of the Middle Ages as it manifested itself in song, sculpture, in art and life.   Heinrich Heine (1833)

To say the word Romanticism is to say modern art – that is, intimacy, spirituality, colour, aspiration toward the infinite.   Charles Baudelaire (1846)

What is Romanticism? ... Intoxication, paroxysm, numbness, madness.   Friedrich Nietzsche (1882/7)

A movement to honour whatever Classicism rejected. Classicism is the regularity of good sense – perfection in moderation; Romanticism is disorder in the imagination, – the rage of incorrectness. A blind wave of literary egotism.   Ferdinand Brunetière (1886)

It is the addition of strangeness to beauty, that constitutes the Romantic character in art.   Walter Pater (1889)

Sentimental melancholy ... vague aspiration.   William Lyon Phelps (1893)

Extraordinary development of imaginative sensibility.   C. H. Herford (1897)

The classic temper studies the past, the Romantic temper neglects it.   Felix Schelling (1898)

Whereas in classical works the idea is represented directly and with as exact an adaptation of form as possible, in Romantic the idea is left to the reader's faculty of divination assisted only by suggestion and symbol.   George Saintsbury (1901)

The renascence of wonder ... knowingness and Romanticism are mutually destructive.   Theodore Watts-Dunton (1903)

The illusion of beholding the infinite within the stream of nature itself, instead of apart from that stream.   Paul Elmer More (1910)

Imagination as contrasted with reason and the sense of fact.   William Allan Neilson (1912).

I object even to the best of the Romantics ... I object to the sloppiness which doesn't consider that a poem is a poem unless it is moaning or whining about something or other ... The thing has got so bad now that a poem which is all dry and hard, a properly classical poem, would not be considered poetry at all.   T. E. Hulme (1913–14)

The cult of the extinct.   Geoffrey Scott (1914)

In general a thing is Romantic when, as Aristotle would say, it is wonderful rather than probable; in other words, when it violates the normal sequence of cause and effect in favour of adventure. ... The whole movement is filled with the praise of ignorance, and of those who still enjoy its inappreciable advantages – the savage, the peasant, and above all the child.   Irving Babbitt (1919)

Romanticism is a bad name for the poetry of the nineteenth century because it sets you looking for a common quality when you ought to be reading or remembering individual poems.   W. P. Ker (1923)

Romanticism does mean something ... The fairy way of writing ... a world of fine fabling.   W. P. Ker (1923)

The spirit counts for more than the form.   Herbert Grierson (1925)

The opposite, not of Classicism, but of Realism – a withdrawal from outer experience to concentrate upon inner.   Lascelles Abercrombie (1926)

Pure Romanticism is distinguished by a naive idealism ... An effort to escape from actuality.   Gilbert Waterhouse (1928)

An accentuated predominance of emotional life, provoked or directed by the exercise of imaginative vision, and in its turn stimulating or directing such exercise.   Louis Cazamian (1928)

A desire to find the infinite within the finite, to effect a synthesis of the real and the unreal. The expression in art of what in theology would be called pantheistic enthusiasm.   H. N. Fairchild (1928)

Applying Bernbaum's methodology to the four decades after the appearance of his book, up until the late 1960s, and similarly extracting key critical quotations about Romanticism, we see debates about this cultural phenomenon becoming rather more definitely the province of scholars of English and comparative literature rather than of creative writers (as in the nineteenth century). That said, from F. L. Lucas's polemical Freudian criticism to René Wellek's attempts to construct a general theory of Romanticism, the same tendency towards over-arching generalisation is as evident here as it was in the previous century. Critics continued to look, in W. P. Ker's words, 'for a common quality' to Romanticism.

1931–1967

The period of the great Romantics, Wordsworth, Coleridge, Byron, Shelley and Keats.   F. R. Leavis (1931)

A liberation of the less conscious levels of the mind; an intoxicating dreaming. Classicism is control by the conscious mind.   F. L. Lucas (1936)

It has been suggested that the fundamental quality of Romanticism is not mere anti-Classicism, nor medievalism, nor 'aspiration', nor wonder, nor any of the other things its various formulas suggest; but rather a liberation of the less conscious levels of the mind.   F. L. Lucas (1936)

Classical and Romantic: private language of a family quarrel, a dead dispute over the distribution of emphasis between man and nature.   Cyril Connolly (1945)

If we examine the characteristics of the actual literature which called itself or was called 'Romantic' all over the continent, we find throughout Europe the same conceptions of poetry and of the workings and nature of poetic imagination, the same conception of nature and its relation to man, and basically the same poetic style, with a use of imagination, symbolism, and myth which is clearly distinct from that of eighteenth-century classicism.   René Wellek (1949)

Historians have recently been instructed to speak only of 'Romanticisms', in the plural, but from our point of vantage there turns out to be one distinctly 'Romantic' criticism, although this remains a unity amid variety.   M. H. Abrams (1953)

It is ultimately misleading to put Blake and Shelley, instead of Wordsworth and Coleridge, at the intellectual centre of English Romanticism.   M. H Abrams (1953)

The French Revolution, the Napoleonic Wars, and the progress of domestic reform enlarged the boundaries and enriched the content of English Romanticism, but these social and political events did not initiate the movement. For its origins, search must be made deep into the past, perhaps into the very nature of the human spirit.   Samuel C. Chew and Richard D. Altick (1959)

In the beginning, modern poetry abandoned most of what had served as the subject matter of European literary tradition from Homer to Pope. Wordsworth was the inventor of modern poetry, and he found no subject but himself ... Our poets were and are Romantic as poets used to be Christian, that is, whether they want to be or not.   Harold Bloom (1961)

The tendency of historic Romanticism was away from authority and toward liberty, away from the acceptance of caked wisdom and toward the exploratory development of the individual, away from the secure fixities and towards the drama of the unforeseeable, away from monarchy and toward the sovereignty of the people. Jacques Barzun (1962)

The anti-Romantic movement, which in Britain and America followed the Hulme–Eliot–Pound broadsides of the early twenties, is now over and done with, and criticism has got its sense of literary tradition properly in focus again. Northrop Frye (1963)

First, Romanticism has a historical centre of gravity, which falls somewhere around the 1790–1830 period. This gets us at once out of the fallacy of timeless characterization ... Second, Romanticism is not a general term like 'Medieval': it appears to have another centre of gravity in the creative arts ... Third, even in its application in the creative arts Romanticism is a selective term ... We think of it including Keats [and] Scott, but not, in general, Jane Austen.   Northrop Frye (1963)

Whenever anyone embarks on a generalisation on the subject of Romanticism ... in Wordsworth and Coleridge, let us say ... somebody will always be found who will produce countervailing evidence.   Isaiah Berlin (1965)

The single propelling force of the age was, to use modern terminology, the trauma of revolution.   J. L. Talmon (1967)

Since the 1970s, Romanticism has been the subject of a great deal of academic argument. Scholars began to interrogate what was seen as the overly reverential and unquestioning nature of existing criticism, its willingness to take Romantic idealisms on their own terms. 'Romantic poems tend to be about Romantic imagination,' wrote W. K. Wimsatt and Cleanth Brooks, and so, it was argued by 'historicist' critics, was Romantic scholarship, which was unable to apply a sceptical cast of mind to Romantic writings, being 'dazzled' (Marilyn Butler's term) by the 'brilliance of the theorists of that movement'. This monomaniacal critical preoccupation with Romanticism's own self-representations had also led, it was argued, to the exclusion of those authors whose work did not suit this governing literary notion of the creative imagination (the critical revision of Marilyn Butler and the American New Historicism of J. J. McGann and others is discussed in 'From Historicism to Ecological Criticism' in the third section of this book). The second, related, critique of traditional Romantic criticism focused on the notion that the 'great Romantics' – in F. R. Leavis's words – were solely confined to 'Wordsworth, Coleridge, Byron, Shelley and Keats' alongside the work of Blake (the so-called 'Big Six' Romantic poets). In particular, feminist critics of Romanticism, noting that there were a number of once critically and commercially successful female poets active in the Romantic period who languished in critical obscurity in subsequent decades, have criticised orthodox accounts of the period as confining it to little more than a 'men's club' (this body of critical work is discussed below in 'Gender Criticism').

1970–2006

Romantic poems tend to be about Romantic imagination.   W. K. Wimsatt and Cleanth Brooks (1970)

A love of revolution for its own sake ... is part of the Romantic outlook ... In France it had resulted in Napoleon, the prototype for every power- and notoriety-seeking villain who has afflicted mankind subsequently.   Malcolm Muggeridge (1972)

General histories of English Romanticism have tended to seem dazzled by the brilliance of the theoreticians of that movement.   Marilyn Butler (1979)

Romanticism is the true beginning of our modern world.   Thomas McFarland (1987)

Romanticism is impossible to define with historical precision because the term itself is historically unsound. It is now applied to English writers of the first quarter of the nineteenth century, who did not think of themselves as Romantics. Instead they divided themselves by literary precept and by ideology into several distinct groups, dubbed by their opponents 'Lakeists', 'Cockneys', 'Satanists', 'Scotsmen'. It was the middle of the nineteenth century before they were gathered into one band as the English Romantics.   Marilyn Butler (1988)

The elision of sexual difference, or occlusion of women, is a by-product of the Romantic master-plot.   Mary Jacobus (1989)

The theory, practice, and style of the Romantic art, music, and literature of the late eighteenth and early nineteenth centuries, usually opposed to Classicism. P. Hanks (1990)

One of those terms historians can neither do with nor make do without.   M. H. Abrams (1991)

We have concurred in grounding English Romanticism on a reading of a highly selective group of texts, almost all poetry, almost all written by men.   Anne K. Mellor (1993)

The familiar and traditional view of Romanticism as privileging emotion, intuition and spontaneity should be understood as a gendered as well as a literary-political construction.   David Simpson (1993)

We must question our tendency to see the beginnings of Romanticism in terms merely of a few distinguished names.   Jonathan Wordsworth (1995)

The truly great – Blake, Coleridge, Wordsworth, Byron, Shelley, Keats (it becomes a litany, now we know it so well) – the truly great were all monomaniacs. They thought they were Milton or Elijah.   Jonathan Wordsworth (1995)

The central tenet of all branches of Romanticism, the creative energy of the imagination.   Peter Gay (1999)

'Romantic Poetry' is a philological term for a style or movement in verse-writing historically located in the late eighteenth and early nineteenth centuries. It is important to realize that the term works according to a fuzzy logic; that is to say, it is the very looseness of the term that can promote helpful critical discussion. Jerome J. McGann (1999)

The 'Romanticism' refined and institutionalized at the end of the nineteenth century was a men's club, and stayed that way a long time.   Susan Wolfson (2006)

Although many definitions are suggested, none command universal agreement. Duncan Wu (2006)

1 Contexts: History, Politics, Culture

British Politics 1789–1815

The French Revolution

One cataclysmic event shaped the entire politics of the Romantic period. Writing to his friend Lord Byron in 1816, the poet Shelley described the French Revolution, which informed European culture for decades afterwards, as 'the master theme of the epoch in which we live'. The fourteenth of July 1789 saw the storming of the Bastille prison in Paris by the masses, mobilised into action by a centuries-old grievance over the power and wealth of the aristocracy and, more particularly, by inflationary prices that threatened to place the cost of everyday staples – bread, wine and so on – beyond the means of the common man and woman. The French political system, dependent on an absolute monarchy, a king with huge powers, and a highly unrepresentative parliament which granted privileges to the nobility and the established Roman Catholic Church, made the British government, with its system of parliamentary representation (though this was actually highly limited by modern standards) and tripartite systemic 'balance' of King, Lords and Commons – which had been established after the 'Glorious Revolution' of 1688 – seem the very model of fairness.

The likes of Voltaire and Rousseau, the so-called *philosophes* of the eighteenth century ('philosophe' means philosopher in French, and the Enlightenment thinkers are generally referred to by this term), had warned of the dangers inherent in the iniquities of the French system of government and lamented the lack of fairness within it. 'Man is born free', wrote the latter in his *Social Contract* (1762), 'but he is everywhere in chains.' The *philosophes* had argued for reform along British lines; however, the actuality of the French Revolution went much further in transforming French society than they could have anticipated as the political reform which they envisaged was replaced by root-and-branch revolution in which previous models of government were abolished along with the system of monarchy and the very fabric of the *ancien régime* (the 'old regime', as the French system of government before the Revolution is generally referred to). The initially fairly moderate party of revolution, the Girondins, was soon displaced from power by the extremist Jacobin faction, led by Maximilien Robespierre (1758–94), who was instrumental in the execution of King Louis XVI in January 1793. Robespierre's pitiless rule climaxed in the bloody Reign of Terror of September 1793 to July 1794 in which tens of thousands of the aristocracy, the former queen Marie Antoinette and other so-called enemies of the state – including many Girondins – were guillotined. The year 1793 also saw Great Britain join the European Revolutionary wars in which a pan-European alliance (Austria, the Dutch Republic, Portugal, Russia and others) fought the French republic, and France simultaneously sought to export revolution. Despite the fall and execution of Robespierre in 1794, hostilities lingered on until the Peace of Amiens in 1802, by which time the French Revolutionary government had been replaced. France found herself once again ruled by another monarch, this time no Bourbon potentate but the brilliant young Corsican general Napoleon Bonaparte (1769–1821), who seized power as first consul in 1799 and eventually proclaimed himself Emperor in 1804.

The Revolution and British Society

The French Revolution had a seismic effect on British society. It seemed to many at the time that events across the channel might inspire a far-reaching reform in Great Britain itself. Initially, before the bloody tidings of the Terror and the lopping off of the king and queen's heads reached British ears, and before the country became involved in the Revolutionary wars, leaving British sympathisers of revolution open to charges of a lack of patriotism, even treason, many people were enthusiastic supporters of the Revolution. Certainly the first generation of Romantic poets rallied to the cause, at least in its early days. Wordsworth famously eulogised his reaction to the fall of the Bastille and the Revolution of 1789, which took place when he was an undergraduate at Cambridge University: 'Bliss was it that dawn to be alive / But to be young was very heaven.' Similarly Coleridge, who went to the same university in 1791, was also an enthusiastic devotee of French liberty and, indeed, anticipated a corresponding transformation of British society, a new millennium of peace and equality throughout Europe (see 'Millenarianism'). However, this was no consensual view. Many English people remained wedded to a Church-and-King Toryism, sneeringly labelling friends of the Revolution such as Coleridge and Wordsworth 'Jacobins', as if they were followers of the loathed Robespierre and, indeed, enthusiasts for Madame Guillotine herself.

It must also be remembered that not all hitherto left-leaning thinkers approved of the revolution. Edmund Burke, the great Irish Whig politician (the Whigs were the – relatively – liberal eighteenth-century opposition to the Tories) who had been sympathetic to the American Revolution of 1776, caused a schism in liberal circles by publishing his highly antipathetic *Reflections on the Revolution in France* (1790) in which he derided French 'liberty, equality and fraternity' as mere chimeras, stressed the importance of tradition and continuity within political systems, and chivalrously leapt to the defence of the former Queen of France as a paragon of female virtue whose elegant personage was threatened by the rough attentions of what he labelled the 'swinish multitude'. The Whig party split and Burke and many of his like-minded colleagues (the 'Rockingham Whigs' as they were known) crossed the floor of the House of Commons to sit with the Tory party under Prime Minster William Pitt the Younger (1759–1806), first minister from 1783 onwards, who as a consequence of what he saw as the potential threat of the French Revolution to the British political system transformed himself and his faction from advocates of systematic parliamentary reform into implacable opponents of any form of change to the status quo.

The 'Revolutionary Controversy'

The *Reflections* ignited a political war of words involving some of the most notable of the English Jacobins in what the critic Marilyn Butler has influentially labelled a 'Revolution Controversy' instigated by Burke. Central to these debates were the set of London-based thinkers and writers clustered around the radical publisher Joseph Johnson, who swiftly ran to the defence of the Revolution. The first sustained rebuttal of Burke was Mary Wollstonecraft's, *A Vindication of the Rights of Men* (1790), which supported the universal rights of mankind in a post-Rousseauian manner (Wollstonecraft also advocated social as well as political reform in her *Vindication of the Rights of Woman* (1792), which argued for a society which would value women as the intellectual and moral equals of men). This was closely followed by Thomas Paine's hugely successful *The Rights of Man* (1791), a central plank in working-class English radicalism for many decades afterwards. The firebrand Paine, an English emigrant to America and acquaintance of both General Washington and one of his successors as President of the United States, Thomas Jefferson, had become the principal propagandist for the cause of the colonists in his incendiary pamphlet *Common Sense* (1776), one of the founding documents of the American Revolution. Sensing the chance of fermenting Revolution in the mother country, he returned to Britain in 1787 and published *The Rights of Man* in which he attacked the 'rancour, prejudice and ignorance' of Burke's *Reflections* and argued that the people themselves should decide a country's constitution rather than having it imposed from on high by kings, noblemen and priests. Paine was joined in the radical chorus by Wollstonecraft's future husband William Godwin in his proto-anarchist treatise, *An Enquiry Concerning Political Justice* (1793), which envisaged the withering away of all state authority, alongside the demise of formal religion and the institution of marriage. Whereas Paine's style was populist, witty and passionate, written in a manner intended to appeal to the common people, Godwin's was measured and stately, advocating highly radical change to the middle classes in a dry and carefully argued manner.

Radical ideas such as Thomas Paine's began to spark mass protest amongst the English working class, especially after Great Britain joined the Revolutionary wars which were convulsing Europe, as the Austrian Empire, Britain, Prussia, Russia and a number of other states fought against France; 1794 and 1795 saw mass protest meetings against the war and in favour of radical political reform, held in London and the provinces. Alarmed by what they saw as the imminent threat of armed revolution, Pitt's Tory government, caught up in European war and besieged by internal dissent, introduced tough and repressive measures. Habeas corpus (the right to a trial before a jury of one's peers) was suspended in May 1794 while the so-called 'Gagging Acts' of November 1795 forbade public meetings of more than fifty people unless specifically licensed by a magistrate, and introduced measures to censor the press, which the government saw as disproportionately Whiggish. Many of the leaders of the leading radical association, the London Corresponding Society (LCS), Thomas Hardy, John Thelwall and John Horne Tooke amongst them, were arrested and charged, unsuccessfully, with high treason in the famous treason trials of 1794. They were acquitted in large part because of the intervention of William Godwin's tract 'Cursory Strictures', which demolished the prosecution case, but the LCS never recovered its influence to the same extent thereafter, and English radicalism waned by the turn of the century, not recovering until after the passing of the Napoleonic age.

The Revolutionary and Napoleonic Wars

As the decade of the 1790s wore on, France enjoyed a measure of military success in continental Europe, notably in its annexation of Switzerland, hitherto the bastion of European republicanism and closely associated – given that it was the birthplace of Rousseau – with the concept of 'liberty'. This event was instrumental in leading both Coleridge and Wordsworth finally to lose patience with the Revolution, a faith which had previously been severely tried by the Terror and tested by their country's war with France. Coleridge lamented in 'France: An Ode' (1798) that he, a 'worshipper' of 'the spirit of divinest Liberty', had been betrayed by that country. He describes his initial ecstasies at the Revolution, when he, in 'slavish' Britain, reacted with 'joy' at events across the channel:

> When France in wrath her giant-limbs upreared,
> And with that oath, which smote earth, air, and sea,
> Stamped her strong foot and said she would be free,
> Bear witness for me, how I hoped and feared!
> With what a joy, my lofty gratulation
> Unawed I sung, amid a slavish band.

Coleridge records his personal shame at Britain joining the crowd of reactionary European tyrants such as the Tsar of Russia and the Emperor of the Austro-Hungarian Empire arrayed against republican France: 'The monarchs marched in evil day, / And Britain joined the dire array.' Even in the face of the French Terror – 'A dance more wild than ever maniac's dream' – Coleridge hoped that once the spasm had passed the French would return to being a sponsor of freedom and liberty, exporting a new vision of 'love and Joy':

> 'And soon', I said, 'shall Wisdom teach her lore
> In the low huts of them that toil and groan!
> And, conqu'ring by her happiness alone,
> Shall France compel the nations to be free,
> Till love and Joy look round, and call the earth their own!'
>
> Forgive me, Freedom! O forgive those dreams!
> I hear thy voice, I hear thy loud lament,
> From bleak Helvetia's icy caverns sent –
> I hear thy groans upon her bloodstained streams!
> Heroes, that for your peaceful country perished,
> And ye that, fleeing, spot your mountain snows
> With bleeding wounds – forgive me, that I cherished
> One thought that ever blessed your cruel foes!

By the 1810s, both Wordsworth's and Coleridge's politics had swung round to the implacable Toryism which led to their denunciation by the likes of Shelley and Byron (to the younger poets, it seemed, in Robert Browning's memorable phrase, that Wordsworth was now 'The Lost Leader'), but it is important to realise that the first generation of Romantic poets and the forging of the Romantic literary project, if that is what we might call it, were fashioned by men then of what we now call the left.

At this stage, and in 1797 to 1798 most particularly, it really seemed as if an invasion of Great Britain was likely. Over 100,000 French soldiers of the 'Army of England' congregated on the channel coast and British newspapers manifested a mixture of fear and paranoia at the prospect of what they saw as an army of *sans culottes* (the term means 'without knee-breeches' and was applied to the poorer adherents of French republicanism) marching through the Home Counties. Historically, when Britain is caught up in European war, Irish revolutionaries, as the Easter Rising of 1916 demonstrates, have frequently sought to take advantage, and so at the same time as an invasion of England seemed imminent, there were the stirrings of domestic revolution in Ireland, in the 1798 uprising of the United Irishmen led by Theobald Wolfe Tone in favour of French ideals of liberty and with the aim of ridding Ireland of British rule. Tone canvassed a number of the French soldiery, General Bonaparte included, and a small invading force arrived from France to support Tone's insurrection, but was swiftly put down. The invasion of England, on the other hand, never happened as the French concentrated on war in Austria and Egypt, and Wolfe Tone died in prison, at his own hand, while awaiting execution.

Exhausted by seven years of war, France and its continental enemies agreed a ceasefire in 1800, followed by peace with Britain in the next year, a cessation of hostilities which lasted until May 1803. William Pitt, lukewarm about the truce, was replaced as Prime Minister by the ministry of Henry Addington, formerly Speaker of the House of Commons. Pitt returned as war leader in 1804 when Europe was convulsed by conflict once again. The fighting spread to the Iberian peninsula by 1807, where the young Duke of Wellington led an army which took until 1814 to drive the Napoleonic army out of Spain after a decade's hard combat, and, most crucially, to Russia where Napoleon, after sensational initial victories and a surge to Moscow, fought an eventually ruinous campaign in 1811–12. In Britain, Pitt, his body emaciated by years of heavy drinking and self-neglect, died in 1806 at the age of forty-six, briefly to be replaced by the coalition 'Ministry of All the Talents', which featured both the Tories and such Whig luminaries as Charles James Fox and the politician-dramatist Richard Brinsley Sheridan. This unlikely ménage lasted less than a year and the Tories were returned to power, remaining there for over twenty years. The following year of 1807 was notable for the abolition of the slave trade (see 'Slavery, Abolition and African-British Literature'), brought about in large part by the efforts of philanthropic Evangelicals such as Thomas Clarkson and William Wilberforce, the culmination of two decades of agitation against the iniquities of slavery (the actual freeing of the slaves in the British West Indian plantations would have to wait more than twenty-five years after that).

The Regency

Throughout Pitt's administration and its successors, the British King, George III, had remained staunchly devoted to the Tory interest. His despised son, however, George, Prince of Wales, favoured the Whig interest, and after the Ministry of Talents the Whigs remained convinced that, should the King die or return to the mental confusion which had disabled him in the 1780s, Prince George would bring them back into power. In this they were mistaken. In 1812, the King lapsed back into madness and the new Prince Regent, now possessed of all the powers of the monarch, retained the Tories in office even after the murder of his Prime Minister, Spencer Perceval, in that year, thereby ensuring his transformation from hero of liberty in Whig opinion to drunken, corpulent traitor to the cause (the Prince had a well-known penchant for fine wine, lavish dinners and middle-aged aristocratic mistresses (see 'Satire')).

In the first few years of the Prince Regent's reign, it seemed as if Napoleon, his military strength sapped by his Russian misadventure and by Wellington's highly successful assault on the French army in the Spanish peninsula, would have to sue for peace. This duly occurred in 1814 when the Emperor abdicated and was banished to the island of Elba and European peace was restored. However, it was short lived. Escaping from his island gaol, Napoleon was enthusiastically welcomed back by the French people and battle swiftly resumed against the anti-Napoleonic alliance of Britain, Russia and Prussia, in the so-called 'hundred days' of Napoleon's return, which ended in June 1815 with his final defeat in Belgium at the Battle of Waterloo by the Duke of Wellington's British forces and the Prussian army led by Marshal Blücher. Unlike the hapless Louis, Napoleon kept his head but was banished to the South Atlantic island of St Helena. With these momentous events, one of the most remarkable periods in British history ended.

See also   Empire and Travel; Ireland and the Catholic Question; Millenarianism; Philosophy; Political Protest; Satire; Slavery, Abolition and African-British Literature.

Further Reading

Asa Briggs, *The Age of Improvement 1783–1867* (1959).
Marilyn Butler, *Burke, Paine, Godwin and the Revolution Controversy* (1984).
J. C. D. Clark, *English Society 1688–1832: Ideology, Social Structure and Political Practice during the Ancien Regime* (1985).
William Doyle, *The Oxford History of the French Revolution* (2nd edition, 2002).
Boyd Hilton, *A Mad, Bad, and Dangerous People? England 1783–1846* (2006).
Roy Porter, *The Enlightenment* (2nd edition, 2001).

British Politics 1815–1832

Post-Napoleonic Britain

In August 1815, Napoleon, after rising from his Elban grave and haunting Europe for the 'Hundred Days' (see previous entry), was finally consigned to living incarceration in the remote South Atlantic island of St Helena, where he wore out his last few years before dying an agonising death, probably from stomach cancer (though some argue as a consequence of poisoning), in May 1821. In the euphoric aftermath of victory at Waterloo, it seemed in Britain that a new era of peace and prosperity beckoned, but this was far from the case. Tens of thousands of demobbed soldiers struggled to find employment on their return from the continent as the economy lurched into depression. Bad harvests inflated bread prices and the spectre of famine raised its unattractive head. Instead of calm and contentment, peacetime Great Britain lurched into political unrest. Around twenty years of war were followed by a period of severe political and economic turmoil.

As a consequence of the post-Napoleonic social travails, British radicalism's stock rose as that of the economy fell, despite the passing of the first of the protectionist and highly contentious Corn Laws in 1815, which were designed to support domestic prices against cheap foreign imports to the advantage of producers rather than of consumers. A series of mass protest rallies demonstrated against what oppositionalists perceived as the iniquities and inadequacies of Lord Liverpool's Tory government. The radical leaders, Henry 'Orator' Hunt, William Cobbett and others, called for parliamentary reform and for the fairer treatment of the working classes. For the first time since the early to mid-1790s, it seemed as if England might descend – or ascend, depending on your point of view – into revolution. A huge gathering at Spa Fields in London in December 1816 led to rioting and an unsuccessful armed march – in the Fall of the Bastille manner – on the Tower of London. Habeas corpus was once again suspended and trials for treason ensued. In February 1820, the so-called Cato Street conspirators, drawn from the most extreme of the Ultra-radicals, led by Arthur Thistlewood (who had been a leading light at Spa Fields), actually plotted to assassinate senior figures in the administration, the loathed foreign secretary Lord Castlereagh in particular, hoping this would spark a wider class struggle and the overthrow of the government (see 'Political Protest and Popular Radicalism'). In the end, informers did for the conspirators, who were led to the customary place of execution at Tyburn Hill.

Perhaps more significant than these somewhat pathetic, doomed attempts at violent rebellion was the radical mainstream of Cobbett and 'Orator' Hunt. Cobbett was proprietor of a number of journals, notably the *Register*, in which he championed the cause of the people, and the rural poor most particularly. Henry Hunt, a firebrand radical but no revolutionary, agitated in a series of mass 'monster' meetings for the cause of radicalism, most importantly in the famous August 1819 meeting at St Peter's Field in Manchester during which he addressed a huge crowd of several thousand people. The Riot Act was read and a panicky local yeomanry charged, killing eleven people in the process. This became known as the 'Peterloo massacre', an iconic moment in the history of English radicalism which encapsulated, for them, the fear and contempt in which the ruling class viewed the common people. In self-imposed exile in Italy, the radical poet Shelley raged against what he saw as the homicidal nature of the British state in *The Mask of Anarchy* (1820):

> As I lay asleep in Italy
> There came a voice from over the Sea,
> And with great power it forth led me
> To walk in the visions of Poesy.
>
> I met Murder on the way –
> He had a mask like Castlereagh –
> Very smooth he looked, yet grim;
> Seven blood-hounds followed him:
>
> All were fat; and well they might
> Be in admirable plight,
> For one by one, and two by two,
> He tossed the human hearts to chew
> Which from his wide cloak he drew.

Post-Napoleonic Europe

Great Britain apart, in wider European terms 1815 saw the second restoration of the French monarchy in the figure of Louis XVIII, younger brother of the headless sixteenth Louis and uncle of the hapless seventeenth (who died in gaol at the age of ten). Following Napoleon's demise, in September 1815 France's old enemies, Austria, Prussia and Russia, established the unyieldingly anti-democratic Holy Alliance as a bulwark against what it saw as the twin threats of revolution and secularism. Testimony to the Alliance's politics was the right-wing British government's unwillingness to join on account of its former allies' reactionary politics. Nonetheless, following the Congress of Aix-la-Chappelle (now Aachen, in Germany) in 1818 which decided on the evacuation of troops from France, Britain – alongside newly monarchical France – joined the Quintuple Alliance, a kind of proto-League of Nations with a conservative bent designed to sustain peace – albeit on its own terms – in Europe. This all said, the French settlement was by no means stable and eventually led to the second French Revolution, the July Revolution of 1830, in which another Bourbon king, Louis XVIII's successor, Charles X, was removed from power (though escaping with his head).

The Queen Caroline Crisis

Back in Britain, 1817 was significant as the year of the death of the heir apparent Princess Charlotte, only daughter of the Prince Regent, as a consequence of complications arising from her delivering a stillborn son. This young woman had been the new great hope of the Whigs, given that she was estranged from her father (as the Prince had been from his in the earlier 1800s). In 1820, George III, the 'old, mad, blind, despised and dying king', in P. B. Shelley's memorable phrase from his sonnet 'England in 1819', finally expired, and Prince George became George IV. Family tragedy was succeeded by family farce with the introduction of a parliamentary 'bill of pains and penalties', designed to remove the title of queen from the new monarch's estranged wife Caroline on account of the queen's alleged dalliance – her 'indecent and offensive familiarity [and] licentious, disgraceful and adulterous intercourse' – as the bill put it – with her Italian manservant Bartolomi Pergami, and end the Royal marriage by act of parliament (this is often referred to as the 'trial' of Queen Caroline).

The reading of the bill and the extraordinary debates and investigations which surrounded it in parliament turned into a voyeuristic delight, with tales of stained sheets, servants' gossip and other unsavoury evidence being paraded before a scandal-hungry public. Ever eager to embarrass the King, the Whig opposition took up the cause of Queen Caroline with alacrity, maintaining (without, it has to be said, a great deal of evidence) the highly unlikely argument that the Queen's relations with Bartolomi had been entirely innocent. The bill never passed, being dropped by a Tory administration worried about incensing popular opinion and inciting civil unrest only a few months after the events at Cato Street. Desperate to keep his despised wife out of the coronation to which she was still legally entitled, the prince hired the most notable boxers of the day, from Tom Cribb, champion of all England, downwards, to act as a phalanx of bouncers to eject her majesty should she turn up at the ceremony (Leigh Hunt scoffed in a contemporaneous satirical poem that the prince had begged the rough pugilists to 'Save us from our wife – O!'). In the end the queen was refused admission at bayonet point by a member of the soldiery, and what was seen as her undignified exhibitionism at the coronation and her acceptance of a pension of £50,000 per year as a sop from the government alienated many of her radical supporters. Queen Caroline had little time to enjoy her bounty, dying shortly afterwards, in August 1821, as a consequence of intestinal problems, possibly stomach cancer (though there were those who said that she, like Napoleon several months earlier, had been poisoned by her enemies).

Catholic Emancipation

Matters improved in general economic terms in Great Britain as the 1820s progressed (though were still undeniably grim if you were a factory worker toiling ten hours a day in one of the new Lancashire factories, or a London seamstress doing piece work for a pittance an hour; see 'Industry and Economics'). In 1827 Lord Liverpool, Prime Minister for fifteen years after the assassination of the Regent's first PM, Spencer Perceval, in 1812, retired on health grounds. He was succeeded by the more moderate George Canning, a Burkean Whig in the late 1780s and the brilliant satirist of the *Anti-Jacobin* (1797–8; see 'Satire'), who died within four months of taking office. Up to the plate stepped the figure of the Duke of Wellington (1769–1852), the fire-eating general and senior cabinet minister who had refused to serve in Canning's administration, fearing that it was too liberal. Within a year the old Tory warhorse, an Anglo-Irish Protestant from Dublin, had overseen the passing of an act of Catholic Emancipation (1829) (see 'Ireland and the "Catholic Question"') which repealed the last of the Irish Penal Laws and finally allowed Roman Catholics to sit in parliament. Robert Peel, Home Secretary, though initially opposed to Emancipation, felt that such a measure was preferable to revolution in Ireland: 'though emancipation was a great danger, civil strife was a greater danger'. George III had been implacably opposed to the cause and had vetoed a previous Emancipation bill in 1801 and equally opposed the efforts at reform of the 1807 Ministry of all the Talents. His son (after abandoning his Whiggism in 1812) felt the same way, and it was only the 'Iron Duke's' threat to resign as Prime Minister if he did not receive royal assent to the bill that carried the day.

Parliamentary Reform

Though the Tories narrowly won the general election of summer 1830 which was held after the king's death, it was clear that a measure of parliamentary reform, like Catholic Emancipation before it, was becoming an inevitability, given that there had been a widespread perception since the 1780s that the system of parliamentary representation was demonstrably unfair (Pitt the Younger himself shared this conviction early in that decade). A 'borough' (a modern-day constituency) could be no more than a hamlet with a few dozen electors in the pay of local dignitaries (a 'pocket borough'); the most notorious of which was the famous 'rotten borough'

'Old Sarum' in Salisbury (which had only five electors in the election of 1802 and only eleven in 1831 in its last parliamentary hurrah, none of whom actually lived there). On the other hand a borough could be a sizeable city such as Leeds, then with a population measured in the tens of thousands. Worse, powerful noblemen controlled several dozen of the pocket boroughs between them; the Whig Sydney Smith proclaimed that 'The country belongs to the Duke of Rutland, Lord Lonsdale, the Duke of Newcastle, and about twenty other holders of boroughs. They are our masters!'

Following the 1830 election, Wellington's resolutely anti-reform views split his party and he lost a vote of confidence in November of that year. After nearly forty years in power the Tories had fallen. Wellington was replaced by the Whig leader Charles Grey, the second Earl Grey (1764–1845). Earl Grey and his lieutenant Lord John Russell attempted to take a reform bill through parliament in the early months of their adminis- tration but were thwarted. As a consequence the new King, William IV, brother of the late George IV, called a general election, held between April and June 1831, in which the Whigs were returned with a sizeable majority of 136 over the Tories, and won a vast majority of all of the English seats which were not in the pockets of Tory aristocrats. Grey then reintroduced a bill intended to 'take effectual Measures for correcting diverse Abuses that have long prevailed in the Choice of Members to serve in the Commons House of Parliament'. Most of the pocket boroughs were swept away and the second Reform Bill, when enacted, significantly extended the franchise. Nonetheless, voters – all male of course – were still required to possess property worth £10 and the working classes, despite their leaders' enthusi- asm for the Act, remained disenfranchised. Adult suffrage would have to wait until 1918 for men (and women over 30) and even later – 1928 – for universal female suffrage. In the aftermath of the Act, the radicals who had agitated for reform were split. While William Cobbett and Henry Hunt were returned to parliament, the radical poor began to turn instead to the leader- ship of the Chartist movement, which agitated for universal male suffrage and a range of other political reforms and which was so important in the Victorian political scene in the later 1830s and 1840s.

See also   Industry and Economics; Ireland and the 'Catholic Question'; Political Protest and Popular Radicalism; Satire.

Further Reading

Asa Briggs, *The Age of Improvement 1783–1867* (1959).
James Chandler, *England in 1819: The Politics of Literary Culture and the Case of Romantic Historicism* (1998).

J. C. D. Clark, *English Society 1688–1832: Ideology, Social Structure and Political Practice during the Ancien Regime* (1985).
Boyd Hilton, *A Mad, Bad, and Dangerous People? England 1783–1846* (2006).

Empire and Travel

The Growth of Empire

The British Empire developed apace throughout the first half of the eighteenth century as Great Britain grew and consolidated its dominions in Asia, North America, the West Indies and the Pacific. By the second half of the century the American colonies had developed into vast and profitable territories, Canada's French had finally been subdued (after the siege of Quebec in 1759), and the British influence in India had developed into rule of significant parts of the sub-continent (the East India Company administered much of India from the 1750s onwards). In this period Captain Cook opened promising trade routes with Polynesia, Australasia began to be colonised, and the Caribbean, with its slave-dominated economy, continued to prove the most lucrative of all the British dominions.

In the midst of this growing power and influence, however, one great and troubling event occurred, the secession of the 'thirteen colonies' in the American Revolution, which began in 1776 and led to the loss of the most important of all the British holdings in the 'New World'. Though it now seems like a given of history, it should be remembered how extraordinary the revolution seemed at the time, and how shocking to the motherland was the colonials' revolt. The defeat of the King's army by what was seen by some in Britain as a coalition of traitorous landowners and soldiers (General Washington most particularly), self-interested merchants and ignorant rabble dealt a terrible blow to national esteem, and helped to ensure that Pitt's government in the 1790s would take severe measures to ensure that there would not be a revolution at home equivalent to those which had occurred in the United States and France.

The events of 1776 also ensured that Britain would subsequently seek to bind its remaining territories and dominions more closely to its embrace. The India Act of 1784 in effect nationalised the East India Company and during the 1790s – as in Great Britain itself – there was a clear emphasis upon counter-revolutionary measures in the wider empire after the French Revolution of 1789 (and Ireland, arguably Britain's oldest colony, became part of the United Kingdom in 1801 as a consequence of the Act of Union). At the same time, there was also an attempt to internalise British manners, social mores and religion into its colonies, notably by zealous missionaries. The founding in 1804 of the British and Foreign Bible Society is symbolic of the contemporary attempt to Christianise home and Empire alike. Indeed, though there were those whom we would now label 'anti-imperialists' in Britain in the Romantic era (the poet Shelley, for instance, called the notion of empire a 'scheme for the enslaving of the most civilised portion of mankind'), the mainstream of public opinion was in its favour, despite what many saw as the one shameful stain on empire, the slave trade (William Wilberforce and his cohorts in the abolitionist movement were against slavery rather than empire *per se*).

As well as sending off Bibles and the message of Christianity to its dominions, Great Britain was also exporting less prized assets in the contemporary system of transportation, in which criminals would be shipped out to toil in the wider reaches of the Empire. After the loss of the American colonies, previously the dumping ground for British criminals, the decision was taken to base the principal penal settlements for the United Kingdom in what is now Australia, notably in Botany Bay (now part of Sydney) and Van Diemen's Land (now Tasmania). Here felons convicted of crimes from shoplifting to picking pockets, alongside those whose capital sentences for burglary and so on had been commuted, laboured in fearsome heat and disease-ridden conditions to found a new country. From what was then seen as the bottom of the world (Botany Bay, Van Diemen's Land and Captain Cook's New Zealand and Polynesia) to the top (Britons made most of the early Arctic explorations, for example in the doomed searches in northern Canada for the North West passage), the late eighteenth and early nineteenth centuries were notable for the way in which British explorers, armies, and colonists willing and unwilling, spread throughout the world.

Travel and its Literature

Simultaneous with the growth of Empire was an increasing willingness to travel both at home and abroad, especially amongst the privileged. Fabulously wealthy and frequently aristocratic young men would undertake the 'Grand Tour' in the mid- to late eighteenth century upon completing their education (often after attending one of the universities) by making a visit, generally accompanied by a tutor, to Europe (indeed, the very word 'tourist' dates from the later eighteenth century). Travel was generally supposed to expand a young man's horizons and complete his gentlemanly education; William Gilpin's treatise *Three Essays: on Picturesque Beauty; on Picturesque Travel; and on Sketching Landscape* (2nd edition, 1794) captures this sense of the pedagogical nature of early tourism very well, stressing the importance of 'travel as a civilising force, alongside the study of the classics, foreign languages, hunting and so on'. Lord Byron's Grand Tour to eastern Europe and the Mediterranean (to Albania, Greece, Malta and

Turkey) is perhaps the most famous of these expeditions, though whether his lordship's tour was a 'civilising force' is a matter of debate, given that many of his adventures on these travels involved sleeping with transient sexual partners of both sexes (its naughtiness exemplified in Byron's description of visits to the Turkish baths, 'marble palace[s] of sherbet and sodomy'). That said, the poet's European sojourn directly informed his early writing; to a certain extent the work which made Byron's name, *Childe Harold's Pilgrimage* (1812–16), draws on his experiences – though certainly not all of them – on the Grand Tour. *Childe Harold* is a piece of imaginative travel writing, and Byron's satirical masterpiece *Don Juan* (1819–24; see 'Satire') is also a kind of travelogue, as its hero moves from Spain to Russia and Great Britain and many points in between. Byron's experiences in the East also informed the successful Oriental tales which he produced in the 1810s such as *The Giaour* (1813) and *The Corsair* (1814).

As the nineteenth century rolled on, the well-heeled British middle classes also began to travel in unprecedented numbers, both in their own country and abroad. There was a vogue to visit famous picturesque sites – in Europe, Mont Blanc, Etna, and the Alps; in the British Isles, the Lake District, Fingal's Cave, Snowdon, and the Scottish Highlands (this last especially after the commencement of Sir Walter Scott's series of 'Waverley' novels in 1814). This phenomenon was exemplified in the spectacle of the British bourgeoisie hastening in large numbers to the continent from 1815 onwards, after twenty years in which this had been well nigh impossible on account of the Revolutionary and Napoleonic Wars. Indeed, 1815 was a watershed for British travel, as the cessation of hostilities saw a host of English tourists pour into France and beyond. As Mary Shelley wrote in 1826, 'after many years of war ... our island prison was opened to us, and our watery exit from it was declared practicable, it was the paramount wish of every English heart ... to hasten to the continent'. The Irish poet Thomas Moore's highly successful satire *The Fudge Family in Paris* (1818) mocked what he saw as the vulgarity of the new travellers enjoying the loosening of the restrictions, portraying the flighty Biddy Fudge on her arrival in Calais lamenting the lack of 'sentimental' scenery. Expecting a land of fashion and finery, instead she encounters the deprived citizenry of post-war France: 'some picturesque beggars, whose multitudes seem / To recall the good days of the *ancien régime*'. In Paris itself, the travelling Fudges look but do not understand, their perception of French culture limited to food, balls and social frippery. The momentous events which had changed Europe after the fall of Napoleon – the rise of the Holy Alliance, the reintroduction of the monarchy, entrenched reactionary governments throughout the continent, and the continued suffering of the poor – mean nothing to these foolish young people.

The ability to travel significant distances began to spread ever wider in social terms in the following decade, which saw the development of the steam-ships which were already changing the speed and topography of tourism along waterways, and, in particular, the emergence of the railway in the late 1820s, which quickly made the old coaching system redundant and initiated a new era of mass travel for all – from the first- to the third-class passenger. To many contemporary eyes the great invention promised to change the world; writing about the new Liverpool railway in *A Practical Treatise on Locomotive Engines upon Railways* (1836), François de Pambour asked excitedly, 'What may not society at large expect in future from this new industry, which will augment, ten-fold, the capital and produce of the country, by the immense influence of speedy and economical conveyance!' For the likes of de Pambour the 'economical conveyance' afforded by the railway democratised travel, and promised great things for 'society at large'. However, some others were not convinced. To social conservatives such as the Tory journalist C. J. Apperley, traditional English life seemed to be threatened by this new-fangled modernity. Apperley lamented what he saw as the deleterious effects of the railway, where sturdy coachmen were transformed into industrial plebs and where honest passengers were treated like the scum of the earth, with all risking life and limb in the notoriously accident-prone railway:

> The healthy-looking coachmen and guards [are] metamorphosed into smoke-dried stokers and greasy engineers; their passengers conveyed through the country like thieves amidst hosts of police officers and constables, and locked in vans as if on the road to Newgate; and all this with the chance of being blown up into the clouds, or decapitated on the spot!

As well as seeing epochal developments in travel itself, the Romantic era was also notable as the period in which travel writing developed as never before in a torrent of travelogues, philosophical treatises, poems and novels. Before the Romantic era, much travel writing was written by navigators telling of their sojourns in fantastically remote, and, indeed, sometimes mythical, places. This was the manner of Marco Polo's famous early fourteenth-century *Travels* and of the fabulous *Travels* of the mid-fourteenth century attributed to Sir John Mandeville, and, more recently, the *Account of a Voyage Round the World, 1768–71*, of Captain James Cook (1773), and Louis-Antoine de Bougainville's *Voyage Autour du Monde* (1771). Alongside the latter, there was also a vogue for fiction which exploited the conventions of the literature of travel, such as Jonathan Swift's *Gulliver's Travels* (1726), in which exotic voyages were pressed into the satirical service of an examination of the state of affairs in Great Britain and Ireland, and in what has been seen as the first English novel, Daniel Defoe's *Robinson Crusoe* (1719). In both of these works, travel is reinterpreted for moral, satirical and religious purposes. Both fed into Romantic travel writing (and before that into the mid-eighteenth-century tradition of picaresque fiction in the work of Henry Fielding, Tobias Smollett and, arguably, Laurence Sterne).

The earliest, most basic form of travel writing, first-hand narratives, was not neglected in the Romantic period, which saw the appearance of such works as James Bruce's *Travels to Discover the Source of the Nile* (1790), Captain James Wilson's *A Missionary Voyage to the Southern Pacific* (1799), Charles Waterton's *Wandering in South America* (1825) and William Ellis's *Tour through Hawaii* (1826). Mungo Park, the surgeon, African explorer and friend of Walter Scott, published his *Travels in the Interior Districts of Africa ... in the Years 1795, 1796 and 1797* (published on his return from the so-called 'dark continent' in 1799), and there was also a taste for books about the Caribbean and the Indian sub-continent in the success of Bryan Edwards's *History ... of the British Colonies in the West Indies* (1793) and Thomas Pennant's *View of Hindoostan* (1798). At the same time the notion of travel providing a vehicle for commenting on British society continued, in such texts as the aforesaid *Don Juan*'s satirical picaresque, or Robert Bage's 'Jacobin' novel *Hermsprong* (1796; scc 'Thc Novel'), in which a young man brought up by American Indians returns to Great Britain bearing with him enlightened views on the equality of women and offers radical views on the unfair class divisions within British society.

This was also the method of Robert Southey, who assumed the voice of a Spanish traveller in England in his *Letters from England: by Don Manuel Alvarez Espriella, Translated from the Spanish* (1807), a conceit which permitted him to range broadly in commenting, often waspishly, on British manners, prejudices and bigotry and to meditate on contemporary politics, religion, sport and medicine among other topics. Writing in 1799, the author Jane West lamented the ideological slant of some current travel writing: 'Books of travels are converted into vehicles of politics and systems of legislation.' Works such as Southey's *Letters from England* and the *Letters* (1790–5) of Helen Maria Williams (*c.*1761–1827) bear her out. Williams, the radical friend of Mary Wollstonecraft (and indeed the recipient of William Wordsworth's first published poem 'Sonnet on Seeing Miss Helen Maria Williams Weep at a Tale of Distress' (1787, written under the pseudonym 'Axiologus')), who lived in Paris from 1788 onwards, wrote and published epistolary accounts of France in its momentous years which expressed her initial enthusiasm for the Revolution, especially for the Girondin faction which held power before the rise of Robespierre's Jacobins.

In none of the historical traditions of British travel-related writing was introspective self-analysis particularly evident. However, and perhaps unsurprisingly given the philosophical preoccupations of Romanticism, this became very important in the Romantic period's tradition of travel writing. Take, for instance, Mary Wollstonecraft's *Travels Written during a Short Residence in Sweden, Norway and Denmark* (1796), a book well received in its day (admiring references appear in the journals or correspondence of Coleridge, Southey, Wordsworth and Hazlitt). Here the author projects her emotions onto the landscape while simultaneously internalising her surroundings. The external vision is here made internal – in the manner of the Romantic nature poet – as the 'cold' heart of the lovelorn Wollstonecraft (who had just been spurned by her lover Gilbert Imlay) finds its mirror image in the Norwegian scenery. Robert Southey wrote enthusiastically to a friend: 'Have you met with Mary Wollstonecraft's [book]? She has made me in love with a cold climate, and frost and snow, with a northern moonlight'; Wollstonecraft added Norway to the list of sublime landscapes loved and admired by the Romantic poets, and her combination of introspection and observation also set a template for a generation of poets. The former abstract thinker of such works as the *Vindication of the Rights of Woman* (1792) here presents herself as engaging emotionally and intuitively with nature; her emotional landscape interacts with her natural surroundings through the vehicle of a pronounced sensibility.

Wollstonecraft's travelling was an emotional as well as a physical journey. Travel in the period as a whole was often associated with mental and spiritual development. The Grand Tour, as we have seen, was supposed to broaden the mind and also serve an educative purpose, and its ethical basis was also shared by much British contemporary writing about travel, which was possessed of a didactic and philosophical bent. The pioneering works here were the *Observations on the River Wye ... Relative Chiefly to Picturesque Beauty; Made in the Summer of 1770* (1782) and the famous *Observations Relative to Picturesque Beauty, made in the Year 1772 ... Particularly the Mountains and Lakes of Cumberland* (1786) by William Gilpin (1724–1804), with their aim to 'examine landscape by the laws of picturesque beauty'. From the late 1760s Gilpin, a man of the cloth, travelled England in search of the 'picturesque' – the striking, the irregular, the angular (a term drawing on and developing Edmund Burke's 1757 treatise on the sublime and the beautiful; Gilpin portrayed the picturesque as lying somewhere in between the two concepts) in his published tours of trips to Wye and the Lake District and, finally, the Scottish Highlands (1800).

In the wake of Gilpin, travellers frequently followed his and other picturesque tours, on routes which had become very familiar by the 1810s, a fact encapsulated by John Keats's letter to Benjamin Robert Haydon of 8 April 1818:

I purpose within a Month to put my knapsack at my back and make a pedestrian tour through the North of England, and part of Scotland – to make a sort of Prologue to the Life I intend to pursue – that is to write, to study and to see all Europe at the lowest expence. I will clamber through the Clouds and exist. I will get such an accumulation of stupendous recollections that as I walk through the suburbs of London I may not see them – I will stand upon Mount Blanc.

As well as inspiring travellers such as Keats, who made it to the Lake District and the north of England and Scotland, though never, sadly, to Mont Blanc, Gilpin's work also initiated a tranche of philosophically informed writing about travel. In the wake of the publication of the Wye *Observations*, there was a vogue for both the picturesque tour and for travel writing, both in straightforward travelogues and in more thoughtful and meditative efforts. As Thomas West wrote in 1788, 'Since persons of genius, taste, and observation, began to make the tour of their own country, and to give such pleasing accounts of the natural history and improving state of the northern part of the kingdom, the spirit of visiting them has diffused itself among the curious of all ranks.' West gave his own 'pleasing account' in his highly successful and pioneering *A Guide to the Lakes* (1784), combining travel guide with philosophy in tempting readers 'to visit the lakes of Cumberland, Westmorland, and Lancashire; there to contemplate, in Alpine scenery, finished in nature's highest tints, the pastoral and rural landscape, exhibited in all their styles, the soft, the rude, the romantic, and the sublime; and of which perhaps like instances can nowhere be found assembled in so small a tract of country'.

West drew on both Burke's theory of the sublime and Gilpin's notion of the picturesque in his description of the Lakeland terrain which was to be so important in Romantic era poetry. That said, he was not the first to portray the Lake District in such a philosophically charged light. Before West, in 1753, Dr John Brown had written that the 'perfection' of Cumberland and Westmorland was attributable to their 'Beauty, horror and immensity'. After West came Wordsworth, who also composed a *Guide to the Lakes*, published in 1823, a volume which drew upon his sister Dorothy's own 'An Excursion on the Banks of Ullswater' (1805) and 'An Excursion up Scawfell Pike' (1818). (Dorothy Wordsworth wrote notable travel journals of trips to Scotland (1803; 1822), Switzerland (1820) and the Isle of Man (1828).) In his lifetime this was Wordsworth's best-selling book; Matthew Arnold recalled the poet telling him that a clergyman who visited the Wordsworths' home at Rydal Mount had 'asked him if he had ever written anything besides the *Guide to the Lakes*' ('"Yes", he answered modestly, "he had written verses"'). Like West, Wordsworth offered both a locodescriptive and a sublimised version of the Lake District, and in the latter his prose travelogue mirrored the imaginative tenor of his verse.

Wordsworth wrote about travel from the very beginning of his poetic career, which began with the publication of his first two books in 1793, *An Evening Walk*, an exercise in the picturesque mode, and the *Descriptive Sketches, in Verse, taken during a Pedestrian Tour in the Italian, Grison, Swiss, and Savoyard Alps* (1793), which drew on his personal experience of European travel. A nineteenth-century contributor to *Fraser's Magazine* wrote that 'Good travel-writing requires a certain sort of egotism. It is indeed autobiography – a narrative of personal adventure.' Wordsworth's imaginative vision – his 'egotistical sublime' in Keats's phrase – owed much to his travelling, and especially to his incessant 'pedestrianism'. Thomas De Quincey once cattily wrote of Wordsworth that 'His legs were pointedly condemned by all the female connoisseurs in legs that I ever heard lecture on that topic,' but certainly the poet was a keen 'peripatetic', to use the other contemporary term; he walked incessantly, often composing as he went, thinking nothing of covering a dozen miles or more on an everyday walk. As an undergraduate in the University of Cambridge, the young radical, enthused by the French Revolution of 1789, decided he wanted to see matters for himself, and in the summer vacation of 1790 set off for Paris, and – the Channel excepted – made his journey entirely on foot. Wordsworth's journey was also significant in terms of both his political and his poetical development. John Keats never saw Mont Blanc but William Wordsworth did. Travel directly informs what has generally been seen as the very heart of British Romanticism in Wordsworth's *The Prelude*, in such moments as his famous and powerful account of seeing Mont Blanc for the first time:

> That day we first
> Beheld the summit of Mont Blanc, and grieved
> To have a soulless image on the eye
> Which had usurped upon a living thought
> That never more could be. The wondrous Vale
> Of Chamouny did, on the following dawn,
> With its dumb cataracts and streams of ice –
> A motionless array of mighty waves,
> Five rivers broad and vast, make rich amends,
> And reconciled us to realities.

After seeing Mont Blanc, P. B. Shelley mused to Thomas Love Peacock that 'I never knew – I never imagined what mountains were before.' 'But how shall I describe to you', the poet wrote of the Alps, 'the scenes by which I am now surrounded. – To exhaust epithets which express the astonishment & the admiration – the very excess of satisfied expectation, where expectation scarcely acknowledged any boundary.' In the preface to his poem *Laon and*

Cythna (1817), Shelley maintained that travel was … in 'the education peculiarly fitted for a poet' and … blessed with such an education. 'I have trodden the gla… lived under the eye of Mont Blanc. I have been a wande… fields.' Mont Blanc shimmers at the heart of the Shelleyan … that of Wordsworth, his poem of that name an opaque but b… …ita-tion on the nature of the imagination, and the role of the lands… in what he saw as a godless universe:

> Far, far above, piercing the infinite sky,
> Mont Blanc appears, still, snowy, and serene.
> Its subject mountains their unearthly forms
> Pile around it, ice and rock; broad vales between
> Of frozen floods, unfathomable deeps
> Blue as the overhanging heaven.

Writing of the Alps in their sublimity, the poem declares that 'these primeval mountains / Teach the … mind'. Travel shaped many of the highest peaks of what the critic Thomas McFarland once called the 'mountain range' of Romanticism.

See also Ireland and the 'Catholic Question'; Satire; Slavery and Abolition.

Further Reading

Malcolm Andrews, *The Search for the Picturesque: Landscape Aesthetics and Tourism in Britain, 1760–1800* (1989).

Peter Bicknell and Robert Woof, *The Discovery of the Lake District 1750–1810: A Context for Wordsworth* (1982).

James Buzard, *The Beaten Track: European Tourism, Literature, and the Ways to 'Culture' 1800–1918* (1993).

Nicholas Canny, *The Oxford History of the British Empire: The Origins of Empire* (1998).

Chloe Chard, *Pleasure and Guilt on the Grand Tour: Travel Writing and Imaginative Geography 1600–1830* (1999).

Benjamin Colbert, *Shelley's Eye: Travel Writing and Aesthetic Vision* (2005).

Robin Jarvis, *Romantic Writing and Pedestrian Travel* (1997).

Nigel Leask, *Curiosity and the Aesthetics of Travel Writing 1770–1840* (2002).

Thomas McFarland, *Romantic Cruxes: The English Essayists and the Spirit of the Age* (1987).

Kathleen Turner, *British Travel Writers in Europe 1750–1800: Authorship, Gender and National Identity* (2001).

ism and the Position of Women

The Legal Status of Women

'Reason and experience convince me that the only method of leading women to fulfil their peculiar duties, is to free them from all restraint by allowing them to participate in the inherent rights of mankind.' So wrote Mary Wollstonecraft (1759–97) in her revolutionary treatise, *Vindication of the Rights of Woman: with Strictures on Political and Moral Subjects* (1792), a text that has since become a foundational work of British feminism in its insistence that women are the equals of men, intellectually and morally, and should therefore share the same social, legal and political rights. In terms of her independence, the position of a woman in eighteenth-century Britain was parlous – her educational, social, financial and marital choices were overseen by a crew of male relatives: fathers, husbands, and brothers; sons, nephews and guardians all had ultimate control over a woman's free-dom, and for married women the situation was still more restricting. After marriage, a woman was required to surrender her legal independence to her husband for the duration of their union. The eminent English judge Sir William Blackstone in his definitive legal text *Commentaries on the Laws of England* (1765–9) defined a married woman as a 'feme covert' [sic], that is, a woman under the cover or protection of her husband: 'By marriage, the husband and wife are one person in law: that is, the very being or legal exis-tence of the woman is suspended during the marriage, or at least is incor-porated and consolidated into that of the husband: under whose wing, protection, and *cover*, she performs every thing.'

Underpinning Blackstone's gendered dictates is what the modern histo-rian might call an ideology of 'separate spheres', that is, the notion that women's biological difference from men orients their cultural destination towards the private domestic sphere – to take up the 'affective' roles of wife and mother – rather than inhabit the public male-dominated realms of law, politics, business and, in general, inheritance. Most women were excluded from owning land and property by the prevailing law of primogeniture (whereby the eldest male heir inherited estates and titles) and by entailment – the system of inheritance designed to keep the estate in the male line, which is the situation confronted by Jane Austen's famous Bennet sisters in *Pride and Prejudice* (1813) when the odious Mr Collins – the closest male relative of their father – descends upon the family with a view to inheriting Longbourn.

The 'Bluestockings'

Land ownership – and by extension political power – was the preserve of the male elite which ruled Britain in the late eighteenth and early nineteenth centuries. Women, however wealthy or titled, did not have any official elec-toral power in Britain and, indeed, were not granted the vote until after the First World War. It was this state of affairs that prompted the post-French Revolutionary Romantic-era feminism exemplified in the work of Mary Wollstonecraft. However, Wollstonecraft was certainly not the first of what one might call British public female intellectuals. The 'Bluestockings' before her were an informal group of intellectual and artistic women (from the monied classes for the most part) who met at London salons during the second half of the eighteenth century and cultivated female accomplish-ments in learning, charity and philanthropy. Their members included Elizabeth Carter (1717–1806), scholar, linguist and poet, whose success enabled her to purchase her own home in Deal; Hannah More (1745–1833), the tremendously successful Evangelical author, abolitionist poet and socially-conservative propagandist of unmarried celibacy and temperance among the lower orders; and Catherine Macaulay (1731–91), the great female Whig historian and promoter of Parliamentary reform. The Bluestockings, although representing an important chapter in the history of women's advancements in learning and philanthropy, stopped short of forming anything that might be recognised as a modern feminist move-ment. Indeed, their members tended to view their intellectual achieve-ments as exceptional and *sui generis*, to be admired by other women but not necessarily emulated.

Mary Wollstonecraft and Revolutionary Feminism

The onset of the French Revolution in 1789 ushered in a new dawn of female radicalism in Britain. A much more radical kind of female thinker than the likes of the conservative More emerged, in the writings of Mary Wollstonecraft, Mary Hays, and Helen Maria Williams. Wollstonecraft, the first of a 'new genus' of female writers, as she styled herself, picked up the revolutionary baton on behalf of her sex and insisted, against the opinion of contemporary educationalists, moralists and writers of conduct litera-ture, that women had the capacity to think rationally. Women, she declared, were capable of becoming the intellectual equals of men, except that society encouraged girls from an early age to play down their intellec-tual attributes and concentrate on fripperies such as their outward appear-ance. Girls were in general reared by their parents for the marriage market ('daughters are chickens brought up for the tables of other men', as the unpleasant brother of Samuel Richardson's heroine Clarissa puts it). Even after marriage and motherhood, a time during which Wollstonecraft urges women to lose the lover in the husband and seek to develop instead a rational companionship based on mutual affection and the duty of care to their children, the generality of her sex continued to be in thrall to the social injunction on a woman to be beautiful and to be judged by men accordingly (what modern feminists call 'the beauty myth'). 'Short-lived queens' is Wollstonecraft's sobering judgement on the coquettes of her day, and she quotes the dissenting poet Anna Laetitia Aiken (later Barbauld) (1743–1825) to prove her point:

> In beauty's empire is no mean,
> And woman, either slave or queen,
> Is quickly scorn'd when not ador'd.

'But the adoration comes first', adds Wollstonecraft archly, 'and the scorn is not anticipated'.

In the 'noon of beauty's power', argues the *Vindication*, women are 'treated like queens only to be deluded by hollow respect … Confined then in cages, like the feathered race, they have nothing to do but to plume themselves, and stalk with mock-majesty from perch to perch.' The image recalls the idle sensuality of the French court of the *ancien régime*; the spectre of a morally corrupt aristocracy haunts Wollstonecraft's middle-class dissenting aesthetic of reform and self-improvement throughout her treatise. She is constantly on guard against the seductive glamour of the French court, epitomised by the beautiful, flirtatious and – in the eyes of Edmund Burke, her Irish defender – ultimately fragile figure of Marie Antoinette. In his *Reflections on the Revolution in France* (1790), a full-scale assault on the theory and practice of the Revolution, to which Wollstonecraft responded with her pro-Revolutionary treatise *A Vindication of the Rights of Men* (1790), the chivalric Burke famously lavished praise on Marie Antoinette as a woman of unprecedented loveliness – a 'delightful vision'. Such a woman was the incarnation of feminine beauty and domesticity, and red meat to the rapacious mob who marched on Versailles in October 1789, who, in Burke's alarmist vision, were a 'swinish multitude' that threatened to desecrate her femininity and destroy French domesticity. To Wollstonecraft, however, the French queen represented all that was corrupt and degrading about modern femininity (she accuses Burke of having been dazzled 'by the fascinating glance of a *great* Lady's eyes, when neither virtue nor sense beamed in them'). It is this image of overtly sexualised femininity that leads her to call upon middle-class English women to effect a 'REVOLUTION in female manners'.

Like her intellectual mentor Richard Price, the distinguished Dissenting minister who, in his *Discourse on the Love of our Country* (1789), celebrated the French Revolution's promise of individual and religious liberty (see 'Religion and Atheism'), Wollstonecraft argues that a rational and cultivated mind is the key to salvation. Her feminist version of that revolutionary promise, however, is notable in her insistence that if women are to realise their rational faculties, they must relinquish to some degree their sexuality:

> Were women more rationally educated, could they take a more comprehensive view of things, they would be contented to love but once in their lives; and after marriage calmly let passion subside into friendship – into that tender intimacy, which is the best refuge from care; yet is built on such pure, still affections, that idle jealousies would not be allowed to disturb the discharge of the sober duties of life, nor to engross the thoughts that might otherwise be employed.

Unlike modern feminism, with its emphasis on female equality and sexual liberation as two sides of the same coin, Wollstonecraft stresses that sexual freedom is the enemy of women's emancipation. If women aspire to the courtly model of flirtatious femininity, then the cause of equality is lost because in prioritising sexual conquests (whether real or merely fantasy) above her duties – to her family and her children especially – a woman diminishes her entitlement to be viewed as a rational subject who is aware of her social responsibilities to participate in the rights of mankind.

Rights entail duties (and vice versa): female independence comes at a price in Wollstonecraft's prospectus. In the critic Cora Kaplan's memorable words, 'Wollstonecraft sets up heart-breaking conditions for women's liberation – a little death, the death of desire, the death of female pleasure.' Even so, while Wollstonecraft venerates the duties of chaste motherhood and decries the pleasures of the flesh, she also rewrites the copybook, so to speak, of eighteenth-century domesticity by resituating the domestic space as a sphere of importance and influence in which women can perform their duties to themselves as rational beings and to their children. In this context the private space of the home becomes a place where the concerns of the (male) public sphere are incorporated and readdressed by women in their overseeing of the moral and intellectual welfare of the family:

> The being who discharges the duties of its station is independent; and, speaking of women at large, their first duty is to themselves as rational creatures, and the next, in point of importance, as citizens, is that, which includes so many, of a mother.

For Wollstonecraft, the duties a woman has to herself (her education and the development of her intellect) and to her family grant her moral authority within the wider sphere and entitle her to be treated as man's equal, thus turning on its head the conservative doctrine of separate spheres. However, many of her female Tory contemporaries used similar ammunition to argue for the naturalness and inevitability of those separate spheres. Just as the

Bluestockings in the mid- to late eighteenth century saw themselves as a select, highly-educated coterie of literary and artistic talent, so in the 1790s a group of so-called Tory anti-Jacobin feminists emerged – women such as the Belfast poet and novelist Elizabeth Hamilton (a close friend of the Anglo-Irish author Maria Edgeworth), the Quaker moralist Priscilla Wakefield and English poet, playwright and novelist Jane West, the afore-mentioned Hannah More and even the sainted Jane Austen herself. These 'literary ladies', conservative in outlook (we borrow the term from the title of Maria Edgeworth's *Letters for Literary Ladies* (1795), a book which, though rightly described by Claire Connolly as 'a witty three-pronged attack on male chauvinism' and a call for feminine education, held back from upset-ting the sexual status quo), tended to denigrate their role of female author (even while they wrote and published reams) and insisted to the last that their family duties took precedence over their writing.

Female education, on the other hand, though a central concern of the above writers, is not attached to a programme of social change, a transfor-mation hinted at in the title of Wollstonecraft's *Rights of Woman*. Indeed, Hannah More is said to have found that very title so 'ridiculous' that she declared her intention of never reading the book. More's antagonism was rooted in her antipathy to the French Revolutionary ideas, and her suspicion that female liberation was tantamount to female licentiousness, a fear that appeared to be borne out by the domestic tragedy of Mary Wollstonecraft's life. Wollstonecraft's 'scandalous' life came to light when, after her prema-ture death in 1797 following the birth of her second daughter, Mary Wollstonecraft Godwin (later Mary Shelley), her distraught husband of six months, the philosopher and novelist William Godwin, published his *Memoirs of the Author of A Vindication of the Rights of Woman* (1798). Intending it as a frank and honest biographical tribute to his remarkable wife, Godwin held nothing back: he revealed that Wollstonecraft's first daughter Fanny Imlay was the illegitimate child of an American army captain Gilbert Imlay, and that Wollstonecraft had twice attempted suicide on discovering the latter's infidelity. In anti-Revolutionary circles, however, Wollstonecraft's life story was seized on as evidence of the pernicious consequences of Jacobin philosophy on female sexual morals. Wollstonecraft, it seemed to many, had fallen foul of her own dictates on women's sexual modesty and she was duly mocked for it, mercilessly in some instances. The *European Magazine*, for example, christened her 'a philosophical wanton' in its 1798 notice of Godwin's book and there followed plenty more insults in this vein such that by the beginning of the nineteenth century it was almost impossi-ble for any respectable female writer to lay claim to feminist ideas. Conversely, there were also some eloquent testimonies to Wollstonecraft's heroism; these came mostly from men, especially poets (Blake, Coleridge, and Wordsworth all wrote poems to or about her). Even so, for many women readers Wollstonecraft's name was too sullied by charges of sexual misconduct for her work to be taken seriously. Only at the end of the nineteenth century, when radical ideas began to be discussed once more in intellectual circles, did her writing again become a force to be reckoned with.

Exceptional Women

It might be pointed out, in conclusion, that not all women in late eighteenth- and early nineteenth-century Britain were victims of what we now call patriarchal oppression. One example, that of the Duchess of St Albans, serves as a cheering reminder of some women's inventiveness, their *joie de vivre*, and their ability to beat the men at their own game. Harriot Beauclerk, Duchess of St Albans (*c*.1777–1837), began her life as the illegitimate daughter of an Irish wardrobe keeper in a company of strolling actors and ended it as one of the richest and most successful businesswomen in England, becoming first the mistress and then the second wife of the powerful and enormously wealthy London banker Thomas Coutts. He was seventy-nine, over twice Harriot's thirty-seven years, when they married in 1815, and he left her his entire fortune, including his partnership in Coutts Bank, on his death in 1822, without leaving any other legacy, either to his children from his first marriage or to any other incumbent. By her innate wit and intelligence Harriot proved an accomplished businesswoman and banker, taking an active part in investment and management decisions; she was also extremely generous to her stepdaughters, giving them each £10,000 per annum, notwithstanding their lifelong hostility to her. She married next William Aubrey de Vere Beauclerk, ninth Duke of St Albans (1801–49). He was twenty-six years of age to her forty-nine but the marriage seems to have been a happy one, Harriot all the while keeping control of her inheritance, which she left in trust for Angela Coutts, the youngest granddaughter of Thomas Coutts and philanthropic friend of Charles Dickens – to which she added her own terms and conditions, namely that should Angela marry an alien, the fortune would go to the next person in the remainder. (Remarkably, Angela did break the terms of the trust when she was sixty-seven by marrying her twenty-six-year-old American-born secretary.) If late Georgian Britain was a man's world socially, financially and politically, then Harriot Beauclerk, Duchess of St Albans, bucked the trend, stupendously. The Romantic era had exceptions as well as rules.

At the other end of the social spectrum working-class women also showed themselves adept at managing and running family businesses. Single women and widows could own property; historians have uncovered evidence of widows successfully taking over the running of a printing business following the demise of the husband, for example. Other women might help run a hostelry, a boarding house, or a shop, and some enterprising middle-class females ran milliners' and other clothes shops. The general picture of feminism in the late Georgian period cannot really do justice to the details of the lives of working women from the lower classes, who tend to slip through the narratives of official history. This said, the revival of interest in Romantic-era women poets in general and the attention that has been paid in recent years to such working-class poets as Elizabeth Hands (a servant whose poetry satirises the ignorance and petty hypocrisies of life above the stairs) or Ann Yearsley (the Bristol 'milk maid' poet who eventually turned on her patron, the bluestocking Hannah More) is drawing a fuller picture of feminism and the position of women in the context of British Romanticism (see '"Peasant" or Labouring-class Poets').

See also   British Politics 1789–1815; Religion and Atheism.

Further Reading

Maria Edgeworth (ed.), Claire Connolly, *Letters for Literary Ladies* (1993).
Margaret Homans, *Bearing the Word: Language and Female Experience in Nineteenth-Century Women's Writing* (1986).
Gary Kelly, *Women, Writing, and Revolution, 1790–1827* (1993).
Jane Moore, *Mary Wollstonecraft* (1999).
Joan Perkin, *Women and Marriage in Nineteenth-Century England* (1989).
Janet Todd, *Mary Wollstonecraft: A Revolutionary Life* (2002).
Janet Todd, *Sensibility: An Introduction* (1986).

Industry and Economics

The Industrial Revolution

When the poet Blake was born in the year 1757, England was rather more of a 'green and pleasant land', as the poet put it in his most famous lyric, 'And did those feet in ancient times' (now generally referred to as 'Jerusalem' after Sir Hubert Parry's musical setting), than when he died, approaching his seventieth birthday, in the year 1827. In the 1750s, England was principally an agrarian and mercantile society, with most people living outside the metropolis in the countryside or in the principal ports: Bristol, Liverpool, Newcastle and so on. The slave trade was then still in full malign flow, industrialisation was unheard of, and the factory system was in its infancy. However, things changed rapidly and markedly during Blake's three score and almost ten. If the late eighteenth century is notable in historical terms as the era of the French Revolution, one of the founding moments in modern

European society, it is also significant as the period in which the 'Industrial Revolution' began (though it should be pointed out that this term is not uncontentious amongst historians, some of whom argue that industrialisation was a more gradual, more evolutionary process in the period between the 1760s and 1840s than the word 'revolution' suggests).

'Industrialism', according to the *Oxford English Dictionary*, is 'a social or economic system in which manufacturing industries are prevalent'. Great Britain was the first society to undergo the process of concerted industrialisation. Whereas its economy had previously relied on manual labour and the toil of what was then called the 'brute creation' – horses and oxen in particular – at the turn of the nineteenth century there was a turn towards machine-based industry in British manufacturing, and later in farming. New industrial technology allowed greater volumes of production, initially in textile, mining and engineering industries but eventually throughout most of the economy. Entrepreneurial capitalism and inventive genius went hand in hand in this period. In the 1760s and 1770s James Watt developed the steam engine to a higher degree of efficiency – and lower cost – than had previously been possible but it was his partnership with the manufacturer and businessman Matthew Boulton which enabled both to prosper, with their engines facilitating the mechanisation of hundreds of English factories. Sir Richard Arkwright's pioneering spinning frame also allowed mills to increase their volumes hugely, especially when linked to hydropower in the shape of a water wheel (powering what became known as the 'water frame'). Capitalist pioneers such as the resourceful industrialist and self-publicist Josiah Wedgwood industrialised the production of hitherto expensive consumer goods (his famous pottery, for instance) whilst simultaneously using sophisticated advertising campaigns to market their wares and increase brand awareness.

Factory Conditions

Alongside mass production, improved roads, especially after John McAdam's invention of tarmac in the 1810s, meant that formerly local products could now be distributed on a nationwide basis, and several long-established brands were founded during the era of the Industrial Revolution (Wedgwood, Guinness, Bass, and Lea and Perrins amongst them). During this period, small-scale manufacturers gave way, in terms of profit and importance to the economy, to large-scale factory production in which hundreds of people – men, women and children – toiled for long hours, often for six days a week, in frequently hot, raucous and unpleasant conditions. As a consequence, population mass, especially in the north of England, began to move from small towns and villages to industrialised cities such as

Leeds, Manchester and Sheffield, and to the rapidly growing mill towns of Lancashire and Yorkshire: Halifax, Oldham, Stockport and the like.

A sense that these events were epoch-making for the British economy – and, after that, those of Europe and North America – was evident very quickly. Whatever modern historians might think about the notion of an 'Industrial Revolution', there was a contemporary sense that this was indeed what was happening, that the new machines, mass production and industrialisation were the equivalent in economic terms of the French Revolution. The French writer Alphonse de Lamartine wrote in 1836 of what is now called the Industrial Revolution as 'le 1789 du commerce et de l'industrie'. Similarly, writing of the inventions which had transformed economic society, in the *Condition of the Working Classes in England* (1845), Friedrich Engels, later co-author of the *Communist Manifesto* (1848), wrote that 'these inventions ... gave the impulse to an industrial revolution, a revolution which at the same time changed the whole of civil society'.

By the 1820s, hundreds of thousands of people now lived in the industrialised towns and cities of the north of England where a large proportion of the workers laboured relentlessly in factories. Within a century of what is often seen as the establishment of the first modern factory – the brothers Lombe's water-powered silk manufactory in Derby in 1721 – and half a century or so after the pioneering Industrial Revolution factories – Boulton's Soho Manufactory in Birmingham (established in 1761) and Arkwright's Cromford Mill in Derbyshire (founded ten years later) – factories proliferated throughout the midlands and the north. Though the likes of Wedgwood and Boulton aspired to decent conditions for their workers, many of their successors were far less scrupulous, exploiting adults and children alike in their factories.

As illustration of this, consider the hearings conducted in the House of Commons in 1819 when Sir Robert Peel, father of the future Prime Minister and himself an industrialist, introduced a bill to prevent children under nine from working in factories and to regulate the hours of those aged nine to sixteen. The records of the evidence taken are both revealing and poignant (William Cobbett called them 'horrid, heart-sinking facts' in the *Register*). In giving testimony to a House of Commons committee, Dr Peter Ashton, a medical practitioner from the Lancashire town of Stockport near Manchester, noted that over 10,000 people were employed in factories in his town, including over 2,000 children. Asked whether he noticed 'any difference in the appearance of the cotton factory children from other children', Ashton replied 'Yes, a very great one ... I could distinguish from their countenances [which] betrayed sickliness, wanness, and ill health ... that they were employed in cotton factories.' The chair of the investigating committee inquired if there were 'any factory children under nine years of age in those schools', receiving the sobering response '623 girls'. Ashton's fellow doctor John Graham was next to give evidence:

> From your experience of 24 years at Stockport, are you of opinion that a greater number of children die in proportion who have been working in cotton factories than have died among children in other employments?
>
> I can have no doubt of it; I think by the bill of mortality for the parish of Stockport, there are not less than 200 who have died of consumptions in the last year.

The bill passed, though to modern eyes the results of the bill might seem very modest; the 1819 Cotton Mills and Factories Act prohibited children under nine being employed in factories, and limited children aged nine to sixteen years to a maximum of twelve hours per working day.

As the above testimonies demonstrate, the relentless economic growth evident in late Georgian England was not without its attendant social cost. The process of developing industrialisation certainly did not guarantee instant national prosperity. Robert Southey's comment was astute; after 'the steam engine and the spinning engines', he maintained in 1807, 'follow in natural and necessary consequence, increased activity, enterprise, wealth, and power; but, on the other hand, greediness of gain, looseness of principle ... wretchedness, disaffection, and political insecurity'. Disaffection and wretchedness certainly followed enterprise and wealth in the Romantic era. Though the metropolis had seen areas of wretched poverty – 'rookeries' such as St Giles in central London – from the turn of the eighteenth century, now slum areas became widespread in some of the northern cities, with their attendant overcrowding, squalor, disease and death. This poverty was exacerbated by the fact that many skilled workers, notably in the textile trade, found their crafts redundant in the light of the new mill technology.

The Luddites

Alongside grinding poverty came industrial strife, as Southey had predicted ('If the manufacturing system continues to be extended, I believe that revolution inevitably must come, and in its most fearful shape'). Some workers – most notably the 'frame-breaking' Luddites – began to take violent action against the hated new machinery. The Luddites – so called after Ned Ludd (sometimes King Ludd, sometimes even Eliza Ludd), the mythical figure on whose behalf the disaffected sometimes signed threatening letters – were textile workers who, furious at the introduction of mechanised looms which could be utilised by relatively unskilled labour, took violent action in the early 1810s against what they saw as the infernal machines which were threatening their livelihoods.

Machine breaking was punished by severe penalties, notably trans-portation, but the government, alarmed by the increase in such activities, introduced a Frame Breaking bill in 1812 intended to make the offence a capital crime. In February of that year, Lord Byron, whose ancestral home Newstead was in Nottinghamshire – a county at the heart of the Luddite unrest – spoke up in his maiden parliamentary speech in the House of Lords to rationalise the behaviour of the frame-breakers and to argue against what he saw as the draconian nature of the proposed legislation:

> During the short time I recently passed in Nottingham, not twelve hours elapsed without some fresh act of violence ... I was informed that forty Frames had been broken ... Whilst these outrages must be admitted to exist to an alarming extent, it cannot be denied that they have arisen from circumstances of the most unparal-leled distress: the perseverance of these miserable men in their proceedings, tends to prove that nothing but absolute want could have driven a large, and once honest and industrious, body of the people, into the commission of excesses so hazardous to themselves, their families, and the community ... There was none to relieve them: their own means of subsistence were cut off.

Byron's pleas went unanswered; the bill passed. In the following year four-teen men were executed – in Voltaire's phrase, 'pour encourager les autres' – after a trial of frame-breakers held in York.

Romantic Writers on Industry and Economics

As the case of Lord Byron demonstrates, there was much literary sympathy for the human consequences of Great Britain's rush towards industrialisa-tion in the Romantic period. In the light of these industrial 'advances', the same humanitarian spirit that had led versifiers to take up the cause of slav-ery and the suffering of animals in the 1780s and 1790s began to inform tender-hearted laments about the plight of the poor and the consequences of the Industrial Revolution, both to people and upon the English landscape. An early example is a 1794 contribution to the *Gentleman's Magazine* which depicts the water frame as a corruption of the natural landscape. In this account, the English river, once at the heart of an unchanging pastoral vision, has become enslaved, made subordinate to the principle of profit:

> The plenteous stream, that spread its fruitful course;
> In many a channel, through the spacious vale,
> Freshening the tender herbage as it sprung,
> And faded flowers that hung the languid head,
> Is stopped – and its collected force applied
> To move one vast machine.

Sentiments such as these were also evident in rather better verse by Romantic poets such as Blake and Wordsworth who, in their work, spoke out against the consequences of industrialisation. Indeed, the idealist Shelley, who wrote in the 'Defence of Poetry' (1821) that 'poets are the unacknowledged legislators of the world', went so far as to consider poetry as an important counterbalance to what he saw as the grasping excesses of contemporary capitalism, arguing in the same essay that 'The cultivation of poetry is never more to be desired than at periods when, from all excess of the selfish and calculating principle, the accumulation of the materials of external life exceed the quantity of the power of assimilating them to the internal laws of human nature.' Poetry, he maintained, could act as a counterbalance to the selfish tenets of modern capitalist economics.

Blake, who lived in Lambeth in South London in the 1790s, and as a consequence saw the effects of industrialisation at first-hand in nearby boroughs, also had little time for the vast machines attacked by the contributor to the *Gentleman's Magazine*, condemning what he memorably called the 'intricate wheels' of industrialisation as a juggernaut which ground the suffering poor beneath it. Blake's long, visionary book *Jerusalem*, etched and written *c.*1804–20 (and not to be confused with 'And did those feet ...', which was composed for his *Milton* (*c.*1804–8)), offers a heartfelt, if to some confusing, lament that the 'arts of life' were now converted into the 'arts of death', and the people were now 'kept ... / In sorrowful drudgery to obtain a scanty pittance of bread':

> And all the arts of life they changd into the arts of death
> The hour glass contemnd because its simple workmanship
> Was as the workmanship of the plowman & the water wheel
> That raises water into Cisterns broken & burnd in fire
> Because its workmanship was like the workmanship of the Shepherd
> And in their stead intricate wheels invented Wheel without wheel
> To perplex youth in their outgoings & to bind to labours
> Of day & night the myriads of Eternity, that they might file
> And polish brass & iron hour after hour laborious workmanship
> Kept ignorant of the use that they might spend the days of wisdom
> In sorrowful drudgery to obtain a scanty pittance of bread.

Blake's *Jerusalem* has something of the book of Revelation about it, offering as it does an apocalyptic vision of hideous, hellish-hot mines which 'belch forth storms of fire'. His is a kind of eschatological view of the age of the machine. This is an unnatural world, and it might be argued that Romantic dystopian visions such as Byron's 'Darkness' (1816), with its apocalyptic vision of a dying world where 'the bright sun was extinguished' (indeed, the sun was literally darkened in 1816 – the so-called year without a summer – by clouds of volcanic dust sent up into the earth's atmosphere following the sudden eruption in the previous year of Mount Tambora, in Indonesia), and Mary Shelley's *The Last Man* (1826), with its vision of a plague-ravaged world, could be seen as symbols, even prophecies, of a world poisoned ecologically and ethically as a consequence of industry.

Wordsworth, like Blake a poet preoccupied with the nature and importance of childhood experience, condemned the effects of industrialisation on children such as the Stockport factory girls. Wordsworth laments the fate of children working in factories in the eighth book of his narrative poem *The Excursion* (1814) in which he compares the plight of a young lad working in a cotton factory with two rural boys at play in the countryside, happily fishing and playing games amidst rural scenery. To Wordsworth, the consequences of industrialisation and new manufacturing techniques threatened the family unit and the way in which the common people traditionally organised their lives. Because their work could now be mass produced in mills, mothers who used to be involved in cottage manufacture now had no 'household occupation; no nice arts / Of needle-work'. Similarly, the father who used to take his sons with him to his rural employment loses them to the factory:

> – The Father, if perchance he still retain
> His old employments, goes to field or wood,
> No longer led or followed by the Sons;
> Idlers perchance they were, – but in *his* sight;
> Breathing fresh air, and treading the green earth;
> 'Till their short holiday of childhood ceased,
> Ne'er to return! That birth-right now is lost.

The 'short holiday of childhood' is replaced by grinding labour; Wordsworth portrays the child in the factory as a hapless 'prisoner':

> He is a Slave to whom release comes not,
> And cannot come. The Boy, where'er he turns,
> Is still a prisoner.

For Wordsworth there could be little more forlorn. The factory child is abased in spirit, denied its right to blossom in the world of nature (the Wordsworthian conceptualisation of the best childhood, of course). William Cobbett once labelled a northern textile factory a 'Cotton-lord's hell' and Wordsworth's sharp social critique shares his perception.

Dr Ashton (referred to above), giving evidence to the House of Commons, contrasted the factory children with the other youngsters in the town: 'the rest of the others, whose employments were different, were ruddy and blooming'. Wordsworth paints a similar picture later in the same book of the *Excursion* in the depiction of the two boys returning from a rural fishing trip:

> two lusty Boys
> Appeared, – confusion checking their delight.
> – Not Brothers they in feature or attire,
> But fond Companions, so I guessed, in field,
> And by the river-side from which they come,
> A pair of Anglers, laden with their spoil.

The narrative voice's admiration of the 'animation in the mien / Of those two boys' and the healthful sport which they enjoy in the Lake surroundings is the idealised counterpart of the dystopian 'Picture of a Child employed in a Cotton-mill' (as Wordsworth's abstract calls it) earlier in Book Eight. The factory lad languishes in a kind of mental and physical captivity; the rural boys live out the idealised Romantic childhood.

The mill boy, in Wordsworth's polemical verse, is a slave to labour, his childhood holiday perverted, and his family torn apart. The poet is withering in his condemnation of those who think that this is good for the economy or easily rationalised in terms of the wealth of the nation:

> Economists will tell you that the State
> Thrives by the forfeiture – unfeeling thought,
> And false as monstrous! Can the Mother thrive
> By the destruction of her innocent Sons?

Presumably the 'economists' Wordsworth is attacking here are those associated with the classical economics generally identified with the likes of Adam Smith (1723–90) and David Ricardo (1772–1823), which espoused the notion that markets can regulate themselves rather than requiring state intervention.

The Scotsman Smith, the author of the *Wealth of Nations* (1776), praised self-interest as the basis of trade and industry, though also arguing that it ultimately also served the greater national interests of 'the State' in building national prosperity. Wordsworth, on the other hand, implies that to foster economic growth based on naked self-interest and a carelessness of the personal circumstances of the workers instrumental in building the wealth of the nation was a pernicious doctrine. Again, in this the Tory poet Wordsworth and the radical iconoclast Cobbett were as one. In 1825 the latter raged in the *Register* against 'unhealthy ... factories', their appalling conditions sanctioned by rascally laissez-faire economists:

> This, Sir, is ... our boasted manufacturing system; that system which Ricardo and the Scotch Economists laud to the skies; that system for the extension of which

they recommend us to 'give up the cultivation of poor lands'; to turn our plough-men and haymakers into spinners and weavers, breathing steam, and gas, and cotton fuz, instead of the air of heaven; and, instead of raising food, making yarn and cloth.

Eventually modern factory-workers also found poetic voices of their own rather than solely having university-educated poets such as Wordsworth speaking on their behalf. The most notable of these was the Chartist poet Ebenezer Elliott (1781–1849), a Sheffield factory worker who published the *Corn Law Rhymes* in 1831. A radical from an industrial city, Elliott – like Shelley before him – was an unashamedly political versifier; 'all genuine poets are fervid politicians', he declared. Elliott's biographer January Searle wrote that his was 'the first melody that ever came from the dead and monotonous mill-wheels of political economy!' As the title of his most notable collection implies, Elliott's principal target was the tariffs on imported bread introduced by the Corn Laws, which kept the price of bread artificially high, much to the detriment of the poor. The *Rhymes* ask rhetor-ically: 'England! what for mine and me, / What hath bread-tax done for thee?' and condemn the entire system of government as deliberately intended to keep the poor in near-starvation and subjection:

> What is bad government, thou slave,
> Whom robbers represent?
> What is bad government, thou knave,
> Who lov'st bad government?
>
> It is the deadly *Will*, that takes
> What labour ought to keep;
> It is the deadly *Power*, that makes
> Bread dear, and labour cheap.

While Cobbett, Elliott and Wordsworth address the industrial growing pains of rural and provincial England, the conditions of the London poor also struck a poetic chord. Blake in his 'London' (published in the *Songs of Innocence and Experience* (1794)) described a city teeming with people:

> I wander through each chartered street,
> Near where the chartered Thames does flow,
> A mark in every face I meet,
> Marks of weakness, marks of woe.

'The chartered Thames'; here, as in the *Gentleman's Magazine* poem, even the primal force of nature, represented by that mighty and emblematic river the Thames, is transformed into a powerfully ironic symbol of oppression.

And as in his later vision of the grinding and oppressive 'intricate wheels' of industry, mental bondage is everywhere in this supposedly great city:

> In every cry of every Man,
> In every Infant's cry of fear,
> In every voice, in every ban,
> The mind-forg'd manacles I hear.

Blake's cityscape of mental and personal bondage was echoed fifty years later, shortly after the conclusion of the Romantic age, in Thomas Hood's famous poem of political protest, 'The Song of the Shirt' (1843), another threnody for the London poor, which movingly articulates the suffering of a worn-out seamstress in the rookeries, paid a pittance for her piece-meal work:

> With fingers weary and worn,
> With eyelids heavy and red,
> A Woman sat, in unwomanly rags,
> Plying her needle and thread –
> Stitch! stitch! stitch!
> In poverty, hunger, and dirt,
> And still with the voice of dolorous pitch
> She sang the 'Song of the Shirt!'

Thomas Hood and William Wordsworth have something in common. In Hood's poem and in Book Eight of *The Excursion*, 'household occupation', the 'arts / Of needle-work', are charged with a wider ideological significance. Both texts testify to a wider economic malaise which prioritises the profit imperative within modern industry over its human consequences.

Further Reading

G. S. Checkland, *The Rise of Industrial Society in England 1815–1885* (1964).
Paul Mantoux, *The Industrial Revolution in the Eighteenth Century: An Outline of the Beginnings of the Modern Factory System in England* (1961).
Peter N. Stearns, *The Industrial Revolution in World History* (3rd edition, 2007).
E. P. Thompson, *The Making of the English Working Class* (1963).
Arnold Toynbee, *The Industrial Revolution* (1956).

Ireland and the 'Catholic Question'

The Act of Union

Ireland ended the Romantic period as part of an enlarged 'United Kingdom of Great Britain and Ireland' following the passing in 1800 of the Act of

Union (under the supervision of William Pitt's Tory administration), which took effect in 1801 and abolished the Irish parliament as an independent governing body. Parliament House, the magnificent neoclassical building on College Green, Dublin, designed in the 1720s by the Irish architect Sir Edward Lovett Pearce and one of the most influential buildings in eighteenth-century Ireland, a proud symbol of the capital city's wealth and cultural prestige in the pre-Union Georgian era, was parliament no more (it was eventually sold to the Bank of Ireland). Following the Union, the British government made provision for Ireland to be represented at Westminster by a mere quartet of bishops and 28 peers in the Lords, and in the Commons by a group of 100 elected MPs.

Some Irish Catholic leaders initially supported the Act of Union because they believed, encouraged by Westminster, that its passage would be followed by rapid progress towards full Catholic Emancipation (the right to sit in parliament and hold positions of high office). In the event, that belief proved false and it was nigh on 30 years before the majority Catholic population of Ireland was released from the so-called 'Penal Laws', which severely restricted their participation in public and political life. Under these stern anti-Catholic statutes, which commenced with the reign of William III in 1689 and continued under Anne and the first two Georges, defenders of the 'old faith' could not sit in parliament or vote in general elections; they were excluded from the law, the university, the navy and all public bodies; they were forbidden to own arms or a horse worth more than five pounds; no Catholic could keep a school or send a child abroad to receive an education. Under the complex rules governing land ownership, almost all of the remaining land owned by Catholics passed into Protestant hands. The eldest son of a Catholic family could, by becoming a Protestant, deprive his Catholic father of management of his property. Catholic bishops and other senior ecclesiastics were banished from the country and threatened with death if they returned. Although the rules governing education, land ownership and civil rights were significantly relaxed during the course of the eighteenth century, especially in the closing revolutionary decade of the 1790s which saw emergency legislation forced through parliament, giving voting rights to those relatively few Catholics who met the property qualifications, the situation remained that Irish Catholics did not have the right to sit in the new UK parliament or hold high office in their country. In Ireland, as in Great Britain (see 'Religion and Atheism'), the established church during the Romantic era was the (Protestant) Anglican Church. However, the majority of the populace were Catholics and thus disenfranchised (as were English nonconformists), and this alongside a national sense that Ireland as a whole was oppressed by England. Irish Catholics during the Romantic period experienced oppression on two fronts: first, from England,

and secondly, from the Anglo-Irish 'garrison' in Ireland, particularly the local governors appointed by the British parliament and the Irish Protestants who held the monopoly on Irish public and political life.

The United Irishmen

Ireland was not a peaceful country in the Romantic age; revolutionary energy radiated across the channel from France, sparking a current of nationalist protest against what many Irishmen saw as misrule from London. Some sought to take action by constitutional reform while others argued for – and took – violent action in the Irish cause. It is important to realise that much of the opposition to the notion of Union and its actuality came from Protestant Irishmen, from the United Irishmen movement, the ideological wing of the radical Ulster Presbyterians. Founded in Belfast in October 1791 and also established in Dublin the following month, the United Irishmen movement operated originally as a radical Presbyterian but genteel middle-class debating club, inspired by the examples of the American and French Revolutions to advance the cause of Irish patriotism (principally the removal of English control in Ireland). However, under the presiding spirit of Theobald Wolfe Tone (1763–98), who sought to make Ireland a republic along French lines, the movement was quickly transformed from a sophisticated constitutional club into a radical French Revolutionary sect, with strong ties to the rural underground of 'Defenderism' – the generic name given to secret, mostly Catholic, agrarian groups such as the 'Whiteboys' and the 'Defenders', formed by an oppressed peasantry to combat (often by violent means – rural killings were not uncommon) the injustice of the penal laws and their representatives, avaricious landlords and their despised agents and middle men. There was much to complain about; absentee landlords left grasping managers in charge who would 'rack-rent' the land above its economic potency and way beyond the means of the subsistence farmer, creating a situation where even minor crop failures could bring about famine conditions.

The speed at which the United Irishmen took on the colour of the agrarian secret societies matched the hasty government crackdown following the declaration of war with France in 1793 on all apparently radical and French Revolutionary activity. Insurgence was not confined, however, to the Catholic population, and the underground United Irishmen clubs had a mirror image in the Protestant Orange Order, founded in 1795 to combat defenderism and the Church of Rome in the wake of continued sectarian confrontation. Wolfe Tone, in the meantime, travelled to France where he represented Irish republicanism to Napoleon and other generals, with striking though eventually disappointing results. Owing to his efforts, a French invasion force made an attempt to land at Bantry Bay in December 1796 but was defeated by bad weather. A second attempt at ridding Ireland of English control was planned by the United Irishmen for the summer of 1798 but a government cull in May that year of known radicals, including the capture and death of the movement's legendary hero Lord Edward Fitzgerald, gave way to a spontaneous and frequently blood-thirsty uprising. The French arrived in August 1798 to assist the insurgents but government forces had by then resumed control; the French were defeated and Tone was condemned to death.

Emmet's Rebellion of 1803

In 1803 the nationalists tried again, in an abortive rebellion, in Dublin, led by Robert Emmet (1778–1803), a Protestant contemporary of the poet Thomas Moore at Trinity College, Dublin. Emmet's plan to seize Dublin Castle and spur a popular uprising across the country petered out in less than two hours after a small group of some three hundred insurgents were dispersed by the soldiers. Emmet was arrested and publicly executed. His speech from the dock requesting that his memory be shrouded in silence until the day of Ireland's liberation quickly became a classic of nationalist literature. The concluding lines in particular inspired a poetic mythologising of Irish martyrdom (notably in Thomas Moore's tremendously popular *Irish Melodies* (see 'Irish, Scottish and Welsh Poetry')).

> Let no man write my epitaph; for as no man who knows my motives dare now vindicate them, let not prejudice nor ignorance asperse them. Let them and me repose in obscurity and peace, and my tomb remain uninscribed, until other times, and other men, can do justice to my character; when my country takes her place among the nations of the earth, then, and not till then, let my epitaph be written.

Shelley and Byron on Ireland

In the years immediately following the Union of 1801 the lines that had blurred Catholic and Protestant dissent under the aegis of the United Irishmen began to crystallise and harden. In the ensuing period 'Protestant' became virtually synonymous with 'Unionist' and the vast majority of Catholics aspired to various forms of self-government, from Home Rule to independence. At the same time, the fate of the Catholic population in Ireland now lay with England's military garrison and their commanders, with the English Tory parliament and, ultimately, with the royal heads of state, George III and George IV after him. In England, the cause of Catholic

Emancipation was closely associated with the Whig opposition and, most particularly, with the Royal champion, the Prince of Wales. So when the Prince assumed the powers of the Regent in February 1812, it seemed a foregone conclusion to many – on both sides of the water – that Catholic Emancipation was imminent. The Regent's decision to retain the King's Tory favourites in power blasted that hope overnight.

Into this political maelstrom there arrived in February 1812 the English Protestant poet – in upbringing if not in conviction – and firebrand aristocrat Percy Bysshe Shelley, armed with two pamphlets on Irish affairs. The first, 'An Address to the Irish People', was aimed at the Dublin Catholic poor, to whom he energetically distributed his fine words – which advocated a pacific and philosophical approach to Emancipation and repeal – by throwing copies to passers-by espied from his balcony in Dublin's upmarket Sackville Street. The second, 'Proposals for an Association of Philanthropists', also fell on stony ground. The Irish people may have welcomed the support of the heir to an English baronetcy but there was no sign that they intended to adopt Shelley's elaborate theorising and every indication that it was to their own leaders that they looked for guidance. Moreover, despite his admiration for Irish nationalism, Shelley had no time for the Roman Catholic Church, in his words, 'a plan according to which the cunning and selfish few have employed the fears and hopes of the ignorant many to the establishment of their own power and the destruction of the real interest of the Irish people'. By 10 April, Shelley's short-lived Irish venture was over and the indefatigable radical headed home to England, 'dissatisfied with my success, but not with the attempt'.

Catholic Ireland found a second noble ally in the poet Byron, who was provoked by the Royal apostate George IV's visit to the country in 1821 to pen an acerbic political satire, ironically titled 'The Irish Avatar' (that is, 'messiah'). The first monarch to make an official state visit to Ireland since Richard II, the King rolled up on the shores of Ireland happily drunk, sporting a shamrock in his hat and with an enthusiastic handshake for any commoner who cared to take it. Greeted on his arrival by loud cheers, the turncoat opponent of Catholic Emancipation declared: 'My heart has always been Irish. From the day it first beat, I have loved Ireland.' Byron, angered by the King's apparently blatant hypocrisy over his treatment of the country and incredulous that the Irish people could so quickly forget how little the House of Hanover had done for their country, radically challenged George's professed love of Ireland by likening it to his (notoriously unsuccessful) marriage. His estranged wife Caroline had passed away just a few days prior to George's visit and for him to embark on a round of drinking and revelry while Caroline was en route to her Prussian grave seemed in very poor taste. Byron's condemnatory opening stanza runs thus:

> Ere the Daughter of Brunswick is cold in her grave,
>   And her ashes still float to their home o'er the tide,
> Lo G[eorge] the Triumphant speeds over the wave,
>   To the long-cherish'd Isle which he loved like his – bride.

O'Connell and the Catholic Association

The struggle towards Emancipation that continued throughout the first decade of Union and well into the second was no longer merely a matter of religion; rather, it seemed to many to be at one with the fight for national liberation, a synergy harnessed by the great Catholic champion Daniel O'Connell – 'the Liberator' – who, via the offices of his 'Catholic Association', founded in 1823, built the first mass political movement in Ireland.

Through the introduction of the 'Catholic rent' (the minimum subscription of one penny per month charged to raise fees for the Catholic Association) O'Connell transformed the Catholic Association from a Dublin-based body to a mass movement with branches across the country. One of the most effective weapons in the fight towards liberation was O'Connell himself, who exerted his commanding presence over huge gatherings of the faithful (the so-called 'monster meetings') held up and down the country to promote the Catholic cause in the years immediately preceding Emancipation. A further boost to morale came in the general election of 1826 with a visible demonstration of Catholic power as activists in several counties campaigned hard to defeat the Protestant monopoly – with some dramatic results as large numbers of 40-shilling freeholders defied their landlords and voted for pro-Emancipation candidates. The real electoral breakthrough, however, was O'Connell's decision to stand in the County Clare by-election of 1828 in which his overwhelming defeat of the government candidate Vesey Fitzgerald confirmed the powerful resistance of Catholic voters to controlling landlords and persuaded both Peel and, after him, Lord Wellington (Tory Prime Minister 1828–30) that Emancipation could be delayed no longer. Catholic Emancipation was finally reluctantly granted in 1829 by Wellington's government, some thirty years after the original debates over the Union when Peel had first used the Emancipation carrot to gain support for the measure from Irish Catholic leaders.

Catholic Emancipation

The Duke of Wellington (the most notable member of the late Georgian-period soldiery) was Anglo-Irish, being born in Dublin to Ascendancy grandees, as indeed was Lord Castlereagh, a figure who might be described as the arch-foe of Catholic Ireland, a man who helped steer the Act of Union through the Irish parliament and in his role of Irish Chief Secretary (1798–1801) gained an unwelcome reputation as the persecutor of Irish rebels, many of whom were either executed or brutally flogged. British Whigs and radicals such as Leigh Hunt, Byron and Shelley raged at Castlereagh as a traitor to his own country. Byron considered him 'the vulgarest tool that Tyranny could want' and after the minister's suicide he wrote a widely-circulated squib which suggested that right-minded folk should urinate on his grave ('Stop, stranger, p--s!')

Emancipation signalled the end of the penal system that had all but written the Catholic majority population of Ireland out of legal and civic existence; it also saw a significant weakening of the 'garrison' stronghold. However, in real terms the lives of many remained in the ultimate control of the government outside Ireland. Not only was the country still in the grip of British rule, but Ireland also continued to be torn by a sectarian divide and ongoing religious discord. What Emancipation delivered to the Catholic people (the right to sit in parliament and occupy senior administrative roles) was arguably of less significance than the *process* of attaining victory, because it was the mass movement built up around it that gave Irish nationalists the groundswell of support needed to begin the next crucial battle, nothing less than for the repeal of the Union itself.

See also   British Politics 1789–1815; British Politics 1815–1832; Irish, Scottish and Welsh Poetry; Religion and Atheism.

Further Reading

R. F. Foster, *Modern Ireland 1600–1972* (1988).
R. F. Foster, *The Oxford Illustrated History of Ireland* (1989).
Hugh Kearney, *The British Isles: A History of Four Nations* (1990).
Oliver McDonagh, *Ireland: The Union and Its Aftermath* (1979).
Theodore William Moody and W. E. Vaughan (eds), *A New History of Ireland: Eighteenth-century Ireland, 1691–1800* (1986).

Leisure, Fashion and Sport

We should not think of the Romantic era, to borrow Lord Tennyson's friend R. J. Tenant's wonderful phrase, as 'nothing but revolutions and reigns of Terror and all that'. Even during the Revolutionary and Napoleonic Wars, such quotidian matters as betting, billiards, boxing and balls were preoccupations of large portions of English society. People in large numbers participated in and were spectators of popular cultural pursuits: the Epsom Derby, the most famous horse race of the day, frequently attracted crowds of over

100,000; the waltz ('the indecent exhibition from Germany', as the *Universal Magazine* called it) was a wild success despite – or possibly because of – the controversy it attracted by the close physical proximity of the gentlemen and ladies who danced it; the controversial State Lottery distributed prizes of up to £20,000 (before its statutory abolition in 1826); pantomimes such as *Mother Goose* had long theatrical runs; crowds of spectators gawped at freakshows such as the 'living skeleton', Claude Ambroise Seurat, who visited London in the early 1820s, and the supposed Javanese 'mermaid' which was exhibited in the metropolis in 1823, and the aeronauts, reckless in their hot-air balloons, became heroes of the age. Similarly, Romantic-period writers did not think elevated thoughts every moment of the day; they also possessed a taste for diversions of various kinds: Wordsworth skated and attended wrestling matches; Byron sparred and befriended prize-fighters; Charles and Mary Lamb played cards for money; De Quincey

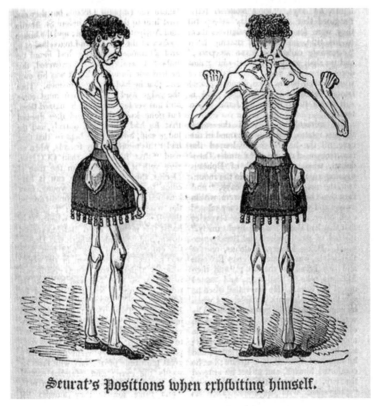

Seurat's Positions when exhibiting himself.

Fig. 1   Anon., 'Seurat's Positions when Exhibiting Himself'. Images of Claude Ambroise Seurat from Robert Chambers's *Book of Days* (1864).

loved the opera, Leigh Hunt played and sang at the pianoforte, and Coleridge bought tickets, unsuccessfully, for the Irish Lottery.

Nor should we imagine that late Georgian print culture was solely attuned to matters of high Romantic argument, the creative imagination, the sublime and so on, or the important political questions of the day, Catholic Emancipation, repeal of the Corn Laws and the like. The fashionable diversions of the day echoed through contemporary print culture in caricature and satire, society miscellany, 'silver fork' fashionable novels and broadside ballads. Alongside much moral condemnation of, and satire upon, the doings of fashionable high society, there were also periodicals devoted to the goings on amongst 'the Upper Ten Thousand' – to use a contemporary term – which salivated over (or voiced mock outrage at) the lifestyles of the rich and famous in a manner reminiscent of modern-day celebrity magazines. Journals, guidebooks and biographies devoted to sport also appeared, from the first publication of the *Sporting Magazine* in 1792 onwards, and manuals dealing with matters of etiquette, dress and behaviour reached a ready audience. From the vast number of social epiphenomena which fascinated the late Georgians, this chapter examines three subjects in particular: gambling, fashion, and sport.

Gambling

The late Georgian period was an age of inveterate gambling, despite much moral disapproval in parliament, pulpit and in the public prints. In the final decades of the eighteenth century, there was a great public interest in and appetite for games of chance of all kinds, from the apprentice tossing up coins with his friends to the aristocrat spending his evenings at the tables of the London gambling clubs of White's and Brooks's, a phenomenon exemplified in the figure of Charles James Fox (1749–1806), the Whig politician and unblinkingly fearless gambler who was said to have lost £15,000 in one session at cards. Matters were little different in the elevated circles of post-Napoleonic England, which indulged in an orgy of gambling after the peace of 1815. Captain Gronow (1794–1865), in his once famous *Reminiscences* (1862), remarked that 'One of the features of high society after the long war was a passion for gambling; so universal was it that there are few families of distinction who do not even to the present day retain unpleasant reminiscences of the period.'

Moralists pounced on sad cases of privileged young men brought down by gambling, from the 1776 suicide of John Damer onwards (this noble heir to a large fortune contracted gaming debts of some £70,000 and his father Lord Milton – despite his immense wealth – refused to settle them). Satirists were also quick to condemn the moral iniquity of gambling. For instance, in her 1793 satire on the superficiality and decadence of the *haut ton* (high fashionables), *Modern Manners. A Poem. In Two Cantos*, Mary Robinson portrayed contemporary high society as being possessed by an avaricious spirit of gambling. Her poem is part of the long-established eighteenth-century satirical tradition of anti-luxurious satire which frequently dwelt on the perils of gaming. Such jeremiads teem with depictions of the ruined heir losing his patrimony at the gaming clubs of St James's or, on a less exalted level, the unfortunate awaiting the drop at Tyburn as a consequence of crimes committed to feed his all-consuming habit of gambling.

Robinson's example of obsessive gambling, however, is rather more remarkable: 'Yet some great souls on gain so keen are set, / They'll *eat* a cat to win a trifling bett.' This is based, as the movie-makers say, on a true story. In 1788, readers of *The World*, a miscellany of society gossip, anecdotes of fashionable life, and salon verse, were confronted with an extraordinary example of aristocratic eccentricity:

> Amongst the curious Betts of the day, may be reckoned the following: The *Duke* of *Bedford* has betted 1,000 guineas with Lord Barrymore, that he does not – *eat a live* Cat! It is said his Lordship grounds his chances upon having already made the experiment upon a Kitten.

The seventh Earl Barrymore (1769–93), the rakish Irish peer and inveterate gambler who ran through much of his family's fortune at the gambling tables only to shoot himself to death in a hunting accident at the age of twenty-four, later thought better of testing his stomach in this curious fashion, writing that he only sought to find 'a man who would eat a Cat' on his behalf (in 1790, such a one was found, the 'Chelsea Cat-Eater', who, according to the *Sporting Magazine*, ate a live nine-pound cat at a local hostelry for a wager. This fearless omnivore 'made a formidable attack on the head of his antag-onist and, with repeated bites, soon deprived it of existence'; the fur, skin and sinew of the deceased beast were then consumed, with only a few bones left as 'memorials of ... the degradation of human nature').

The prospect of feline-eating wagers was diverting to the late Georgian audience because of the bizarre grounds of the bet rather than the weight of the sum at stake, which, though sizeable, was by no means spectacularly large by the standards of the day. Contemporary readers were used to anec-dotes of family inheritance lost at the wheel or squandered at cards. Late Georgian society contained many upper-class rakehells who, in Richard Owen Cambridge's phrase, 'In races, routes, the stews, and White's [a London club], / Pass['d] all their days and all their nights'. Much middle-class opinion such as Robinson's condemned rich and poor alike for their gambling proclivities. Similarly, radical orators attacked the upper classes for wasting more money in an evening's entertainment than a footman would earn in several lifetimes, and some patrician aristocrats (William Wilberforce the most notable) who espoused philanthropic causes rather than indulging in fox-hunting, boozing and playing cards, lamented the effects of gaming on rich and poor alike.

Robinson herself criticised the morally deleterious effects of gambling on women in her drama *Nobody* (1794), which satirised the debased moral standards of female gamesters in high society, especially among the Whig aristocracy which had once patronised the dramatist, during her days as an actress. Robinson's comedy flopped after receiving a great deal of heckling and jeering, and closed after a mere three performances at Drury Lane. Perhaps Robinson was seen as biting the hand that had fed her, in her satire on the avariciousness, obsession with gambling and hypocrisy about sexual matters of the *haut ton*. Her daughter writes that elements of high society 'had decided that "*Nobody* should be damned!"' and that some of its members had sent their lackeys to boo and hiss: 'On the drawing up of the curtain, several persons in the galleries, whose liveries betrayed their employers, were heard to declare that they were sent to *do up "Nobody"*. Even women of distinguished rank hissed through their fans.'

Mary Robinson's campaign against gambling took the form of satire, drama and narrative verse. Her poem 'The Gamester' (1800), published under the pseudonym 'Laura Maria' in the *Monthly Visitor* (a journal 'particularly addressed to the rising generation'), is a typical example of contemporary anti-gambling literary polemic, and is worth examining at some length. The unfortunate gambler in Robinson's poem is an abject figure. His miseries are etched on his physiognomy, fevered of lip, pale of cheek, and bloodshot of eye as he is:

> Say, what is he, whose haggard eye
>   Scarce dares to meet the morning ray?
> Who, trembling, would, but cannot fly
>   From man, and from the busy day?
> Mark how his lip is fever'd o'er,
>   Behold his cheek, how deathly it appears!
> See! how his bloodshot eye-balls pour
>   A burning torrent of unpitied tears!

'Despis'd, suspected, ruin'd, lost' though he might be, Robinson's moral tale makes clear that it was not ever thus for this hopeless wretch, who was once young, happy and financially secure ('Once were his prospects bright and gay / And Independence blest his hours'). However, all of this has disappeared since he started to visit the gambling 'Hells' and 'learn[ed] the lesson of the gamesters' school!':

> One hour elate with ill-got gold,
>> And dazzled by the shining ore,
> In plenitude of joys behold
>> The Prodigal display his store!
> The next in poverty and fear,
>> He hides him, trembling at approaching fate,
> While greedy creditors appear,
>> And with remorseless rage lurk round his gate.

The gamester, 'On Mis'ry's stormy ocean tost', is alone, without parent or wife to support and succour him. He declines into insanity and self-destruction, and Robinson takes a grim relish in apportioning him the destiny of pain eternal:

> Then comes the horror-breeding hour!
>> While recreant Suicide attends;
> Or Madness, with impetuous pow'r,
>> The scene of desolation ends!
> Upon his grave no Parent mourns,
>> No widow'd Love laments with graceful woe;
> No dawn of joy for him returns,
>> For Heav'n denies that peace his frenzy lost below!

Even in suicidal death the gambler's sorrows are not over, so dire are the consequences of gaming. Gambling, in this account, is ruinous to the family, the nation and even to the immortal soul.

Fashion

If frittering away money at the gaming table was seen as a sign of unconscionable decadence to many moralists in the Romantic period, so, for some, was the near obsessive attention to dress and personal appearance frequently evident in high society, alongside its slavish willingness to follow fashion and the latest sartorial innovations, however ludicrous or ephemeral. Mary Robinson was one author who, in both poetry and prose, mocked what she saw as the misplaced values of a womanhood unhealthily obsessed with clothes and fine display (see 'Satire' for discussion of her attitude to 'Preposterous Fashion' in *Modern Manners*). In this she followed the example of Mary Wollstonecraft, who wrote in the *Vindication of the Rights of Woman* (1792) that 'An air of fashion ... is but a badge of slavery.' 'The varnish of fashion', declares Wollstonecraft, 'may dazzle the weak', but women should learn to rise 'above the fumes of vanity'.

Not everyone felt this way, however. The late Georgian period, which was a significant time in the development of modern fashion, was populated by many who relished fashion, both as a diversion from European conflict during the Revolutionary and Napoleonic Wars and for its own sake. This preoccupation was summed up in the figure of the Prince of Wales, later George IV (1762–1830), who, alongside his fondness for huge dinners, middle-aged aristocratic mistresses and oriental furnishings, was the leader of a fashionable set which expressed, in part, its social difference and separation from the common herd through conspicuous consumption and elegance in fine, and sometimes exotic, clothing. The Carlton House circle (named after the Prince's residence), which included such men as the foppish playwright Sir Lumley St George Skeffington (1771–1850) and William Arderne (1789–1849), 2nd Baron Alvanley, paid meticulous attention and – particularly in the Prince's case – large sums of money for their tailoring.

'When turned out of the hands of his valet', wrote the society journalist C. J. Apperley of the upper-class dandy, 'he presents the very *beau-ideal* of his caste. The exact Stultz-like fit of his coat, his superlatively well-cleaned leather breeches and boots, and the generally apparent high breeding of the man, can seldom be matched.' Such styling betokens the exquisite man of fashion, and the reference to the ultra-fashionable St James' tailor Stultz & Co. is not innocent; this is a particularly mannered and exclusive avant-garde mode of fashion, consciously adopted to gesture to one's peers (a very small set) and to exclude one's inferiors (a very large one). The divisions in society between those that had and those that did not were incarnate in the dress of the fashionable gentleman.

During the 1790s, in his Whig days, Prince George patronised a dashing young army officer, George Bryan Brummell (1778–1840), generally known as 'Beau Brummell', who, after leaving the soldiery, became the exemplary figure of the modern fashionable set (*Tait's Edinburgh Magazine* described him in 1844 as the 'Dictator of the World of Fashion for about twenty years'). Brummell wore no wig or powder on his head, and he popularised cravats, tight-fitting jackets and full-length trousers (indeed, he has been described as the inventor of the modern man's suit). He was famous for his languid humour; Hazlitt described Brummell as the 'greatest of small wits' (his favourite, the Beau's remark to a friend who 'found him confined to his room from a lameness in one foot [and] expressed his concern at the accident. "I am sorry for it too," answered Brummell very gravely, "particularly as it's my favourite leg!"' Hazlitt comments that it is 'as if a man of fashion had nothing else to do than to sit and think of which of his legs he liked best'). Though some have thought of Brummell as the epitome of a somewhat effeminate exquisite, there was actually something of the hypermasculine about his styling given the clean, unfussy lines of his clothing, and especially when compared with the powdered and bewigged exquisites of

the previous fashionable upper-class grouping, the 'macaronis' of the mid-
to late eighteenth century. (It all ended in salt tears for Brummell. He fell out
with his patron, once seeing 'Prinny' with their mutual friend Lord Alvanley,
and loudly asking 'Alvanley, who's your fat friend?', and eventually financial indiscretions led to self-imposed exile in France.)

The fresh, increasingly streamlined, tailoring of male fashion was
complemented on the distaff side by the clean, flowing lines of the Empire-
line dress in vogue from the late 1790s through to the Regency, with its
'waist' tied just under the bust, beneath which flowed a long skirt. Certainly
less restrictive than the anti-functional bustle worn by her later, Victorian
sisters, the loose revealing muslins and calicos sported by the late Georgian
society beauty have been seen as striking a temporary note of sartorial freedom for the female sex which was arguably analogous to their brethren
beginning to leave their heads wig-less and unpowdered during the 1790s
(this latter trend was prompted, in part, by Pitt's infamous tax on hair
powder, introduced in 1795). The neoclassical style, generally worn without corsetry or a half-dozen protective petticoats, fashionable at the turn of
the nineteenth century, gave the appearance of simplicity and a lack of clut-
ter, before Victorian corsetry and crinoline and after the elaborate wiring
and ruching of the eighteenth century (fig. 2 shows an 1805 image from the
women's magazine *La Belle Assemblée* which contrasts the styling of the
present day with that of fifty years since).

Writing in the *Quarterly Review* in 1854, W. M. Thackeray imagined a
child asking her grandmother about the forward, if not indecent, dress of
the old lady's youth: 'Grandmamma, did you wear such a dress as that,
when you danced at Almack's [the ultra-exclusive assembly rooms]? There
was very little of it, grandmamma'. In a manner similar to the way in which
gambling was condemned, so the fashions of the day were sometimes
viewed in scandalous terms as the very height of foolishness, even of ethical perniciousness. In an essay published in 1821, the renowned poetic
anthologist of the *Elegant Extracts* (1784) and moral philosopher the
Reverend Vicesimus Knox (1751–1821) thundered that 'They who are
exempted by their elevated condition from the confinement of commercial
and professional life, involve themselves in voluntary slavery by engaging
in the service of the tyrant Fashion,' a service which he condemns as 'profligate, extravagant, intemperate, or even wicked [and] ungenteel'. Knox
attacks fashion in its widest sense – with its drinking, gambling and sexual
intemperance – as destructive of family:

> For this, the stripling squanders his patrimony, and destroys his constitution. For this,
> the virgin bloom of innocence and beauty is withered at the vigils of the card-table.
> For this, the loss of integrity, and public infamy, are willingly incurred; and it is

Fig. 2   Anon., 'Full Dress for July 1805; Dress of the Old Woman in 1755'. From *La Belle Assemblée* (1805)

agreed by many, that it were better to go out of the world, than to live in it and be unfashionable.

Better, indeed, to live in middle-class sobriety declares Knox; 'The middle ranks of mankind are the most virtuous, the best accomplished, and the most capable of enjoying the pleasures and advantages which fall to the lot of human nature.' Only the bourgeoisie could save the nation, given that the upper classes were turning away from the old sense of *noblesse oblige* and, indeed, leading the lower orders astray. The contagion was seen as spreading from fine ladies to their inferiors; servants were accused by some, in the 1806 words of the *Saunterer*, of 'applying their wages to purchase the insignia of pride, of loading themselves with indecent finery, and rivalling their superiors by the splendor of their dress'.

Alongside such soap-box oratory came satire such as George Cruikshank's 'Monstrosities' series (1816–28), which lampooned the vanity and slavish following of fashion – no matter how grotesque – among both men and women (see fig. 13 in 'Satire', below, for an example of this series). The caricaturist's father, the elder Isaac Cruikshank, has also been credited with an early lampoon of the neoclassical style, the 'Parisian Ladies in their Winter Dress for 1800' (fig. 3; 1799), which takes the notion of *déshabillé* to its logical conclusion, at least in terms of satirical *reductio ad absurdum*.

Alongside standard Horatian satire on the follies of humanity, frequently the attacks on the thoughtless frippery of the rich had a political tinge about them. The Parisian ladies in Cruikshank's caricature are sexual *sans culottes*, their nakedness indicative of France's social, political and sexual decadence

Fig. 3   Attrib. Isaac Cruikshank the Elder, 'Parisian Ladies in their Winter Dress for 1800' (1799)

after the Revolution. Similarly, lampoons on the Prince Regent had much of the somatic (physical) about them, stressing Prince George's corpulence and unloveliness. William Hone's brilliant satire on the Tory establishment *The Political House that Jack Built* (1819), illustrated by George Cruikshank (see fig. 14 on p. 255), portrayed the Prince as a fat 'Dandy of Sixty', and in so doing confirmed him as the unshakeable figure of satirical fun among Whig satirists from Charles Lamb's 'The Triumph of the Whale' (1812) onwards (see 'Satire' for discussion of this poem). Attacking the Regent's inappropriate vanity and dress, his vainglorious obsession with clothes, signifies the misplaced moral priorities of the upper class; while fat Prince George was being poured into his man corset, the post-Napoleonic recession made life appalling for the poor, who needed no assistance in slimming down. Mocking George's girth and obesity implied that the system of kingship which he epitomised was busily hogging the continent's wealth and resources. The heedless greed of the existing system, to radical satirists such as Hone, is emblematised in the Prince of Wales's huge girth. In such satire, mocking dandyism was charged with a sharp political resonance.

Sport

Writing of British society in 1886, the critic Andrew Lang declared that 'Fifty years ago we were a cruel ... people. We had bull-baitings, and badger-drawings [and] prize-fights, and cock-fights; we went to see men hanged.' It is undeniable that sport in the late Georgian era was often bloody and violent, but it should also be acknowledged that British sport was in a transitional phase in the period, a curious hybrid where a widespread taste for the pitiless and ancient amusement of cocking (practised by the ancient Greeks but criminalised, alongside animal baiting, by the 1835 Cruelty to Animals Act) coexisted with the establishment of the governing bodies of modern horse-racing and cricket, the Jockey Club and the Marylebone Cricket Club, institutions of some power to this day. Sport between 1780 and 1840 was characterised by a mixture of the athletic activities of England, cricket, rowing, football and so on, with more questionable pursuits drawn from what George Orwell once called 'the boxing, racing, cock-fighting, badger-digging, poaching, rat-catching side of life'.

Sport resounded through the wider print culture of the age with an explosion of printed material devoted to it. There were unprecedented numbers of press columns on the subject: newspapers covered it in greater detail than ever before, specialist periodicals devoted in part or whole to sport were established (the *Annals of Sporting and Fancy Gazette* and the *Sporting Review*, for instance, but most notably the *Sporting Magazine* and *Bell's Life in London*), and several literary journals (*Blackwood's Edinburgh*

Magazine most significantly) enthusiastically championed sports, especially those of the river (angling), the field (horse-racing and various forms
of hunting) and the Fancy (the fraternity of boxing devotees). The rise of
sports publishing is one of the great success stories of late Georgian print
culture. Following the success of Peter Beckford's groundbreaking
Thoughts on Hunting (1781), enterprising publishers began to take sport
seriously as an income generator, producing a range of new or hitherto
underdeveloped forms of sporting literature: advice manuals for the
sportsman, the earliest sporting biographies, lavishly illustrated and
expensive collections of prints, picaresque tales of amusing Cockney
sportsmen, encyclopaedias, almanacs, memoirs, commemorative broadsides and so on. The first important sporting journalists appeared: Pierce
Egan (1772–1849), the most notable of all boxing writers, and the chroni-
clers of the hunt 'Nimrod' (Charles James Apperley (1777–1843) and 'Nim
South' (Robert Smith Surtees (1805–64)). All three of these men also wrote
highly popular books of some literary distinction: Apperley's *The Chace,
the Turf, and the Road* (1831–2) and the remarkable *Memoirs of The Life of
The Late John Mytton, Esq.* (1835), the first best-selling sporting biography,
Egan's multi-volume pugilistic history *Boxiana* (1812–29) and his novel
Life in London (1821), a populist triumph; and the distinguished sporting
satirist Surtees's successful series of hunt-related comic tales which
began with *Jorrocks' Jaunts and Jollities* (serialised in the *New Sporting
Magazine* between 1831 and 1834) and continued deep into the Victorian
age.

The three most popular spectator sports of the day were cricket, horse-
racing and bare-knuckle fighting. Perhaps surprisingly, the most literary of
these – and of sport in general in this period – was the most violent, Lord
Byron's favourite, pugilism. Prompted by the publication of the first two,
highly successful, volumes of Egan's *Boxiana; or Sketches of Modern
Pugilism* (1812 and 1818), there were a significant number of literary treatments of boxing, the most famous example being William Hazlitt's great
essay 'The Fight' published in the *New Monthly Magazine* in February 1822
(see 'Reviews, Magazines and the Essay'). Then, as now, there were those
who sought to identify the national temper in terms of sport. In 1819, the
satirist and critic John Wilson (1785–1854; a keen cock-fighter and amateur
wrestler) declared in *Blackwood's* that 'The character of a people is to be
sought for and found in their amusements.' The amusement which Wilson
identified as most emblematic of the British spirit was that most
contentious (bloodsports apart) of all contemporary sports, bare-knuckle
boxing. For pugilistic pressmen such as Wilson and Pierce Egan, the fighter
represented the national character stripped to white breeches: boxing
became a highly literary sport in the late Georgian age, albeit one praised

and damned in equal measure. Here the amusements of the people became an arena for debating issues of national character, for exploring matters of identity and masculinity and those of race, social class and gender.

During and immediately after the Napoleonic Wars, the skilled violence of pugilism, with its mixture of sustained courage and real danger, held a special appeal, providing a new outlet for narratives of male bravery and national superiority. Certainly Egan saw sport as socially suggestive, maintaining in the first volume of *Boxiana* that boxing was 'a national trait': 'we feel no hesitation in declaring, that it is wholly – BRITISH!' 'The manly art of boxing', according to Egan, has conditioned the martial spirit of the nation – warlike but humane, fierce but honourable – having 'infused that true heroic courage, blended with humanity into the heart of Britons'.

Egan complemented his prose with boxing poetry which reiterated the polemical convictions of his journalism and historical writing; all articulate his conviction that settling disputes with the 'naked fist' was a particularly British and honourable custom, especially when contrasted with the perfidious continental who ends an argument by pulling out a dagger. 'Britain', declares Egan in *Boxiana*, is 'a country where the stiletto is not known – where trifling quarrels do not produce assassination, and where revenge is not finished by murder. Boxing removes these dreadful calamities; a contest is soon decided, and scarcely ever the frame sustains any material injury.' Similarly, in Egan's best-selling novel *Life in London* (1821), Bob Logic, when shown a picture of an Italian knife killing, waxes philosophical: 'When comparisons are made, the above plate speaks volumes in favor of the manly and generous mode resorted to by Englishmen to resent an insult or to decide a quarrel.'

Egan makes the same point in verse in 'A Boxing we will go' (1811), which begins by toasting maiden fair and boxer brave, and in particular Thomas Cribb, then champion of England (the variant 'Crib' is often used in contemporary writing), but moves on to tavern philosophising about the honest Briton and the foreign stabber:

> Come move the song, and stir the glass,
>   For why should we be sad;
> Let's drink to some free-hearted lass,
>   And Crib, the boxing lad.
>   And a boxing we will go, will go, will go,
>   And a boxing we will go.
>
> Italians stab their friends behind,
>   In darkest shades of night;
> But Britons they are bold and kind,
>   And box their friends by light.

> The sons of France their pistols use,
>   Pop, pop, and they have done;
> But Britons with their hands will bruise,
>   And scorn away to run.

Drunken pothouse singalong though this might be, it also has a certain combative logic. Here Egan's conviction that boxing embodies the good-natured temper of the national spirit, in contradiction to the Mediterraneans' perfidy, is given poetic shape, part of his three-pronged assault on the national consciousness on behalf of pugilism.

Britain was, of course, at war with France when Egan wrote these words. Boxing was in more senses than one a serious game during the Napoleonic period. It is clearly linked to the notions of 'Britishness' and 'manliness':

> Since boxing is a manly game,
>   And Briton's recreation;
> By boxing we will raise our fame,
>   'Bove any other nation.

Egan portrays pugilism as a matter of national pride, of real utility in time of war, and his poem gives metaphorical life to this notion, whimsically imagining the boxers of England defeating the French Emperor, as if Tom Cribb's fists were instruments of British military power rather than just its symbol. A roaring patriotism fills the air:

> If Boney doubt it, let him come,
>   And try with Crib a round;
> And Crib shall beat him like a drum,
>   And make his carcase sound.
>
> Mendoza, Gulley, Molineaux,
>   Each nature's weapon wield,
> Who each at Boney would stand true,
>   And never to him yield.

Interestingly, Egan's anti-Gallican cohort is a rainbow coalition of Caucasian, Jew and black: Thomas Cribb (1781–1848), Daniel Mendoza (c.1765–1836) the East Ender who fought as the 'Hebrew', and 'the tremendous man of colour', the gifted black Virginian pugilist and freed slave Tom Molineaux (c.1785–1818) who fought two epic bouts with Cribb in 1810 and 1811. If the granitic Molineaux had the misfortune to be born outside Albion's shores, and a 'Negro' to boot, in his pluck and bottom he has shown himself capable of behaving like an Englishman. Egan's vision of boxing unites the nation, both native and immigrant. Sport was, in its rough-hewn way, seen as morally significant in the Romantic period.

See also   Reviews, Magazines and the Essay; Satire.

Further Reading

John Ashton, *The History of Gambling in England* (1899).
Dennis Brailsford, *A Taste for Diversions: Sport in Georgian England* (2001).
Ian Kelly, *Beau Brummell: The Ultimate Dandy* (2005).
George Orwell, 'Charles Dickens' (1939), in *Shooting an Elephant: and Other Essays* (2003), pp. 49–97.
Lawrence Stone, *Road to Divorce: England 1530–1987* (1990).
Norah Waugh, *Corsets and Crinolines* (1954).
Norah Waugh, *The Cut of Men's Clothes 1600–1900* (1964).

Medicine and Science

Romantic-Era Medicine

The Romantic period was an age of pandemic, of ever-present illness and high rates of infant mortality. We are fortunate today inasmuch as the death of a child or young adult is now a relatively rare and shocking event, and sudden death – heart attacks excepted – is highly unusual even among the middle aged. But every adult of the Romantic period knew of hitherto healthy people struck down one day by illness – smallpox or cholera, for example – and dead very soon thereafter. Consider the lives of the 'Big Six' Romantic poets themselves, the youngest of whom, John Keats, died of consumption (tuberculosis) at the age of 25. The disease was a scourge, as the medically-trained Keats well knew. The poet's mother and his younger brother Tom also died from the condition. Of his compatriots in the 'Big Six' Romantic poets, the patriarch Wordsworth, who lived to 80, also knew grief. Two of his six children died in infancy and another adult child predeceased him. Coleridge had four children, of which number his second son, Berkeley, died when a baby. Of the four children born to the poet Shelley and his second wife, Mary Godwin Shelley, only one grew to adulthood. Byron, who died of a fever at 36, had three daughters, one of them, Allegra, was illegitimate and passed away just before her sixth birthday. Blake, winner of this grim lottery of mortality, did not have any children and lived happily with his near illiterate wife Catherine until his death when he was nigh on 70.

Prior to the dramatic developments in bacterial medicine forged by Louis Pasteur in the 1870s, the field of contemporary medicine during the Romantic period, in contrast to those of politics, philosophy and science, was not one of revolutionary activity and change. With the notable exception of the smallpox vaccination developed by Edward Jenner from 1796 onwards (and even that had early problems; young Berkeley Coleridge died aged 7 months in an adverse reaction to the vaccine), the medical situation in the Romantic period ended much as it began, with large sections of the population falling foul of a range of ailments from such major epidemical scourges as tuberculosis and cholera down to the generally less harmful but still potentially fatal conditions for infants of dysentery, influenza, and measles. Jenner's contribution to eradicating death from smallpox was considerable but, even so, the very young remained vulnerable to deadly diseases and the toils of birth such that in some accounts an estimated two out of every five infants died before the age of five. Meanwhile childbirth itself endangered the female adult population, with poor obstetrics, lack of anaesthetics, and puerperal fever (blood poisoning) frequently leading to death. Mary Wollstonecraft herself died at the age of 38 from puerperal fever following the complicated delivery by a local midwife of her second daughter, Mary Shelley. (Wollstonecraft's husband of six months, William Godwin, desperate to save his wife from a premature death, had promptly called in the 'experts' – four male physicians arrived in succession to treat Mary's post-partum condition but to no avail.)

The urban adult population in general faced grave health risks resulting from poverty, crowded housing and poor ventilation as the so-called 'filth diseases' (notably, typhoid and cholera morbus, ran rampant through workhouses and prisons, but also barracks and schools). In the face of widespread health risks, domestic self-help manuals and quackery flourished as, indeed, did the medical profession (of surgeons, physicians and apothecaries), which expanded in wealth and status throughout the period, in part as a consequence of the increased disposable income of the upper, middling and merchant classes. Even so, the British Medical Association was not founded until relatively late in the Romantic period, in 1832, before which date quacks mingled freely with earnest medical pioneers.

To the mass of people desperate for a cure for ailments, from the ubiquitous toothache to the common ravages of venereal disease, the charlatan was indistinguishable from the trained physician. The promotion and administering of dubious (and sometimes fatal) medical cures took place without a system of nationally or professionally agreed standards, such that the chief empirics of the age could advertise and peddle their wares with bold abandon – and sometimes with remarkable showmanship. Take, for instance, the case of physician and dentist Martin Van Butchell (1735–c.1812) who famously exhibited the embalmed corpse of his first wife in the window of his home-based surgery to attract potential clients among the onlookers; take also the notorious Doctor Samuel Solomon (1768/9–1819), proprietor of the Cordial Balm of Gilead, a brandy-based mixture, which claimed to cure the epidemic of the nervous disorders (anxiety, hysteria, melancholia and the like) that afflicted those many who saw themselves as fashionably sensitive and delicate. It should be remembered that the Romantic period came on the heels of the eighteenth-century cult of sensibility: the cultivation of heightened physiological responses (both to one's own suffering and to the suffering of others) involving feelings of melancholy and empathy. A nervous or melancholic temperament was seen in genteel circles to be a sign of taste and refinement, as, indeed, was the 'white plague' of consumption. That 'gentle disease', as Edgar Allan Poe later called it, seemed peculiarly matched to the febrile victims among the artistic – or would-be artistic – community.

Melancholy (the eighteenth-century term for depression) also infiltrated a Romantic poetic sensibility, famously in John Keats's 'Ode on Melancholy'. Keats, of course, had first-hand knowledge of suffering and death, owing to his training as an apothecary and, indeed, from seeing the ravages of tuberculosis visited upon his mother and brother. The death of the latter, Tom Keats, in December 1818, plainly has direct influence on perhaps Keats's most famous poem, the 'Ode to a Nightingale' (1819):

> Fade far away, dissolve, and quite forget
>   What thou among the leaves hast never known,
> The weariness, the fever, and the fret
>   Here, where men sit and hear each other groan;
> Where palsy shakes a few, sad, last grey hairs,
>   Where youth grows pale, and spectre-thin and dies.

Other Romantic sufferers of medical ailments which acted as a spur to creativity were S. T. Coleridge and Thomas De Quincey, opium addicts both (and men for whom the process of imaginative creation was in part enhanced by artificial stimulation). Indeed, pain itself is recurrently fetishised in Romantic-period writing in such stuff as De Quincey's 'Pains of Opium' in the *Confessions of an English Opium Eater* (1821) (see 'Reviews, Magazines and the Essay'). We can see something of this in the opium-infused passions of Coleridge's famous poem 'Pains of Sleep', written in 1803 when the poet's unfulfilled love for Sara Hutchinson, Wordsworth's sister-in-law, was the cause of a deep-rooted emotional torment:

> But yesternight I prayed aloud
> In anguish and in agony,
> Upstarting from the fiendish crowd
> Of shapes and thoughts that tortured me;
> A lurid light, a trampling throng,
> Sense of intolerable wrong

Similar levels of Romantic suffering are even found in descriptions of such mundane conditions as a stomach ache. Take, for instance, Thomas Carlyle's description in a letter of 1821 of the psychological pains trigged by intestinal malfunction: 'today the guts are all wrong again, the headache, the weakness, the black despondency are overpowering me ... my curse seems deeper and blacker than any man'. The discourse is positively Byronic. Unembarrassed by this rhapsodic agony, Carlyle's letter is testimony to what might be called the Romantic sublimation of pain.

Romantic-era Science

Unlike the somewhat halting progress of medical advancements during the Romantic age, scientific research developed at an unbridled pace. Some of the most famous scientific discoveries of the modern age occurred during the Romantic period, from Joseph Priestley's (1733–1804) discovery of oxygen to Sir Humphry Davy's (1788–1829) invention of the miners' safety lamp, which he presented to the Royal Society in January 1816. In the same year, John Keats, in his first notable poem, 'On First Looking into Chapman's Homer', envisaged himself a traveller in the world of poetry, 'the realms of gold', in terms of a scientific explorer, his lines echoing the excitement of William Herschel's (1738–1822) discovery of Uranus thirty-five years previously: 'Then felt I like some watcher of the skies / When a new planet swims into his ken.' In the Royal astronomer Herschel's telescopic investigations of the size and scope of the Milky Way and the discoveries of botanist Sir Joseph Banks (1743–1820) on Captain James Cook's first exploratory round-the-world voyage of 1768–71, the notion persisted throughout the Romantic period of a natural, physical and chemical world whose infinite mysteries were waiting to be unfolded.

In contrast to the scientific rationalism of the Enlightenment, epitomised by the exactness of Newtonian physics, Romantic science, as Richard Holmes puts it in his fine study of the subject, *The Age of Wonder: How the Romantic Generation Discovered the Beauty and Terror of Science* (2008), 'favoured a softer "dynamic" science of invisible powers and mysterious energies ... of growth and organic change'. This is one of the reasons, Holmes also observes, why Romantic scientists – and not just scientists but poets and novelists also – were fascinated by 'Vitalism', the existence of a Life Force or Life Principle, a notion that arose from the insufficiency of anatomical science – the pulses of the heart and the circulation of the blood – to explain the mystery of human existence. The physician John Abernethy (1764–1831), who would later count the poet Coleridge among his patients, speculated that the 'Life Force' – analogous to the theological notion of the soul – was something superadded by a power outside man. On the other hand, scientific men such as Davy focused attention on 'animal magnetism', human animation and the potentialities of volcanic or electrical charge, an investigation that bore literary fruit most famously in Mary Shelley's visionary novel *Frankenstein* (1818).

Romanticism and Science

The idea of Romanticism as a cultural force that is generally hostile to science, its ideal of the creative imagination and fluid subjectivity forever opposed to a rigorous scientific objectivity, has been successfully overturned by the growing body of modern scholarship on Romantic science. Such works as Holmes's study demonstrate the interconnectedness between literature and science in the Romantic period, a mutuality of concerns evident in the work of the 'Big Six' Romantic poets as well as that of a number of women writers, including Mary Shelley, Anna Laetitia Barbauld and Charlotte Smith (consider, for example, the botanically precise descriptions of the local flora and fauna in Smith's posthumously published blank verse poem *Beachy Head* (1807)). In their turn, the most famous botanist (Erasmus Darwin) and the best known scientists of the age (Humphry Davy and Joseph Priestley) also wrote poetry and, in the case of Priestley, who was an early supporter of Anna Barbauld, encouraged the literary efforts of others. Indeed, much of Darwin's scientific output was expounded in poetry and, significantly, he declared of his botanical garden established at Lichfield that its general design was 'to enlist imagination under the banner of Science'. Not for Darwin love lyrics or satire; his verse deals with the reproduction of plants and the like. His long poem *The Loves of the Plants* (1789), which was gleefully ridiculed in the pages of the satirical Tory magazine the *Anti-Jacobin, or Weekly Examiner* (see 'Satire') as 'The Loves of the Triangles' in 1798, was succeeded by the 1791 poem *The Botanic Garden*. There also appeared in 1802 the poem *The Temple of Nature*, from which come the following lubricious (sexually-charged) lines:

> Hence on green leaves the sexual Pleasures dwell,
> And Loves and Beauties crowd the blossom's bell;
> The wakeful Anther in his silken bed
> O'er the pleas'd Stigma bows his waxen head;
> With meeting lips, and mingling smiles they sup
> Ambrosial dew-drops from the nectar'd cup;
> Or buoy'd in air the plumy Lover springs,
> And seeks his panting bride on Hymen-wings.

Joseph Priestley and Anna Laetitia Barbauld

The scientist, religious divine and grammarian Joseph Priestley was one of the earliest embodiments of what we might now call Romantic science in terms of his interlocked pursuit of religious, scientific and social questions (for Priestley's religious thought, see 'Religion and Atheism' and 'Millenarianism'). He was also the lynchpin of a network of liberal-minded philosophers and intellectuals, among them Thomas Paine, Mary Wollstonecraft, Anna Barbauld and (through her father Richard Lovell Edgeworth) Maria Edgeworth. A Fellow of the Royal Society, and a radical in politics (he supported the colonists' cause in the American Revolution) and in religion (he was a Unitarian, that is a Christian unconvinced of the divinity of Jesus Christ), Priestley did not see his religious faith as incompatible with his scientific endeavours. He welcomed the French Revolution and was one of the original members of the Lunar Society of Birmingham (an informal learned society of prominent industrialists and intellectuals), alongside Darwin and the industrialists James Watt, Matthew Boulton, and Josiah Wedgwood. A man of the Enlightenment, Priestley had many talents; he was a grammarian (author of *The Rudiments of English Grammar* (1761)), and a religious polemicist (his *History of the Corruptions of Christianity* (1782) attacks the established church), as well as an experimental chemist who participated in the Europe-wide race to identify and separate chemical elements and identify a number of gases, including so-called 'laughing gas', nitrous oxide.

Anna Barbauld, for her part, penned a witty poetic riposte, 'The Mouse's Petition' (written under her maiden name of Aiken), to Priestley's scientific experiments on mice, which humorously ridicules the self-proclaimed champion of liberty for keeping caged members of the divine creation for his own research. In a gesture typical of the Romantic poet's empathetic identification with the natural world and with God's creatures, Aiken ventriloquises the plight of the captive mouse thus:

> If e'er thy breath with freedom glow'd,
> And spurned a tyrant's chain,
> Let not thy strong oppressive force
> A free-born mouse detain.

Let us consider Barbauld in more detail as a female Romantic poet whose verse also engaged seriously with the concerns of modern science. Following the piece of whimsy that is 'The Mouse's Petition', which appeared in Aiken's first volume of poetry in 1772, the poet, who was a close of friend of Priestley, publicly acknowledged her support of his scientifically experimental and politically radical stance in a daring poem of her own, 'Eighteen Hundred and Eleven' (1812). This portrays the dissolution of intellectual life in a Britain under oppressive Tory rule, in strident heroic couplets, providing both a poetic theme and a measure that was more commonly associated with public poetry written by men. She was fiercely attacked for this supposed transgression of her poetic feminine role by the Tory reviewer John Wilson Croker, who in 1812, in the *Quarterly Review*, scorned her impropriety in turning 'satirist' and mocked her attempt at political commentary, the first in a series of politically hostile notices that would destroy Barbauld's confidence and effectively bring her literary career to a premature end. Joseph Priestley, her erstwhile mentor, had been forced to flee to America in 1794 after being hounded out of his Birmingham laboratory by a 'Church and King' rabble who set fire to his premises in protest at his Revolutionary sympathies; Barbauld's poem pays tribute to him alongside his fellow discoverers of 'Nature's coyest secrets', Davy and the American Benjamin Franklin (1706–90; who, like Priestley, conducted experiments with electricity in the 1790s):

> Join with their Franklin, Priestley's injured name,
> Whom, then, each continent shall proudly proclaim.

Barbauld's father had been during her youth a schoolmaster at the Warrington Academy for Dissenters, which is where the young aspiring poetess first received Priestley's encouragement and support.

An earlier poem, 'A Summer Evening's Meditation' (1773), poeticises the night sky and by association glosses it as feminine. Barbauld renders the starlit sky as an alternative, metaphorically feminine realm where female 'wisdom' takes flight.

> This dead of midnight is the noon of thought,
> And wisdom mounts her zenith with the stars.

As Barbauld's intellectual musings soar skywards there is a parallel movement of something within her: the 'self-collected soul / Turns inward' towards God and the creative imagination which, released, begins its own ascent into an unknown world of infinite mystery: 'Fearless thence, / I launch into the trackless deeps of space', until 'Fancy droops' and 'thought astonished stops her bold career'. In an optimistic flourish, Barbauld prophesied that one day her sex would gain easier access to the sublime, which was likened to the scientific unveiling of the wonders of the universe:

> the hour will come
> When all these splendours bursting on my sight
> Shall stand unveiled, and to my ravished sense
> Unlock the glories of the world unknown.

It is difficult not to detect here the influence of Barbauld's familiarity with contemporary advancements in science; what she does quite remarkably is to blend that understanding into the poetic language of sensibility and feeling. She, in effect, feminises the science of astronomy.

Mary Shelley and Romantic Science

Barbauld notwithstanding, the most famous woman writer of the period to be influenced by contemporary experiments in science was Mary Shelley, whose novel *Frankenstein, or The Modern Prometheus* (1818) is predicated on the notion of inert matter being sparked into life, and constitutes the most remarkably literary response of her day to the so-called 'Vitalism' debate. As is well known, the novel charts the tale of Victor Frankenstein, a quondam student of natural philosophy and chemistry at the Swiss University of Ingolstadt, whose several solitary years spent researching the secret of life come to a dramatic head one dark night, when in the seclusion of his own apartment, he brings to life his creation, the famed monster. Richard Holmes has noted that the genus of the work can be traced back to the time when Mary Shelley's father William Godwin took her to hear Humphry Davy's lectures on chemistry at the Royal Institution. This said, the fiction, rather than a championing of modern science, has frequently been seen as a warning against the dangers of the obsessive pursuit of knowledge and the scientific quest for the ultimate secret of life. That the monster – created from stolen body parts – turns in his loneliness and pain upon his creator Victor, and destroys all that he held dear, has been read as a sign both of his unnaturalness and of the unnaturalness of the male scientific usurpation of the right to create life, the province of the Almighty and, indeed, of the female (Anne K. Mellor has read the novel as a parable of P. B. Shelley's shortcomings as a father in Victor's swift abandonment of his 'offspring').

Even so, Davy's scientific speculations resonate throughout the literature of the Romantic period, influencing in various ways the poetry of nearly all of the 'Big Six': Coleridge, Wordsworth, Byron, Keats, and Mary Shelley's husband, Percy Bysshe. Coleridge's poems on the 'One Life' of the 1790s might be seen, Richard Holmes suggests, as a poetical and theological accompaniment to Davy's work on the 'carbon cycle', which he presented as the key to earthly existence, a continuous recycling of carbon and oxygen between plants and humans. And that Coleridge and Wordsworth were well aware of the 'labours of Men of science', is apparent in the revised Preface to *Lyrical Ballads* of 1802, which brings modern science into the discussion of the question 'What is a Poet', thus:

The remotest discoveries of the Chemist, the Botanist or Mineralogist, will be as proper objects of the Poet's art as any upon which it can be employed, if the time should ever come when these things shall be familiar to us, and the relations under which they are contemplated by the followers of these respective Sciences shall be manifestly and palpably material to us as enjoying and suffering beings. If the time should ever come when what is now called Science, thus familiarized to men, shall be ready to put on, as it were, a form of flesh and blood, the Poet will lend his divine spirit to aid the transfiguration, and will welcome the Being thus produced, as a dear and genuine inmate of the household of man.

Poetry, in other words, is potentially the companion of science rather than its opposite, both arts rejoicing in the beauty and terror of new discovery, whether that be the machinations of the inner life or the outward workings of physical matter.

See also   Millenarianism; Religion and Atheism; Reviews, Magazines and the Essay; Satire.

Further Reading

Tim Fulford, Debbie Lee and Peter J. Kitson, *Literature, Science and Exploration in the Romantic Era* (2004).
Richard Holmes, *The Age of Wonder: How the Romantic Generation Discovered the Beauty and Terror of Science* (2008).
Clark Lawlor, *Consumption and Literature: The Making of the Romantic Disease* (2006).
Anne K. Mellor, *Mary Shelley: Her Life, Her Fictions, Her Monsters* (1989).
Alan Richardson, *British Romanticism and the Science of the Mind* (2001).
Sharon Ruston, *Shelley and Vitality* (2005).

Music

Romanticism and Music

Music was an important aspect of the leisure habits of the Romantic period. The majority of people attended public worship and sang in church, and this was but the most visible manifestation of the national musical life. Country people sawed on fiddles, beat on drums and played other folk instruments with varying levels of accomplishment, and the fashionable town and city dance – a quadrille or waltz – was performed to a band of musicians, rather than to previously recorded music as often happens today. Learning to play the pianoforte was considered a desirable accomplishment for young ladies, northern choral societies, then, as now, belted out Handel's *Messiah* and glee clubs (where men gathered to sing part songs) were established in the metropolis and other cities.

People also often paid their money, hard-earned or otherwise, to listen to music. The opera was wildly popular in the metropolis, there were symphonic recitals in all of the major cities, and religious oratorios – such as the *Messiah* – were frequently performed. As well as conventional drama, London and regional theatres often featured plays with musical numbers to serve the widespread appetite for ballad operas or 'burlettas' (short comic plays which generally featured a handful of songs). At the same time, the then exalted state of European classical music did not go unnoticed in Great Britain. Indeed, there was a tendency towards genuflection to continental, especially German, music (the 'population' of Germany, declared Leigh Hunt, the Romantic author who wrote most about music, 'learn music as they do their ABC'). Mozart (1756–91), who had visited England to great acclaim as a boy, died early in the period, in 1791, at the early age of 35, and the Romantic age was also the heyday of Beethoven, Rossini and Schubert, and of the great violin virtuoso Paganini, whose visits to England in the 1820s and 1830s caused much excited comment amongst British Romantic writers, notably Hunt, Felicia Hemans and Mary Shelley.

In 'To –' (published posthumously in 1824), P. B. Shelley wrote mellifluously that 'Music, when soft voices die, / Vibrates in the memory'; Romantic thinkers were keen to examine the nature of the aesthetic, emotional or spiritual experiences involved in listening to music. In his *Confessions of an English Opium Eater* (1821), Thomas De Quincey, a musical obsessive (especially of the opera which fed his narcotic rhapsodies), describes the feelings he experienced during frequent visits to the Opera House, notably his love for the voice of the renowned Italian singer, the 'angelic [Giuseppina] Grassini' as – in that great, rather Keatsian phrase – 'she poured forth her immortal soul' in song. 'Music', De Quincey writes, 'is an intellectual or a sensual pleasure according to the temperament of him who hears it'. For the essayist, music was a sensual – in a non-pejorative sense of that term – phenomenon, a matter of both feeling and imagination. De Quincey did not believe that 'musical sounds' should be programmatic or attempt to conjure up intellectual 'ideas' in the listener: 'Ideas! My dear friend! there is no occasion for them,' he exclaims in the *Confessions*; music, rather than offering something to understand – a 'class of ideas' – actually plays to the heart, in bestowing a 'language of representative feelings'.

'There is an infinity about the violin,' De Quincey once remarked to James Hogg, and in this high Romantic conception of the nature of music he was not alone. Indeed, the German fantasy writer and music critic E. T. A. Hoffman (1776–1822) provocatively maintained that music 'is the most Romantic of the arts; almost one might say, it alone is truly Romantic, for only the infinite is its subject' (Mozart himself wrote that poetry should be 'the obedient daughter' of music). William Blake, a musical fellow who composed a number of melodies (unfortunately now lost) for his early lyrics, also believed that music, like poetry, offered an insight into everlasting things, writing in 1809 that it 'exists and exults in immortal thoughts'. Music is part of Blake's re-imagined, exalted version of the everyday human world; 'In Eternity', he writes in *Milton* (c.1804–8), 'the Four Arts, Poetry, Painting, Music and Architecture, which is Science, are the Four Faces of Man.' 'Music ... is Inspiration and cannot be surpassed' declared Blake pithily; it, like poetry, offers emotional, spiritual and imaginative expression.

Blake's friend J. T. Smith once recalled that in the 1780s, though 'entirely unacquainted with the science of music', the poet's 'ear was so good, that his tunes were singularly beautiful, and were noted down by musical professors'. We do not know if Blake wrote airs to any of his *Songs of Innocence* (1789), but the very title of that work is significant. Song was deeply entwined with the early Romantic tradition, in Blake's lyrics, in the brilliant songs of Burns, and in Scott's collections of ancient ballads (eventually published as the *Minstrelsy of the Scottish Border* (1802–3)). Furthermore, though they did not intend their poems as songs as such, in calling their collection *Lyrical Ballads, with a Few Other Poems* (1798), Wordsworth and Coleridge were aligning their work with the medieval tradition of the ballad, lyrics more often sung than recited in their early days. This was a poetic development of the antiquarian interest in the ballad (and medieval culture in general) evident in the second half of the eighteenth century in such works as Bishop Percy's *Reliques of Ancient English Poetry* (1765) (see 'Medievalism, the Sublime and the Gothic').

'To simple national melodies Blake was very impressionable,' writes the poet's early biographer Alexander Gilchrist; 'he was very fond of Mrs Linnell [wife of the Romantic painter John Linnell] singing Scottish songs, and would sit by the pianoforte, tears falling from his eyes'. There was a widespread taste for the songs of the Celt amongst the English in the Romantic period. Burns's poetry and songs sold in huge numbers, Thomas Moore's *Irish Melodies* (1808–34), with verses by Moore arranged for music by Sir John Stevenson and Sir Henry Bishop, enjoyed a tremendous vogue, as did Felicia Hemans's *Welsh Melodies* of 1821 (see 'Irish, Scottish and Welsh Poetry'). Lord Byron also had much success with a collection of national songs set less close to home, the *Hebrew Melodies* of 1815, a mixture of scriptural songs and love lyrics published by the composer Isaac Nathan (c.1790–1864) who arranged many of them to traditional Jewish melodies. This volume includes some of Byron's most well-known lyrics, including 'She walks in beauty' and 'The Assyrian came down like the wolf on the fold'.

Mournful minor-key lamentations like some of the *Irish Melodies* were not the delight of Moore's literary best friend, Lord Byron. Where music summoned grief, ecstasy and emotional transcendence in such febrile Romantic encounters as De Quincey's visits to the opera, Byron preferred a vigorous tune, at least according to Leigh Hunt's memoir of the poet: 'All the best music, he said, was *lively*' (this was 'an opinion', Hunt sniffed, with 'which few lovers of it will agree'). Byron much admired Rossini, who was seen as rather vulgar in some quarters. In a passage in his notes to the sixteenth canto of *Don Juan* (1823), he described himself as 'a liege and loyal admirer of Italian music' and praised Rossini as 'the successor to Mozart'. 'Rossini was his real favourite,' wrote Hunt of Byron; 'he liked his dash and animal spirits'. The essayist himself did not concur, writing in the *Companion* in 1828 that Rossini's gifts were of 'a species as inferior to that of Mozart, as the cleverness of a smart boy is to that of a man of sentiment'. 'There is genius of many kinds,' writes Hunt with reference to the difference between the two composers, 'and of kinds remote from each other, even in rank.' Coleridge, according to his nephew and son-in-law H. N. Coleridge, felt the same way, 'requir[ing] from music either thought or feeling; mere addresses to the sensual ear he could not away with; hence his utter distaste for Rossini and his reverence for Beethoven and Mozart.'

Genius and the Virtuoso

Where Coleridge valued 'thought' and 'feeling' in music, Hunt wrote of the 'union of passion and feeling' with 'science' which 'constitutes the style of Mozart and the other great German composers'. Wordsworth, it is worth recalling, had described the highest kind of verse as a fusion of 'powerful feelings' with deep 'thought' in the 1800 'Preface' to the *Lyrical Ballads*, and it is not difficult to draw comparisons between contemporary notions of poetic creation and those dealing with musical composition. Wordsworth, indeed, whose masterpiece was published by his wife shortly after his death in 1850 under a title resonant with musical metaphor, *The Prelude*, was born in the same year as Beethoven, and the early German theorists of Romanticism had no doubt that music and literature served the same exalted artistic principles. Hoffman, for instance, wrote that 'Beethoven's music ... arouses exactly that infinite yearning which is the essence of Romanticism.' There is a clear analogy between the Romantic poet and the Romantic musician, something perhaps most apparent in the figures of the great poet, the inspired composer and the instrumental virtuoso. These notions cohered in Great Britain in the figures of W. A. Mozart, 'divine Mozart' as Keats called him, seen after his death as a natural genius responsible for the very music of the spheres, and in that of the most remarkable instrumentalist of the day, the Italian Niccolò Paganini (1782–1840). It is worth looking at the British reception of the latter as illustration of this important critical tendency within contemporary discourses about music.

Paganini, 'the pale magician of the bow', as Hunt called him, toured Great Britain and Ireland in 1831–2 to huge acclaim. Mary Shelley saw him play at the King's Theatre in London in 1831 and praised his 'divine' performance, recording breathlessly in her journal that 'I heard Paganini today – he is divine – he had the effect of giving me hysterics – yet I could pass my life listening to him'. In this idealising account, it is as if the violinist – to borrow Coleridge's phrasing in 'Kubla Khan' – with his 'music loud and long' had 'drunk the milk of Paradise'. His listener shares the fine excess of his performance in a 'hysterical' frenzy of ecstatic listening. Paganini was also seen to play the emotions as skilfully as his fiddle; he was 'the Spectacular Virtuoso', wrote Hunt in the same year as Shelley's effusions; he could 'move both the tears and the laughter of his audience [and] melt you into grief and pity'.

Some years after seeing him play, Shelley recalled Paganini's physical travails as he made music; he, like his literary auditor, had something of the 'hysterical' about him: 'Paganini excited and agitated violently – it was rather nervous hysterics than gentle sorrowing – it was irresistible.' This encapsulates the Romantic notion of the fruitful creative self-torment of the 'genius', whose creative energies spark his imagination. The role of the suffering, tortured artist was one that Paganini performed with the self-consciousness of a Byron. One contemporary source said of him that he cultivated 'romance and mystery, as the inseparable attributes of genius'. Felicia Hemans, who saw Paganini perform twice in Dublin in 1831, wrote that the sounds of his violin were 'more aerial than you would suppose it possible for human touch to produce'. She, too, portrays the other-worldly nature of the music, as if she metaphorically slept, only to 'waken ... in what a German would call the "music-land"'.

Hemans, who compared Paganini's music to Byron's verse, also recorded the virtuoso's own self-dramatisations, 'the sufferings ... by which he pays for his excellence': 'he scarcely knows what sleep is, and his nerves are wrought to such almost preternatural acuteness, that harsh, even common sounds, are often torture to him'. Hemans particularly admired Paganini's encore piece, the 'Dance of the Witches'; this – by someone said by the credulous to have sold his soul to the devil for his talent – was 'a complete exemplification of the grotesque in music'. According to a friend of Hemans who had conversed with the musician, he was possessed by his art as by some benign spirit gifted by heaven: 'His passion for music [Paganini] described as an all-absorbing, a consuming one; in fact he looks as if no other life than that ethereal one of melody were circulating within his veins: but he added with a glow of triumph kindling through deep sadness *"mais c'est un don du ciel!"* ["But it is one given of heaven"].'

Paganini was welcomed to England in verse several times, but one of the earliest treatments of the musician is actually a poetic raspberry blown in doggerel verse by the rough-edged satirist and singer of popular comic songs Thomas Hudson (c.1791–1844), the 'New Verses to Adam and Eve' (1818–27), in which the narrative voice – a bluff plain-speaking Englishman – mocks the very notion of John Bull being entranced by a money-grubbing foreigner:

> But now there's a man makes fiddling shine high,
> The astonishing, wonderful Paganini!
> Who gets, while John Bull's mouth is gaping,
> Twelve hundred pounds for one hour's scraping.

One almost cherishes a dissenting voice, given the near-universal adoration shown the fiddler, but it has to be said that this is very definitely a minority poetic report. Rather more conventional is the attitude summed up in Louisa Anne Twamley's bathetic 1835 sonnet to the 'Great hero of the Fiddlestick!' and Leigh Hunt's verse tribute 'Paganini. A Fragment', first published in 1834, though earlier, which portrays the lovely mystery of his music and the dark Byronic mournfulness of the artist himself, and also glances at the soul-selling yarns·

> The exceeding mystery of the loveliness
> Sadden'd delight; and with his mournful look,
> Dreary and gaunt, hanging his pallid face
> 'Twixt his dark flowing locks, he almost seemed,
> To feeble or to melancholy eyes,
> One that had parted with his soul for pride.
> And in the sable secret lived forlorn.

Hunt hears the range of human emotions, from joy to despair, from love to grief, incarnate in the sound of Paganini's violin, and the abrupt changes of register in his performance, as the human gives way to the bewitched in a turn to Romantic grotesquerie:

> Or behold
> In his despair, (for such, from what he spoke
> Of grief before it, or of love, 'twould seem)
> Jump would he into some strange wail uncouth
> Of witches' dance, ghastly with whinings thin
> And palsied nods – mirth wicked, sad, and weak.
> And then with show of skill mechanical.
> Marvellous as witchcraft, he would overthrow
> That vision with a show'r of notes like hail,

Hunt's description of Paganini's 'Witches' Dance' is reminiscent of the witches' Sabbath in Robert Burns's 'Tam O'Shanter' (see 'Irish, Scottish and Welsh Poetry'), and, indeed, Hemans, writing of the same number, maintained that 'I think Burns's "Tam O'Shanter" ... a parallel in poetry to this strange production in music.' Paganini captures the Romantic grotesque as surely as Burns – or Byron and Coleridge – before him.

Hunt builds to a Romantic crescendo, to borrow a musical term, in hearing a longing for joyous solitude and transcendence of the world as Paganini's music builds to its climax:

> now rising fine
> Into some utmost tip of minute sound,
> From whence he stepped into a higher and higher
> On viewless points, till laugh took leave of him:
> Or he would fly as if from all the world
> To be alone and happy, and you should hear
> His instrument become a tree far off,
> A nest of birds and sunbeams, sparkling both.

The echo here of Hunt's friend Keats's 'viewless wings of poesy' in the 'Ode to a Nightingale' (1819) is doubtless conscious, but in the final analysis Hunt's poem is less ambiguous than Keats's in enacting the uplifting movement of Paganini's playing and its final transformation into that joyous image of 'a nest of birds and sunbeams', a metaphor emphatically poetical, and testimony to the widespread Romantic likening of music and verse.

See also   Irish, Scottish and Welsh Poetry; Medievalism, the Sublime and the Gothic.

Further Reading

Cyril Ehrlich, *The Music Profession in Britain Since the Eighteenth Century: A Social History* (1985).
Maureen N. McLane, *Balladeering, Minstrelsy, and the Making of British Romantic Poetry* (2008).
Gillen D'Arcy Wood, *Romanticism and Music Culture in Britain, 1770–1840* (2010).

Political Protest and Popular Radicalism

British Radicalism and the French Revolution

In an undemocratic age when the right to vote was restricted to property-owning men (and even that qualification was highly restricted), street protest – whether impromptu or organised – and mass meetings were important methods of signifying dissent to an unpopular government. This was certainly the case in the two most turbulent periods in Britain of the Romantic age: the 1790s after the French Revolution of July 1789 and the post-Napoleonic period from 1815 onwards. Mass demonstrations led to government legislative repression in the former period and to violent suppression of radical demonstrators in the latter, notably in the so-called 'Peterloo' massacre, which occurred at a 'monster meeting' in Manchester in August 1819.

However pure the motivations for much political protest in Great Britain at the turn of the nineteenth century and beyond might have been, such occasions could also be less idealistically motivated, providing an opportunity to parade religious bigotry, or to fight and loot. Just before the start of the Romantic period the latter urges prevailed in the so-called Gordon riots of 1780, in which a London mob called violently for 'No Popery' in a paroxysm of anti-Catholic feeling instigated by the leader of the Protestant Association, Lord George Gordon. For nearly a week, 'multitudes, violence and fury', to use Charles Dickens's description, engulfed London in riotous attacks on property, the opening of prisons, and violence which led to over two hundred deaths (there is a powerful portrait of these events in Dickens's historical novel *Barnaby Rudge* (1841)).

Lord North's Tory government vigorously persecuted the Gordon rioters, though Gordon himself escaped from a charge of high treason, and the recent memory of civil unrest was partly responsible in ensuring that the subsequent administration of William Pitt the Younger clamped down hard on the mass demonstrations held in favour of the French Revolution in the following decade. Adding to the Tory paranoia was the fact that the storming of the Bastille prison in July 1789 by riotous Parisians had led directly to the outbreak of the French Revolution and the eventual overthrow of the *ancien régime*. In the aftermath of the Revolution it seemed to many that there was a possibility that the same thing might happen in Great Britain.

In the middle of the 1790s, Pitt and his cohorts, engaged in pursuing a war against the French which had begun in 1793, became increasingly concerned about the spread of radical ideas in England. August 1795 saw massive demonstrations in favour of radical reform and, in November 1795, the month after an anti-monarchical riot at the state opening of parliament, the government introduced the so-called 'Gagging Acts', which prohibited meetings of more than fifty people unless specifically licensed by a magistrate, and introduced measures censoring the press. The government sought to weaken the influence of the principal non-parliamentary radical organisation, the London Corresponding Society (LCS), by charging some of its leaders with the capital crime of high treason. Thomas Hardy, John Thelwall and John Horne Tooke amongst others were tried in the famous Treason Trials of 1794, though subsequently acquitted (with help from both a sympathetic jury and the publication of William Godwin's eloquent pamphlet 'Cursory Strictures', which demolished the prosecution case).

Some of the LCS principals were of a literary bent. Thelwall, friend of Wordsworth and Coleridge, was a journalist and poet, and Horne Tooke a distinguished historian of the English language, and both proselytised (sought converts) for radicalism in print. However, the organisation's most energetic literary advocate was Thomas Spence (1750–1814), the tireless radical pressman, bookseller and satirist who denounced the notion of private property, and called for root-and-branch political reform in a torrent of popular journals, broadsheets and satires in both verse and prose. Spence, originally from Newcastle, moved to London where he became a member of the Corresponding Society in the early 1790s. He published *The Real Rights of Man* in 1793 and edited several radical journals such as *One Penny Worth of Pig's Meat: Lessons for the Swinish Multitude* (a dig at Burke's notorious description of the Parisian plebs in his *Reflections on the Revolution in France* (1790)). A sense of Spence's rough and ready radical satire is given in 'Burke's Address to the Swinish Multitude', published in *Pig's Meat* in 1793, which envisages the Irish statesman addressing the English poor:

> YE vile SWINISH Herd, in the Sty of Taxation,
> What would you be after? – disturbing the Nation?
> Give over your grunting – Be off – To your Sty!
> Nor dare to look out, if a KING passes by:
>   Get ye down! down! down! – Keep ye down!
>
> …
>
> Do you think that a KING is no more than a Man?
> Ye Brutish, ye Swinish, irrational Clan?
> I swear by his Office, his Right is divine,
> To flog you, and feed you, and treat you like Swine!
>   Get you down! &c.

Radical popular print culture like that sold on Spence's Chancery Lane bookcart burgeoned in the early 1790s, alongside the more genteel work of William Godwin and Mary Wollstonecraft (see 'British Politics 1789–1815'). Most influential of all was Tom Paine, most notably in the first part of his *Rights of Man* (1791), an early riposte to Burke's *Reflections*, which sold in thousands to working-class radicals. Paine's republicanism and religious freethought led to furious denunciations by Tory luminaries such as Richard Watson, the Bishop of Llandaff, near Cardiff (Wordsworth penned a 1793 response, 'A Letter to the Bishop of Llandaff … by a Republican', which described Watson as 'an enemy lurking in our ranks', but prudently – some say cravenly – decided against publishing the work, which could have led to his arrest). He was indicted on a charge of treason (Paine wisely removed himself to France before he could be tried). However, and as in the wider oppositional movement, radical enthusiasm for France diminished as the 1790s wore on and the acquittal of the LCS radicals had something of the Pyrrhic victory about it. English radicalism waned by the turn of the century, not recovering until after the defeat of the Napoleonic regime in 1815.

Post-Napoleonic Radicalism

The return of radical protest after the end of the continental conflicts was in large part the consequence of economic depression. War can be a boost to an economy, of course, and the British economy staggered through the war years of 1793 to 1815 without too many severe setbacks. However, after the defeat of Napoleon at Waterloo, it lurched into a deep depression. Thousand of discharged soldiers were unable to find work, there were bread shortages (and antipathy to the protectionist Corn Laws, which inflated the price of what bread there was) and renewed discontent at the lack of parliamentary representation for all but a tiny minority of the population. Mass protests developed once again, culminating in the meeting of some 60,000 radicals at St Peter's Field in Manchester in August 1819 which saw the local yeomanry cut down eleven protesters in the so-called 'Peterloo massacre'. The intended speakers at Peterloo, led by the Lancastrian demagogue Henry 'Orator' Hunt, included the radical journalist Richard Carlile (see 'Religion and Atheism'), who wrote furiously in his journal *The Republican* on 27 August 1819 that 'The massacre ... should be the daily theme of the Press until the murderers are brought to justice ... Every man in Manchester who avows his opinions on the necessity of reform, should never go unarmed – retaliation has become a duty, and revenge an act of justice'. (Shelley advised the people of England in his 'Men of England: A Song' (1819), his great poem of political protest inspired by Peterloo, 'Forge arms – in your defence to bear'.)

Carlile was not the first to recommend physical force as a way to change the world. From 1811 onwards the frame-breakers or Luddites had sabotaged the factory heavy machinery which threatened their trades (see 'Industry and Economics') and there were also efforts to effect wider change through violent means in Great Britain in the period. It is well known that Ireland also saw armed insurrection in the Romantic age, in the 1798 revolt of the United Irishmen under the Belfast Protestant Theodore Wolfe Tone, and the ill-fated 1803 uprising of the poet Thomas Moore's boyhood friend Robert Emmet (see 'Ireland and the "Catholic Question"'). What is less well appreciated is the fact there were also a number of plots for armed uprising amongst English radicals in the wake of Peterloo, as

Carlile's call to arms was taken up. The most notable of these was the Cato Street conspiracy of February 1820 (see 'British Politics 1789–1815') led by Arthur Thistlewood, which plotted to assassinate the hated Foreign Secretary Lord Castlereagh and other Tory parliamentarians in an attempt to trigger revolution. The principal conspirators were executed after being betrayed by an informant. Two months later, in April 1820, a small group of Scots radicals, inspired by the Cato Street crowd, announced a general strike and marched on Stirling in an attempt to provoke an insurrection. After an armed skirmish at the 'Battle of Bonnymuir', nigh on fifty men were charged with high treason (the three ringleaders were executed and the majority of the rest went the way of Botany Bay). In June of the following year, armed radicals from the Derbyshire village of Pentrich, under the leadership of one Jeremiah Brandreth and labouring under the illusion that they were part of a nationwide revolution intended to establish a British republic, marched on Nottingham. Captured by the soldiery, Brandreth and two of his lieutenants were executed and many of the rest of the co-conspirators transported to New South Wales.

This catalogue of insurrection was the sharpest end of radicalism, however, and the generality of radicals tended to remain in favour of non-violent reform. Alongside 'Orator' Hunt, the most notable non-parliamentary oppositionalist spokesmen were William Cobbett, editor and populist, who also happened to be a writer of real genius, Robert Owen, proto-Socialist entrepreneur, and Thomas Jonathan Wooler, journalist, editor and mischievous satirist in the mode of Spence (for the brilliant propagandist William Hone, see 'Satire'). The indefatigable Cobbett (1763–1835) was initially on the conservative side and made his name in the United Sates in rabble-rousing polemics attacking President Jefferson and the wicked works of Tom Paine. On returning to England in 1800, he rejected invitations from Pitt's administration to act as a Tory propagandist and subsequently set off in a more radical direction in his *Political Register* (founded in 1802) and, later, the populist, somewhat cheaper, *Cobbett's Register* ('Cobbett's Twopenny Trash', to the editor's enemies), a periodical aimed at the common people whose cause he so passionately and eloquently advocated. Cobbett, who spent two years in Newgate gaol for attacking flogging in the military, was an iconoclast, who looked back to an English golden age before 'The Thing' (corruption in high and low places), the pernicious influence of the 'Great Wen' (London), industrialisation, Jewish financiers (Cobbett was an enthusiastic anti-Semite) and the nouveau riche 'Spinning Jenny Baronets' had ruined life for honest Englishmen. The country, he warned, was in near-terminal decline on account of these malign influences: 'Commerce, Opulence, Luxury, Effeminacy, Cowardice, Slavery: these are the stages of national degradation. We are in the fourth!'

T. J. Wooler (c.1786–1853), radical journalist and editor, was the publisher of *The Republican* (established 1813) and, most notably, the *Black Dwarf* (1817–24), a controversial and combative journal with a gleeful satirical tenor, the success of which was attributable to its mixture of broad *ad hominem* humour and steely-eyed reformism. Like his oppositionalist contemporaries, the author was no stranger to the court of law and was three times tried for seditious libel and eventually dispatched to gaol in 1820. On 8 September 1819, Wooler raged against the events at St Peter's Fields in an address to the 'magistrates of M[anchester]' which condemned the massacre while calling for peaceful counsel to prevail amongst radicals:

> A dreadful scene of terror and confusion ensued. Several persons were murdered, and hundreds of others badly wounded! Thus was our peaceable meeting dispersed by an armed force! Thus was war made, by your orders, upon defenceless men, women and children! These are your exploits! They will never be forgotten! You did not prevent the crowd from assembling – you did not order them to disperse after they had assembled, but when quietly congregated together, in a legal way, you let in your executioners among them! Thus it is, you, ye magistrates, who have set the example of a brutal violence to a suffering and famished population. Dangerous proceedings! Impolitic step! – MAY IT NEVER BE IMITATED BY REFORMERS!

Robert Owen (1771–1858), factory reformer, freethinker, and Utopian, was a man of practical action as well as a political theorist. Owen was the manager and proprietor of the New Lanark Mill in Scotland, where he settled in 1800 and set about organising his business along egalitarian and rational principles. The mill's employees included some five hundred pauper children dispatched to his premises for both work and schooling from surrounding parishes (Owen stressed the importance of treating young children kindly, without automatic recourse to punishment). Other innovations at New Lanark included a shop for the workers, selling, Owen maintained, better-quality goods at fairer prices and paying decidedly higher wages than in the wretched factories of Lancashire and Yorkshire. On the basis of his New Lanark experiment, Owen proposed his famous 1817 'Plan' (of 'Amelioration and Reformation'), which aimed to solve national poverty by removing the able-bodied poor from the charity registers and into self-sustaining, classless communities of men, women and children who would work for profit and submit to the rules of industry and sobriety.

As the 1830s approached, the 'freedom of the press' heroics once evident in the fearlessness of men such as Cobbett and Carlile were succeeded by those of Henry Hetherington (1792–1849), publisher and radical journalist, who made his name as the fiercest opponent of the 'tax on knowledge', the fourpenny duty – or 'stamp' – on newspapers. In a direct challenge to the law, Hetherington introduced several illegal unstamped newspapers in the early 1830s, most notably the *Poor Man's Guardian* (1831–5), and experienced three spells of imprisonment for his pains. Hetherington used populist methods to sugar the pill of Radical instruction, declaring that his recipe for success was 'Police Intelligence ... Murders, Rapes, Suicides, Burnings, Maimings, Theatricals, Races, [and] Pugilism'. This was a catchpenny mixture which directly influenced the mass market newspapers of the Victorian era, notably the *News of the World* (established 1843), but Hetherington's motives were ideological rather than financial – he once declared that 'Our object is not to make money, but to beat the Government!'

Towards the tail end of the Romantic era, in the late 1820s and early 1830s, the print culture of radical protest was focused on parliamentary reform. William Pitt had attempted to introduce a measure of change in the 1780s before the French Revolution did for his reformism, and it was not until 1832 that Earl Grey's Whig government introduced a Reform Act, though this did not by any means approach universal suffrage (see 'British Politics 1815–1832'). Hetherington's *Poor Man's Journal* was at the forefront of radical debate on the Act, advocating universal male suffrage and the repeal of the Corn Laws, and attacking Cobbett for what it saw as an unseemly willingness to compromise these goals. Other radical unstamped newspapers, unlike Hetherington's, supported armed uprising to ensure the passing of the Act; the *Cosmopolite* declared in a front page banner of 1832 that 'The finale of Reform must be settled by Physical Force!!' After the passing of the Reform Act, a disappointment to many radicals, Hetherington became a mainstay of the Chartist movement, the Victorian equivalent of the Corresponding Society which was set up as a consequence of the Act, espousing the centrist 'knowledge' arm of the movement as opposed to its ultra 'physical force' members. The same tensions which had divided Romantic-era radicalism persisted long afterwards.

See also   British Politics 1789–1815; British Politics 1815–1832; Ireland and the 'Catholic Question'; Religion and Atheism; Satire.

Further Reading

Ian Dyck, *William Cobbett and Rural Popular Culture* (1992).
Iain McCalman, *Radical Underworld: Prophets, Revolutionaries and Pornographers in London, 1795–1840* (1988).
Marcus Wood, *Radical Satire and Print Culture, 1790–1822* (1994).

Religion and Atheism

Anglicanism, Nonconformity and Dissent

In the Romantic era, the Church of England retained, as it had since the Reformation of the sixteenth century and as it does to this day, a formal position as the state-aligned, or 'established' Church. While establishment today means not a great deal in practical terms, it certainly did in the late Georgian period. Only Anglicans could attend the major public schools and universities or sit in parliament and the whole of British society was structured to favour members of the Church of England. English Protestants who were not Anglican (Baptists, Unitarians and so on) were known as 'dissenters' and 'nonconformists', and experienced various forms of discrimination. Perhaps unsurprisingly, they were amongst the leading contemporary enthusiasts for the French Revolution (for the position of Roman Catholics, see 'Ireland and the "Catholic Question"', above).

Whereas 'Church and King' loyalists supported the established church and the political system incarnate in the figure of George III, those accustomed to political and religious disempowerment tended to approve of events across the channel. The Welsh nonconformist divine the Reverend Dr Richard Price, for instance, gave a famous sermon, 'A Discourse on the Love of our Country', in the months after the fall of the Bastille in which he saluted the events of July 1789 in the biblical words of the 'Nunc Dimittis', the episode in the book of Luke in which Simeon the Righteous rejoices at living long enough to see the infant messiah at the temple (in the version from the Book of Common Prayer, 'Lord, now lettest thou thy servant depart in peace: according to thy word. For mine eyes have seen thy salvation ...'). Price (1723–91) gloried in living to see the emergence of a new epoch of liberty in Europe and, he anticipated, also in Great Britain, a new dawn symbolised in the extraordinary spectacle of the King of France pledging allegiance to the French revolutionary government, the National Assembly.

Republished in pamphlet form in 1790, the 'Discourse', in which, as the *Monthly Review* noted, Price candidly 'inform[ed] the King, in plain English, that he is only *the servant of the people*', became a stirring call to arms for the radical cause or a blasphemous misuse of scripture, depending on your political persuasion. Edmund Burke, who argued that 'the church is a place where one day's truce ought to be allowed to the dissensions and animosities of mankind', was not keen, and opened his *Reflections on the Revolution in France* (1790) with a systematic attack on Dr Price, whom he considered as someone motivated by conspiratorial extremist politics rather than religious enthusiasm: 'a man much connected with literary caballers, and intriguing philosophers; with political theologians, and theological politicians, both at home and abroad'.

Of the numerous versions of Christianity evident during the Romantic period, dissent, and particularly – at least in literary terms – the Unitarianism espoused towards the end of his career by the Reverend Price, was hugely important for contemporary radicalism, especially during the Revolutionary decade of the 1790s. Unitarianism, though not characterised by doctrinal uniformity in those days, was united in emphasising the centrality – to borrow a phrase from S. T. Coleridge – of 'something one and indivisible', in denying the Trinity and stressing the divinity of God alone (here Jesus is a man – albeit a prophet – rather than the son of God, and the Holy Spirit simply another name for God). Alongside its contentious theology, Unitarians also called for a comprehensive transformation of earthly politics; Price argued for a democratising of power where the destiny of humankind lay with individual men and women rather than tyrannical human agencies such as an untrammelled monarchy and the established Church.

Price, Welsh-born but living in London, influenced a generation of radical philosophers and poets with his 'Nunc Dimittis' sermon, including some who were born in nonconformity but who had lost their faith (such as William Godwin, who was present at Price's peroration) and others raised in Anglican orthodoxy (such as Mary Wollstonecraft, who knew Price in the last decade of his life). Wollstonecraft rallied to his defence in her *Vindication of the Rights of Men, in a Letter to the Right Honourable Edmund Burke* (1790) in which she took issue with the author of the *Reflections*:

> You further proceed grossly to misrepresent Dr Price's meaning; and, with an affectation of holy fervour, express your indignation at his profaning a beautiful rapturous ejaculation, when alluding to the King of France's submission to the National Assembly; he rejoiced to hail a glorious revolution, which promised an universal diffusion of liberty and happiness.

After Price's death in April 1791, he was replaced as the most notable Unitarian churchman-cum-political philosopher by his fellow scientist and radical clergyman Dr Joseph Priestley (1733–1804), who agitated for root and branch reform before his home and meeting houses were burned down by a Church and King mob in Birmingham in July 1791. After this, Priestley emigrated to the United States in search of greater levels of liberty and democracy (his settlement at Northumberland, Pennsylvania, inspired Coleridge and Southey's abortive scheme to establish a Pantisocratic commune on the banks of the Susquehanna River in the same state), having decided that the Second Coming, which he initially thought the French Revolution heralded, was not as imminent as he had thought (for

Priestley's millennial thought, see 'Millenarianism'). After his Birmingham travails Priestley was saluted in verse in Anna Laetitia Barbauld's 'To Dr Priestley, Dec. 29, 1792' as a victim of 'hooting crowds' and 'A mark for Power to shoot at' (see 'Science and Medicine' for Barbauld's later tribute to Priestley in 'Eighteen Hundred and Eleven'). Barbauld was one of the most notable literary dissenters. She charged her religion with oppositionalist political overtones, arguing in her *Remarks on Mr Gilbert Wakefield's Enquiry Into the Expediency and Propriety of Public or Social Worship* (also 1792) that communal worship brings the whole of humanity together regardless of rank; it 'is the public expression of homage to the Sovereign of the Universe. It is that tribute from men united in families, in towns, in communities, which individually Men owe to their Maker'. 'Joy', she writes in a marvellous phrase, 'is too brilliant a thing to be confined within our own bosoms.'

Coleridge and Religion

The most significant of all the Romantic-era literary Unitarians, Priestley notwithstanding, was Coleridge, who converted, albeit fairly briefly, in the early 1790s when he was an undergraduate at Cambridge, from the Anglicanism into which he was born (his father was a vicar in the Church of England). Coleridge's decision was influenced by his college mentor, the incendiary Unitarian don the Reverend William Frend (1757–1841) – himself forced to resign by the High Anglican Cambridge authorities for his political radicalism as a consequence of espousing 'representative government' in his pamphlet 'Peace and Union Recommended to the Associated Bodies of Republicans and Anti-Republicans' (1793). Coleridge, after leaving the university, trained for the Unitarian ministry before – as was his wont – bolting, and settling for a life of authorship and journalism. Nonetheless, the idea of the Unitarian 'God is One' clearly informed the 'One Life' philosophy which was so influential in his poetry of the later 1790s, in his collaboration with Wordsworth and in the development of the *Lyrical Ballads* (1798).

Coleridge was a man who, despite veering from Anglicanism to Unitarianism and back again, was always a thoroughgoing transcendentalist (unlike Wordsworth, whom Coleridge described as being 'at least a semi-Atheist' in the mid-1790s). At Cambridge, he believed that the French Revolution heralded a new dawn of peace and liberty, which would be followed, he hoped, by the return of Christ in a new spiritual millennium. Such beliefs are articulated in Coleridge's 'Religious Musings' (1796), a poem that fuses visionary Christianity with proto-socialistic politics:

O return!
Return pure Faith! return meek Piety!
The kingdoms of the world are yours: each heart
Self-governed, the vast family of Love
Raised from the common earth by common toil
Enjoy the equal produce.

Both Coleridge and Priestley were millenarians, who believed in the imminence of the Second Coming; Priestley, despite his scientific rationalism, wrote to a friend in the early 1790s that 'the second personal appearance of Christ was very near ... It cannot, I think, be more than twenty years.'

Blake and Religion

The poet Blake also believed that the millennial age was nigh, and responded accordingly in his visionary prophetic works *The French Revolution* (1791) and *America: A Prophecy* (1793). Price had characterised the Revolution as 'a blaze that lays despotism in ashes, and warms and illuminates Europe!' and his eschatological tone is echoed in Blake's prophecy in America that 'the tempest must fall'. Blake's poem begins, ominously, 'The dead brood over Europe, the cloud and vision descends ...', and his is a vision of imminent apocalypse, with 'thunderclouds ready to burst'. Critics of Blake have maintained that the poet's realisation in the mid-1790s that apocalypse was not actually and literally at hand transformed his work, leading him from a sense of the power of revolution in the world of the here and now towards a psychological and visionary notion of revolution in his extraordinary later works such as *Milton* and *Jerusalem: The Emanation of the Giant Albion* (*c*.1804–20); as John Beer has argued, Blake 'internalised' his 'sense of apocalypse'. Similarly, in discussing the earlier visionary narrative poems such as the *Book of Urizen* (1795), Blake's remarkable retelling of the book of Genesis, Beer argues that the poet was 'no longer concerned with apocalyptic events but rather with setting up his own creation myth in order to account for the state in which humanity ... found itself' (for further discussion of Blake and religion, see 'Millenarianism').

Calvinism

Another key form of religion during the Romantic era, and one possessed of a similarly powerful literary resonance (though generally being portrayed unsympathetically), was Calvinism, the rigorous form of Puritanism which insisted that God preordains – even before one's birth – whether one is to be saved or damned. In this account, good works or personal faith were not enough to deserve eternal redemption. The poet William Cowper (1731–1800), a life-long Calvinist, was so sorrowfully sure of his own exclusion from the ranks of the 'elect' that he lapsed into madness as a consequence of the pain which his religious convictions inflicted upon him. His narrative poem 'The Castaway' (1799) symbolises the plight of the unelect in its portrayal of a mariner who falls overboard, 'unnoticed, into the sea'. The ship sails off, its crew having 'left their outcast mate behind'. Cowper explicitly compares the sailor's fate with such 'a destin'd wretch as I'; his fate is to drown in far worse waters, in the biblical 'lake of fire':

> No voice divine the storm allay'd,
>   No light propitious shone;
> When, snatch'd from all effectual aid,
>   We perish'd, each alone:
> But I beneath a rougher sea,
> And whelm'd in deeper gulphs than he.

Cowper apart, Calvinism is most notable in Romantic-period literature because of its representation in two great Scottish satirical works. The first is Burns's antipathetic representation of the doctrine and its followers in 'Holy Willie's Prayer' (published 1799), a dramatic monologue which contains strong satire on Calvinism in its portrait of a self-righteous Calvinist elder rejoicing in the implacable nature of his God:

> O Thou, that in the heavens does dwell,
> Wha, as it pleases best Thysel',
> Sends aen to Heaven an' ten to Hell,
> A' for Thy glory,
> And no for onie guid or ill
> They've done afore Thee!

Though Willie boasts that he is 'a pillar o' Thy temple', as his self-incriminating narrative goes on he unconsciously reveals himself to be a hypocrite, a fornicator and boozer. Instead of a biblical god of love, Willie's deity is vengeful and cruel, and the poem ends with the old sinner calling down maledictions on the heads of his enemies:

> Lord, in the day o' vengeance try him!
> Lord, visit him wha did employ him!
> And pass not in Thy mercy by them,
> Nor hear their pray'r,
> But for Thy people's sake destroy them,
> An' dinna spare!

> But, Lord, remember me and mine
> Wi' mercies temporal and divine,
> That I for gear an' grace may shine
> Excell'd by nane;
> And a' the glory shall be thine!
> Amen, Amen!

Willie's sense that his own moral lapses are immaterial because of his eternally-fixed status as a member of the elect offered a hint to James Hogg, Burns's poetic successor and great admirer. In *The Private Memoirs and Confessions of a Justified Sinner* (1824), a novel in the Gothic tradition of supernatural fiction but also a satirical engagement with contemporary Scottish religious life, Hogg pushes the Calvinist logic to its extreme in envisaging a young man, Robert Wringham, utterly convinced of his own election, who ends up as a murderer and a fratricide at the prompting of a mysterious 'friend' Gil-Martin, who turns out to be none other than the 'deil' – the devil – himself. Wringham's belief that he is of the elect and therefore invulnerable from damnation – no matter what sins he commits – in the end leads him to a pact with Satan and a suicide's grave. Though the innovative use of the Doppelgänger motif (the Gothic double or evil twin) in the novel eventually became influential in Scottish and wider European culture from R. L. Stevenson's *The Strange Case of Dr Jekyll and Mr Hyde* (1886) onwards, it was the theological aspects of Hogg's work – his satire on the hypocrisy and double standards of a perverted form of Calvinism – which were most remarked on by contemporary readers and reviewers. The *Monthly Critical Gazette*, for example, noticed the book in its 'Theology' section and agreed with Hogg on the dangers of Calvinism, observing 'the dreadful fact that our mad-houses are peopled with individuals whom the doctrines which this gentleman has so ably exposed have driven to insanity'.

Barbauld, in her *Remarks on Mr Gilbert Wakefield's Enquiry*, called for 'juster ideas of Christianity' than those available in Calvinism and attacked its implacable nature:

> The age which has demolished dungeons, rejected torture, and given so fair a prospect of abolishing the iniquity of the slave trade, cannot long retain among its articles of belief the gloomy perplexities of Calvinism, and the heart-withering perspective of cruel and never-ending punishments.

In the face of the relentless contemporary nonsense about Hell, Leigh Hunt – like his schoolfellow Coleridge, born the son of an Anglican minister – went so far as to invent his own benevolent brand of faith which he labelled 'Christianism'. Hunt, appalled by the Hell-fire sermons which he had heard in the chapel at his school, Christ's Hospital, and by what he saw as the impossible conventional notion that a loving God would torture unbelievers in Hell for Eternity, wrote a spiritual treatise, *Christianism* (1832; later developed into *The Religion of the Heart* (1853)), which attacked the notion of eternal damnation in ironical terms:

> Without threats to terrify us, and impossibilities to bend reason to faith, God ... would never be thought of, nor man kept in order. The Divine Teacher must succeed differently from all others, and make his children love him by dint of fear and terror; by setting pits of torment beside lessons incapable of comprehension.

Towards the end of his life, in 1850, Hunt published a poem called 'Death', in which he envisaged eventual salvation for all of mankind, given his belief in the true benevolence of the Almighty:

> Soft is the travelling on the road of Death.
> But guilt has pass'd it? Men not fit to die?
> Oh, hush – for He that made us all, is by.
> Human were all; all men; all born of mothers;
> All our own selves, in the worn shape of others;
> Our *used*, and oh! be sure, not to be *ill*-used brothers.

Evangelicalism

Turning from Leigh Hunt's splendid iconoclasm to a rather more widespread religious phenomenon, the late Georgian age is notable for the rise of Evangelicalism, a form of Protestantism which, unlike Calvinism, stressed the centrality of the doctrine of salvation by faith and personal conversion. Evangelicalism, though generally associated with its founding fathers, the Methodists John and Charles Wesley, who eventually left the Church of England, was also influential amongst many Anglicans such as William Wilberforce and Hannah More. As well as espousing the notion of a widespread Christian revival, many Evangelicals also possessed a philanthropic social conscience. In practical terms, this led them actively to oppose various disgraceful activities – slavery, the state lottery, gambling, animal-baiting and cruel sports amongst them. Whereas the Unitarians failed in their campaigns of the 1790s for national political reform, the Evangelicals were frequently successful in the series of single-cause campaigns that they espoused, and were instrumental in the abolition of the state lottery in 1826 and in the passing of the Cruelty to Animals Act of 1836. Indeed, many of the early animal rights and care organisations were motivated by religion, and were often dominated by Evangelicals. The Association for Promoting Rational Humanity towards the Animal Creation, for instance, was rational rather than rationalist and humane rather than humanist, and was founded in 1830 upon explicitly Christian grounds, as its annual report for 1832 noted: 'Your Committee were always convinced that there could be no true humanity which was not based on CHRISTIAN principle.' Similarly, the Society for the Prevention of Cruelty to Animals (the Royal Society from 1840), founded by the Reverend Arthur Broome in 1824, was also dominated by orthodoxy in its earlier days.

Foremost of the Evangelical causes was slavery (see 'Slavery, Abolition and African-British Literature'); William Wilberforce, the principal advocate of the abolitionist case, was a member of the Evangelical 'Clapham Sect'. However, though Wilberforce published his once famous *A Practical View of the Prevailing Religious System of Professed Christians* (1797), in which he advocated 'vital religion', the leading literary exponent of Evangelicalism in England at the turn of the nineteenth century was the Bristol-based philosopher, novelist, poet, and abolitionist, Hannah More, who asked in 'Slavery. A Poem' (1788): 'While Britain basks in thy full blaze of light, / Why lies sad Afric quench'd in total night?' That said, though on the side of the angels when it came to slavery, More was also a High Tory, determined on maintaining the power of a patriarchal and privileged elite. Certainly she insisted on a very conventional set of standards for her own sex, and her theological convictions now seem as vengeful to the modern eye as Holy Willie's. A series of didactic verses she and others published under the title of *Cheap Repository Tracts*, sold cheaply to be read and remembered among the lower orders, counselled its readers, especially female ones, to remain subordinate and conform to moral standards at the cost of their souls.

More's ballad 'The Story of Sinful Sally' (1796) is a case in point. It relates the tale of a vain young country maiden, who, all too conscious of her personal charms, is happy to receive the attentions of the local landowner, Sir William. Putting aside her simple rustic garments, clad in London fashion and 'bedecked in ribbons gay' she becomes 'the mistress of a rake'. From then it is but a short step to a life of reading 'filthy novel[s]', whoredom, boozing and consorting with low life criminals. As the narrative concludes, Sally, now alcoholic and dying from venereal disease, approaches her end and – More cheerfully implies – an after-life of eternal damnation (More was very fond of hell, at least for others):

> Hark! a well known sound I hear,
> 'Tis the Church's Sunday bell;
> No; I dread to venture near;
> No, I'm now the child of hell.
>
> ...

Still at every hour of leisure
Something whispers me within,
'O! I hate this life of pleasure,
For it is a life of sin'.

Thus amidst my peals of laughter
Horror seizes oft my frame?
Pleasure now – Damnation after,
And a never-dying flame.

Atheism

Contemporaneous with Hannah More's unyielding Old Testamentism was the beginnings of a challenge to theism. Modern-day militant atheists such as Richard Dawkins are working in a tradition which began in the late eighteenth century. Indeed, David Berman in *A History of Atheism in Britain from Hobbes to Russell* (1988) dates 'the birth of avowed atheism' to as recently as the early 1780s. This was a period where the charge of godlessness was a scandal and atheism was – generally correctly – associated with what we would now call left-wing politics. In the 1790s the word 'atheist', like 'Jacobin', became an insult to throw at radical politicians. For example, 'Smelling out a Rat; or The Atheistical-Revolutionist disturbed in his Midnight "Calculations"' (fig. 4), a 1790 graphic satire on Dr Price's Old Jewry sermon by the great Tory caricaturist James Gillray, portrays the author of the 'Discourse' startled by the huge face of Edmund Burke in the act of writing a treatise 'On the Benefits of Anarchy, Regicide, Atheism'. However, there were a small number for whom atheism became a proud, if bold, boast, most importantly the poet Shelley, someone who in post-Napoleonic Europe could defiantly sign after his name – in the guest book of a Swiss inn – the Greek words for 'democrat, great lover of mankind, and atheist'. Shelley was also willing to publish his opinions in a manner unprecedented even amongst fellow literary radicals. His father-in-law and early philosophical hero William Godwin strongly objected in his 'Of Religion' (1818) to the notion of a punitive God 'perpetually controlling us with his lash'. However, the author, at one time ordained as a nonconformist cleric but someone who wrote privately that 'I became ... in my 36th year [1792] an atheist,' was not willing to declare as much in print. But perhaps this is not so surprising in a Christian age where blasphemy could be published by imprisonment, and one where the free-thinker and publisher Richard Carlile (1790–1843) could be repeatedly sent to prison for blasphemy and seditious libel. Carlile, who was explicitly styling himself an 'atheist' in his radical journalism by the early 1820s, collaborated later in the decade with Robert Taylor (1784–1844), himself Cambridge-educated

Smelling out a Rat;—— or The Atheistical-Revolutionist disturbed in his Midnight "Calculations".

Fig. 4   James Gillray, 'Smelling out a Rat; or The Atheistical-Revolutionist disturbed in his Midnight "Calculations"' (1790)

and once ordained into the Church of England, in a self-styled missionary tour on behalf of unbelief, advertising themselves thus in 1829 handbills:

CIRCULAR
The Rev. Robert Taylor, A.B., of Carey Street, Lincoln's Inn, and Mr Richard Carlile, of Fleet-street, London, present their compliments as *Infidel Missionaries* ... and most respectfully and earnestly invite discussion on the merits of the Christian religion, which they argumentatively challenge, in the confidence of their competence to prove, that such a person as Jesus Christ, alleged to have been of Nazareth, never existed; and that the Christian religion has no such origin as has been pretended; neither is it in any way beneficial to mankind; but that it is nothing more than an emanation from the ancient Pagan religion.

By the end of the following year Carlile was back in prison, having been convicted of seditious libel.

Atheism such as that of the 'Infidel Mission' was rarely clamorous before the Romantic period, but in Shelley it found its John the Baptist. Carlile and Taylor were following in the wake of the poet, who was behind one of the very first explicitly atheistic works to be published in Great Britain, 'The Necessity of Atheism' (1811), the notorious pamphlet which he published with his friend T. J. Hogg while both were undergraduates at University

College, Oxford (Berman calls this the 'second' avowedly atheistic publication in Britain after the anonymous 'Answer to Dr Priestley's Letters to a Philosophical Unbeliever' (1782)). Deploying the religiously sceptical arguments of David Hume and also co-opting the thought of John Locke, the young men argued that as there was no rational basis on which a belief in God could be proved, then atheism was the only tenable position. They ended the pamphlet with a breezy 'Q.E.D.' The dons of the young men's college, all in holy orders (as was the requirement in those days), were not impressed and both men were sent down (expelled) from the university. Though he came to admire the life, and some of the thought, of Jesus, a man whom he eventually viewed as a great executed iconoclast, Shelley had no time for organised Christian religion, which he considered a system designed to enslave the people ('the opium of the people', as Karl Marx was later to call it). Two years after the 'Atheism' pamphlet, Shelley's incendiary notes to his poem *Queen Mab* (1813) anticipate a future world in which mankind has dispensed with religion, part of Shelley's attack on what he characterised as 'God the Father, & the King, & the Bishops, & Marriage, & the Devil knows what'. In the main body of the poem Queen Mab herself mounts the soapbox, her perorations clearly articulating Shelley's passionately-held views:

> There is no God!
> Nature confirms the faith his death-groan sealed.
> ...
>   human pride
> Is skilful to invent most serious names
> To hide its ignorance.
>   The name of God
> Has fenced about all crime with holiness,
> Himself the creature of his worshippers,
> Whose names and attributes and passions change,
> Seeva, Buddh, Foh, Jehovah, God, or Lord,
> Even with the human dupes who build his shrines.

See also   Literary and Philosophical Key Concepts I; Millenarianism; Medicine and Science.

Further reading

John Beer, 'Romantic Apocalypses', in *Romanticism and Millenarianism*, ed. Tim Fulford (2002), 53–70.

David Berman, *A History of Atheism in Britain from Hobbes to Russell* (1988).

John Mee, *Romanticism, Enthusiasm and Regulation: Poetics and the Policing of Culture in the Romantic period* (2003).

Martin Priestman, *Romantic Atheism: Poetry and Freethought, 1780–1830* (1999).

Sexualities

There are two historical generalisations about the eighteenth and nine-teenth centuries which have resonance in the popular imagination to this day. The first is the conceptualisation of the Victorian period as a buttoned-up time of sexual repression, moral decorum and a cheerlessly ethical cast of mind (a po-facedness summed up in Queen Victoria's supposed remark, 'We are not amused!'). The second is the perception of the eighteenth century as a dissolute age – 'Drunk for a penny, dead drunk for tuppence' – emblematised in William Hogarth's riotous vision of 'Gin Lane' (1751), in which the poor drank themselves into insensibility and the rich knew no better, with wealthy rakes pleasuring themselves with boozy and pox-ridden lightskirts (prostitutes) before going off to the cock-fight, to wager large sums at the gaming table, or to leer at the lunatics at Bedlam. Both of these truisms have rightly been put under great pressure by historians (there was moral probity in the Georgian age and vice in the Victorian), but another related commonplace also retains its power, the sense of the late Georgian, Romantic era as a transformational period between the naughtiness of the mid-eighteenth century and the prudery and philanthropy of the mid-nineteenth century. 'Between 1780 and 1850', wrote the social historian Harold Perkin in *The Origins of Modern English Society 1780–1880* (1969), 'the English ceased to be one of the most … brutal, rowdy, outspoken [and] riotous, nations in the world and became one of the most inhibited, polite, orderly, tender-minded, prudish and hypocritical.'

Boyd Hilton says something similar in his volume in the prestigious Oxford New History of England series *A Mad, Bad, and Dangerous People?: England 1783–1846* (2006): 'Slowly but surely, the raffish and rakish style of eighteenth-century society … was succumbing to the new norms of respectability popularly known as "Victorianism".' The notion implicit here, of the Romantic era possessing both respectability and raffishness, is a fair one. Alongside the campaigns against slavery, cruelty to animals and the state lottery, amid increasing literacy among the working classes (the so-called 'march of mind'), and campaigns for factory reform, temperance (abstinence from alcohol) and reform of the bloody penal system, the early nineteenth century undeniably had a scandalous side. Allied to the reformist zeal of the age was a fascination with the seamier side of life. Contemporary newspapers were enthralled by divorce cases involving the wealthy and aristocratic (divorce needed a special act of parliament and was, as a consequence, beyond the means of the middle and 'lower classes'), and featured lurid accounts of 'crim. con.' ('criminal conversa-tion', that is adultery), there was gambling on a colossal scale among all social classes, and a taste for gawping at cruel sports (cock-fighting, bull and bear-baiting and so on) and at public executions.

To illustrate the naughtiness of the Romantic period, it is illuminating to focus upon two examples of what would, later in the nineteenth century, be described as 'deviant' sexuality, one from each gender: female prostitution and male homosexuality. The widespread nature of the former was, at least in part, the consequence of the moral conventions of the day.

Prostitution

In an age where unmarried couples, according to the tenets of the Church, were supposed to abstain from sexual relationships, in a society in which 'respectable' married women were not encouraged in sexual expressiveness, and one in which a seduced unmarried woman – especially a pregnant one – was considered a 'fallen woman' and was likely to be placed outside the moral pale, small wonder that prostitution was, as they say, rife in late Georgian Britain. In her *Vindication of the Rights of Woman* (1792), Mary Wollstonecraft protested against the moral censoriousness which surrounded the seduced woman and its social consequences. 'Highly as I respect marriage', she writes, 'I cannot avoid feeling the most lively compassion for those unfortunate females who are broken off from society, and by one error torn from all those affections and relationships that improve the heart and mind':

> It does not frequently even deserve the name of error; for many innocent girls become the dupes of a sincere affectionate heart, and still more are, as it may be emphatically termed, *ruined* before they know the difference between virtue and vice.

In such a context, simultaneously morally adamantine and hypocritical, often women had little choice than to become mistresses, 'kept' women, 'demireps' (short for demi-respectables, courtesans) and even prostitutes on the street or in the 'bawdy house' ('A house of ill-fame, kept for the resort and commerce of lewd people of both sexes', as an 1811 dictionary of the law put it). Wollstonecraft writes that 'A woman who has lost her honour imagines that she cannot fall lower, and as for recovering her former station, it is impossible ... prostitution becomes her only refuge.'

The revolutionary feminist Mary Hays (1759–1843) says something similar in her *Appeal to the Men of Great Britain in Behalf of the Women* (1798), which maintains that society is 'not entitled ... to despise or condemn too rigorously, that unfortunate portion of the sex who have fallen victims to vice – Or rather let me say to the arts of men'. Hays also fictionalised the plight of the fallen woman in the depiction of the unfortunate Mary in her novel *The Victim of Prejudice* (1799). The heroine, who is raped, subsequently refuses to marry her violator, and is thereafter abused, persecuted and imprisoned, with her gaoling providing a clear metaphor for the contemporary plight of women. In the 'Advertisement' to her novel, Hays states that the purpose of her work was to portray 'the mischiefs that have ensued from the too-great stress laid upon the *reputation* for chastity in *woman*'.

Wollstonecraft and Hays's feminist contemporary Mary Robinson protested directly against the sexual double standard of society of the time, in *A Letter to the Women of England* (1799; published under the pseudonym 'Anne Frances Randall'), in which she argued that erring men were granted forgiveness and indulgence not afforded the women concerned in sexual indiscretion:

> If he has the temerity to annihilate the bonds of moral and domestic life, he is acquitted; and his enormities are placed to the account of human frailty. But if WOMAN advance beyond the boundaries of decorum, 'Ruin ensues, reproach, and endless shame, / And one false step, entirely damns her fame'.

Robinson, a former actress (see 'Literary and Philosophical Key Concepts I'), a profession frequently associated in the mind of the public with prostitution, or at least courtesanship, knew whereof she spoke. The lot of women, experience had taught her, was unjust:

> Such partial discriminations seem to violate all laws, divine and human! If WOMAN be the weaker creature, her frailty should be the more readily forgiven. She is exposed by her personal attractions, to more perils, and yet she is not permitted to bear that shield, which man assumes; she is not allowed the exercise of courage to repulse the enemies of her fame and happiness; though, if she is wounded, – she is lost for ever!

Whether prompted by social hypocrisy, economic reasons or through coercion by pimp or bawd, vendors of sexual favours abounded both in the metropolis and in provincial towns. In the seventh book of his verse autobiography *The Prelude* (1805), Wordsworth recalled seeing prostitute women for the first time as he travelled to Cambridge to begin his inauspicious career as an undergraduate in October 1787:

> Southward two hundred miles I had advanced,
> And for the first time in my life did hear
> The voice of woman utter blasphemy –
> Saw Woman as she is to open shame
> Abandoned, and the pride of public vice.

The poet writes of his almost sublime horror at the scene ('Full surely from the bottom of my heart I shuddered') and his sense that the women's abandonment rendered them 'from humanity divorced'. This dehumanisation makes an immoral Doppelgänger of 'The human form, splitting the race of man / In twain, yet leaving the same outward shape'. In more 'mature' years, Wordsworth goes on, his 'Distress of mind' at prostitution had taken a more empathetic cast:

> afterwards
> A milder sadness on such spectacles
> Attended: thought, commiseration, grief,
> For the individual and the overthrow
> Of her soul's beauty.

Perhaps related to these latter feelings is the 'Reverie of Poor Susan' (1797, published in the *Lyrical Ballads* of 1800), in which Wordsworth offers a tender-minded depiction of a country girl adrift in the metropolis who hears the song of the thrush in the heart of the City of London. The sound conjures up visions of 'green pastures' and the 'small cottage' ('The one only dwelling on earth that she loves') from which she has been banished for some nameless sin:

> She looks, and her heart is in heaven: but they fade,
> The mist and the river, the hill and the shade:
> The stream will not flow, and the hill will not rise,
> And the colours have all passed away from her eyes!
>
> Poor Outcast! return to receive thee once more
> The house of thy Father will open its door,
> And thou once again in thy plain russet gown,
> May'st hear the thrush sing from a tree of its own.

The final stanza (which was excluded in subsequent republications of the poem) suggests that Susan is a fallen woman (indeed, Wordsworth's friend Charles Lamb wrote to the poet in 1815 that 'to term her a poor outcast seems as much as to say that poor Susan was no better than she should be'). Wordsworth draws a contrast in the figure of the 'outcast' between the symbolic corruption of the city and the lost Eden – before the Fall, so to speak – of the countryside.

The phenomenon of prostitution was particularly evident in poor Susan's London (or, at least, it is best documented in literary and historical terms in the metropolis), where there subsisted, in G. M. Trevelyan's phrase, 'a great army of prostitutes'. Indeed, the Wordsworthian critic Mary Jacobus claims that in 1803 there were between 50,000 and 70,000 prostitutes active in London. There were also, unsurprisingly, a legion of men who lived off their immoral earnings; Pierce Egan editorialises in his *Life in London* (1821) that 'however degrading it might appear ... it is too true that there are to be found in the Metropolis thousands of men who *exist* entirely on the *prostitution* of women'. Such women, writes Egan, 'daily and nightly walk the streets of London, for the sole purpose of getting a livelihood, and to support such a set of wretches'.

It was amid such circumstances, according to his *Confessions of an English Opium Eater* (1821; 1856), that Thomas De Quincey, as a seventeen-year-old runaway in the winter of 1802–3, encountered the saintly Ann of Oxford Street, a fifteen-year-old prostituted girl who helps him in his misery and near-starvation. This young woman he describes, accurately, as one of 'that unhappy class who belong to the outcasts and pariahs of our female population'. De Quincey identifies with the 'outcast' status of the women working as prostitutes, describing them as his 'sisters in calamity', and, indeed, as 'sisters amongst whom, in as large measure as amongst any other equal number of persons commanding more of the world's respect, were to be found humanity, disinterested generosity, courage that would not falter in defence of the helpless, and fidelity that would have scorned to take bribes for betraying'. Some of De Quincey's biographers have argued that what the author called his 'studies of the working poor' in adult life included visits to prostitutes which were prompted by less virtuous feelings, but here he portrays himself as a disinterested friend of suffering humanity; no-one, De Quincey maintains, should be beyond the pale:

> But the truth is that at no time of my life have I been a person to hold myself polluted by the approach or touch of any creature that wore a human shape. I cannot suppose, I will not believe, that any creatures wearing the form of man or woman are so absolutely rejected and reprobate outcasts that merely to talk with them inflicts pollution.

Rather than sketching a picture of degradation, some disreputable parts of the print culture of the Romantic period saw a sordid glamour in the depiction of 'Cyprians' (a slang term for prostitutes). There was a thriving trade in pornographic prints (as Iain McCalman's *Radical Underworld: Prophets, Revolutionaries and Pornographers in London, 1795–1840* (1988) has demonstrated), and a relish for scandal-mongering publications such as Charles Molloy Westmacott's *The English Spy* (1825). Such works glee-fully portrayed commercial sex, often while disingenuously condemning it. Westmacott, for instance, describes Covent Garden at the turn of the century as a 'gay scene' which 'partook of the splendour of a Venetian carnival', where ladies of easy virtue 'whose names are enrolled in the cabi-net of Love's votaries' paraded their charms:

> In the centre of Covent Garden market at midnight might be found the bucks, bloods, demireps, and choice spirits of London, associated with the most elegant and fascinating Cyprians, congregated with every species of human kind that intemperance, idleness, necessity, or curiosity could assemble together.

There were also *vade mecums* to the world of prostitution, notably in the notorious *Harris's List* of Covent Garden whores (the subject of Hallie Rubenhold's study *The Covent Garden Ladies: Pimp General Jack and the Extraordinary Story of Harris' List* (2005)), which supposedly featured their names, addresses and sexual specialties. In the 1793 edition, for instance, those not in the first flush of youth were recommended Mrs Hamblin (of 'No. 1 Naked-Boy Court in the Strand'); 'The young lady in question is not above 56 ... we know she must be particularly useful to elderly gentlemen.' Devotees of what was once referred to as the 'English vice', flagellation, were directed to a woman on Drury Lane described as 'Very impudent and very ugly; chiefly a dealer with old fellows. It is reported that she uses more birch rods in a week than Westminster school in a twelvemonth.'

Given that to use a single room for the purposes of paid sexual transaction could potentially render the prostitute guilty of keeping a bawdy house, then it is likely that the Harris list was more an example of comic erotica rather than active advertisement. This of another pride of Drury Lane:

> Known in this quarter for her immense sized breasts, which she ... makes use of ... to indulge those who are particularly fond of a certain amusement. She is what you may call, at all; backwards and forwards, all are equal to her, posteriors not excepted, nay indeed, by her own account she has most pleasure in the latter. ... Entrance at the front door tolerably reasonable, but nothing less than two pound for the back way.

In her *Purchasing Power: Representing Prostitution in Eighteenth-Century English Popular Print Culture* (2004), Sophie Carter writes that ' "Harris's List" represented the client/prostitute relationship as a happy coincidence of supply and demand.' The text, she maintains, 'resembles nothing so much as a shopping list. Here prostitutes are paraded like a range of diverse and differently packaged commodities competing for the attention ... of the male consumer.'

Attitudes towards prostitution in the period varied from winking indulgence as found in *The English Spy* and *Harris's List* through to fear, 'shuddering' (Wordsworth's term), and moral indignation. However, the most common literary attitude was one of sentimental sympathy, or 'sadness' to use a Wordsworthian phrase once again. Here we can see the emergence of the Victorian preoccupation with the subject of the 'Fallen Woman', in turns philanthropic and deeply patronising, which is evident from Thomas

Hood's ostentatious show of poetic compassion in his portrayal of the suicide of a 'Fallen Woman' in 'The Bridge of Sighs' (1844) (her 'evil behaviour' having prompted a 'cold inhumanity' in the society around her) to Dickens's prostitute Nancy in *Oliver Twist* (1837–8) and fallen girl Little Em'ly in *David Copperfield* (1849–50; the author was also closely involved in Urania House, a home for 'redeemed' prostitutes), and beyond.

Homosexuality

The homosexual counterpart of the London bawdy houses for 'lewd persons of both sexes' were the 'molly houses', homosexual brothels (the metropolis has had these establishments for a long time before the modern days of gay rights). Visitors were treading dangerously. Sodomy carried the death penalty in this period, though executions for this so-called crime were not as common as the act itself, given that an eye witness had to testify that he or she saw the actual act of penetration. But there were some, and they continued until the mid-1830s when the offence lost its capital status. Indeed, the historian A. D. Harvey has demonstrated a hardening of the legal mind towards 'sodomites' in the Romantic era; in the period between 1749 and 1804, he claims, executions for the offence occurred about once in a decade, but after that they averaged once a year until judicial abolition of the punishment three decades later.

Perhaps the shift in judicial attitudes towards sodomy was attributable to the context of war. Over half the Romantic period (1793–1815, with one short ceasefire in 1802–3) took place in a time of European conflict in which Great Britain was centrally involved. In a society which stressed manliness and the martial spirit, and in which some delighted in what we now see as cruel sports and in the spectacle of execution, the supposed effeminacy of what we now call homosexual men – 'those who perverted the instincts of humanity in unnatural acts of sensuality', as the *Monthly Review* called them in 1782 – could be seen as a threat to the aggressive masculinity which was necessary to a central group within contemporary society. William Dickinson's *A Practical Exposition of the Law* (1813) sums up the implacability of much contemporary social and legal opinion: 'Buggery is an abominable sin, committed by carnal knowledge, against the ordinance of God, and the order of nature, by man, with his own kind, or with brute beast' (there was but one concession: 'If the party buggered be within [under] the age of discretion [14] it is no felony in him, but in the agent only. But if committed upon a man of the age of discretion, it is felony in both').

Matters were not helped by the fact that sodomy was seen as a kind of statutory rape, with consent to the act being legally immaterial. The famous legal textbook *The Justice of the Peace,* in its twenty-sixth edition (1831),

pointed out that 'In a prosecution for this crime, an admission by the prisoner that he had committed such an offence at another time and with
another person, and that his natural inclination was towards such practices,
ought not to be received in evidence.' That said, a social double standard
was sometimes evident in the punishment of sodomy. In the 1820s there
were executions for the offence, as in the hanging of three 'common men' at
Grantham in 1825, but the establishment was also capable of closing ranks
to protect one of its own. In 1822 the Bishop of Clogher (an Ireland bishopric)
was discovered in a London tavern engaged in sodomy – or just about to
(accounts vary) – with a member of the soldiery. One contemporary source
described the case delicately: 'On the evening of July 19, the Hon. and Rev.
Percy Jocelyn, Bishop of Clogher, was detected, in a back room of the White
Lion public-house, in St. Alban's Place, St. James's, in a situation, with a
private in the foot guards, which led to his instant apprehension.' The Bishop
was tried on the capital charge of sodomy but was bailed – to the surprise of
many – and subsequently escaped to France, allegedly as a consequence of
the intervention on his behalf of an unknown government agency.

One contemporary source, William Bailey, pointed out the contrast
between the treatment of the Lincolnshire nobodies and the Bishop in 1826:
'Had any one of the three wretches of Grantham, who were last year
executed for their unnatural crimes, been a lord, a bishop, or a clergyman,
the Constitutional Association would have looked quietly on, while he was
bailed and screened away.' The author goes on to contrast what he saw as
healthsome heterosexuality (one celebrated in Thomas Moore's translation
of the amatory *Odes of Anacreon* (1800)) and the Bishop's unsavoury
predilections:

> The holy scoundrel, with his contrite heart, is now in France, to do the same with
> the private soldiers of the French guards. It is even said that this favoured and
> protected miscreant has taken up his abode near Paris, in the identical house
> which Anacreon Moore had occupied the year preceding: thus defiling the
> dwelling of Love's highly-lifted poet, where the Graces and the Muses have danced
> and sung to a thousand of his effusions to love and beauty.

When, in the month after Jocelyn's arrest, the Foreign Secretary Viscount
Castlereagh committed suicide after receiving (or having said he received),
from an effeminate cross-dresser, blackmail threats to 'out' him, in the
modern parlance, some radicals saw their conspiracy theories confirmed.
The ultra-Radical and religious freethinker Richard Carlile (see 'Religion
and Atheism') argued that 'the ministers can expect no other distinction by
the future historian than as having been the patrons of sodomy among the
clergy and army, and the murderers of poor men who fell into the same
error'. Carlile goes on to hint at the prevalence of such behaviour (a sign of

the decadence and moral corruption, to his mind, of the Tory government): 'There is a strong rumour prevalent, that the Bishop of Clogher wrote to Castlereagh from the watch-house, and threatened to impeach near a hundred of the leading men in church and state, whom he knew to be guilty of the same practices, if he were prosecuted.' Carlile concludes, with mordant relish, by expressing his 'strong suspicion' that this 'was in some measure an inducement to Castlereagh's throat-cutting!'

Byron and the Love of Men

It is not known if Lord Byron ever visited a London house of sodomitical ill-repute. Such a thing was unlikely in the years of his fame, given the poet's sensitivity to the possible threat of exposure of his taste for participating in homosexual acts – 'Even to have such a thing *said* is utter destruction & ruin to a man, & from which he can never recover,' he once lamented to his half-sister and lover, Augusta Leigh. In this period Byron could, in general, only physically express his homosexual side on the continent in such places as the Turkish baths, renowned for their tolerance, which he once described as 'marble palaces of sherbet and sodomy'. In December 1818, P. B. Shelley ranted to Thomas Love Peacock of Byron's 'sickening vice' in consorting in Venice with 'wretches who seem almost to have lost the gait and physiog-nomy of man & do not scruple to avow practices which are not only unnamed but I believe seldom even conceived in England'. Byron also traded with female prostitutes in this period of his life, says Shelley, with 'the lowest sort of these [Italian] women', and 'allow[ed] father & mothers to bargain with him for their daughters' ('for an Englishman to encourage such', lamented Shelley, 'is a melancholy thing').

Byron's feelings for members of his own sex was by no means just a matter of sexual desire. From his schooldays Byron had strong feelings for boys and young men. His intense affection at Harrow for his school friend John Edleston, who died, young, in 1811, is well known (Byron's elegy 'Thryza' was written in October 1811 for his beloved, though the poet judi-ciously changed the gender of the lost love in his poem). Indeed, in his last months, even to Missolonghi, Byron's entourage included the fifteen-year-old boy Loukas Chalandritsanos. Older critics such as G. Wilson Knight (1897–1985) have sometimes seen such liaisons as Platonic, as evidence of a 'Youthful, pre-sexual harmony'. Writing in 1966, Knight declares that 'the prevailing note ... characteristic of what such love meant to Byron – his acquaintance with Edleston started with his saving the boy from drowning – is that of *care*'. Byron was acting *in loco parentis*, it seems, in such cases: 'From Harrow onwards Byron's protective, almost maternal, instincts were a driving force.' However, whatever may or may not have happened with

Edleston, on his Grand Tour in 1809 Byron might be seen, in the modern phrase, as behaving as a kind of 'sex tourist' in the Levant (in modern-day Albania, Greece and Turkey), where he indulged in sexual liaisons with young men and boys as well as cultivating passionate relationships with the 'dearly-beloved' Greek youth Eustathios Georgiou (with his 'ambrosial curls hanging down his amiable back') and a teenage Athenian schoolboy, Nicolo Giraud.

Louis Crompton's study *Byron and Greek Love: Homophobia in Nineteenth-Century England* (1985) has no truck with the ethereal love posited by the likes of Wilson Knight and argues strongly for the physical nature of Byron's love of boys. Crompton examines Byron's homosexual side, beginning with the 'Georgian homophobia' of which the poet was all too well aware and contrasting the situation in Great Britain with what he sees as the greater tolerance of the attitudes that Byron encountered in Europe, such as 'the Turkish passion for boys'. Following Crompton's study, there has been a deal of discussion about Byron's sexuality (for discussion of recent critical work on Byron's friend M. G. Lewis and other Gothic novelists who would now be identified as 'gay', see 'Gender Criticism'). The poet has become, in the words of Michael O'Rourke and David Collings, 'something of a poster boy for queer Romanticism'.

See also   Feminism and the Position of Women; Gender Criticism; Literary and Philosophical Key Concepts I; Religion and Atheism.

Further Reading

Sophie Carter, *Purchasing Power: Representing Prostitution in Eighteenth-Century English Popular Print Culture* (2004).

Louis Crompton, *Byron and Greek Love: Homophobia in Nineteenth-Century England* (1985).

A. D. Harvey, *Sex in Georgian England: Attitudes and Prejudices from the 1720s to the 1820s* (1994).

Boyd Hilton, *A Mad, Bad, and Dangerous People?: England 1783–1846* (2006).

G. Wilson Knight, *Byron and Shakespeare* (1966).

Mary Jacobus, ' "Splitting the Race of Man in Twain": Prostitution, Personification and *The Prelude*', in *Romanticism, Writing and Sexual Difference* (1989), 206–36.

Iain McCalman, *Radical Underworld: Prophets, Revolutionaries and Pornographers in London, 1795–1840* (1988).

Michael O'Rourke and David Collings, 'Queer Romanticisms: Past, Present, and Future', *Romanticism on the Net* (2004), http://id.erudit.org/iderudit/011132ar

Harold Perkin, *The Origins of Modern English Society 1780–1880* (1969).

Laura Jean Rosenthal, *Infamous Commerce: Prostitution in Eighteenth-Century British Literature and Culture* (2006).

Hallie Rubenhold, *The Covent Garden Ladies: Pimp General Jack and the Extraordinary Story of Harris' List* (2005).

G. M. Trevelyan, *English Social History* (1944).

Slavery, Abolition and African-British Literature

The Slave Trade and the Campaign for Abolition

Slavery is an ancient vice. We know the importance of slaves to the empires of classical Greece and Rome, and that that latter day imperial colossus, the British Empire, was for nigh on two centuries dependent in some of its colonies – the United States and the West Indies most particularly – upon black slaves, bought in large part on the west coast of Africa and then shipped to the plantations of the New World. Indeed, some of Great Britain's most notable ports, namely Bristol and Liverpool, owe much of their development into sizeable cities to the slave trade, with ships leaving for Africa, taking slaves stacked 'close to each other, like books on a shelf', in the ex-slave-captain John Newton's phrase, to the West Indies, and then returning to Great Britain with cargoes of cotton, sugar and so forth. The slave trade was lucrative, and the plantations in which the unfortunates toiled even more so. The novelist and travel writer William Beckford, for instance, 'England's wealthiest son' in some accounts, inherited a fortune of over £150,000 from his father's West Indian plantations.

Defences of slavery are as old as that implacable system itself. Aristotle, for example, wrote in the fourth century BC that there was a class of man who was 'intended by nature to be a slave'. 'Some', he maintained, were 'marked out for subjection, others for rule'. Though physically powerful, a slave was no more fit to look after himself than a beast of burden. Both needed a master: 'the use made of slaves and of tame animals is not very different; for both with their bodies minister to the needs of life'. Even in the eighteenth century, some believed that 'negroes' were not fully human or so inferior in mental capacity that enslaving them (and giving them Christianity) was actually doing them a favour. As late as 1754, the mainstay of the Scottish Enlightenment, the philosopher David Hume, had maintained that 'I am apt to suspect the negroes to be naturally inferior to the whites ... No ingenious manufactures amongst them, no arts, no sciences' (over twenty years later he heard of a black poet in Jamaica, Francis Williams, who wrote Latin verses, and unflatteringly compared him to 'a parrot, who speaks a few words plainly'). Less abstractly, as calls for the abolition of the slave trade and the system of slavery began to be heard in the later eighteenth century, supporters of slavery stressed what they saw as the importance of the trade to the wealth of empire. The planter politician Bryan Edwards's *History, Civil and Commercial of the British Colonies in the West Indies* (1793), for instance, defended the system for its economic paramountcy and argued that its effects would in the end be benign and civilising, and eventually inculcate 'humanity' and 'improvement' amongst the negroes, people who were not, as yet, ready for liberation (and better to be enslaved by the enlightened British than by the other colonial powers active in the trade, the French or Dutch, for instance).

Edwards (1743–1800) became MP for Grampound, a Cornish 'pocket borough' (see 'Empire and Travel'), in 1796 and staunchly defended slavery as in Britain's best interest. He was described as a powerful adversary by the leader of the abolitionist cause in parliament, William Wilberforce (1759–1833), the Cambridge-educated Member of Parliament for Yorkshire. A lay theologian and leading light in the Evangelical Clapham Sect (see 'Religion and Atheism'), Wilberforce devoted himself to philanthropic causes but principally to the cause of slavery, notably with his influential lieutenant, the firebrand Thomas Clarkson (1760–1846), the co-founder in 1787 of the Society for Effecting the Abolition of the Slave Trade. In his *A Letter on the Abolition of the Slave Trade* (1807) Wilberforce argued passionately for the cause, maintaining that as well as oppressing fellow human beings, slavery also corrupted the moral fabric of England, declaring that 'The system of slavery, especially of slavery in its more hateful forms, never did nor ever will prevail long in any country, without producing a most pernicious effect.' Wilberforce, Clarkson, and their cohorts both parliamentary and extra-parliamentary were influential in the passing of the 1807 Act which abolished the slave trade (and Wilberforce lingered on his death bed to hear the tidings of the success of the second reading of the bill which eventually abolished slavery in 1833).

Wilberforce and Clarkson were the figureheads of an abolitionist movement with thousands of supporters, which became innovative and resourceful in its campaigning. Trade boycotts of West Indian goods such as sugar were organised, thousands of pamphlets were distributed, and publicity materials endorsing the cause became fashionable. Figure 5 shows Josiah Wedgwood's famous image which was what we would now call the 'logo' of Clarkson's society, in which a supplicant slave asks 'Am I not a Man and a Brother?' Plainly there is an element of paternalism in the emblem – the slave beseeches rather than revolts – but the image was in any case well judged to appeal to philanthropic sentiment and, indeed, to prompt sympathy in parliament, the place where the future of the slaves would be resolved. The image was used in a variety of abolitionist paraphernalia: not only in books and broadsheets, but also on medallions, brooches, snuff boxes, plates and such like.

Benjamin Franklin declared that the impact of Wedgwood's propagandist image was 'equal to that of the best written pamphlet'; visual and written word went hand in hand to support the cause. Many of the principal abolitionists were culture warriors, pressing the case of the slave in pamphlet, published sermon and in prose polemics of various kinds. The Reverend Legh Richmond (1772–1827), to give but one example, published

Fig. 5   Anon., 'Am I not a Man and a Brother?' Seal of the Society for Effecting the Abolition of the Slave Trade (designed at the Josiah Wedgwood company, 1787)

a number of works dealing with 'slavery ... the cause of everything that is bad' about the British West Indies. Richmond called 'aloud for the ardent prayers and active exertions of Christians [on] behalf' of the slaves, envisaging a time when they would have both liberty and a strong Christian faith (the day when 'the poor benighted Negro will look from the ends of the earth unto Jesus, and be saved').

Abolitionist Literature

Orthodox abolitionist polemic such as this was also complemented by didactic verse and prose, with imaginative literature and more conventional oratory linked in a twin-pronged rhetorical attack. Richmond himself proselytised for the cause in *The Negro Servant* (1804), a fiction where the subtitle tells all: 'An Authentic Narrative of a Young Negro, Showing How He Was Made a Slave in Africa, and Carried to Jamaica, Where He was Sold to a Captain in His Majesty's Navy, and Taken to America, Where He Became a Christian, and Afterwards Brought to England and Baptised' (the story offers tales of conversion in which black folks tell of their salvation in comical negro speak: '"Me believe", said he, "dat Jesus Christ came into de world to save sinners; and dough me be chief of sinners, yet Jesus will save me, dough me be only poor black Negro"').

However, the most notable literary attacks on slavery were evident in poetry. An early example is 'The Dying Negro' by Thomas Day (1773), one of the most celebrated abolitionist poems, which tells the forlorn story of a slave taken to London who falls in love with – and seeks to marry – a white woman, a fellow-servant. 'Being detected' in his intention, says the preface, 'he was sent on board the Captain's vessel then lying in the River; where, finding no chance of escaping, and preferring death to another voyage to America, he took an opportunity of shooting himself'. The poem is supposedly the slave's last epistle to his betrothed:

> And better in th'untimely grave to rot,
> The world and all its cruelties forgot,
> Than, dragg'd once more beyond the Western main,
> To groan beneath some dastard planter's chain,
> Where my poor countrymen in bondage wait
> The slow enfranchisement of ling'ring fate.
> Oh! my heart sinks, my dying eyes o'erflow,
> When mem'ry paints the picture of their woe!
> For I have seen them, ere the dawn of day,
> Rouz'd by the lash, begin their chearless way;
> Greeting with groans unwelcome morn's return,
> While rage and shame their gloomy bosoms burn.

As the abolitionist cause grew in strength and popularity, several of the most popular Christian poets of the day such as William Cowper and Hannah More began to play an important part in abolitionist propagandising. Cowper, described by Thomas Clarkson as a 'great coadjutor' in the cause, wrote several poems in that direction in the late 1780s. 'The Negro's Complaint' (1788), a work which was circulated widely by the Committee for the Abolition of the Slave Trade in pamphlet form, begins thus:

> Forced from home and all its pleasures
> Afric's coast I left forlorn,
> To increase a stranger's treasures
> O'er the raging billows borne.

Men from England bought and sold me,
Paid my price in paltry gold;
But, though slave they have enrolled me,
Minds are never to be sold.

Still in thought as free as ever,
What are England's rights, I ask,
Me from my delights to sever,
Me to torture, me to task?
Fleecy locks and black complexion
Cannot forfeit nature's claim;
Skins may differ, but affection
Dwells in white and black the same.

A related poem, written in the same year, was Cowper's powerful satire 'Pity for the Poor Africans', which indicts those who refused to participate in trade boycotts as being motivated by a blinkered appetite for West Indian consumer goods such as rum, tea and sugar. Such people, Cowper suggests, are complicit in the very system of slavery:

I own I am shock'd at this Traffic of Slaves,
And fear those who buy them, and sell them, are Knaves.
What I hear of their Hardships, their Tortures and Groans
Is almost enough to draw pity from stones.

I pity them greatly, but I must be mum,
For how could we do without sugar and rum?
Especially sugar, so needful we see,
What? give up our desserts, our coffee and tea!

To the abolitionist movement, tea, as Robert Southey wrote, was 'a blood-stained beverage'.

Though an anti-Radical conservative, Hannah More (1745–1833), who considered the consumption of slave-produced goods 'an atrocity', was an enthusiastic proponent of abolition both in popular-cultural and in more genteel verse. She produced 'The Sorrows of Yamba, or, The Negro Woman's Lamentation' (1795), one of the pamphlets written for the Cheap Repository Tracts which were widely distributed amongst the poor. Yamba, 'parted many a thousand mile' from her African home and made to toil in the West Indies, tells her heart-rending story. Though hers has been in one sense a 'fortunate fall' – to use Milton's phrase – inasmuch as she has become baptised, she still awaits freedom on this earth, given that 'British laws shall ne'er befriend me / They protect not slaves like me':

> Ye that boast 'Ye rule the waves',
> Bid no Slave Ship soil the sea,
> Ye that 'never will be slaves'
> Bid poor Afric's land be free.

As well as populist material such as this, aimed at what were then called the 'lower orders', More also published more elevated – though not necessarily any better – poetry in heroic couplets to preach abolition to a more elevated audience. The conclusion to her *Slavery. A Poem* (1788) (see also 'Religion and Atheism'), with its abstract moral personifications and heroic couplets, echoes the end of Pope's *Dunciad*. However, whereas Pope had envisioned a dystopian world where 'Dulness' reigned supreme, More anticipates a day where the 'dusky myriads' would be free. Though current British policy was to deny the slaves their freedom, this was, More implies, an aberration from the great political tradition of British 'liberty'. She envisages a day when the country would return to the moral high ground by freeing its slaves:

> And, LIBERTY! thy shining standard rears!
> As the bright ensign's glory she displays,
> See pale OPPRESSION faints beneath the blaze!
> The giant dies! no more his frown appals,
> The chain untouch'd, drops off; the fetter falls.
> Astonish'd echo tells the vocal shore,
> Opression's fall'n, and Slavery is no more!
> The dusky myriads crowd the sultry plain,
> And hail that mercy long invok'd in vain.
> Victorious Pow'r! she bursts their two-fold bands,
> And FAITH and FREEDOM spring from Mercy's hands.

In subsequent editions, the word 'Mercy's' was altered to 'Britain's'; Britain, in More's account, can demonstrate its national superiority by freeing the hapless negroes.

There were also many prose narratives dealing with personal experiences of the slave trade, by colonialists and travel writers but also by ex-slavers and ex-slaves themselves. The aforesaid Captain John Newton (1725–1807), slave trader turned abolitionist and friend of Wilberforce, drew upon his personal experiences in his *Thoughts upon the African Slave Trade* (1788), offering a powerful account of the slaving voyages:

With our ships, the great object is, to be full ... The cargo of a vessel [is] from 220 to 250 slaves. Their lodging-rooms below the deck [are] five feet high, and sometimes less ... the poor creatures, thus cramped for want of room, are likewise in irons ... both hands and feet, and two together, which makes it difficult for them to turn or move. [T]he heat and smell of these rooms, ... would be almost insupportable to a person not accustomed to them. [E]very morning, perhaps, more instances than one are found, of the living and the dead ... fastened together.

Epidemical fevers ... often break out ... nearly one-half of the slaves on board, have, sometimes, died; and that the loss of a third part [is] not unusual ... one fourth of the whole purchase may be allotted to the article of mortality: that is, if the English ships purchase sixty thousand slaves annually, upon the whole extent of the coast, the annual loss of lives cannot be much less than fifteen thousand.

Newton railed against the 'nature and effects of that unhappy and disgraceful branch of commerce, which has long been maintained on the coast of Africa', and his work was taken up by abolitionists; the *Critical Review*, for instance, commended the work to 'the public attention. They will convince everyone that the farther importation of Africans should be stopped.'

One of the most compelling accounts of slavery is John Stedman's gruesome *Narrative of a Five Years' Expedition against the Revolted Negroes of Surinam* (1796), a book for which William Blake engraved some of the illustrations. While Stedman was not for the freeing of the slaves at that time, arguing only for a curb to the excesses with which they were treated, his descriptions of the indignities and agonies suffered by slaves were taken up and much quoted by the abolitionists. Blake's figures stress the latter aspect of slavery, his portraits of the suffering of tortured slaves offering a powerful testimony against the practice. Figure 6 shows one of Blake's most enduring images, the unlovely portrait of a slave hung by the chest.

Slave Narratives and African-British Literature

It should be pointed out that white authors did not entirely dominate the debates over slavery. For the first time in British history, black people began to speak for themselves in print in the late eighteenth and early nineteenth centuries, a period when a series of remarkable slave testimonies were published in London. The pioneer volume was Ukawsaw Gronniosaw's *A Narrative of the Most Remarkable Particulars in the Life of James Albert Ukawsaw Gronniosaw*, published as early as 1770, the story of a freed slave – once 'a prince' in Africa – who served in the British navy and settled in England where he married a white wife. That said, Gronniosaw's book – the work of a devout Christian – is more in the tradition of the spiritual autobiography and instead of dwelling on his experiences of slavery constantly stresses 'the glory and beauty of God', emphasising the former slave's spiritual rather than worldly liberation.

Ottobah Cugoano (*c*.1757–1803), a freed slave who lived in London (and who knew Blake himself) and was active in abolitionist circles, was more

Fig. 6   William Blake, illustration to John Stedman's *Narrative of a Five Years'
Expedition against the Revolted Negroes of Surinam* (1796)

forthcoming than Gronniosaw about his experiences. Sold into slavery
from what is now Ghana and shipped to the West Indies, Cugoano argued
passionately against the trade in his *Thoughts and Sentiments on the Evil and
Wicked Traffic of the Slavery and Commerce of the Human Species* (1787),
which bluntly declared that 'the base treatment which the African Slaves
undergo ought to be abolished'. The most notable of the early slave narratives was that of Olaudah Equiano (1745–97), whose *The Interesting
Narrative of the Life of Olaudah Equiano … The African. Written by Himself*
was published in 1789. As well as telling the story of his early days in Africa
(he angrily denied rumours that he had been born in the West Indies) and
his period as a slave, Equiano's aim in his eloquent and passionate book
was clear: to demonstrate 'the enormous cruelties practised on my sable

brethren, and strengthening the generous emulation now prevailing in this country, to put a speedy end to a traffic both cruel and unjust'.

Towards the end of the period of British slavery, Mary Prince offered her own account of her life as a Bermudan slave, *The History of Mary Prince, a West Indian Slave* (1831). In his preface to the book, Thomas Pringle, secretary of the Anti-Slavery Society, for whom Prince had worked as a domestic servant on her arrival in England, writes that the 'idea of writing Mary Prince's history was first suggested by herself. She wished it to be done, she said, that good people in England might hear from a slave what a slave had felt and suffered.' Prince's appeal is heartfelt and direct:

> Oh the horrors of slavery! – How the thought of it pains my heart! But the truth ought to be told of it; and what my eyes have seen I think it is my duty to relate; for few people in England know what slavery is. I have been a slave – I have felt what a slave feels, and I know what a slave knows; and I would have all the good people in England to know it too, that they may break our chains, and set us free.

Where once blacks had been congregated in slave ships 'like books on a shelf', now they were, so to speak, putting books on shelves, a sure sign – the abolitionists argued – that the African shared a common intelligence and humanity with the European.

See also   Religion and Atheism.

Further Reading

Adam Hochschild, *Bury the Chains: Prophets and Rebels in the Fight to Free an Empire's Slaves* (2005).

Peter J. Kitson and Debbie Lee (gen. eds), *Slavery, Abolition and Emancipation: Writings in the British Romantic Period*, 8 vols (1999).

Debbie Lee, *Slavery and the Romantic Imagination* (2002).

Emmanuel Sampath Nelson, *African American Autobiographers: A Sourcebook* (2002).

Anne Stott, *Hannah More: The First Victorian* (2004).

Helen Thomas, *Romanticism and Slave Narratives: Transatlantic Testimonies* (2000).

Marcus Wood, *Slavery, Empathy and Pornography* (2002).

2 Texts: Themes, Issues, Concepts

Literary and Philosophical Key Concepts I: The First Generation Romantic Poets (Wordsworth, Coleridge, Blake, Smith, Robinson)

Neoclassicism and Romanticism

In his renowned study of historical literary theory, *The Mirror and the Lamp: Romantic Theory and the Critical Tradition* (1953), the distinguished critic of Romanticism M. H. Abrams drew a distinction between the neoclassical and Romantic manners. The former he compared to a mirror, in its dependence on a 'mimetic' literary model (the notion derives from Aristotle's fragmentary fourth-century BC treatise *Poetics*, 'mimesis' being the Greek word for imitation). Here poetry is seen as holding up a glass (to use the Georgian term) to nature, offering a faithful reflection of the world. The mimetic mode of neoclassicism was dominant in English verse from the 1660s to the turn of the nineteenth century. Whereas Wordsworth worried about the notion of the artist as mere copyist (in the words of the 'Immortality Ode', 'As if his whole vocation / Were endless imitation'), the quintessential neoclassical poet Alexander Pope (1688–1744), in his great effort in metrical lit. crit., *An Essay on Criticism* (1711), argued that it was the duty of literature 'to copy nature'. Here there is no striving for originality in the later Romantic fashion; good poetry should 'Avoid extremes', and aspire to an elegant summary of received opinion: 'True wit is nature to advantage dress'd / What oft was thought, but ne'er so well express'd.'

On the other hand, rather than offering a mirror's reflection, Abrams likens Romantic verse to a lamp throwing out internally generated light. The Romantic poet, he argues, works within an 'expressive' mode of creation, much of his or her inspiration coming from within, from the creative imagination; 'that inward eye', as William Wordsworth memorably put it in his famous lyric 'Daffodils' (1804). 'Poetry', Wordsworth maintains in words almost as well known in the 1800 'Preface' to the *Lyrical Ballads*, 'is the spontaneous overflow of powerful feelings'. Instead of literature

offering pleasingly articulated versions of 'the most kn⌐
received observations' – Pope's friend Joseph Addison's ⌐
Romantic 'imagination', writes Wordsworth in 1815, 'has no re⌐
images that are merely a faithful copy ... but is a word of higher impo⌐   ⌐e
Romantic author aspires to offer something new and original, clothing 'his
idea in an individual dress', as Wordsworth put it. The *avant garde* poet must
shape rather than follow the literary taste of the age. In Coleridge's formulation, 'Every great and original writer, in proportion as he is great and original, must himself create the taste by which he is to be relished.' Abrams's
summary of these positions is word perfect: 'Poetry is the overflow, utterance, or projection of the thought and feelings of the poet [and] the artist
himself becomes the major element generating both the artistic product
and the criteria by which it is to be judged.'

To qualify Abrams' central distinction slightly, for William Wordsworth
poetic creation was, strictly speaking, a hybrid of both the mimetic and
expressive modes, 'an ennobling interchange', as he put it in the poetic
autobiography of his youth *The Prelude* (1805), 'of action from within and
from without'. To Wordsworth and Coleridge, his collaborator in the book
which has generally been seen as the founding document of British
Romanticism, the *Lyrical Ballads* of 1798, the best poetry was born of the
fruitful relationship between the creative imagination 'within' and nature
'without'. The 'imagination, by which word I mean the faculty which
produces impressive effects out of simple elements', as Wordsworth put it
in an 1800 note to his poem 'The Thorn', gives birth to poetry in its creative
intercourse with nature, which is itself often characterised in Romantic-era
thought as fecund and generous. 'The love of Nature is ever returned
double to us,' declares Coleridge in his *Anima Poetæ* (first published posthumously in 1895); 'even in sickness and nervous diseases she has peopled
our imagination with lovely forms'.

Abrams was certainly right to see the first generation of male Romantics
as poets engaged in a quarrel with what might be called their overbearing
literary parents of the eighteenth century. The so-called 'first generation' of
Romantic poets repudiated their neoclassical predecessors just as surely as
T. S. Eliot and the Modernists rejected the post-Romantic consensus which
had prevailed in English verse since the 1830s (see 'Twentieth-Century
Criticism from Modernism to the New Criticism'). Coleridge, for instance,
tartly maintained that 'To read Dryden, Pope, &c, you need only count sylla-
bles'; the new poetry, he implied, would be written from the heart rather
than merely offer a metronomic display of empty metrical cleverness along
the lines of 'Pope's cuckoo-song verses' (Leigh Hunt's phrase). Indeed, so
successful was the poetic patricide of the late eighteenth and early nineteenth century effected by the poets whom we now label 'Romantic' that by

the middle of the Victorian period the likes of Pope and Thomas Gray could be dismissed as tinny versifiers, their lines seen as little more than a soulless exhibition of poetic showmanship. The words of the poet-critic Matthew Arnold (1822–88) are this view made incarnate: 'The difference between genuine poetry and the poetry of Dryden, Pope, and all their school, is briefly this ... their poetry is composed in their wits, genuine poetry is conceived and composed in the soul.'

Wordsworth's 'Preface' to the *Lyrical Ballads* and the 'Real Language of Men'

Abrams, with most conventional twentieth-century literary opinion, views Wordsworth's 1800 'Preface' to the *Lyrical Ballads* as the most important theoretical document of early English Romanticism, as emblematic of a 'change in sensibility' from classical to Romantic. This manifesto has often been seen as heralding a kind of poetic regime change from neoclassical to Romantic, the literary equivalent, indeed, of the French Revolution of 1789. Certainly Wordsworth's polemical, contentious 'Preface' consciously positions itself against that which had come before. A key part of his theoretical positioning takes aim at the very language of neoclassicism, notably in condemning the 'poetic diction' of much eighteenth-century verse, which is dismissed in Wordsworth's account as overwrought, stilted, and far removed from everyday language. Wordsworth quotes as an example the 'Sonnet on the Death of Richard West' by Thomas Gray (1716–71) and considers the 'curiously elaborate structure of [its] poetic diction'. In the 'false refinement' of such verse, the sun does not come up; no, here 'reddening Phoebus lifts his golden fire'. Wordsworth argues that such mannerisms are stale and worthless. A fine poet damages his work in such tired conventions; Gray, he maintains, was capable of much better and, indeed, is on much surer ground later in the same poem – 'the only part of this Sonnet which is of any value' – where his language is plainer and less self-consciously poetic, in the simple though stately Elizabethan tenor of the sonnet's last two lines: 'I fruitless mourn for him that cannot hear / And weep the more because I weep in vain.'

Thomas Gray once claimed that 'the language of the age is never the language of poetry'. In this account, poetry, as the most elevated of all artistic forms, should be couched in an ornate linguistic register which is consciously set apart from everyday language in order to signify its importance. Wordsworth, on the other hand, argues for the importance of a 'plainer language' within English verse. What Augustan periphrasis (the habit of dignifying and poeticising everyday subject matter by using more words than are strictly necessary) would call 'a member of the feathered tribe' or, indeed, the 'finny race', he – in aspiring to an unadorned poetic diction – would simply label 'a bird' or 'a fish'. Wordsworth warns, in the words of the 'Advertisement' to the 1798 *Lyrical Ballads*, that contemporary poetry was addicted to 'gaudiness and inane phraseology'. Trite cliché had replaced real feeling in English verse, he argues, calling instead for the use of a poetic idiom close to 'the real language of men'.

A key literary innovation of the *Lyrical Ballads* and their 'Preface' was this willingness to endorse a plain-speaking idiom and an attendant and inter-related valorisation of the poetic representation of 'low and rustic life' (in contradistinction to neoclassicism's attention to a sophisticated, metropol-itan and classically-educated literary coterie). The imagination, as Wordsworth put it in 1800, can be fired up by 'simple elements' (early Romanticism's theorisation of simplicity and plainness of language is captured wonderfully in a 1796 letter of Charles Lamb to Coleridge: 'Cultivate simplicity, Coleridge ... banish elaborateness; for simplicity springs spontaneous from the heart, and carries into daylight its own modest buds and genuine, sweet, and clear flowers of expression'). In the 'Preface', Wordsworth declares his intention to fashion verse crafted from the 'language of man in a state of vivid sensation' and maintains that 'Low and rustic life was generally chosen because in that situation the essential passions of the heart find a better soil in which they can attain their matu-rity, are less under restraint, and speak a plainer and more emphatic language.'

In his *Biographia Literaria* (1817), Coleridge describes the composition of the *Lyrical Ballads*, which were intended as 'a series of poems ... composed of two sorts'. While his subject matter would be 'supernatural' (as in 'The Rime of the Ancient Mariner'), Wordsworth's 'subjects were to be chosen from ordinary life. The characters and incidents were to be such as will be found in every village and its vicinity, where there is a meditative and feel-ing mind to seek after them or to notice them when they present them-selves.' Wordsworth had the capacity, in Walter Pater's fine phrase, 'to appreciate passion in the lowly'. He was willing to portray a country pedlar as a font of philosophical knowledge, consider conversation with a leech-gatherer as an elevating experience and to view the experiences of chil-dren, gypsies and female vagrants as profound and moving to the soul. Like Robert Southey before him, a poet who had written verse on the suffering of the poor and the agonies of the homeless (and had been roundly mocked by the Tory wits of the *Anti-Jacobin* for his pains (see 'Satire')), Wordsworth paid great attention to the dispossessed and marginal in English society. Though quickly superseded by Wordsworth in the critical consciousness of the day as the leader of the 'Lake Poets', Southey, in his 1797 *Poems*, antic-ipated some of the poetic experimentation of the *Lyrical Ballads* (another key precursor to Wordsworth and Coleridge was Robert Burns – see 'Irish, Scottish and Welsh Poetry').

The Romantic willingness to offer a sympathetic account and, indeed, to attempt a realistic portrayal of the experience of rural folk, and especially the rural poor, sounded a new note in English poetry (in much neoclassical pastoral verse after the manner of Pope's *Pastorals* (1709), shepherds and their shepherdesses recline in front of haystacks, the sun shines and little visible work is done). These attitudes were rightly seen in their day as ideo-logically significant, as betokening a political radicalism. To espouse the cause of the poor in verse in the decade after the French Revolution was to risk the charge of poetic subversion; the 'Lake School', in the 1797 words of the Tory satirist George Canning, was also frequently seen as a 'Jacobin School of Poetry'. Lord Byron himself, no admirer, wrote that Wordsworth in the 1790s 'seasoned his [poems] with democracy'. Wordsworth, Southey and Coleridge's later conversion to Toryism should not blind us to the radi-calism of both their early politics and their early poetics.

Abrams writes that 'Wordsworth's "Preface" [is] a convenient document by which to signalize the displacement of the mimetic ... by the expressive view of art in English criticism.' The key statement here is the author's contention that 'poetry is the spontaneous overflow of powerful feelings'. 'It takes its origin', Wordsworth maintains, 'from emotion recollected in tranquillity.' This notion is given practical incarnation in the 'Daffodils', which begins by describing the bald fact of seeing the 'host of golden daffodils' as the poet walks beside the lake at Grasmere. It is only later that the experience, 'recollected in tranquillity', fires his imagination:

> For oft when on my couch I lie
> In vacant or in pensive mood,
> They flash upon that inward eye
> Which is the bliss of solitude.
> And then my heart with pleasure fills
> And dances with the daffodils.

Memory, the trace of lived and loved experience, sparks the creative faculty of imagination. The emphasis is not on precise description of the flowers – Wordsworth was not a professional botanist – but upon the poet's imagina-tive engagement with them.

At the same time, alongside Wordsworth's notion of the poet as some-one blessed with a privileged sensibility is an insistence on the concomitant necessity for thought and contemplation. 'Poems to which any value can be attached', he writes, 'were never produced on any variety of subjects but by a man, who being possessed of more than usual organic sensibility, had also thought long and deeply.' As well as owing much to the spontaneous

overflow of the once 'vacant' creative imagination, a
also indebted to the 'pensive' state of the mind (here
'thoughtful' rather than 'worried'). Walter Pater's
Wordsworth is right to stress the poet's belief in the centra
contemplation in the conduct of life'.

Poetic vision

Wordsworth, Coleridge and the Romantic Imagination

A 'more than usual organic sensibility': there was an emphasis in Romantic
literary theory upon the grandeur and splendour of the poet's vision (even
as an undergraduate at Cambridge Wordsworth considered himself someone with a special calling, a 'bard elect'). The critic Harold Bloom maintains
that after the *Lyrical Ballads* 'the best poetry internalized its subject matter,
particularly in the mode of Wordsworth after 1798. Wordsworth had no true
subject except his own subjective nature, and very nearly all significant
poetry since Wordsworth ... has repeated Wordsworth's inward turning.'
The second part of this statement is decidedly overstated but it is undeniable that from Wordsworth to Keats, (male) Romantic poetry was preoccupied with the poetic subject, whether in moments of power and inspiration
or, indeed, in times of doubt and anxiety.

Romanticism, rather than seeing poetry – as per neoclassicism – as the
well-wrought expression of commonly held truths, pays great attention to
the 'original' and 'spontaneous' power of the creative imagination, which
from the turn of the nineteenth century was celebrated – some would say
fetishised – as never before in English literary history. Whereas Dr Johnson's
Imlac warns (in *Rasselas* (1759)) against 'that hunger of imagination that
preys incessantly upon life', the first generation of Romantic poets, in S. T.
Coleridge's phrase (in 'Dejection. An Ode' (1802)), celebrated the 'shaping
spirit of imagination' (a power which 'nature gave me at my birth', says the
poet). Both Wordsworth and Coleridge, indeed, saw the imagination as
possessing something of the divine. In his 1815 'Essay, Supplementary to
the Preface' Wordsworth declared that there was a spiritual dimension
to artistic creation, maintaining that imagination 'is given ... to incite and to
support the eternal' (in contradistinction to 'fancy', which has but 'the
power of evoking and combining').

Two years later, in the *Biographia Literaria*, Coleridge developed this
notion of the metaphysical nature of the imagination even further. He has
little time here for mimetic Fancy, which is dismissed as having 'no other
counters to play with but fixities and definites'. Turning to the imagination,
however, in famous if somewhat opaque words Coleridge attributes our
very perceptual awareness itself to what he called the 'primary imagination'. This, he declared, was nothing less than an echo of God's own act of

.on as described in scripture: 'a repetition in the finite mind of the eter-
act of creation in the infinite I AM' (the last two words are a synonym for
.od in the Old Testament book of Exodus). Closely allied to this was the
'secondary', artistic form of imagination from whence springs the highest
manifestations of art, music and poetry. In this loftiest of Romantic-era
notions of poetic creation, Coleridge declares that the secondary imagination possesses something of the same 'living power' as that of the god-like
primary imagination:

> The secondary imagination I consider as an echo of the former ... identical with the
> primary in the *kind* of its agency, and differing only in *degree*, and the *mode* of its
> operation.

Coleridgean thought in its most optimistic and idealistic mode saw something of the divine in the act of poetic creation. 'Poets', writes Coleridge, are
'Gods of love that tame the chaos'. Poetry in its most elevated cast echoes
God's creation. The power and beauty of the 'lovely forms' of nature are met
with a response which proceeds from the creative power of the human soul,
again in the words of 'Dejection':

> from the soul itself must issue forth
> A light, a glory, a fair luminous cloud
> Enveloping the earth.

'One Life' Philosophy

In the famous passage from the thirteenth chapter of the *Biographia*
discussed above, Coleridge portrays the secondary imagination as a force
which 'dissolves, diffuses, dissipates, in order to recreate ... it struggles to
idealize and to unify'. This is central to the poet's thinking, which manifested a life-long quest for philosophical and spiritual unity. As he wrote in
a letter to John Thelwall of October 1797, 'My mind feels as if it ached to
behold and know something *great*, something *one* and *indivisible*' (and in
the *Biographia* he similarly refers to the 'high spiritual instinct of the human
being impelling us to seek unity'). During the 1790s this longing for unity
was expressed in the Unitarian brand of Christianity which Coleridge
espoused for most of the decade (see 'Religion and Atheism' for a discussion of Coleridge's spiritual faith), but also in the philosophical concept of
the 'One Life' which preoccupied him in the mid-1790s and that
Wordsworth also briefly espoused around the time of the composition
between 1797 and 1799 of the *Lyrical Ballads* and the *Two-Part Prelude*
(1797–9). In a fragment written in 1799 Wordsworth writes of:

> the one interior life
> that lives in all things ...
> In which all beings live with God, themselves
> Are God, existing in the mighty whole.

In this notion there is One Life, to use Coleridge's coinage, 'within us and abroad', a power binding all of creation together in one united and tremendous whole, uniting all of creation in – to use two quintessentially Coleridgean words – love and joy. This notion is encapsulated in a stanza added to his 1796 poem 'Effusion XXV' in that poem's re-publication in Coleridge's *Sibylline Leaves* (1817):

> Oh the one life within us and abroad,
> Which meets all motion and becomes its soul,
> A light in sound, a sound-like power in light,
> Rhythm in all thought, and joyance everywhere –
> Methinks it should have been impossible
> Not to love all things in a world so filled.

The recast 'Effusion' is retitled 'The Eolian Harp'. A key Romantic-era conceit compared the 'wondrous interchange' of nature and imagination with the workings of the Aeolian harp – a musical instrument not played by human hands, which, when placed at a window, would make sounds as the wind blew through its strings:

> And what if all of animated nature
> Be but organic Harps diversely framed,
> That tremble into thought, as o'er them sweeps
> Plastic and vast, one intellectual breeze,
> At once the Soul of each, and God of all?

Again Coleridge stresses the creative power of the God-given intellectual breeze which leads 'animated nature' through what Keats later called 'the vale of Soul making'. The creative imagination is like the harp; as God and nature 'roll through' it (to adapt a phrase from 'Tintern Abbey'), it responds in music of its own making.

There is a clear logic underpinning Coleridge's assertion in 'The Eolian Harp' that it would be 'impossible / Not to love all things in a world' created by a benign creator. 'No sound is dissonant which tells of Life,' as the final line of another Coleridgean poem of the One Life, 'This Lime Tree Bower my Prison' (1797), puts it. Even creatures of ill omen and supposed ugliness – the line refers to a rook (to some country folk a harbinger of death) which flies 'creeking' overhead. The bird is still part of the ultimately benign force of the One Life.

\id passage of the *Biographia Literaria* on the composition of
's Coleridge describes his role as to provide verse dealing
_ uoes the 'Rime of the Ancient Mariner' (the only poem of this
nature Coleridge actually finished in time to be published in the first
volume) – 'persons and characters supernatural, or at least romantic' (that
is, 'exotic' or 'fanciful' in the contemporary senses of that term). At the
same time, he was to add both 'a human interest' to such narrative and 'a
semblance of truth' to it, thereby 'procur[ing] for these shadows of imagination that willing suspension of disbelief for the moment, which constitutes
poetic faith'. Our scepticism and insistence upon rational logic are put
aside, and we can afford a measure of empathy, 'human interest', to the
macabre tale of the mariner, his dying confreres, the albatross, and the
Nightmare-Life-in-Death. And to the conceptual framework of the poem is
added a verisimilitude, a 'semblance of truth' – or at least Coleridgean truth.
Thus, for example, the episode with the sea snakes, in which the Ancient
Mariner sees and blesses them in the waters – thereby ensuring his deliver-
ance from his unwelcome avian burden – is simultaneously dramatic
grotesquerie and testimony to the thematic concerns of the wider
Coleridgean philosophy. A conventional interpretation of the 'Rime' is that
the Mariner's shooting of the albatross 'is a crime against the One Life ...
possible only to a man who had not seen the unity of all life in the world' (as
John Beer puts it) and that his serpentine benedictions allow him to be
reconciled once again with that mighty power.

Coleridge and Nature

In his 'Frost at Midnight' (1798), one of his meditative 'conversation poems'
of the late 1790s, the poet's finest achievements in blank verse (perhaps
paradoxically, these 'conversations' are generally addressed to someone
either absent – Charles Lamb in 'This Lime Tree Bower' – or incapable, as
here, of understanding what the poet is saying to him), Coleridge added
further dignity to the natural world by portraying it as the 'eternal language'
of God. The landscape bears the trace of the all-creating hand of the
Almighty. The poem, addressed to its author's infant son Hartley who
'slumbers peacefully' beside him, envisages the 'dear Babe' as a growing
lad close to nature, living amid the sublime and educative scenes of the
natural landscape:

> beneath the crags
> Of ancient mountain, and beneath the clouds,
> Which image in their bulk both lakes and shores
> And mountain crags: so shalt thou see and hear

The lovely shapes and sounds intelligible
Of that eternal language, which thy God
Utters, who from eternity doth teach
Himself in all, and all things in himself.

This is, of course, very close to a Wordsworthian childhood. Coleridge, though born in the West Country, describes himself as 'reared / In the great city', London (he attended Christ's Hospital school), where 'pent 'mid clois-ters dim, [he] saw nought lovely but the sky and stars'. Better far for his own son to 'wander like a breeze / By lakes and ... ancient mountain' learning the lessons of the 'Great universal Teacher'.

Romanticism and Childhood

As 'Frost at Midnight' and *The Prelude* demonstrate, both Coleridge and Wordsworth believed in the central importance of childhood experience in shaping adult consciousness; 'the child is father of the man', as Wordsworth puts it in his short lyric 'The Rainbow' (1802). In an inspired passage from his *Suspiria de Profundis* (1845), Thomas De Quincey says something similar in writing of the lingering power of the deepest emotional moments of childhood, 'the deep, deep tragedies of infancy, as when the child's hands were unlinked for ever from his mother's neck, or his lips for ever from his sister's kisses, these remain lurking below all, and these lurk to the last'. William Wordsworth, hero-worshipped by the young De Quincey, labelled key moments of power in his own youth 'spots of time' in a famous passage from the 1799 *Prelude*:

There are in our existence spots of time
That with distinct pre-eminence retain
A fructifying virtue, whence ... our minds
Especially the imaginative power
Are nourished and invisibly repaired.
Such moments chiefly seem to have their date
In our first childhood.

Such episodes do not have to bear the emotional weight of losing a mother as in De Quincey's prose-poem peroration. Indeed, they can seem mundane – the spots include descriptions of skating, birds' nesting, and the boy Wordsworth stealing a boat at Patterdale. Nonetheless they serve a dual purpose in Wordsworth's singular account, being educative of the child and creatively nourishing to the adult poet. This is despite the fact that some of the memories, as Jonathan Wordsworth has written, notwithstand-ing 'their vividness ... have in common the presence of fear'; the boy

Wordsworth was, to borrow his Burkean phrase from the *Prelude*, 'fostered alike by beauty and by fear' (see 'Medievalism, the Sublime and the Gothic' for Burke and the sublime). However, whether in moments of fear – Wordsworth's description of his guilt as he propels the stolen boat over Ullswater – or beauty – his joy as he skates alone over Esthwaite Water – the spots of time, later in life, nourish 'the imaginative power' of the poet.

Whether in short lyric ('The Rainbow'), extended lyric ('Lines Composed a Few Miles above Tintern Abbey on Revisiting the Banks of the Wye Valley During a Tour, July 13, 1798') or fourteen-book autobiographical epic (the 1850 *Prelude*), this relationship between the child and the man is a central concern of many of Wordsworth's finest poems. 'Tintern Abbey', of course, draws an explicit contrast between Wordsworth's younger and older selves and their response to the natural landscape. Even though the ecstasies of his childhood response to nature (its 'aching raptures' and 'dizzy joys') are gone, for 'such loss', he says, he has received 'Abundant recompense':

> For I have learned
> To look on nature, not as in the hour
> Of thoughtless youth; but hearing oftentimes
> The still, sad music of humanity,
> Nor harsh nor grating, though of ample power
> To chasten and subdue.

Poetry has a moral function for Wordsworth ('each of these poems has a purpose' he declares in the 1800 'Preface' to the *Lyrical Ballads*) and here he links the love of nature to the love of his fellow man, a humanistic aria that flies in the face of those critics from Byron onwards who see solipsism or lack of human empathy in his work. Taught by experience, he can now hear 'the still sad music of humanity', and this also informs his mature love for nature ('Therefore am I still / A lover of the meadows and the woods, / And mountains'). Here, too, Wordsworth dwells on the 'ennobling interchange' which he saw as giving rise to imaginative creation; in 'Tintern Abbey' poetry is described as the product of the relationship between 'the mighty world / Of eye and ear' and 'all that we behold / From this green earth' (in that brilliant phrase 'what they half create, / And what perceive').

Charles Lamb, who shared an exalted view with Wordsworth and Coleridge of 'what the soul of a child is' ('how apprehensive! how imaginative! how religious!'), rightly noted in his *Quarterly Review* notice of Wordsworth's *The Excursion* (1814) that 'His verses shall be censured as infantile by critics who confound poetry "having children for its subject" with poetry that is "childish".' How true this was. Byron's notice chastised the *Poems in Two Volumes* (1807) as being composed in 'language not simple, but puerile', Lord Jeffrey called many verses in the same collection 'low, silly, [and] uninteresting', and satirists scoffed, in such works as Richard Mant's *The Simpliciad* (1808), that Wordsworth, in Mant's phrase, 'lisp[ed in] the accents of the nursery' (see 'Satire').

William Blake and Enlightenment Philosophy

The mockery of Wordsworth's 'simplicity' notwithstanding, at least Wordsworth was not described in print as 'an unfortunate lunatic, whose personal inoffensiveness secures him from confinement', unlike his great contemporary William Blake (the description is Robert Hunt's in his 1809 *Examiner* review of the only art exhibition which Blake mounted in his lifetime). Some of this perception of Blake's supposed 'madness' was the result of his remarkable, visionary, nonconformist religious convictions (see 'Millenarianism' for an account of Blake's spirituality); Southey, for instance, called Blake a 'decided madman' on the grounds of his supposed conviction that 'Oxford Street is in Jerusalem'. Perhaps a little of this was also attributable to the remarkably combative and iconoclastic ambition of the poet's writings in verse and prose. If Blake was going to tilt at windmills they needed to be very tall ones indeed: Sir Isaac Newton and John Locke in philosophy, Homer and Virgil in poetry, and Sir Joshua Reynolds and the entire British artistic establishment in terms of the visual arts (for Blake's attitude to contemporary art, Reynolds and the Royal Academy, see 'William Blake and Romantic-Era Art'). Blake did not waste his time aiming criticism at second-rate thinkers.

The aesthetic philosophy of Romanticism developed after eighteenth-century empiricism and rationalism, and is in profound ways antagonistic to them. Blake's cherishably iconoclastic philosophy is arguably the most extreme British reaction against Enlightenment-era thought. He challenged the empiricist position that all knowledge is derived from experience (which emphasises the passivity of the human mind as it receives sense perceptions from the external world), labelling it as crass and limiting, confining the divinity of the human spirit to the 'filthy rags of memory'. To Locke (1632–1704), knowledge comes from the way in which external objects act upon the senses and are manifested in the mind as 'ideas'. The problem with this epistemology (a theory of knowledge, a philosophical attempt to account for how we learn) for certain key eighteenth-century thinkers from Burke (see 'Medievalism, the Sublime and the Gothic') to poets such as Blake and Coleridge is that, in the latter's phrase, it leaves the human mind 'a lazy Looker on an external World'. It also fails to account for humanity's perception of the grandeur of the natural landscape and, particularly for Blake, the imaginative faculty, especially as this is manifested in poetic inspiration.

Blake was loudest in the Romantic-era shout against the 'filthy

garments' of rationalism ('Rational Demonstration'), as the personal manifesto in his *Milton* (1804–8) demonstrates:

> I come in Self-annihilation & the grandeur of Inspiration,
> To cast off Rational Demonstration by Faith in the Saviour,
> To cast off the rotten rags of memory by Inspiration,
> To cast off Bacon, Locke & Newton from Albion's covering,
> To take off his filthy garments & clothe him with Imagination,
> To cast aside from Poetry all that is not Inspiration,
> That it no longer shall dare to mock with the aspersion of Madness.

The poet here repudiates the Enlightenment *bêtes noires* Locke and
Newton, throwing in the Renaissance philosopher, essayist and scientist Sir
Francis Bacon (1561–1626) for good measure ('Bacon's philosophy has
ruined England', Blake wrote in the margin of his copy of Reynolds's
Discourses). Bacon, who 'had no notion of anything but Mammon' (one of
the many ill-tempered annotations in Blake's copy of Bacon's *Essays*), is
emblematic of a society that values material things over the things of the
mind and imagination. It is telling that Blake once wrote: 'What it will be
Questiond When the Sun rises, do you not see a round Disk of fire somewhat like a guinea O no, no, I see an Innumerable company of the Heavenly
host crying, "Holy, Holy, Holy is the Lord God Almighty".'

Blake felt 'Contempt & Abhorrence' for what he described as the 'Barren
Waste' of Newtonian thought and for the natural philosophy of Locke.
Against Locke's notion of the mind as a 'tabula rasa' (a blank sheet of paper
on which experience inscribes external ideas), Blake declared that 'Innate
Ideas are in every man, Born with Him. They are truly Himself.' Though
Blake's Christianity was very far from being orthodox, a degree of his
antipathy to materialist philosophy is what he saw as its tendency towards
unbelief; 'Locke and Newton', he maintains, 'deny a Conscience in Man &
the Communication of Saints or Angels'. Blake also defends himself from
the trite charges of lunacy in the heartfelt words: 'That it no longer shall
dare to mock with the aspersion of Madness'. That said, there was also a
sense in which Blake half-delighted in the charge. In 1819, he wryly plays
with the accusation in describing an encounter in a vision with the 'mad' –
and now dead – poet Cowper who tells him, sounding very like Blake
himself, that 'You retain health and yet are as mad as any of us all – over us
all – mad as a refuge from unbelief – from Bacon, Newton and Locke.'

Blake and the Imagination

Like Wordsworth, a poet about whom he had equivocal feelings (simultaneously 'the *only poet* of the age' and, in his obsession with nature rather than

God, also 'No Poet but a Heathen Philosopher at enmity against all true Poetry or Inspiration', as a Blakean annotation to Wordsworth's 1815 *Poems* puts it), Blake sees a redemptive power in the Imagination, which he judges as capable of raising Albion (a poeticism for England) beyond the current state where it is mired, literally, in a malign materialist philosophy. Like Coleridge, Blake insists upon the spiritual nature of the imagination; another of his annotations to Wordsworth maintains that 'One Power alone makes a Poet: Imagination, the Divine Vision.' Also like Coleridge, in that poet's concept of the primary imagination, for Blake imagination is the defining faculty of God and his creation. Blake's copy of the works of the philosopher George Berkeley (1685–1753) is adorned with the words 'The Eternal Body of Man is The Imagination, that is, God himself.' Yet, he goes further than Coleridge, who always believed in a God-in-the-skies deity (however fully he was manifested in this earth), in implying an identity between God and the imaginative Man, and, indeed, raising the possibility in both his pre- and post-1790s thought that God does not exist outside of the human. Northrop Frye's *Fearful Symmetry. A Study of William Blake* maintains that Blake 'identif[ies] God with human imagination ... man in his creative acts and perceptions is God, and God is Man'. 'Man is All Imagination,' writes Blake in a note of around 1820 to a volume of Bishop Berkeley's works, 'God is Man & exists in us & we in him.'

Blake and Classicism

While Wordsworth's repudiation of neoclassicism involved fairly restrained, if undeniably antipathetic, commentary on Thomas Gray's 'poetic diction' and the use of the medieval, 'Gothic', ballad tradition (see 'Medievalism, the Sublime and the Gothic'), which positioned itself implicitly against the favoured Augustan neoclassical genres of satire, verse epistle and ode, Blake baldly and directly attacked the inheritance of Greece and Rome and, indeed, the ancient poets themselves. His is the most acerbic and ambitious attack on classicism outside of Germany in this period (for the latter, see 'What is Romanticism?'). In his 'On Virgil' (*c*.1822), Blake declares that 'Greece and Rome ... so far from being parents of Arts & Sciences, as they pretend, were destroyers of all Art.' Where Pope insisted in *An Essay on Criticism* that a poet should 'Learn hence for ancient rules a just esteem' (the works of Homer, Virgil, Horace, Ovid and Juvenal were seen for centuries as the highlights of European literary civilisation, and learning from their example, Pope implies, is only logical), Blake raged against this notion: 'The Classics it is', he says, 'the Classics, and not Goths or monks, that desolate Europe with wars'. Pope, says Blake, 'did not understand Imagination' and 'did not understand Verse'. Indeed, the poet wrote dismissively that his work was suited to what Napoleon called the nation of shopkeepers rather than to the Imagination of Albion: 'While the works of Pope and Dryden are looked upon as the same art as those of Shakspeare and Milton ... there can be no art in a nation but such as is subservient to the interest of the Monopolizing Trader.'

William Blake had no time for the Greek and Roman empires, which he saw as militaristic, imperialist pseudo-democracies built on slavery. Nor did he, unlike Pope, care for the great poets of ancient times, whom he dismissed as 'silly Greek & Latin slaves of the Sword' – not only Virgil (patronised as he was by the first Roman Emperor, the implacable Augustus Caesar), whose epic first-century poem *The Aeneid* begins 'Arms and the Man I sing', but also 'the perverted writings of Homer' which saluted battle and slaughter. In the 'Preface' to *Milton*, Blake's prose concludes – just before the first appearance of that famous lyric 'And did those feet in ancient time' – with a resounding flourish, in what might be seen as the ultimate endorsement of the Romantic creative imagination against the neoclassical temper: 'We do not want either Greek or Roman Models if we are but just & true to our own Imaginations, those Worlds of Eternity in which we shall live for ever.'

Charlotte Smith and Melancholy

'There is something in the madness of this man that interests me more than the sanity of Lord Byron and Walter Scott', remarked Wordsworth of Blake to Henry Crabb Robinson in 1812. Wordsworth, a man not given to easy praise, thought even more highly of Charlotte Smith, 'a lady', he maintained, 'to whom English verse is under greater obligations than are likely to be either acknowledged or remembered' (both Wordsworth's sonnets and aspects of his blank verse are indebted to Smith's verse). Sir Walter Scott, the most famous novelist of the age, was also an admirer of Smith's fiction (see 'The Novel'); in his *Lives of the Novelists* (1826) he labels her 'one of our most distinguished Novelists'. Scott regretted, however, 'the tone of melancholy which pervade[d Smith's] compositions', which, he argued, 'was derived too surely from the circumstances and feelings of the amiable Authoress'.

Though it is tendentious to judge a work's themes by reference to its author's life, it is plain that Smith's poetry of melancholy has at least something to do with her forlorn personal life. Scott attributed this mournfulness to Smith's unfortunate marriage. Born into a life of privilege, she was blessed, in her account, by a happy childhood, most influentially, her time at Arun in Sussex (the landscape of the South Downs affected Smith deeply as a child and informs much of her best poetry). Smith's apparently propitious destiny quickly shifted course when she was 'sold into slavery' (as she herself put it) by her father, a spendthrift and gambler, who arranged for his daughter, at fifteen, to marry the son of a prosperous West India merchant, Benjamin Smith. Though the couple had twelve children, the marriage was unhappy, with Mr Smith financially profligate, possibly violent and a reckless gamester. Financial need pushed Mrs Smith into a professional writing career: in 1783 her husband was imprisoned on a charge of embezzlement, at the King's Bench (the main London debtor's prison), for seven months and Smith began a career as an author in order to raise funds. She considered poetry her literary vocation although she also achieved considerable success as a novelist (Scott, indeed, much preferred her prose to her poetry). As an author, Smith was able to make sufficient money to support her children, though not without difficulty, and she eventually separated from her husband.

In 1784 Smith published her *Elegiac Sonnets*, written from the debtors' prison, which were an almost instant success (running to a sixth, much expanded, edition, by 1790). Their popularity owed something to their author's affecting sentiment and the air of sadness struck, as Smith called it, by 'the chords of the melancholy lyre'. She argued that this was not mere posturing but was based on her experience of real personal sorrow: 'That these [poems] are gloomy, none will surely have a right to complain; for I never engaged they should be gay. But I am unhappily exempt from the suspicion of *feigning* sorrow.' Smith maintained that her poetry was not written for public consumption; 'its notes were never intended for the public ear', she states in the 'Preface' to the sixth edition of the *Sonnets*. Indeed, Smith implies that her poetry was the unmediated product of powerful feelings within her; 'It was unaffected sorrows drew them forth. I wrote mournfully because I was unhappy.' (She adds, in a tone of lamentation, 'I have no reason yet, though nine years have since elapsed, to change my tone.') In the high Romantic manner, Smith portrays her art as spontaneous and possessed of emotional truth. (More recently, however, this notion has been challenged and qualified by Jacqueline M. Labbe's warning of the dangers of seeing an unqualified equivalence between the mournful narrative voice of the sonnets and Charlotte Smith's personal life. To Labbe, her poetry is artful as well as heartfelt; rather than 'offering a sustained picture of personal sorrow, the *Sonnets* are a compendium of identities and voices, linked by an "I" who changes costume with ease, and stage-managed and directed by Smith'.)

Smith and Nature

Smith's major poetic achievement was to develop – and adapt to the formal restrictions of the sonnet – a plainer, simpler style of poetry in which she combined fresh and vivid descriptions of the natural world with the intense expression of her personal sorrow. Although never specified, her domestic troubles shape the elegiac mood of her poems, adding an affecting poignancy to her detailed, tender recollections of the rural Sussex land-scape of her childhood, a landscape, however, in which the adult Smith can find no relief from her overwhelming despair. This is her 'Sonnet. To the South Downs' (1782):

> Ah! hills beloved! – where once, an happy child,
>   Your beechen shades, 'your turf, your flowers among',
> I wove your blue-bells into garlands wild,
>   And woke your echoes with my artless song.
> Ah! hills beloved! – your turf, your flowers remain;
>   But can they peace to this sad breast restore,
> For one poor moment soothe the sense of pain,
>   And teach a breaking heart to throb no more?
> And you, Aruna! – in the vale below,
>   As to the sea your limpid waves you bear,
> Can you one kind Lethean cup bestow,
>   To drink a long oblivion to my care?
> Ah! no! – when all, e'en Hope's last ray is gone,
>   There's no oblivion – but in death alone!

Smith writes these words in the midst of a large family of children but the intellectual tone is the same throughout: loneliness, isolation and lack of hope. Nature and the beauty of the South Downs were hugely important to her. Like Wordsworth she had a natural childhood inspired by the beauties of the natural landscape. Unlike the adult Wordsworth, however, Smith portrays herself as unable to regain the vision of nature as an adult. In Wordsworth's Romantic crisis lyric, the 'Immortality Ode', the poet begins in a situation of pain and imaginative loss but is restored by the contempla-tion of the landscape. Such consolations of nature are not available in Smith's work. Indeed, nature can be seen as troubling in her work, as a forlorn reminder of all that she has lost: 'But can they [scenes of nature] peace to this sad breast restore, / For one poor moment soothe the sense of pain?' The answer for Smith, unlike Wordsworth, is 'No'.

Smith's heightened response to nature possesses an elevated sensibility and a Romantic sensitivity to nature which marks something new in English poetry and the English sonnet. Wordsworth remarked that 'She wrote ... with true feeling for rural nature, at a time when nature was not much regarded by English poets' and acknowledged her as the true innova-tor of the form – 'the first *Modern*' to be distinguished in the sonnet. Smith, like Wordsworth, writes about the calling of a poet as if it were a vocation, as if she were a gifted person, a chosen one, one possessed of imagination and creativity. However, and this is where she varies from Wordsworth, Smith sees her creativity rather more as a burden than a gift: 'how dear the Muse's favours cost', she writes in the opening sonnet of the *Elegiac Sonnets* (a title heavy with overtones of loss and absence), and a poem which articulates a link between artistic creation and suffering: '*those paint sorrow best – who feel it most!*'

The Emigrants

While Smith's *Elegiac Sonnets* would seem to place her among the ranks of what Anne K. Mellor has termed the feminine 'poetess', her next poetic endeavour, a long narrative poem about the plight of French émigrés fleeing the Revolutionary Terror, complicates that designation with its overtly public and political concerns. *The Emigrants* (1793) portrays émigré French aristocrats escaping from the Terror and looking back at France as a 'ruin'd mass, / Flush'd with hot blood', especially the blood of one (King Louis XVI) whose 'only crime / Was being born a Monarch'. France, which once aspired to liberty, has now resorted to horror and anarchy. Smith, like Wordsworth and Coleridge, was initially a supporter of the French Revolution. Like them she also changed her mind about that event, and she did this more quickly than the male poets, directly as a response to the Terror, and, most particularly, the execution of the French king. This is not to say that Smith thought highly of the English political system; she attacks the government's treatment of the people and, in particular, the corrupt legal system, which she saw as denying her rights (Smith fought a long legal case to obtain a disputed inheritance left by her father-in-law for her children).

In *The Emigrants*, Smith toys with what would eventually be known as the 'Wordsworthian' solution of 'abjuring' or leaving society and taking solace in nature:

> How often do I half abjure Society,
> And sigh for some lone Cottage, deep embower'd
> In the green woods, that these steep chalky Hills
> Guard from the strong South West; where round their base
> The Beach wide flourishes, and the light Ash
> With slender leaf half hides the thymy turf! –
> There do I wish to hide me.

This is a classic encapsulation of the Romantic consolations of nature. Yet Smith cannot 'derive relief' from nature and she concludes, in these final, forlorn words, that nature cannot aid her. To lose oneself in nature is, in a sense, to lose sight of human communality and human suffering ('affliction') and to turn away from empathy with the sorrows of others:

> For never yet could I derive relief,
> When my swol'n heart was bursting with its sorrows,
> From the sad thought, that others like myself
> Live but to swell affliction's countless tribes!

Mary Robinson, Life and Work

Matrimonial unhappiness was a circumstance not unknown to Smith's younger contemporary Mary Robinson, née Darby (1758–1800). She, too, was married early as the result of parental pressure (at the age of fifteen, in 1773), and to a husband who hid significant debts before the marriage and contracted more thereafter. (Robinson, like Smith, spent time in the Fleet debtor's gaol with her imprisoned spouse.) Robinson packed an astonishing amount into her forty-two years. She published her first volume of verse as a teenage girl (*Poems*, 1775, a work which earned her the patronage of the famous Georgiana Cavendish, Duchess of Devonshire), and thereafter took to the stage ('The drama, the delightful drama, seemed the very criterion of all human happiness', she wrote in her memoirs). Sponsored by the famous actor-manager David Garrick, Robinson's most notable role was Perdita (which became her nickname) in a famous 1779 Drury Lane production of *The Winter's Tale*. In 1780, she became the mistress of the Prince of Wales, was then disposed of without the £20,000 'Prinny' had promised her, escaped the scandal-mongers by fleeing to Paris (where she met the ill-fated Queen of France, Marie Antoinette), became involved with the soldier, gambler and pro-slavery MP Colonel Banastre Tarleton (1754–1833) (a war-hero to the British but the implacable 'Bloody Ban' to many Americans), became partially 'crippled' from arthritis and also probably as the result of a miscarriage (1783), and from the late 1780s onwards supported herself as a poet, dramatist, feminist polemicist and novelist (in fictions such as *Vancenza* (1792) and *Walsingham* (1799); see 'The Novel').

It was in the last decade of her life that Smith wrote the verse for which she is remembered today: as a member of the Della Cruscan coterie, as a 'Jacobin' poet, as a social satirist, as a chronicler of metropolitan life, as a sonneteer and as a poet associated with the Lakes circle, especially Coleridge. At the close of the 1780s she came to notice as part of the poetic movement known as the 'Della Cruscans', led by Robert Merry ('Della Crusca'; 1755–98) and Hannah Cowley ('Anna Matilda'; 1743–1809), which was characterised by effusively self-conscious displays of emotion and the use of pseudonyms; Robinson appeared most frequently as 'Laura Maria' (she also wrote as 'Oberon', 'Tabitha Bramble' and 'Horace Juvenal' during her poetic career). In her 'Ode to Della Crusca' (1791), Robinson addressed Merry as the 'Enlighten'd Patron of the sacred Lyre / Whose ever-varying, ever-witching song / Revibrates on the heart'. The Della Cruscans were savagely ridiculed by William Gifford (see 'Satire') in the *Baviad* (1791), which 'ungallantly' – Leigh Hunt's term – mocked Robinson's moral reputation. Critics frequently attacked 'Perdita' on sexual grounds, alleging that she was promiscuous, and Gifford sneers at her sexuality and her disability in envisaging Robinson 'move / On crutches tow'rds the grave, to "Light o'Love"' (a euphemism for whoredom).

Robinson, Politics and the City

Robinson, like her contemporaries, espoused liberal political sentiments in her verse. She supported the Whigs during her principal acquaintance with the Duchess of Devonshire, and come the French Revolution she wrote *Ainsi va le Monde* (1790), one of the earliest British poetical salutes to events across the channel. Despite her lover's defence of the indefensible in parliament, Robinson also espoused the anti-slavery cause in poems such as 'The Storm' (1796; republished as 'The Negro Girl' in 1800). Less political but just as elevated as *Ainsi va le Monde*'s heroic couplets was Robinson's sonnet sequence *Sappho and Phaon* (1796), which relates the story, in sonnets imitative of 'that sublime Bard' John Milton (i.e. rather than Shakespeare), of the poet Sappho's ill-fated love for the boatman Phaon. (Previous versions of the tale by Ovid and Pope, writes Robinson boldly, actually served rather to 'depreciate than to adorn the Grecian Poetess'; she will offer 'the most liberal accounts of that illustrious woman').

Robinson was also an able satirist both in her fiction and in her verse, most notably in terms of the latter in *Modern Manners* (1793) (see 'Satire' for discussion of this poem). She published extensively in newspapers and magazines, especially in the *Morning Post* (a liberal newspaper to which Wordsworth and Coleridge also contributed). Perhaps her finest effort in the *Post* was 'A London Summer Morning' (1794). If the stereotype of Romantic poetry is that it is rural, provincial and celebrates nature, here Robinson walks on the other side of the street in engaging with the vibrant hustle and bustle of London life. Where Wordsworth's sonnet 'Composed upon Westminster Bridge, September 3, 1802' depicts the paradoxically tranquil beauty of the metropolis in the morning and the gliding Thames, Robinson portrays 'noisy London', as 'the poor poet wakes from busy dreams, / To paint the summer morning':

> Who has not wak'd to list the busy sounds
> Of summer morning, in the sultry smoke
> Of noisy London? On the pavement hot
> The sooty chimney-boy, with dingy face
> And tatter'd covering, shrilly bawls his trade,
> Rousing the sleepy housemaid. At the door
> The milk-pail rattles, and the tinkling bell
> Proclaims the dustman's office; while the street
> Is lost in clouds imperious. Now begins
> The din of hackney-coaches, waggons, carts;
> While tinmen's shops, and noisy trunk-makers,
> Knife-grinders, coopers, squeaking cork-cutters,
> Fruit-barrows, and the hunger-giving cries
> Of vegetable venders, fill the air.
> Now ev'ry shop displays its varied trade.

The noises of communal, urban activity and the shouts of commerce conjure up a busy vista of modern culture and industry. Indeed, critics have seen a vibrancy and life-affirming quality to the portrayal of the chimney-boy, maid and dustman amidst the 'din of hackney-coaches'. Anne Janowitz, for example, noting that 'these poems are not tied to her sentimental feminine pseudonyms', argues that Robinson's lines are 'life-affirming and celebratory. [They] actively acknowledge and celebrate London as the source of personal freedom and autonomous identity.'

Robinson and the 'Lake Poets'

Robinson was always quick to notice the latest poetical trends and her *Lyrical Tales* (1800) were influenced, in part, by the 1798 *Lyrical Ballads* of Wordsworth and Coleridge. The debt was not just taxonomic; the Gothic atmospherics of the central poem of that collection 'The Haunted Beach', for instance, owe much to 'The Rime of the Ancient Mariner'. Indeed, Robinson contracted a poetic and personal friendship with Coleridge (she visited Keswick in 1800). The poet who had apostrophised Robert Merry turned her affections to Coleridge in praise verses such as 'To the Poet Coleridge' and the 'Ode inscribed to the Infant Son of S. T. Coleridge' (both 1800). The latter was addressed to young Derwent Coleridge, who was born on 14 September 1800, only weeks before the poet's death. Just as Coleridge had envisaged a Lake District childhood – very different from his own in London – for his son Hartley, so Robinson sees Derwent treading a route more blest than her wanderings through, in those heartfelt words, 'life's disastrous maze':

And blest, amid thy mountain haunts sublime,
  Be all thy days, thy rosy infant days,
And may the never-tiring steps of time
    Press lightly on with thee o'er life's disastrous maze.

Mary Robinson knew Coleridge's 'Kubla Khan' in manuscript, and one of the earliest references in print to that poem occurs in 'To the Poet Coleridge' in which she vows to 'mark thy *sunny dome*, and view / Thy *Caves of Ice*, thy fields of dew!' This poem, indeed, sees Robinson assume the mantle of the Romantic poet, in portraying herself as 'Rapt in the visionary theme!' 'Spirit Divine!', she declares of Coleridge, 'with thee I'll wander'; here Robinson, so to speak, joins the boys' club. In the verses for Derwent, she portrays herself as the untutored daughter of the Muse, an 'untaught Minstrel'; the poet, towards the end of her poetic career, represents herself as a fully fledged Lake poet, blessed with the gift of spontaneous poetic creation.

Coleridge, in return, was an admirer, albeit qualified, of Robinson's verse, describing her as a 'woman of undoubted Genius' to Robert Southey in 1800: 'I never knew a human Being with so *full* a mind – bad, good, & indifferent, I grant you, but full, & overflowing.' On reading 'The Haunted Beach' in the *Morning Post* in February 1800 – that 'poem of fascinating metre' – Coleridge noted that the images 'are new and very distinct – that "silvery carpet" is so *just* that it is unfortunate it should *seem* so bad, for it is *really* good – but the metre – aye, that woman has an ear!' Robinson's own assumption of the oracular power of the poet's song and her hymns to the sublime genius of Coleridge were returned by the male poet in 'A Stranger Minstrel', written in the last few weeks of Robinson's life, in which Coleridge portrayed the elder poet as a 'Lady of sweet song' and paid elegant compliments back, couched in sublime terms, in praising Robinson's 'magic song' and 'divinest melody'.

Like Charlotte Smith and, indeed, many other authors in literary history, Robinson wrote to make money, and she wrote in a variety of poetic styles and genres and under a variety of pseudonyms. She was also frequently associated with the poetic *avant garde*, from the now little-read Della Cruscans to the Lake Poets. As Judith Pascoe writes, 'her poetry participates in the chief aesthetic innovations of the decade'. This is indubitable; in just over ten years Robinson was sentimental poet, Jacobin poet, verse satirist, new-fangled sonneteer, and, finally, a poet of the lakes. Like Byron (see 'Literary and Philosophical Key Concepts II'), she is generally seen to have assumed a series of poetic personae. However, where Byron is held to have constructed a series of versions of himself, Robinson was more of a 'chameleon poet', to use Keats's phrase. Whereas Smith, with her attention to nature and preoccupation with the nature of poetic selfhood, fits the

template of the 'Romantic poet', Robinson, the subject of much recent critical attention, is generally seen as rather a different poetic animal. Pascoe
maintains that 'her adoption of a retinue of alternate poetic identities,
coupled with her frank pursuit of commercial success, clash with the
prevailing stereotype of the Romantic poet with its emphasis on naturalness,
authenticity, and spirituality'. Janowitz sees Robinson's gist as that of a
mimic, one 'drawn to the forms and subjects conceived by others'. To her
this was the way in which Robinson compensated for, and made good, her
'personal insecurity [and] feelings of being an outsider in the world'. This is
certainly a different spin on what constitutes Romanticism – in emphasising
studied imitation over the spontaneous outpouring of powerful feelings –
and it may be that it underestimates Robinson's own originality (just
because two trees of the same species grow from the same earth it does not
mean that the one planted second is mimicking the other). But either way,
Pascoe is right to maintain that 'Robinson's writings reflect the extent to
which her poetry serves as a kind of cultural barometer of aesthetic change.'

See also   Satire; William Blake and Romantic-Era Art.

Further Reading

M. H. Abrams, *The Mirror and the Lamp: Romantic Theory and the Critical Tradition* (1953).
Peter Ackroyd, *Blake* (1995).
Matthew Arnold, 'Thomas Gray', in *The English Poets*, 3 vols (1881), 3, 303–16.
Walter Jackson Bate, *Coleridge* (1968).
G. E. Bentley, Jr, *Blake Records* (1969; revised 2004).
Harold Bloom, *Agon* (1982).
Morris Eaves (ed.), *The Cambridge Companion to William Blake* (2003).
David V. Erdman, *Blake: Prophet against Empire* (1954; revised 1977).
V. A. De Luca, *Words of Eternity: Blake and the Poetics of the Sublime* (1991).
Kelvin Everest, *Coleridge's Secret Ministry: The Context of the Conversation Poems 1795–1798* (1979).
Northrop Frye, *Fearful Symmetry: A Study of William Blake* (1947).
Stephen Gill, *William Wordsworth: A Life* (1989).
Stephen Gill (ed.), *The Cambridge Companion to Wordsworth* (2003).
Geoffrey H. Hartman, *Wordsworth's Poetry, 1787–1814* (1964).
Richard Holmes, *Coleridge: Early Visions* (1989).
Richard Holmes, *Coleridge: Darker Reflections* (1998).
Anne Janowitz, *Women Romantic Poets: Anna Barbauld and Mary Robinson* (2004).
Jacqueline M. Labbe, *Charlotte Smith: Romanticism, Poetry and the Culture of Gender* (2003).
Alan Liu, *Wordsworth: The Sense of History* (1989).
Paul Magnuson, *Coleridge's Nightmare Poetry* (1974).
Charles Mahoney, *Romantic and Renegades: The Poetics of Political Reaction* (2003).
Anne K. Mellor, *Romanticism and Gender* (1993).
Lucy Newlyn (ed.), *The Cambridge Companion to Coleridge* (2002).
Judith Pascoe (ed.), *Mary Robinson, Selected Poems* (1999).

Walter Pater, *Appreciations* (1889).

Seamus Perry, *Coleridge and the Uses of Division* (1999).

Nicholas Roe, *Wordsworth and Coleridge: The Radical Years* (1988).

Mark Storey, *Poetry and Humour from Cowper to Clough* (1979).

E. P. Thompson, *Witness Against the Beast: William Blake and the Moral Law* (1993).

Carl Woodring, *Politics in the Poetry of Coleridge* (1961).

Jonathan Wordsworth, 'The Romantic Imagination', in *A Companion to Romanticism*, ed. Duncan Wu (1999), 486–94.

William Wordsworth, *The Pedlar, Tintern Abbey, the Two-Part Prelude*, ed. Jonathan Wordsworth (1985).

Literary and Philosophical Key Concepts II: The Second Generation Romantic Poets (Byron, Shelley, Keats, Hemans, Landon)

Byron

Everyone knows at least one thing about the man thought in his day to be the iconic figure of what we in our day think of as the post-Wordsworthian cohort of poets (the 'Second Generation Romantic Poets', as they have been known since the turn of the twentieth century). Lord Byron, in the famous words of his spurned mistress Lady Caroline Lamb, was 'mad, bad, and dangerous to know'. This was someone whose attraction, wit and personal incandescence could both trouble and enchant. Coleridge, once charmlessly mocked as a poetic donkey in his lordship's literary satire *English Bards and Scotch Reviewers* (1809; see 'Satire'), declared of Byron that 'So beautiful a countenance, I scarcely ever saw.' 'His eyes', said Coleridge, were the 'open portals of the sun, things of light'. Byron's work was similarly fascinating to his peers; the poet had a Europe-wide audience receptive to what John Wilson of *Blackwood's* (a diehard Tory who had no time for Byron's political radicalism) called 'the almost incomprehensible charm, and power, and enchantment of his poetry'.

At the same time, there were also those who saw the poet as something of a misanthropic genius. The French novelist Flaubert (1821–80) identified 'a spirit of malice toward the human race' in Byron's verse and, indeed, the poet's 'intention of laughing in its face'. Wilson himself, more charitably, saw both high moral aspiration in Byron's work and a conviction therein that mankind was far from what it should be: the 'contrast between his august conceptions of man, and his contemptuous opinions of men' (this latter scorn was, indeed, expressed both in Byron's narrative and in his satirical poetry). This mixture of radiance and darkness might be seen as emblematic of much post-Napoleonic and Byronic-era literature, the age of the 'Byronic hero', the beautiful but damned protagonists of his lordship's early narrative poems, of that most fascinating of monsters in Mary Shelley's *Frankenstein* (1818), and of Thomas De Quincey's narcotic fantasia *Confessions of an English Opium*

Eater (1822), a book which offers in turn an account of the imaginative pleas-ures and – perhaps more strikingly – the imaginative pains of drug addiction. The Romantic imagination which Wordsworth and Coleridge had celebrated at the turn of the nineteenth century as nurturing and nourishing is frequently seen in this later literature as rather darker, sometimes even as wounding. Wordsworth's watery metaphor of the 'spontaneous overflow of powerful feelings' is replaced by the fiery incandescence of Byron's imagery in his memorable conceptualisation of the 'lava of the imagination', that powerful creative force 'whose eruption prevents an earthquake'.

The Byronic Hero

Emblematic of what might be called this tormented side of second-generation Romanticism is the Byronic hero, the versions of himself which the poet served up to great popular success in works such as *Childe Harold's Pilgrimage* (1812–18), *The Giaour* (1813) and *Manfred* (1817). Thomas Babington Macaulay acutely described the Byronic (anti-)hero as 'a man proud, moody, cynical, with defiance on his brow and misery in his heart, a scorner of his kind … yet capable of deep and strong affection'. In his portrayal of these men, fascinating outsiders above the normative values of contempo-rary society, often preoccupied with pain, loss and death, Byron drew on his own transgressive personality, his reputation as the rakish wit, as the sexual rebel, the lover of both women and boys who, gossip (rightly) had it, impreg-nated his own half-sister Augusta Leigh, and as the constant opponent to the Tory government which governed Great Britain in all but one of his 36 years.

Bertrand Russell once called 'Byronism' an act of 'Titanic cosmic self-assertion'. Some, like Russell, have seen the Byronic hero as – in Friedrich Nietzsche's phrase – someone 'beyond good and evil', as if normal moral and social codes do not apply to him. Manfred repudiates God, Satan and his devils, organised religion, and the personification of Nature, instead relying on the power of his nihilistic will. At the same time as they assert their indomitable spirit, the most notable of the Byronic heroes, such as Childe Harold and Manfred, are also capable of guilt. Manfred, in particular, laments the love of his sister Astarte which had led to her death and, in part, to his desire for 'Oblivion, self-oblivion!':

> She was like me in lineaments – her eyes,
> Her hair, her features, all, to the very tone
> Even of her voice, they said were like to mine:
> But soften'd all, and temper'd into beauty …
> …
> Her faults were mine – her virtues were her own –
> I loved her, and destroy'd her!

Whatever its moral or immoral force, this passage indubitably contains a veiled reference to Byron's own incestuous relationship with Augusta. The author of *Manfred* was willing to trade on his notoriety, and the fascinated gossip about his scandalous sexual behaviour, from the moment of the publication of his *Succès de scandale*, the first canto of *Childe Harold's Pilgrimage* (the day in 1812 in which, he recalled, he 'awoke one morning and found myself famous'). Mark Storey maintains that Byron's self-portrayals allowed him to achieve 'what so many of the other major Romantic poets were anxious to achieve – the dramatisation of the self in poetry'. This was done via a series of dramatic personae, from Childe Harold to Don Juan, rather than, as was the way of Wordsworth and Coleridge, talking about himself in what the older poets presented as a direct and sincere first-person poetical manner. Indeed, opinion was divided in the nineteenth century as to how 'real' Byron's representations of the self actually were. Francis Jeffrey of the *Edinburgh Review* wrote of the 'dreadful air of sincerity' which surrounded Byron's verse, while W. M. Thackeray, on the other hand, maintained 'That man never wrote from the heart. He got up rapture and enthusiasm with an eye for the public.' In this latter account, the poetry of the Lake poets is 'sincere', whilst that of Byron is attitudinising, involving little more than the cynical marketing of the author's fascinating and dangerous personality in a meretricious attempt to sell more books.

Byron and the Lake Poets

Apart from his brief immersion, in the Wordsworthian manner, in the 1816 third canto of *Childe Harold*, the result of Shelley, in Byron's words, 'dosing him to physic' [that is, drugging him to the point of nausea] with Wordsworth' (he would as a result, he jested, happily 'have blown my brains out, but for the recollection that it would have given pleasure to my mother-in-law'), Byron treated the Lake Poets with some contempt, his literary antipathy allied to disappointment at what he saw as their political Iscariotism, their transformation from 'the Republican Trio' of the 1790s to hard-line Tories, which was all too evident by the 1810s. In the Dedication to *Don Juan* (1819–24), for instance, Byron offers a spoof tribute to 'Bob Southey!', the 'Poet Laureate' who – in Byron's comical feminine rhyme – has 'turn'd out a Tory at / Last', and in the same poem he mocks the Tory convictions of Wordsworth, an author who once 'season'd his Pedlar Poems with democracy'.

To some extent, all of the second-generation Romantic poets found their poetic feet by aiming kicks at papa, but of the various degrees of scepticism expressed by these poets, Byron's was the sharpest. In one of his earliest publications, a review of Wordsworth's 1807 *Poems in Two Volumes*, he had dismissed the elder poet's experiments as couched in 'language not simple but puerile'. In *English Bards and Scots Reviewers*, he mocked the 'simple Wordsworth' as an 'Idiot in his glory' and the asinine Coleridge as the 'Laureat [*sic*] of the long-ear'd kind'. Alongside the high Romantic posturings of *Manfred* and the third canto of *Childe Harold* Byron also manifested an admiration for Augustan poetics, notably the work of his poetic hero Alexander Pope, which was not generally evident in the work of his predecessors (see 'Literary and Philosophical Key Concepts I'). Writing of Wordsworth, Southey, Thomas Moore and himself, Byron once maintained that 'we are upon a wrong revolutionary poetical system – or systems – not worth a damn in itself'. Where Blake had maintained that Pope 'did not understand Imagination' and 'did not understand Verse', Byron actively proselytised for the satirist in a series of articles in 1821 on 'The Life and Writings of Pope', and in *Don Juan* set out his famous commandments in which he endorses the poets of the neoclassical age over those of the modern:

> Thou shalt believe in Milton, Dryden, Pope;
>   Thou shalt not set up Wordsworth, Coleridge, Southey;
> Because the first is craz'd beyond all hope,
>   The second drunk, the third so quaint and mouthy.

Don Juan

Like Pope, Byron's greatest work is generally seen as his satire, especially the late satirical poems *Beppo* (1818) and, most significantly, *Don Juan* (1819–24). The latter was an attack on – and conscious attempt to provoke – what Byron ironically calls 'moral England' and was intended as 'a satire on the abuses of the present state of society'. It was, Byron wrote to his publisher John Murray, 'a little quietly facetious upon everything'. 'Quietly' is not perhaps the right word, but Byron's satire is certainly wide-ranging. Alongside the literary satire on the Lakers (for fuller discussion of this aspect of the work and *Don Juan*, see 'Satire'), Byron's poem also contains much socio-political satire, mocking what he saw as widespread sexual hypocrisy, the tyrannical political systems found all over Europe, and, in the later 'English cantos', the social and political condition of contemporary Britain.

Shelley: Poetics and Politics

Lord Byron's friend and political ally Percy Bysshe Shelley also employed a post-Wordsworthian expressive model of poetic creation, declaring, for instance, that his great poem 'Mont Blanc' (1817) sprang, in part, from the 'undisciplined overflowing of the soul'. 'It was composed', he writes in the 'Preface' to the *History of a Six Weeks' Tour through a Part of France, Switzerland, Germany and Holland* (1817), 'under the immediate impression of the deep and powerful feelings excited by the objects which it attempts to describe'. Again like William Wordsworth, Shelley saw the imagination as possessed of ethical power. 'The great instrument of moral good is the imagination', he declared in his famous essay 'A Defence of Poetry' (1821). Shelley, a ruminative, idealising, and sceptical poet in turn, lived amidst a world which the author – a radical, atheistical free-thinker – viewed as far from ideal, confronted as he was by a European geopolitical reality in which, in the words of his *Prometheus Unbound* (1820), 'Despair smothers the struggling world, / Which slaves and tyrants win.' Shelley's verse, with its visionary philosophy, Neo-Platonic 'ideal forms', and preoccupation with love and beauty, was not a matter of abstraction ('mere speculation and fancy', in Hazlitt's dismissive description of the elevated philosophical longings evident in Shelley's more Empyrean flights); for him it served the cause of liberty.

Shelley was the most politically radical of the Romantic poets, a genera-tion of poets all of whom, at least in their youth, espoused radical convic-tions. Indeed, Karl Marx 'regret[ted] Shelley's death at the age of twenty-nine, because he was a revolutionary through and through and would consistently have stood with the vanguard of socialism' (it was, on the other hand, 'fortunate that Byron died in his thirty-sixth year, for he would have become a reactionary bourgeois had he lived longer; conversely'). At the heart of Shelley's life and work was this search for 'Moral good' in its widest sense. To him this included the search for justice in many things: personal ethics, philosophy, politics, sexuality and religion. From boyhood the 'Eton atheist', as he was known at school, demonstrated the philosophical fearlessness evident when he was sent down (expelled) from University College, Oxford, for refusing to recant the pamphlet he had co-authored with T. J. Hogg which bore the uncompromising title 'The Necessity of Atheism' (for Shelley's religious views – or lack of them – see 'Religion and Atheism'). Undaunted, the youthful radical soon after published a studiedly subversive philosophical poem *Queen Mab* (1813), composed when he was twenty-one, a poem in mixed metre (Shelley explained that 'The didactic [part] is in blank heroic verse, and the descrip-tive in blank lyrical measure') which is accompanied by extended, discur-sive prose notes ('long and philosophical – and antichristian' in its author's description) on subjects close to the poet's heart – human perfectibility, love, the vegetable diet, philanthropic treatment of animals – and those not so close to it – war, religion, marriage, prostitution, and private property.

The whole is garnished with supporting citations from religiously sceptical British philosophers (such as William Godwin and David Hume) and also continentals (notably Baron d'Holbach (1723–89) and the Marquis de Condorcet (1743–94)). As Shelley later put it, his notes set their face 'against Jesus Christ, & God the Father, & the King, & the Bishops, & Marriage, & the Devil knows what'.

In a note to the incendiary *Queen Mab*, Shelley attacks marriage and declares that 'Love is free.' 'To promise for ever to love the same woman', he maintains, 'is not less absurd than to promise to believe the same [Christian] creed.' Allied to this sexual radicalism, which Shelley certainly put into practice in his tangled private life, is a more philosophical, less earthy notion of love which echoes through Shelleyan thought. 'Love' is 'the great secret of morals', the poet writes in the 'Defence'. If Byron in his non-satirical verse was a poet of the passions, then Shelley, with his preoccupation with love, was a poet of the heart. To Shelley, a Platonic ideal of love shapes the universe (in a manner analogous to Coleridge's notion of the 'One Life'): he writes in his fragmentary essay 'On Love' (*c*.1815) that 'This is the bond and the sanction which connects not only man with man, but every thing which exists.' In this period, both Keats and Shelley were simultaneously bestowing great theoretical weight on the notion of human empathy, but where the former sees this quality as the font of poetic creation in the Shakespearean manner, Shelley views it in ethical terms: 'A Defence of Poetry' declares that 'The great secret of morals is love; or a going out of our own nature, and an identification of ourselves with the beautiful which exists in thought, action, or person, not our own.' In Shelley's opinion, this was something that Wordsworth, whatever his magnificent poetic talents, was incapable of appreciating; in his Wordsworthian parody, *Peter Bell the Third* (1819), Shelley calls the elder poet 'a kind of moral eunuch'.

Despite his constant engagement with moral issues, Shelley did not see himself as a systematic moral philosopher or political scientist (though his second wife said that he combined 'a brilliant imagination' with 'a logical exactness of reason'). Indeed, he maintained that these were roles not appropriate to the poet. In the 'Preface' to *Prometheus Unbound*, he argues that it 'is a mistake to suppose that I dedicate my poetical compositions solely to the direct enforcement of reform, or that I consider them in any degree as containing a reasoned system on the theory of human life'. Some might see this as something of an act of deliberate poetical amnesia, given the unequivocal political tenor of the previous year's sonnet 'England in 1819' and the furious soap box oratory of 'The Mask of Anarchy' (also 1819), the poet's response to the 'Peterloo' massacre (see 'British Politics 1815–1832'), but Shelley's point here is that poetry is not 'solely' dedicated to reform and nor does it have the responsibility to offer a 'reasoned system' (otherwise it may as well be expressed in a prose pamphlet or philosophical treatise).

Poetry serves other purposes, Shelley suggests, its role to offer 'beautiful idealisms' to the service of mankind:

> Didactic poetry is my abhorrence; nothing can be equally well expressed in prose that is not tedious and supererogatory in verse. My purpose has hitherto been simply to familiarize the highly refined imagination of the more select classes of poetical readers with beautiful idealisms of moral excellence; aware that, until the mind can love, and admire, and trust, and hope, and endure, reasoned principles of moral conduct are seeds cast upon the highway of life which the unconscious passenger tramples into dust, although they would bear the harvest of his happiness.

This may have something of the Oedipal to it, offering an implicit rebuke to Wordsworth's declaration in the 'Preface' to the *Lyrical Ballads* that 'Each of these poems has a purpose' (1800). It might also be said that it was Shelley himself who wrote of 'the didactic' nature of his *Queen Mab*'s 'blank heroic verse' (the vast majority of the poem, in fact). Ian Jack, indeed, describes Shelley's words here, 'Didactic poetry is my abhorrence', as 'The most misleading sentence he ever wrote'. However, great poets are not required to be intellectually consistent throughout their careers, and, besides, this passage has its own power and logic, in being part of Shelley's belief that moral reform, to allow 'the mind [to] love, and admire, and trust, and hope', must precede practical reform if true renovation of the human mind and human society was to be achieved. Shelley seems to have in mind by 'didactic poetry' a syllogistic method such as that found in Pope's *Essay on Man* (see 'Literary and Philosophical Key Concepts I'); instead of logical conclusiveness or lectures in verse, in his own poetry he aspires to offer grand and improving symbolic ideals.

'A Defence of Poetry'

Shelley's central account of 'the imaginative and creative faculty' is found in the 'Defence of Poetry', which was begun as a response to his friend Thomas Love Peacock's witty treatise 'The Four Ages of Poetry' (1820). Peacock maintains that in the current 'Age of Bronze' poets no longer have the important social role that they possessed in Shakespeare's time, the 'Golden Age' of modern poetry where verse 'had no rivals in history, nor in philosophy, nor in science', or, indeed, during 'the age of Homer, the Golden Age of [classical] poetry'. Nowadays, wrote Peacock provocatively, the role of poet is atavistic ('a poet in our times is a semi-barbarian in a civilised community') and clever young men should 'withdraw attention from frivolous and unconducive to solid and conducive studies', and concentrate on useful disciplines – economics, ethics and science, for instance – in order to become 'mathematicians, astronomers, chemists, moralists, metaphysicians, historians, politicians, and political economists'.

Against this, Shelley maintains that poets still have the potential to fill the social and political roles they possessed in less modern times. Inasmuch as they are prophets and seers they have a paradoxical 'utility', to borrow Peacock's criterion of value. Though not lawmakers in practical or parliamentary terms, the poet can fulfil the role of 'legislator' as their 'beautiful idealisms of moral excellence' can provide an example to mankind:

> Poets are the hierophants of an unapprehended inspiration; the mirrors of the gigantic shadows which futurity casts upon the present; the words which express what they understand not; the trumpets which sing to battle, and feel not what they inspire; the influence which is moved not, but moves. Poets are the unacknowledged legislators of the world.

Shelley's disappointment with the 'slave' Wordsworth derives in large part from the poet reneging on his duty of philosophical legislation. In his sonnet 'To Wordsworth' (*c.*1815), he writes that the Lake poet who once, in 'honoured poverty', composed 'songs consecrate to truth and liberty', is now guilty of 'deserting these' elevated principles. It was the early 'libertarian' Wordsworth who declared in the 1802 version of the 'Preface' to the *Lyrical Ballads* that 'the Poet binds together by passion and knowledge the vast empire of human society'; Shelley's 'Defence' is a magnificent reaffirmation of that notion.

Shelley's treatise goes on to maintain that contemporary poetry, 'the expression of the imagination', is characterised by a kind of creative incandescence (Shelley's verse contains a number of related fiery metaphors of volcanic eruption and so on) in being possessed of an 'electric life':

> It is impossible to read the compositions of the most celebrated writers of the present day without being startled with the electric life which burns within their words. They measure the circumference and sound the depths of human nature with a comprehensive and all-penetrating spirit, and they are themselves perhaps the most sincerely astonished at its manifestations; for it is less their spirit than the spirit of the age.

Rather than being a 'semi-barbarian', the poet is the most modern of creatures, the foremost incarnation of 'the spirit of the age', and, furthermore, is bound by the moral responsibility that goes with that role. The renegade Wordsworth had written in 1802 that 'the objects of the Poet's thoughts are everywhere' and his successor Shelley, possessed – in T. L. Peacock's description – by an 'enthusiastic prospect of the future destiny of the world', offers a highly exalted notion of poetic creation and the 'comprehensive and all-penetrating spirit' of creation.

Keats, Poetry and Negative Capability

One of Shelley's most notable poems, *Adonais* (1821), is an elegy for John Keats, who, five years before his death, first came to prominence of a sort when Leigh Hunt included him as one of the 'Young Poets' – alongside Shelley and J. H. Reynolds – in an article published in the *Examiner* in December 1816. Keats never published a poetic manifesto equivalent to Wordsworth's 'Preface' to the *Lyrical Ballads*, or composed a counterpart of Shelley's 'Defence of Poetry', which was published after that poet's death. Instead, his critical ideas were formulated in remarkable correspondence with friends and family in which Keats detailed the key literary concepts with which he is associated today: negative capability, the 'unpoetical' nature of the greatest poets, a preoccupation with beauty and its proximity to truth, the grand march of intellect, the egotistical sublime, the notion of the poet as chameleon, and so on. The soil for Keats's verse was tilled by his correspondence, and the author achieved greatness as a letter writer before he did so in poetry.

The most famous of these ideas is that of 'negative capability', a concept Keats articulated in a letter to his brothers George and Tom of 21 December 1817:

> [A]t once it struck me, what quality went to form a Man of Achievement especially in Literature & which Shakespeare possessed so enormously – I mean *Negative Capability*, that is when a man is capable of being in uncertainties, Mysteries, doubts, without any irritable reaching after fact & reason ... This pursued through Volumes would perhaps take us no further than this, that with a great poet the sense of Beauty overcomes every other consideration, or rather obliterates all consideration.

The poet relished what he called 'the intense pleasure of not knowing' (a phrase he had recently used in annotating his well-thumbed copy of *Paradise Lost*). Being told is passive; better to live in a world of multiple possibilities and to cherish 'uncertainties, Mysteries [and] doubts'. Creative vacancy, in this account, grants 'a sense of independence, of power, from the fancy's creating a world of its own by the power of probabilities' (this from the same marginalia to Milton). Keats's biographer Walter Jackson Bate writes incisively of the negative capability passage in what remains the standard life of the poet, published in 1963, and his words are worth quoting at some length:

> [We] could paraphrase these famous sentences as follows. In our life of uncertainties, where no one system or formula can explain everything ... what is needed is an imaginative openness of mind and a heightened receptivity to reality in its full and diverse concreteness. This, however, involves negating one's own ego [which would be] dissatisfied with such insights as one may attain through this openness ... unless they can be wrenched into a part of a systematic structure of one's own making, in an egoistic assertion of one's own identity.

There is a certain anti-rationalism about this (a part of Keats's philosophy best exemplified in his wish 'for a life of sensations rather than of thoughts!'), but in Keatsian terms – as opposed to those of a logician – the position has distinct creative advantages. Sacrificing the ego and setting aside 'systematic structure' allows the poet a full immersion in his subject. Bate again:

> For a 'great poet' especially, a sympathetic absorption in the essential significance of his object (caught and realised in that active cooperation of the mind in which the emerging 'Truth' is felt as 'Beauty') ... overcomes every other consideration (considerations that an 'irritable reaching after fact and reason' might otherwise itch to pursue).

Keats viewed Coleridge, strange as it might seem, as the epitome of a poet wedded to irritable reaching ('Coleridge, for instance, would let go by a fine isolated verisimilitude caught from the Penetralium of mystery, from being incapable of remaining content with half-knowledge') and Wordsworth, rather more plausibly, as the supreme example of a poet incapable of surrendering ego. Keats saw Wordsworth, that is, as a self-absorbed poet of the 'egotistical sublime'.

W. J. Bate's Harvard colleague Douglas Bush once maintained that Keats, 'alone among the Romantic poets, consciously strove to escape from self-expression into Shakespearean impersonality'. This is a point well made. To Keats, Shakespeare was the supreme poet of negative capability, especially when compared favourably to the dominant poetic force of his own day. In a letter of February 1818 to John Hamilton Reynolds, Keats asked, with reference to Wordsworth, 'are we to be bullied into a certain Philosophy engendered in the whims of an Egotist'? Better to cultivate a poetic character in the manner of the author of *Othello*, as Keats writes to Richard Woodhouse in October 1818:

> As to the poetical character itself (I mean that sort of which, if I am anything, I am a member – that sort distinguished from the Wordsworthian or egotistical sublime, which is a thing per se and stands alone), it is not itself – it has no self – it is everything and nothing – it has no character – it enjoys light and shade – it lives in gusto,

be it foul or fair, high or low, rich or poor, mean or elevated. It has as much delight in conceiving an Iago as an Imogen. What shocks the virtuous philosopher delights the chameleon poet. It does no harm from its relish of the dark side of things, any more than from its taste for the bright one.

Part of Shakespeare's negatively capable poetry is his capacity to empathise with his subject matter, whether malign (as is the murderous schemer Iago in *Othello*), or benign (the virtuous Imogen in *Cymbeline*: 'the most tender' of Shakespeare's heroines in Hazlitt's opinion). Keats's brand of poet, who identifies empathetically with other people's natures and beings, is a poetic chameleon with 'no identity' and 'no self' of its own (Keats describes this tendency as a kind of involuntary reaction of his mind: 'If a sparrow come before my window I take part in its existence and pick about the gravel'). The letter proceeds:

> A poet is the most unpoetical of any thing in existence, because he has no identity, he is continually in for – and filling – some other body. The sun, the moon, the sea, and men and women who are creatures of impulse, are poetical, and have about them an unchangeable attribute; the poet has none, no identity – he is certainly the most unpoetical of all God's creatures.

The poet, in this highly un-Wordsworthian conceptualisation, is capable of losing all sense of self in the contemplation of external reality, making it possible for him to be anything he wants, at least in terms of the imagination.

Though no poetic 'chameleon', able to take on the aspect of external subjects, Keats saw Wordsworth as superior to the older poets in at least one capacity, in his ability, in the younger poet's fine phrase, to 'think into the human heart'. This was testimony to what Keats optimistically saw as a gradual intellectual improvement which was evident in human thought and in the progress of poetry. Writing to Reynolds in May 1818, Keats maintains that Milton 'did not think into the human heart ... as Wordsworth has done – Yet Milton as a Philosopher, had sure as great powers as Wordsworth – What is then to be inferr'd? O many things – It proves there is really a grand march of intellect.'

Keats, Suffering and the Soul

Keats was also, like all of the canonical Romantic poets, concerned with matters of religion. A free thinker, though not a Shelleyan atheist, he rejected the Christian notion of redemption in a journal-letter to George and Georgiana Keats of 21 April 1819: 'The common cognomen of this world among the misguided and superstitious is "a vale of tears" from which we are to be redeemed by a certain arbitrary interposition of God and taken to

Heaven – What a little circumscribed straightened notion!' Instead, as John Barnard has written, Keats proposed that 'the world is a vale of "soul making" in which the individual must work out his or her own salvation. Only if the individual heart feels and suffers the realities of the world can it transcend itself.' Keats writes:

> Do you not see how necessary a World of Pains and troubles is to school an Intelligence and make it a soul? A Place where the heart must feel and suffer in a thousand diverse ways! Not merely is the Heart a Hornbook [a child's reading book], it is the Minds Bible, it is the Minds experience, it is the teat from which the Mind or intelligence sucks its identity – As various as the Lives of Men are – so various become their Souls, and thus does God make individual beings, Souls, Identical Souls of the sparks of his own essence.

In Barnard's words, 'Experience and suffering are essential for the self-education of the individual intelligence into a soul.' Perhaps this is what one might call a more optimistic version of Byron's bleak existentialism ('The emphasis on the individual', writes Barnard, 'is at the centre of Keats's formulation of his spiritual existentialism'). It is also striking that Keats characterises the heart – 'the teat from which the Mind or intelligence sucks its identity' – as being feminine here, though Susan J. Wolfson argues that 'the telos is [despite this] patrilinear: "As various as the Lives of Men are ..."' ('The feminine', in Wolfson's account, 'subserves a male soul-story').

Keats and Beauty

In his discussion of the negative capability letter, Bate writes of the 'active cooperation of the mind in which the emerging "Truth" is felt as "Beauty"'. The concept of beauty is very close to the heart of Keats's poetry, and this is a reference to the final lines of the 'Ode on a Grecian Urn' (1819), which characterises the message of the urn to man in these famous words: 'Beauty is truth, truth beauty'. Similarly, the first line of Keats's most contentious poem, Endymion (1818), begins 'A thing of beauty is a joy forever' (for the controversies stirred by that volume see 'Contemporary and Victorian Criticism' and 'Satire'). Nonetheless, Keats's attitude to the ideal world of art and its symbols – the urn, the nightingale and so on – was deeply ambiguous (as in his description of the urn as a 'Cold pastoral'). Keats's lyricism, despite what some Victorian commentators thought, was not escapist. In the 'Ode to a Nightingale' (1819), for instance, the poet articulates the attraction of pure song, the world encapsulated by the nightingale, but this both enticed and at a deep level somehow repelled him. Keats is tempted – hearing the song of the bird – by the possibility of 'fad[ing] away into the forest dim' but eventually draws away from the human implication of this:

> Fade far away, dissolve, and quite forget
> What thou among the leaves hast never known,
> The weariness, the fever, and the fret
> Here, where men sit and hear each other groan;
> Where palsy shakes a few, sad, last gray hairs,
> Where youth grows pale, and spectre-thin, and dies;
>> Where but to think is to be full of sorrow
>> And leaden-eyed despairs,
> Where Beauty cannot keep her lustrous eyes,
>> Or new Love pine at them beyond to-morrow.

The 'Ode to a Nightingale' is perhaps the finest expression of the theme which echoes through much of Keats's mature work: the attraction, in a universe of suffering and pain, of an escape into an idealised realm of the imagination, and, simultaneously, the drawbacks of such transcendence: the troubling awareness, most particularly, that the desire to escape earthly imperatives and 'fade away' into the world symbolised by the nightingale involves losing touch with one's humanity, given that the bird has no experience of death, pain and suffering, those ineluctable aspects of human life. 'The "immortal bird"', as Nicholas Roe has written, 'which sings beyond the boundaries of human life, brings an intimation of the unescapable facts of existence.' As Keats put it in his journal-letter, 'a World of Pains and troubles' is 'necessary ... to school an Intelligence and make it a soul'.

Felicia Hemans, Life and Work

Felicia Dorothea Hemans (*née* Browne, 1793–1835) was the most successful female poet in terms of sales in the Romantic and early Victorian periods. Hailed in her lifetime by two of the countries of Great Britain – England and Wales – as a national poet (see 'Irish, Scottish, and Welsh Poetry'), she was also highly praised by Wordsworth (the admiration was mutual and Hemans addressed particularly admiring verses to the Lake bard), adored by the *Edinburgh Review*'s Francis Jeffrey (a sometimes stern reviewer but in her case something of a pussycat) and admired by thousands of female readers. She in turn honoured the achievements of her sex in her most famous collection, *Records of Woman* (1828), which is dedicated to the great contemporary playwright Joanna Baillie (see 'Joanna Baillie and Romantic-Era Drama').

Hemans was born in Liverpool, raised in Welsh-speaking North Wales (where she moved with her family as a girl aged seven) and died in Dublin (where her brother George was then living). A gifted child-poet, her first volume of verse, *Poems*, was published in 1808 when she was just 14. This early collection mixes poems addressed to the beauties of local Welsh scenery, such as the 'Vale of Clwyd', with celebrations of British naval successes. 'To Patriotism', for example, opens 'Genius of Britannia's land …'. (Hemans, in fact, came from a military family: two of her three brothers fought in Wellington's army and her future husband, whom she married in 1812, was a wounded veteran of the Peninsular War.)

One of the most accomplished female poets of her age, Hemans was the upholder of what later came to be seen as a Victorian ideology of domestic femininity. In *The Domestic Affections* (1812), she celebrated 'domestic bliss'. While man's domain was the public sphere of politics and war, woman had a more domestic mission:

> Domestic bliss has fix'd her calm abode,
> Where hallow'd innocence and sweet repose
> May strew her shadowy path with many a rose:
>
> …
>
> Thus, while around the storms of discord roll,
> Borne on resistless wing, from pole to pole;
> While war's red lightnings desolate the ball,
> And thrones and empires in destruction fall;
> Then, calm as evening on the silvery wave,
> When the wind slumbers in the ocean-cave,
> She dwells, unruffled, in her bow'r of rest,
> Her empire, home! – her throne, affection's breast!

Hemans's own home life, it has to be acknowledged, was by no means blissful. As did her predecessor Charlotte Smith (see 'Literary and Philosophical Key Concepts I'), Hemans had a physically fecund if ultimately emotionally unsuccessful marriage, alongside an equally fertile and significantly more successful writing career. The mother of five sons, Hemans separated from her husband in 1818 (he left her to live in Italy – claiming the couple had nothing in common – in the year after the birth of their youngest boy). The *Oxford Dictionary of National Biography* speculates that the demands of Hemans's writing career contributed to the marital breakdown; immediately prior to the break up she had published two books of verse: *The Restoration of the Works of Art to Italy. A Poem* (1816; a revised second edition, also published in 1818, came out with the eminent London publisher John Murray, an early marker of Hemans's status) and *Modern Greece: A Poem* (1817; again published by Murray). Subsequently, she wrote prolifically – producing a book a year (sometimes two) between 1818 and

1823's *The Siege of Valencia*. Following the momentous *Records of Woman* (1828) – to which we will return – she continued her extraordinary output with a further four substantial works appearing by 1834, the year before her death.

Hemans: Suffering, War and the Domestic Affections

Unlike Smith's writing, which occasionally hints at her unfortunate marriage, Hemans's poetry does not dwell on her predicament as a single parent estranged from her husband. This is not to say that her verse lacks the preoccupation with suffering associated particularly with women poets and the second generation of Romantic poets. However, what distinguishes Hemans's verse is her emphasis on the *nobility* of suffering, experienced by both men and women. She writes about male bravery in the face of fear and danger, most famously in her remarkable poem 'Casabianca' (1829). A poem much in vogue in the Victorian period, especially amongst the impressionable youth taught to recite it at school, it tells of the extraordinary courage of Giocante Casabianca, a boy aged twelve, the son of a French naval commander in the Napoleonic Wars, who remains at his post after all his shipmates have fled the flame-tossed man-o'-war and heroically goes down with his vessel (he has not received the order to abandon ship from his father who – unbeknown to the lad – lies, dying, below deck):

> The boy stood on the burning deck
>   When all but he had fled;
> The flame that lit the battle's wreck,
>   Shone round him o'er the dead.
>
>   Yet beautiful and bright he stood,
> As born to rule the storm;
>   A creature of heroic blood,
> A proud though childlike form.
>
>   The flames rolled on; he would not go
> Without his father's word;
>   That father, faint in death below,
> His voice no longer heard.

Once as well known (and as often parodied – a sure sign of its status) as Rudyard Kipling's inspirational 'If' (1910), Hemans's verses were seen as useful in inculcating a spirit of obedience and duty among the young. Her iconic poem about the bravery of a French boy, perhaps paradoxically, came to be seen as emblematic of the best of the British masculine spirit. Even so, it is a poem that many modern readers find alien – disturbing even (given the boy's age and the celebration of his death as an 'heroic' sacrifice). Some express surprise that a woman poet – and moreover one who writes elsewhere of the delights of domesticity – should choose such a militaristic, 'masculine' subject. But it is of a piece with Hemans's poetic vision. As they were in the poet's own family, in 'Casabianca' war and family feelings – the 'domestic affections' – are intertwined.

The simple emotional force of 'Casabianca' is characteristic of Hemans's art. Fortitude – both male and female – is a favourite theme. Much of her poetry celebrates women's emotional resilience. Take 'Gertrude, or Fidelity till Death' from the *Records of Woman*. This is the historical narrative of the breaking on the wheel of the German nobleman Baron Rudolph von der Wart on an 'unjust' charge of treason. Hemans portrays the sorrows of his wife Gertrude as her husband is tortured to a slow death: 'Up to the fearful wheel she gaz'd – / All that she lov'd was there'. The husband urges her to leave but Gertrude refuses:

> 'And bid me not depart', she cried,
> 'My Rudolph, say not so!
> This is no time to quit thy side,
> Peace, peace! I cannot go.
>
> ...
>
> I have been with thee in thine hour
> Of glory and of bliss;
> Doubt not its memory's living power
> To strengthen me thro' this!
>
> And thou, mine honour'd love and true,
> Bear on, bear nobly on!
> We have the blessed heaven in view,
> Whose rest shall soon be won.'

While the Baron, his limbs broken, is left to die slowly on the wheel, Gertrude abides physically and emotionally, offering her love and feminine consolation. Indeed, the narrative voice comments directly on her heroic fortitude:

> And were not these high words to flow
> From woman's breaking heart?
> Thro' all that night of bitterest woe
> She bore her lofty part.

The *Eclectic Magazine* praised Gertrude as 'a noble story', a compliment which Hemans would have cherished. 'They also serve who only stand and wait' as Milton put it; Gertrude's heart, as she watches and empathises with her husband's agonies, is as 'broken' as her husband's pitiful body. This 'most heroic devotedness', in Hemans's phrase, offers – as it does in 'Casabianca' – a model of devotion and of what Hemans calls 'humble, patient love'.

Records of Woman and **Romantic Cosmopolitanism**

Records of Woman (1828) belongs to what one might term the international republic of letters. Although she never travelled further afield than Ireland, Hemans had European antecedents – her mother was of Venetian/German origin – and she was a polyglot familiar with French, Italian, Spanish, Portuguese and German. She writes in *Records of Woman* with a broad cultural knowledge of the world, translating for her English-speaking readership stories and myths from other cultures about women – both famous and anonymous. A good example of the latter is 'The Switzer's Wife', a poem about a Swiss woman who urges her fearful husband into battle during Switzerland's medieval war of independence from Austria (the Swiss republic during the Romantic period represented to many the ideal of liberty and freedom from oppression). The poem opens in pastoral and domestic mode with a description of husband and wife gathered under the linden tree watching their young child at play. Mindful of the approaching conflict, the wife gently stirs her husband from his quiet and rouses him to battle, upon which 'He sprang up like a warrior youth awakening / To clarion sounds upon the ringing air.' Before taking his leave, he blesses her as the mother of his child and, implicitly, the Swiss nation:

> My bride, my wife, the mother of my child!
> Now shall thy name be armour to my heart:
> And this our land, by chains no more defiled,
> Be taught of thee to choose the better part!

Hemans and Sir Walter Scott, whose work she admired greatly, describe the histories and traditions of individual nations – onto which they inscribe wider universal themes of love, loss, loyalty and so on – by reference to minor 'bit-players' (individual soldiers, wives, children) rather than key participants in the actions (kings, generals and the like). At the same time Hemans also resembles Byron in what William D. Brewer describes as her 'cosmopolitan' vision; she was arguably an early representative for the globalisation of culture that has become the watchword of the early twenty-first century. Alongside patriotic poems honouring British victories in the Napoleonic War, the homes and hearths of England, and Welsh history, her trans-national verse also commemorates the heroism of the Greek and Spanish armies in such volumes as *England and Spain; or, Valour and Patriotism* (1808), *Modern Greece* (1817), and *The Siege of Valencia* (1823).

Hemans, Wordsworth and Nature Poetry

Notwithstanding her celebrations of valour and heroism, Hemans can also be viewed as a poet of nature. She shares William Wordsworth's pleasure in nature and, like him, recognises its inspirational power over the poet. Hemans's poetry not infrequently echoes Wordsworth, as in her brilliant capturing of the cadence of the 'Immortality Ode'; in 'The Hour of Death', which appeared in *The Forest Sanctuary and Other Poems* (1825): 'Youth and the opening rose / May look like things too glorious for decay ...' The two were personally acquainted, though not as closely as either of them wished. In personal terms, wrote Hemans, Wordsworth 'treated me with so much consideration, and gentleness, and care'. In 'To Wordsworth' (1828), Hemans describes Wordsworth, in the high Romantic manner, as a 'True bard and holy!':

> thou art even as one
> Who, by some secret gift of soul or eye,
> In every spot beneath the smiling sun,
> Sees where the springs of living waters lie.

The poet is a visionary, a seer, seen in Hemans's transcendental terms as possessed of a secret gift. Wordsworth replied, memorialising Hemans in highly exalted terms, using his own watery metaphor of creativity in describing her as a 'holy Spirit / Sweet as the spring, as ocean deep' in his 'Extempore Effusion upon the Death of James Hogg' (1835).

Lucy Newlyn finds in 'To Wordsworth' 'diction and cadences uncannily mirroring Wordsworth's own'. She quotes the first stanza as evidence of the observation:

> Thine is a strain to be read among the hills,
>   The old and full of voices; – by the source
> Of some free stream, whose gladd'ning presence fills
>   The solitude with sound; for in its course
> Even such is thy deep song, that seems a part
> Of those high scenes, a fountain from their heart.

Here, 'in this allegory of the reception process', writes Newlyn, 'Wordsworth becomes merged with the landscape that is the stuff of his poetry', a poetry, she adds, that is 'quietly transliterated into the domestic ideology which underpins Hemans's poetic art', evidenced in the homely hearth and gentle female voice found in stanza three:

> Or by some hearth where happy faces meet,
>   When night hath hush'd the woods, with all their birds,
> There, from some gentle voice, that lay were sweet
>   As antique music, link'd with household words;
> While, in pleased murmurs, woman's lip might move,
> And the raised eye of childhood shine in love.

The 'gentle [female] voice' gives 'new meaning', as Newlyn puts it, to Wordsworth's art, her verse arguably representing a feminising of the art of conventional male Romantic poetry.

Landon ('L.E.L.') and Love

The youngest of this generation of significant Romantic-era poets was Letitia Elizabeth Landon (1802–38), whose verse – unlike that of John Keats and P. B. Shelley – was highly successful in commercial terms in its day. Indeed, Landon, like John Keats a precocious poet, was – unlike the unfortunate Keats – able to make a living as a professional author from an early age. She published several volumes of poetry, notably *The Improvisatrice; and Other Poems* (1824), novels such as *Ethel Churchill* (1837) and a large number of contributions to magazines, particularly the *Literary Gazette* (a journal with which she was closely involved; see 'Reviews, Magazines, and the Essay'), and to literary annuals. Landon generally published her verse under her initials, 'L.E.L.'. At the start of her career, this granted the poet a measure of anonymity and mystery. Indeed, the teasing acronym came to acquire a kind of enchantment in the eyes of the public, and added to the allure of Landon's poetical persona, which was most frequently that of the adoring but inevitably rejected female lover – soft, devoted, yet melancholy.

As in the poetry of Felicia Hemans, love was a central theme of Landon's verse, although, as Jerome McGann and Daniel Reiss have written, 'the domestic and maternal love infusing so much of Hemans' work gets replaced in Landon with the subject of erotic love'. 'Erotic love' certainly, and, one might add, female suffering, something which is another central theme of Landon's poetry. 'Sappho's Song', published in *The Improvisatrice*, is a good example of both, a narrative in which the ancient Greek poet laments the loss of her lover, the ferryman Phaon, and contemplates self-destruction. Landon's Sappho, significantly, maintains that she took to poetic composition as a consequence of the sharp promptings of 'love':

> It was my evil star above,
>> Not my sweet lute that wrought me wrong;
> It was not song that taught me love,
>> But it was love that taught me song.

The link between women's poetry, sorrow and disappointment implicit in much of Landon's work is given literary form in Sappho's death song. For her, poetry cannot offer succour to the heart broken by love. Landon's thematic melancholy itself recalls the verse of her predecessor Charlotte Smith (see 'Literary and Philosophical Key Concepts I').

Sappho, argues Duncan Wu, 'was the exemplar not just of the female poet, but of the jilted lover'. She laments the inconstancy and faithlessness of her beloved:

> If song be past, and hope undone,
>> And pulse, and head, and heart, are flame;
> It is thy work, thou faithless one –
>> But no, I will not name thy name!

Both hope and song are extinguished for Sappho; one can imagine no worse fate for a poet of love. The twenty-two-year-old Landon, however, found the prospect of doomed love creatively enlivening. Wu rightly remarks of the poet's verse that 'the kind of subject-matter that appealed to her was romantic not in the sense of the sublime set-pieces of *The Prelude*, but in its melancholy preoccupation with thwarted or deceived love'. It is in Landon's focus on altered states of mind – minds made distraught by disappointment and minds distracted by beauty – in which her variant form of Romanticism resides.

The critical notion of the central importance of love in L.E.L.'s work is not new; as early as August 1824, William Maginn, reviewing the *Improvisatrice* in *Blackwood's Edinburgh Magazine*, declared that 'We have heard it said that in Miss Landon's volume there was too much love, and that it would be desirable if she would write something else. We beg your pardon – it would not.' Indeed, dwelling on love is exactly how matters should be for the female poet; in Maginn's narrow view of literary gender roles, 'lady' writers, rather than penning historical novels, philosophical treatises or political tracts, should confine themselves to 'their own ground, LOVE'. Where Maginn praised Landon for confining herself to the 'ground' of love, the modern-day feminist scholar Anne K. Mellor suggests that in her obsessive treatment of love and suffering Landon took her society's limited conceptualisation of what it meant to be female too much to heart: 'Once Landon accepted her culture's hegemonic definition of the female, she could only repeat the same story over and over. Her poetry obsessively details every nuance of female love, of female sympathy, of female imagi-nation in the service of the affections.' That said, though Mellor sees Landon as unable to transcend her patriarchal confines, she also discerns a measure of resistance in the poet's work: Landon's verse, rather than shar-ing in or bolstering up the ideology of romantic love, functions in part as a critique of that ideology; she 'always arriv[es] at the same narrative conclu-sion: such love is futile'. Landon's highly self-conscious, amatory verse which engages with the suffering of the female lover and the female poet (indeed, the two themes merge in her work) produces what McGann and Reiss call an 'art of disillusion'.

The Improvisatrice

Maginn's rambling notice of *The Improvisatrice* reads the poem – and the poet – in gendered terms, and his overall tone has much of the patronising about it (it is 'a very sweet volume of poetry' written by 'a very pretty girl, and a very good girl'). Nonetheless, he does pay some attention to the liter-ary worth of Landon's volume, praising the 'real and true warmth and tenderness of delicate feeling' of the best of her verse. *The Improvisatrice* provided Landon with a measure of critical and popular success. The title poem is a long verse narrative set in Italy which recounts the doomed love of a beautiful young female poet – the 'improvisatrice' of the poem's title – for the handsome, raven-haired, pale-cheeked, and rather Byronic youth, Lorenzo, with whom she is infatuated (loving him, in her own words, 'wildly'). Though Lorenzo is drawn to this young woman, he does not declare his love, and marries another. In the face of this inconstancy, the Improvisatrice wastes away with grief. When she is on the very brink of death, Lorenzo returns to claim her as his own, explaining that his wife (whom he married out of duty because of a childhood betrothal, and whom he loved purely as a dear friend) died following their wedding. But the Improvisatrice has sunk too low, and Lorenzo's declaration fails to rescue her from an untimely demise.

In *The Improvisatrice*, Landon feeds the age's taste for exotic tales, popularised by Byron, and arguably shares the Keatsian fondness for poems of febrile passion and desire ('The Eve of St Agnes', for instance). At the same time, the lamentable circumstances of the title tale, related in the Improvisatrice's own words, is intermixed with other, shorter, narratives, such as the aforementioned 'Sappho's Song', 'A Moorish Romance', and 'The Hindoo Girl's Song', that call forth similar scenes of doomed love affairs and female suffering, portending the Improvisatrice's own fate. The device of the interpolated narratives allows the Improvisatrice's individual tale to become every woman's story, and the whole can be read as a lament for – and perhaps also a vindication of – erotic and passionate female love.

Landon claimed to have composed her poem at speed, having written it in 'less than five weeks' (indeed, negative critics have argued that she wrote too much and too quickly). This is not insignificant; an 'Improvisatrice' in Landon's sense is a female poet who improvises, who is gifted with spontaneous poetic utterance. The term might be seen to recall Wordsworth's famous definition of poetry in the 'Preface' to *Lyrical Ballads* that 'all good poetry is the spontaneous overflow of powerful feelings'. Indeed, Jonathan Wordsworth has argued that Landon stands in the Romantic tradition of creative 'outpouring': 'Her work at this early period is characterized by outpourings (more artless than Wordsworthian spontaneity), by beauty of sound and image, and by a glow that is more than anything else an expression of personality.'

At the start of the poem, the Improvisatrice recalls her childhood in radiant verse which describes the artistic and natural worlds which shaped her:

> I am of Florence ...
> My childhood pass'd 'mid radiant things,
> Glorious as Hope's imaginings;
> Statues but known from shapes of the earth,
> By being too lovely for mortal birth;
> Paintings whose colours of life were caught
> From the fairy tints in the rainbow wrought;
> Music whose sighs had a spell like those
> That float on the sea at the evening's close;
> Language so silvery, that every word
> Was like the lute's awakening chord;
> Skies half sunshine, and half starlight;
> Flowers whose lives were a breath of delight;
> Leaves whose green pomp knew no withering;
> Fountains bright as the skies of our Spring;
> And songs whose wild and passionate line
> Suited a soul of romance like mine.

Discussing these lines, Jonathan Wordsworth locates a Keatsian element in Landon's yoking together of the sensuous realms of poetry, painting and beauty alongside the Byronic trope of love in a foreign clime. He claims Landon for 'high Romantic argument', to borrow Wordsworth's famous phrase:

> L.E.L.'s 'soul of romance' unites the roles, and the sensuous worlds, of poet and painter. In the lyricism of her verse she is music-maker too. Added to which she [the improvisatrice] is young, beautiful, Italian, and a lover ... This truly is high

Romanticism, Byronic in its origins, Keatsian in the value it sets upon beauty as the essence of poetry.

Landon and Death

In an essay on L.E.L., Adam Roberts writes that Landon links poetry to self-destruction in ways that are not true of 'male' Romanticism:

> There is something peculiar about the configuration of youth, beauty and death that is so strongly associated with Landon. Not only is it specifically gendered (which is to say, it not only depends fundamentally upon the fact that Landon was a woman, but it also goes towards defining what a certain sort of woman – a woman poet – ought to be), but it is also linked to notions of self-destruction in ways that are not true of male Romanticism.

Some Keatsians might disagree with the tendency of these remarks, but Roberts's point is well made as far as L.E.L. is concerned. Though capable of such poetry as the cityscape 'Scenes in London' (1836), which portrays the throng and hubbub of daily life and 'the crowded street', Landon was much preoccupied with female death and self-destruction in her verse; Sappho and the Improvisatrice are but two of the women who expire for love within that body of work.

There are two ways of looking at this morbid preoccupation. There is something very self-conscious, if not contrived, about the melancholic, mysterious voice of Landon's verse and the first, perhaps cynical, position is that she self-consciously assumed the persona of the suffering poet, as a conscious post-Byronic marketing device to sell more books. The second view is that there was nothing meretricious in Landon's handling of disillusionment and self-torment, that this was as much a poet of sincerity as Wordsworth and Coleridge. Indeed, the tenor of Landon's own unfortunate later emotional life has been seen by some as somehow being anticipated in her early verse. Landon's unprotected position as a woman in the literary world gave rise to various scandals in the 1830s which linked her to Maginn and, more plausibly, to William Jerdan, the editor of the *Literary Gazette*. Dismissing her fiancé John Forster (later the biographer of Dickens) for momentarily countenancing this gossip, in June 1838 she married one George Maclean, with whom she travelled to West Africa, where she died in October of that year, in mysterious circumstances – either by suicide or accident – from swallowing prussic acid.

In her 'Stanzas on the Death of Mrs Hemans' (1835), the elder poet is cast in the role of the quintessentially feminine poet, and her work is linked to suffering and death. For Landon, Hemans's 'song is sorrowful': 'The hopes of which it breathes, are hopes / That look beyond the tomb':

> Ah! dearly purchased is the gift,
>   The gift of song like thine;
> A fated doom is hers who stands
>   The priestess of the shrine.
> The crowd – they only see the crown,
>   They only hear the hymn; –
> They mark not that the cheek is pale,
>   And that the eye is dim.

Suffering is woman's lot, and most particularly the poet's lot. Landon stresses the emotional burden of being a poet, once more linking creativity with suffering and death. As so often in her verse, the female poet here appears as a creature of feeling, of suffering, someone defined by love and tragedy as much as by her 'gifts' and talents.

See also   Joanna Baillie and Romantic-Era Drama; Irish, Scottish and Welsh Poetry; Literary and Philosophical Key Concepts I; Satire

Further reading

John Barnard, *John Keats* (1987).

Walter Jackson Bate, *John Keats* (1963).

William D. Brewer, 'Felicia Hemans, Byronic Cosmopolitanism and the Ancient Welsh Bards', in Gerard Carruthers and Alan Rawes (eds), *English Romanticism and the Celtic World* (2003), 167–81.

Douglas Bush, *Mythology and the Romantic Tradition in English Poetry* (1963).

P. M. S. Dawson, *The Unacknowledged Legislator: Shelley and Politics* (1980).

Cian Duffy, *Shelley and the Revolutionary Sublime* (2005).

Caroline Franklin, *Byron: A Literary Life* (2000).

Robert J. Griffin, *Wordsworth's Pope: A Study in Literary Historiography* (1995).

Richard Holmes, *Shelley: The Pursuit* (1974; biography).

Ian Jack, *English Literature 1815–1832: Scott, Byron, and Keats* (1963).

Peter Manning, *Byron and His Fictions* (1978).

Leslie Marchand, *Byron: A Biography* (3 vols, 1957) (there is a one-volume version, *Byron: A Portrait* (1970)).

Anne K. Mellor, *Romanticism and Gender* (1993).

Jerome McGann, *'Don Juan' in Context* (1976).

Jerome McGann and Daniel Reiss (eds), *Letitia Elizabeth Landon: Selected Writings* (1997).

Lucy Newlyn, *Reading, Writing and Romanticism: The Anxiety of Reception* (2000).

Donald Reiman, *Percy Bysshe Shelley* (1990).

Nicholas Roe, *John Keats and the Culture of Dissent* (1997).

Adam Roberts, 'Letitia Landon (L.E.L.), *The Improvisatrice*', in Duncan Wu (ed.), *A Companion to Romanticism* (1998), 294–300.

Stuart M. Sperry, *Keats the Poet* (1973).

Stuart M. Sperry, *Shelley's Major Verse* (1988).

Jane Stabler, *Byron, Poetics and History* (2002).

Glennis Stephenson, *Letitia Landon: The Woman Behind L.E.L.* (1995).

Timothy Webb, *Shelley: A Voice Not Understood* (1977).
Susan J. Wolfson, *Borderlines: The Shiftings of Gender in British Romanticism* (2006).
Jonathan Wordsworth, *The Bright Work Grows: Romantic Women Poets* (1997).
Duncan Wu, 'Letitia Elizabeth Landon', in *Romanticism: An Anthology* (3rd edition, 2006), 1442–8.

Joanna Baillie and Romantic-era Drama

Romantic Drama

We do not normally think of the Romantic era as a time of great drama, characterising it instead chiefly as an age of poetry, and, after that, as notable for remarkable achievements in the novel and in the essay. Some of the most successful dramas of the age – Joanna Baillie's *The Family Legend* (1810 – a 'complete and decided triumph', in her friend Walter Scott's account), Barry Cornwall's *Mirandola* (1821), Charles Robert Maturin's *Bertram* (1816), Henry Hart Milman's *Fazio* (1815), even the stage adaptation of Pierce Egan's rather disreputable picaresque novel *Life in London* (1821) – have been rarely read and even more rarely performed since their heyday. Chris Baldick's untroubled declaration in the sixth edition of the *Oxford Companion to English Literature* (2000) that 'Drama written for the theatres is generally agreed to be by far the weakest side of Romantic literature' can be seen as summarising the critical consensus of many decades. John Keats's drama *Otho the Great* (1819), for example, was waspishly described by Thomas McFarland, also in 2000, as a 'wasteful churning of his genius': inaptly named, written merely for money and an unwelcome diversion from the sounding of the muse's lyre. Great poets, in this line of argument, could do much better than dissipate their energies in writing plays for Drury Lane.

Notwithstanding this disesteem for the Romantic-era stage, it would be unwise to argue that there was any lack of interest in the drama during the late Georgian period. Shakespeare was a god of the Romantic idolatry, and writings on his tragedies by Coleridge, Lamb and Hazlitt remain some of the most important in the canon of Shakespearean criticism. Furthermore, all of the 'Big Six' Romantic poets wrote drama of one kind or another, from William Wordsworth's exercise in the manner of Shakespeare, *The Borderers* (1797), to the aforesaid *Otho* of Keats (a collaboration with Charles Armitage Brown (1786–1842)), and from Coleridge's *The Fall of Robespierre* (1794) (a collaboration with Robert Southey) and *Remorse* (originally *Osorio* (1797), produced at Drury Lane in 1813), to Lord Byron's *The Two Foscari* (1821). It might also be said that as part of the critical revisionism evident in the wider field of Romantic Studies since the late 1970s (see 'The Expansion of the Romantic Canon'), there has been a recent tendency to reinterrogate Romantic-period literary culture in search of its neglected theatrical traditions and, indeed, a concomitant willingness to value these achievements much more highly than the *Companion*'s summary judgement might encourage.

'Closet' Drama

Chris Baldick's generalisation, it should be pointed out, has an important qualification in its midst: 'for the theatres'. The critic refers to the fare written to be performed at the likes of Covent Garden and Drury Lane rather than to the entire range of Romantic drama, for some of the Himalayan peaks of Romantic-period poetry, so to speak, were hewn from dramatic blank verse – Byron's *Manfred* (1817) and Shelley's *Prometheus Unbound* (1820), for mighty instance. These were 'closet dramas', works written to be read or acted privately rather than produced upon the boards. Quite apart from the practical problem of mounting a performance of a work such as P. B. Shelley's mythological masterpiece, there was also a contemporary sense that dramatic writing was somehow sullied by its realisation on the stage. Lord Byron, for example, professed on a number of occasions what David V. Erdman once described as his 'vociferously expressed intention to keep his own plays off the English stage'.

There were also those in the Romantic period who argued explicitly that there was something amiss about acting, a sense that great works of drama were much better enjoyed in the mind's eye rather than being reduced by over-literalising representation in the theatre. The most winning airing of this argument is that of Charles Lamb, in his 'On the Tragedies of Shakespeare Considered with Reference to Their Fitness for Stage Representation' (1811), which maintains that the principal characters in the dramatist's tragedies are individual 'objects of meditation' and that having an actor interpret Shakespeare's words tended to obscure rather than to assist in their imaginative enjoyment:

> Such is the instantaneous nature of the impressions which we take in at the eye and ear at a playhouse, compared with the slow apprehension oftentimes of the understanding in reading, that we are apt not only to sink the play-writer in the consideration which we pay to the actor, but even to identify in our minds, in a perverse manner, the actor with the character which he represents. It is difficult for a frequent playgoer to disembarrass the idea of Hamlet from the person and voice of Mr K. We speak of Lady Macbeth, while we are in reality thinking of Mrs S.

Lamb admits the 'very high degree of satisfaction which [he] received some years back from seeing for the first time a tragedy of Shakespeare performed', but argues that, in the final analysis, the experience of watching tends to reduce rather than realise Shakespeare's imaginative grandeur: 'When the novelty is past, we find to our cost that, instead of realising an idea, we have only materialised and brought down a fine vision to the standard of flesh and blood. We have let go a dream.' Better, to borrow Michael Bradshaw's fine phrase, the 'ascendancy of intense poetry over stageable action'; better, to Lamb's mind, the vivid flow of words on the page rather than on the boards.

Setting aside his provocative views on the stage, as a dramatic critic Lamb also deserves credit as the editor of works by Beaumont and Fletcher, Marlowe, Webster and others in the *Specimens of English Dramatic Poets who Lived about the Time of Shakespeare*, published in 1808, an important contribution to the Romantic-era revival of interest in Jacobean and Elizabethan dramatists prompted by the likes of Lamb, Francis Jeffrey and William Gifford. Some of the *Specimens*, it might be pointed out, contain material of a kind not everywhere in favour in an age which was receptive to Thomas Bowdler's *Family Shakespeare* (1818; the bard without blasphemy and bawdiness), but Lamb includes some of the naughtiness, revenge and blood, declaring himself willing to give 'an airing' to themes 'beyond the diocese of strict conscience'.

Lamb on the Theatre

A cynic might hazard a guess that some of Lamb's antipathy to the realities of the stage could, in part, have arisen from his own mixed experience of the theatre. Early in his literary career, Charles Lamb did write for the boards in *John Woodvil* (1799), a mock-Elizabethan tragedy, and his farce *Mr H---; or, Beware a Bad Name* (1806). This latter was accepted and staged at one of the two principal theatres of the day, Drury Lane, where it flopped ignominiously. That said, in having a play accepted at the theatre, at least Lamb went one better than his friend Wordsworth, whose blank verse drama *The Borderers* was returned to sender by Covent Garden (the poet was not, nonetheless, particularly distressed at this, declaring that he 'incurred no disappointment when the piece was judiciously returned as not calculated for the Stage'). The catalogue of misfortune goes on: Keats and Brown's *Otho* was 'accepted', in the latter's account, by Drury Lane in 1819, 'with a promise ... to bring it forward during that very season' (with the greatest actor of the day, Edmund Kean himself, 'desir[ous] to play the principal character'), but nothing came of it. In the same hapless vein, P. B. Shelley, the author of arguably the finest of Romantic era closet dramas, declared that his play *The Cenci. A Tragedy* (1819) was – unlike *Prometheus Unbound* – 'expressly written for theatrical exhibition' and submitted it to Covent Garden. The house – which had previously said no to William

Wordsworth – would have none of it. However, Shelley was less equani-mous than the Lake poet at the slight, and expressed his fury that the theatre had 'rejected it with expressions of the greatest insolence'. The dramatist suspected, probably with some justification, that this decision was attributable to the playhouse's distaste for his incendiary politics rather than his dramatic talents (but it would have been a very risky enterprise, it might be pointed out, for a mainstream theatre to put on a play which deals with incest, let alone a play which deals with incest written by a self-proclaimed atheist, radical and sexual revolutionary).

Hazlitt and the Reform of the Stage

Lamb's critical peer William Hazlitt was also a Bardolator. In his *Characters of Shakespear's* [*sic*] *Plays* (1817) Hazlitt takes issue with his critical prede-cessor Samuel Johnson for what he saw as an unimaginative handling of the dramatist and praises the 'magnanimity' of the artist's vision. Indeed, for Hazlitt, Shakespeare's very greatness as a playwright only served to show how paltry were his modern-day successors. The critic poured scorn on 'modern romantic tragedy', dismissing the Reverend Maturin's *Bertram*, for instance, as a 'mixture of fanciful exaggeration and indolent sensibility', and as representative of a drama that 'courts distress, affects horror, indulges in all the luxury of woe, and nurses its languid thoughts, and dainty sympathies, to fill up the void of action'. What was required, Hazlitt declared, was a return to the tenets of 'the old tragedy', principally that of Shakespeare and his contemporaries.

Hazlitt was not alone in seeing the contemporary theatre as going to the dogs. Nostalgia for the lost golden age of drama and a perception that the modern stage had lurched to the bad and needed to be reformed were common laments in the late Georgian age. In *English Bards and Scotch Reviewers* (1809), Byron himself called for the return of the most notable living dramatist, Richard Brinsley Sheridan (1751–1816), the author of *The Critic* (1779) and *The School for Scandal* (1777), urging him to resume his satirical work: 'Give, as thy last memorial to the age, / One classic drama, and reform the stage.' The plea went unheeded (Sheridan's last original play was *The Critic* and for the remaining near forty years of his life, he considered himself first and foremost a politician). In *English Bards*, Byron also envisages another lapsed – and then highly thought of – satirist, the poet William Gifford (1756–1826), resuming his work and scourging the poetasters (weak versifiers) of the day (Wordsworth, Coleridge and Southey amongst them). Gifford had, himself, previously attacked the corruption of the stage and 'the wretched state of dramatic poetry among us' in his *The Maeviad* (1795): 'It seems', Gifford writes in the introduction to that work, 'as if all the blockheads in the kingdom had started up, and exclaimed with one voice, "Come, let us write for the theatres".' The English stage, once the province of Shakespeare, was now, in Gifford's mordant phrase, populated solely by 'the abortions of the Muse'. Gifford, like William Hazlitt, saw the contemporary stage as debased when compared with the works of Elizabethan and Jacobean days, and he, like Charles Lamb, was also a textual scholar of its drama, editing Philip Massinger's *Plays* (1805), Ben Jonson's *Works* (1816), and John Ford's *Dramatic Works* (1827).

The need to 'reform the stage' which Byron, Gifford and Hazlitt identified was taken up by a number of contemporary dramatists themselves. Henry Hart Milman (1791–1868), for instance, described his *Fazio* (1816; successfully staged at Covent Garden in 1818), a tragedy set in Italy and written in a post-Jacobean tenor, as an 'attempt at reviving our old national drama with greater simplicity of plot'. Its language, a contemporary reviewer pointed out, was recidivist, mimetic of the diction of the turn of the seventeenth century: 'as obviously an imitation of our elder dramatic writers, as the plot'. Here is a sample (the reader can judge of its post-Shakespearean qualities):

> *Bianca.*
> What hath distemper'd thee? – This is unnatural;
> Thou could'st not talk thus in thy stedfast senses.
> Fazio, thou hast seen Aldabella!
> *Fazio.*   Well,
> She is no basilisk – there's no death in her eyes.
> *Bianca.*
> Aye, Fazio, but there is; and more than death –
> A death beyond the grave – a death of sin –
> A howling, hideous, and eternal death –
> Death the flesh shrinks from. No, thou must not see her!
> Nay, I'm imperative – thou'rt mine, and shalt not.

Joanna Baillie

A perhaps more significant reformist agenda lay in the efforts for the stage of the Scottish dramatist and poet Joanna Baillie (1762–1851), who, as an important female playwright, has attracted particular critical attention in recent years. She published three volumes of her *Plays on the Passions* (1798; 1802; 1812), each of which foregrounded some individual spur to human behaviour (such as hatred in *De Montfort* and love in *Basil* (both 1798)). In the polemical, reformist 'Introductory Discourse' to the first volume of the *Plays* (1798), Baillie declared that her attention was to portray the passions in a literary language 'genuine and true to nature'. This anticipates Wordsworth's 'Preface' to the *Lyrical Ballads*, published two years later (see 'Literary and Philosophical Key Concepts I'), in which the poet vowed to use the 'real language of men' and, indeed, to foreground the 'passions of the heart' in his verse. Baillie offers an empathetic vision familiar today from the prose writings of Keats and, indeed, those of Wordsworth. She argues that the best drama is founded on the fact of the 'strong sympathy felt by most creatures, but the human above all, for others of their kind'. For her, as a consequence, 'nothing has become so much an object of man's curiosity as man himself' (Wordsworth, remember, described his literary mission as to meditate 'on Man, on Nature and on Human Life'). Joanna Baillie describes herself, two years before Wordsworth's attack on the crass and overblown nature of some contemporary plays, as 'the advocate of nature' in her drama, 'against the false refinements and exaggerations of art'.

In many ways, Baillie anticipates wider Romantic literary theory. Indeed, Janice Patten reads Baillie as the first of the British Romantics, in terms which use the language of high Romantic argument to describe her work, in arguing that in the *Series of Plays* Baillie 'inaugurates a new poetics which raises the importance of imagination to new heights, and dramatizes in beautiful natural language persons of "humble and lowly class" as they respond to "beauty", or labour under self-doubt, haunted by memories, often wandering alone in nature'. It might also be pointed out that this perception of Baillie's primacy is not new. In a *Blackwood's* essay of 1824, the Reverend William Harness (1790–1869) saw her as the progenitor of 'the distinguished fraternity of bards ... who have united in forming of the reigns of George the Third and Fourth another Age of Genius, only second to that of Elizabeth'. The Lake School and the Byron group 'have laboured in a region which was opened to them by the hand of a woman':

> The evidence to substantiate its truth is seen in the state of our national poetry before the publication of the ... preliminary Essay ... and in the state of our present national poetry ... every one of the master spirits, who have arisen into subsequent celebrity, have received ... the impressions of her genius, and have either avowedly or unconsciously followed ... her example.

Using the terminology then of the highest critical approbation, Harness proclaims that Baillie's work is reminiscent of the writings of 'our elder dramatists ... with which it may boldly challenge a comparison'. One of the passages he especially cherishes is the scene in *Basil* between Princess Victoria and Isabella where Victoria speaks of her adopted son, the 'sweet, fair-hair'd Mirando':

Vict. He is the orphan of a hapless pair,
A loving, beautiful, but hapless pair,
Whose story is so pleasing, and so sad,
The swains have turn'd it to a plaintive lay,
And sing it as they tend their mountain sheep.
Besides, (to *Isab.*) I am the guardian of his choice.
When first I saw him – dost thou not remember?
Isab. 'Twas in the public garden.
Vict.   Even so;
Perch'd in his nurse's arms, a rustic quean,
Ill suited to the lovely charge she bore.
How stedfastly he fix'd his looks upon me,
His dark eyes shining through forgotten tears,
Then stretch'd his little arms and call'd me mother!
What could I do? I took the bantling home –
I could not tell the imp he had no mother.

Frederick Burwick wrote in 2004 that it was Baillie's 'intention to reveal how a character succumbs to a compulsive emotion, which then wreaks its dramatic consequences'. This is well put, though at the same time as she attends to her characters' emotional nuance, the playwright was also concerned with the effect of the drama on her audience; in particular, Baillie's 'Discourse' examines an audience's fascination with dramatic works of art which foreground individuals prompted by turbulent and destructive emotions of 'violent agitation'. What is the pleasure to be derived from the contemplation of tragedy, given that few people would wish horrible things upon themselves? Baillie answers the question: at one remove there is pleasure in the contemplation of horrors: 'No man wishes to see [a] Ghost himself ... but *every* man wishes to see one who believes that he sees it, in all the agitation and wildness of that species of terror.' She maintains that there is a human fascination with the darkest side of emotional experience, even with paroxysms of uncontrolled anger, despite the fact that 'Anger is a passion that attracts less sympathy than any other':

> Yet the unpleasing and distorted features of an angry man will be more eagerly gazed upon ... than the most amiable placid countenance in the world. Every eye is directed to him; every voice hushed to silence in his presence: even children will leave off their gambols as he passes, and gaze after him more eagerly than the gaudiest equipage. The wild tossings of despair; the gnashing of hatred and revenge; the yearnings of affection, and the softened mien of love; all the language of the agitated soul, which every age and nation understand, is never addressed to the dull or inattentive.

Gothic Drama

In the 1800 'Preface' to the *Lyrical Ballads*, Wordsworth had decried the contemporary taste for the contemplation of bloody modern drama, notably in his contemplation of 'sickly and stupid German Tragedies', the 'Sturm und Drang' (Storm and Stress) dramas (by Goethe, Schiller and a number of lesser dramatists) which had a vogue in English translation in the 1790s (famous testimony to this is the satire on August von Kotzebue's *Lovers' Vows* (1790) as a disagreeable play of moral ill-tendency in Jane Austen's *Mansfield Park* (1814)). Whatever Wordsworth's views, there was, nonetheless, a large appetite both for contemporary tragedy and for Gothic drama on the British stage in the Romantic period, tragedy such as Baillie's *Constantine Paleologus; or The Last of the Caesars* (1804) (concerning which John Stuart Mill made the exalted claim that this was 'one of the best dramas of the last two centuries') and Gothic drama such as the stage version of Mary Shelley's *Frankenstein*, which was successfully adapted as a play by Richard Brinsley Peake as *Presumption; or, the Fate of Frankenstein* at the English Opera House in 1823, only five years after its first publication as a novel. In this latter genre, the Gothic novelist C. R. Maturin (1780–1824) had one of the great stage successes of the age in combining Gothic atmospherics and tragic drama when his tragedy *Bertram* was produced by Edmund Kean at the Drury Lane theatre in 1816. Maturin wrote *Bertram*, he frankly admitted, 'in 'the hope of the profit' ('the only object of any consequence to me in the disposal of my literary attempts'), and here he hit the public taste in his portrayal of the 'high-hearted man', the anti-hero Bertram, who is 'sublime even in [his] guilt'.

S. T. Coleridge reacted to Maturin's success with a lacerating review, later re-published in chapter 23 of the *Biographia Literaria* (1817), expressing the 'mingled horror and disgust with which [he had] witnessed' the drama, which he considered 'a melancholy proof of the depravation of the public mind'. As we have seen, Coleridge was joined in the onslaught on *Bertram* by William Hazlitt. Nevertheless, the latter was somewhat more charitable; though he attacked the dramatic logic of the piece ('it is a tragedy without business ... no action: there is neither cause nor effect'), Hazlitt conceded that there was much 'very beautiful and affecting writing' in the play and quotes Imogine's soliloquy from Act 1 as she looks at a picture of Bertram – her former lover – as evidence:

> The limner's [painter's] art may trace the absent feature,
> And give the eye of distant weeping faith,
> To view the form of its idolatry.

But oh! the scenes 'mid which they met and parted –
The thoughts, the recollections sweet and bitter –
Th' Elysian dreams of lovers, when they loved –
Who shall restore them?
Less lovely are the fugitive clouds of eve.
And not more vanishing – if thou couldst speak,
Dumb witness of the secret soul of Imogine,
Thou might'st acquit the faith of woman kind –
Since thou wert on my midnight pillow laid.

Though *Bertram* owes something to the blackheart villains of Ann Radcliffe – Schedoni in *The Italian* (1797) most notably – many people saw a Byronic cast to the character and to Maturin's work as a whole (indeed, Byron, like Sir Walter Scott, had recommended the play to Drury Lane), inasmuch as the dramatist's Satanic hero has an 'angel sin', his 'pride that rivals the star-bright apostate's'. Though Maturin's first drama proved – as he had hoped – profitable and successful, the tragedy's successors *Manuel* (1817) and *Fredolfo* (1819) did not succeed.

Byron's Drama

Though willing to endorse C. R. Maturin's work and aid its progress to the stage, Lord Byron did not – as we have seen – approve of the production of his own plays (as Michael Bradshaw has written, there was 'a slightly perverse tendency among Romantic dramatic manifestoes to offer to regenerate "the stage" apparently by writing for the closet'). *Manfred* apart, Byron's principal efforts in closet dramatic terms were *Sardanapalus*, *The Two Foscari*, and *Cain. A Mystery*, first published together in 1821 (it might be added that his *Marino Faliero, Doge of Venice*, a blank verse drama published in the same year, was actually staged at Drury Lane without the author's permission and much to Byron's annoyance). Featuring dark oriental theatre of blood, quasi-Jacobean tragedy, and bleak Biblical story in that order, this trio of plays caused some controversy. John Wilson of *Blackwood's* praised Byron's portrayal of 'the dark, dim, disturbed, insane, hell-haunted Cain' and 'the passionate, princely, philosophical, joy-cheated, throne-wearied' Sardanapalus. On the other hand, the freedom with scripture in *Cain* caused intense annoyance amongst some readers, and Wilson's friend John Gibson Lockhart, though generally an admirer of his lordship, scoffed in the same periodical at the very idea of plays not meant for the playhouse: 'What would people say to a new song of Tom Moore's, prefaced with an earnest injunction on man, woman, and child, never to think of singing it? A tragedy, *not meant to be acted*, seems to us to be just about as reasonable an affair as a song not meant to be sung.'

In his influential study *In the Shadows of Romance: Romantic Tragic Drama in England, Germany and France* (1987), Jeffrey N. Cox writes of the metaphysical and political nature of Byron's *Cain*. To Cox, the portrayal of Cain, whose rebellion against God leads only to suffering, exile and death, is symbolic of much of 'the action of Romantic tragic drama', which he summarises thus: 'revolt seeks transformation but brings destruction'. This is certainly the trajectory of *Cain*, and it also applies to Wordsworth's *The Borderers*, to give but one other notable example, a work through which pulse – in Cox's excellent description – 'the rhythms of revolt'. The well-intentioned protagonist Mortimer causes the death of Baron Herbert after listening to the promptings of the villainous Rivers, someone who implies that assassination can serve the cause of liberty and that summary violence can serve a good cause (in the end Rivers himself is killed and Mortimer is consigned to a Cain-like life of exile). Wordsworth wrote of his play that 'The study of human nature suggests this awful truth, that, as in the trials to which life subjects us, sin and crime are apt to start from their very opposite qualities.' Though *The Borderers* is set in the reign of Henry III it also – as in Shakespearean drama – has contemporary political resonances, notably in its treatment of 'Man's intellectual empire' and its attention to the ideals of liberty which were so resonant in Europe after 1789. From well-meaning revolt to unforeseen violence is a progression, as Cox notes, which brings to mind both Romantic tragedy and the progress of the French Revolution itself. From overt accounts of the Revolution as per the *Fall of Robespierre* to the obliquity of the *Borderers*, drama was capable, like the age's poetry, of dealing with the largest political issues of the Romantic period.

Further Reading

Michael Bradshaw, ' "Bloody John Lacy": *The London Magazine* and the Doldrums of English Drama', in *The British Periodical Text, 1797–1835*, ed. Simon Hull (2008), 121–41.

Frederick Burwick, 'Joanna Baillie, Matthew Baillie, and the Pathology of the Passions', in *Joanna Baillie, Romantic Dramatist: Critical Essays*, ed. Thomas C. Crochunis (2004), 48–68.

Frederick Burwick, *Romantic Drama: Acting and Reacting* (2009).

Jeffrey N. Cox, *In the Shadows of Romance: Romantic Tragic Drama in England, Germany and France* (1987).

Jeffrey N. Cox and Michael Gamer (eds), *The Broadview Anthology of Romantic Drama* (2003).

David V. Erdman, 'Byron's Stage Fright: the History of his Ambition and Fear of Writing for the Stage', *English Literary History*, 6 (1939), 219–43.

Thomas McFarland, *The Mask of Keats* (2000).

Judith Pascoe, *Romantic Theatricality: Gender, Poetry and Spectatorship* (1997).

Janice Patten, 'Joanna Baillie, *A Series of Plays*', in *A Companion to Romanticism*, ed. Duncan Wu (1999), 169–78.

William Blake and Romantic-era Art

William Blake

'I must create my own system or be enslaved by another man's', scribbled William Blake in a margin of Sir Joshua Reynolds's *Discourses* (1769–90). Blake's annotations to Reynolds's treatise on art are certainly representative of their author's singular nature; on the title page of his copy is written 'This man was hired to depress art.' Blake had an entrenched anti-establishment ethos, constantly questioning and attacking the actions, motivations and legitimacy of the institutions and authorities of his day. In Sir Joshua, Blake found an artistic *bête noire* – the equivalent, in his unenthusiastic account, of the despised Locke and Newton in modern philosophy – to add to his cata-logue of malign, 'stony law', authority figures. Reynolds (1723–92), the President of the Royal Academy for over thirty years, was – at least in Blake's imaginatively creative caricature – the epitome of the sterile academic and neoclassical style of art, and his attempts to dignify British society portraiture in elevated allusions to Italian masters such as Michelangelo and to the European Grand Style were little more than foolish.

Blake himself had studied at the Academy (or, in his own more colourful terminology, had 'spent the Vigour of my Youth and Genius under the Oppression of Sir Joshua and his Gang of Cunning Hired Knaves') and his iconoclasm about its presiding spirit was fruitful. Blake was no part of any contemporary artistic or literary scene. This man's refusal to be 'enslaved' by the conventions of the day resulted in his own brilliantly iconoclastic work. Blake was both great poet and frequently magnificent artist. There is much truth in M. H. Abrams's assertion that he 'favoured innovation instead of traditionalism in … materials, forms, and style … without regard to … precedent'. Blake's primary innovation was to fuse his poetry with art; the artist/author considered his verse incomplete without its illustrations. The one complements the other in what Blake labelled his 'illuminated' books; his methodology was to engrave his works on a steel plate (in a reverse mirror image), print them on paper and then hand-colour the resulting pages himself.

Blake's poetry was never conventionally published during his lifetime. That said, he was no stranger to the book trade, having illustrated volumes from 1779 onwards, including contemporary editions of Geoffrey Chaucer, of Robert Blair's gloomy meditation on death *The Grave* (1743) – which Blake found enlivening – and of the Book of Job. Fig. 7, for an instance, shows one of his extraordinary early nineteenth-century illustrations of John Milton's nativity ode, 'On the Morning of Christ's Nativity' (1629).

Blake's own books are frequently both poetical and visual, his figures setting off his verse in the illuminated manner. Take Fig. 8, 'The Lamb', the

Fig. 7   William Blake, 'Annunciation to the Shepherds' (c.1809). Illustration to John Milton's 'On the Morning of Christ's Nativity'

first of the *Songs of Innocence* (1789). Alexander Gilchrist (1828–61), Blake's earliest biographer, described this poem as a 'sweet hymn of tender infantine sentiment, appropriate to that perennial image of meekness', and the lines are 'imaged' in a union of poem and picture, with the naked child and the lamb – symbols of innocence both – in the foreground. The vision of spiritual harmony is also symbolised by the interlinked vines at the top of the image, as well as by the pair of doves on the roof of the thatched house, with the open door of the latter adding to the atmosphere of welcome. Interestingly, the plate's punctuation – or lack of it – might be said to suit its theme: the answer to the child's insistent questions – assuming that he is

Suit a theme

Fig. 8   William Blake, 'The Lamb' (1789)

the speaking voice in the poem – being so obvious that the interrogations do not possess question marks ('Little Lamb who made thee / Dost thou know who made thee').

In the later *Songs of Innocence and Experience* (1794) this lyric is juxta-posed with that justly famous poem 'The Tyger' ('Tyger, Tyger burning bright, / In the forests of the night ...'). Fig. 9 shows the original plate, with Blake's verse accompanied by his rather gentle-looking image of a tiger. This remarkable animal does not seem unduly threatening, it might be said. As the great Blakean critic David V. Erdman once wrote, 'The tiger in Blake's illustration of this poem is notoriously lacking in ferocity.' Perhaps Blake's draughtsmanship did not extend to the portrayal of feline malevolence, but

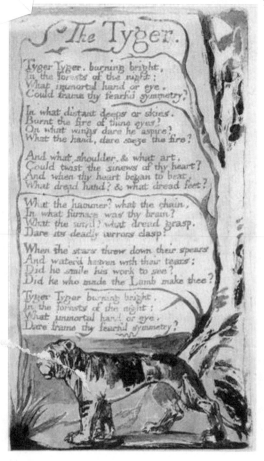

Fig. 9   William Blake, 'The Tyger' (1794)

perhaps more likely is the notion that the *Songs of Innocence and Experience*'s preoccupation with 'contrary states' here extends to a dichotomy between verse and image absent in 'The Lamb', and one, indeed, which finally implies that oppositions such as those emblemised in the contrast between lamb and tiger will, eventually, unite in divine harmony.

Despite his considerable artistic talents, William Blake only had one – poorly received – exhibition in his lifetime, in 1809 (Leigh Hunt's brother Robert – in the sole review of the show – airily described Blake as 'an unfortunate lunatic, whose personal inoffensiveness secures him from confinement'). Blake did not trouble the popular taste of the age, which reserved its enthusiasm for Sir Joshua and his hired knaves, the landscapes of Thomas Gainsborough (and latterly those of J. M. W. Turner), the animal portraiture of George Stubbs, the sporting art of Henry Alken, and for the satirical caricature of James Gillray and the like (see 'Satire'). In later years Blake came to feel that his art was unjustly neglected, though the attentions in his last decade of Samuel Palmer (1805–81) and a younger generation of artists known as 'The Ancients' who were devoted to his work were gratifying to him. Nevertheless, and as with his poetry, it was not until the second half of the nineteenth century that Blake's art began to achieve its due measure of renown.

Henry Fuseli

William Blake was not without his visionary compeers in the Romantic age, and a number of these – unlike him – became highly successful artists. Foremost amongst them was Blake's friend and collaborator Henry Fuseli (1741–1825), who was originally Swiss but who lived in London from his early twenties. Blake memorably memorialised this man in doggerel verse:

> The only man that e'er I knew
> Who did not make me almost spew
> Was Fuseli.

Fuseli is best known for his famous piece of grotesquerie 'Nightmare' (1782), a painting in which a ghostly horse's head glares through a window as a sleeping maiden lies supine on her bed while, in the meantime, a diabolical imp sits glaring malignly at the woman. This painting was much influenced by Edmund Burke's writings on the sublime (see 'Medievalism, the Sublime and the Gothic'), which the artist admired greatly, and, indeed, by contemporary Gothic fiction. Though seen as trite and melodramatic by a number of contemporary critics – that frustrated painter William Hazlitt most particularly – the image became a *succès de scandale*, being reproduced throughout Europe (and Fuseli cannily painted a number of versions of the work in oils to cash in on its notoriety).

Fuseli was the most literary of contemporary painters, Blake excepted. Setting aside the suggestion made by his female admirer Mary Wollstonecraft of a *ménage à trois* cohabitation with him and his wife Sophie (vetoed, unsurprisingly, by the latter, who consequently forbade the author of the *Vindication of the Rights of Woman* the house), Fuseli's engagements with the greats of English literature were imaginative and laudable, notably in the pictures he made for John and Josiah Boydell's famous

Shakespeare Gallery in Pall Mall (scenes from *Hamlet*, *Macbeth* and *A Midsummer Night's Dream*), and in paintings based on the works of Dante, Milton and 'Ossian'. Figure 10, for instance, shows Fuseli's 'Silence' (*c*.1800), which was painted for the second of his 'Milton Gallery' exhibitions of 1799 and 1800, a collection of around forty illustrations of Milton intended as a rival to the Boydells' Shakespeare Gallery. The picture, a revision of an earlier illustration (significantly entitled 'Sorrow') of Milton's 'Il Penseroso' ('The Contemplative Man', *c*.1631, the poet's invocation to the goddess Melancholy), is an atmospheric study of sorrow and misery as the (presumably) lachrymose woman, who seems self-confined to a dark and featureless space, is enervated by overwhelming dejection.

Fig. 10   Henry Fuseli, 'Silence' (*c*.1800), painted for the Milton Gallery

Fig. 11 John Martin, illustration to Book 4 of John Milton's *Paradise Lost* (1824)

Burkes theory of sublime

John Martin

Younger than Blake and Fuseli, though no less visionary, was the Northumbrian painter John Martin (1789–1854), brother of the lunatic millenarian Jonathan, who tried to burn down York Minster in 1829 (see 'Millenarianism'). Painter John had a similar taste for extremity to that of the hapless Jonathan, though this cast of mind was figured in his art rather than his life. He specialised in vast oil paintings featuring Biblical scenes of apocalypse and destruction, as in his colossal images of the fall of the ancient cities of Nineveh and Babylon and, still more powerful, the destruction of Sodom and Gomorrah. John Martin, like Henry Fuseli, was directly influenced by Burke's theory of the sublime, and he too illustrated literature both classical (John Milton; see Fig. 11) and contemporary (Mary Shelley) (and the latter's husband P. B. Shelley wrote letterpress for an engraving of Martin's famous 'Sadak in Search of the Waters of Oblivion' (1812)).

Benjamin Robert Haydon

William Hazlitt, an accomplished draughtsman in his youth, gave up his artistic vocation for literary criticism and philosophy. Oddly, it is the fate of his flamboyant friend Benjamin Robert Haydon (1786–1846), the painter

...number of colossally ambitious historical and Biblical subjects in oils, to be remembered rather more – despite his early artistic success and the labours of four decades – for his literary production and brilliant acquaintance than for his art, principally in vivid accounts of his friendship with his 'Cockney School' colleagues Leigh Hunt and John Keats. Haydon was familiar with many of the most remarkable men of his day, the poet Wordsworth, the artist Fuseli and, perhaps surprisingly, the great Irish soldier the Duke of Wellington amongst them. His splendid journals, first published in 1853 – less than a decade after Haydon's suicide nine years previously – contain much fascinating material, offering a measure of critical and aesthetic insight alongside polemical ranting, highly entertaining anecdotes about his acquaintance, and despondent breast-beating.

Haydon was a thoughtful theorist of art as well as a practitioner, and his *Lectures on Painting and Design* (1846) address the importance of artistic education, the need for state patronage, and the centrality of design in a newly industrialised economy. On a more exalted personal level, he also considered himself someone destined to the task of 'redeeming English art'. This redemption was to be achieved in epical manner. Haydon espoused grand historical painting, frequently on the biblical subjects which Martin later retailed so successfully, in works such as 'The Judgement of Solomon' (1814) and 'Christ's Entry into Jerusalem' of the following year. 'Vastness does not confound him', wrote Hazlitt of his compeer. Even so, it was to be the 'vastness' of John Martin's work which was to find a greater contemporary audience than that achieved by Haydon, and matters were not helped by the perfectionism which led him to spend years on individual paintings, nor, indeed, by his reputation as a scrounging, argumentative spendthrift who contrived to quarrel with both friends and patrons alike.

B. R. Haydon once wrote of the 'immortal dinner' which he hosted in December 1817 at which Wordsworth, Keats, Charles Lamb, and others were present, and it is worth quoting part of his extended recollection of this event at length to obtain a sense of his gifts as an anecdotalist:

Wordsworth was in fine cue, and we had a glorious set-to – on Homer, Shakespeare, Milton, and Virgil. ... 'Now', said Lamb, 'you old Lake poet, you rascally poet, why do you call Voltaire dull?' We all defended Wordsworth, and affirmed there was a state of mind when Voltaire would be dull. 'Well', said Lamb, 'here's [to] Voltaire' ... It was delightful to see the good humour of Wordsworth in giving in to all our frolics without affectation and laughing as heartily as the best of us.

In the morning of this delightful day, a gentleman, a perfect stranger, had called on me. He said he knew my friends, had an enthusiasm for Wordsworth, and begged I would procure him the happiness of an introduction. He told me he was a comptroller of stamps ... I thought it a liberty; but still, as he seemed a gentleman, I told him he might come.

... In introducing him to Wordsworth I forgot to say who he was. After a little time the comptroller looked down, looked up, and said to Wordsworth: 'Don't you think, sir, Milton was a great genius?' Keats looked at me, Wordsworth looked at the comptroller. Lamb, who was dozing by the fire turned round and said: 'Pray, sir, did you say Milton was a great genius?' 'No, Sir: I asked Mr. Wordsworth if he were not'. 'Oh', said Lamb, 'then you are a silly fellow'. 'Charles! my dear Charles!' said Wordsworth; but Lamb, perfectly innocent of the confusion he had created, was off again by the fire.

After an awful pause the comptroller said: 'Don't you think Newton a great genius?' I could not stand it any longer. Keats put his head into my books ...

Haydon, as this demonstrates, was quite capable of splendid gossipy anecdotes about Wordsworth, but he was nonetheless aware of that poet's literary stature. We should be grateful to the artist, in his sublime mode, for his great portrait of Wordsworth (Fig. 12), completed in 1842, the very image of

Fig. 12   B. R. Haydon, 'Wordsworth on Helvellyn' (1842)

the Romantic conception of the creative genius engaged at the work of inspired poetic composition.

See also   Medievalism, the Sublime and the Gothic; Millenarianism; Satire.

Further Reading

David Bindman, *Blake as an Artist* (1977).
David Bindman (gen. ed.), *Blake's Illuminated Books*, 6 vols (1991–5).
Morris Eaves, *William Blake's Theory of Art* (1982).
B. R. Haydon, *Life of Benjamin Robert Haydon, Historical Painter, from his Autobiography and Journals, Edited and Compiled by Tom Taylor* (1853).
Penelope Hughes-Hallett, *The Immortal Dinner: A Famous Evening of Genius and Laughter in Literary London, 1817* (2002).
W. J. T. Mitchell, *Blake's Composite Art: A Study of the Illuminated Poetry* (1982).
Paul O'Keeffe, *A Genius for Failure: The Life of Benjamin Robert Haydon* (2009).
J. Viscomi, *Blake and the Idea of the Book* (1993).
Richard Wendorf, *Sir Joshua Reynolds: The Painter in Society* (1996).

Irish, Scottish and Welsh Poetry

While literary scholars have long acknowledged the predominance of Scotland in the production and reception of the Romantic-era novel in the work of Sir Walter Scott, James Hogg and others, it remains the case, historically, that the canon of British Romantic poetry has generally been seen as dominated by English names. Blake, Coleridge, Wordsworth, Byron (though he spent much of his early childhood in Aberdeenshire), Keats, and Shelley were all born in England and while the latter three died overseas (Byron in Greece, Keats and Shelley in Italy), the weight of their combined presence has led to the perception of England as the birthplace and even the home of British Romanticism, in terms of poetry at least.

More recently this notion has been put under pressure. Burns's status as a hugely important progenitor of Romanticism is being acknowledged and scholars have begun to reassess the poetry of Scotland, Ireland and Wales. Two other poets, from the Irish and Welsh traditions, Thomas Moore and Felicia Hemans (both tremendously popular in their day yet subsequently relegated to the foothills of canonical British Romanticism), have also received renewed attention from contemporary literary historians of those traditions, students of women's writing (in Hemans's case), and scholars working within what has been called 'archipelagic' criticism of literature from Scotland, Ireland, Wales and England (a critical perspective which focuses on the linked cultural histories of those four nations). This chapter examines the work of Burns, Moore and Hemans as representative of Scottish, Irish and Welsh poetry in the Romantic period.

Scotland and Romanticism

The founding document of the poetry of Romanticism was a slim book of verse that appeared towards the end of the eighteenth century and which can be seen as marking the beginning of a new poetical age. Printed in the provinces, well outside the metropolitan mainstream of contemporary eighteenth-century publishing, this collection of lyrics, tales, and other poems, composed in a vivid and straightforward idiom, was simultaneously experimental and also looked back to medieval balladry in a manner foreign to the dominant 'Augustan' eighteenth-century literary tradition, which had appealed for its authority to the age of Greece and Rome. This groundbreaking volume, which valorised the experience of the rural poor in a manner unprecedented in English verse and was politically liberal in articulating the voices of socially marginalised groups who had not hitherto featured in conventional poetry, quickly became a work that directly influenced a generation of Romantic poets.

Though the foregoing narrative might easily be applied to William Wordsworth and Samuel Taylor Coleridge's *Lyrical Ballads* (published in Bristol in 1798), a book seen in much conventional literary history as the starting point of Romantic-era verse, it could without difficulty describe an earlier collection, *Poems, Chiefly in the Scottish Dialect* (1786), by Robert Burns (1759–96), now generally referred to as the 'Kilmarnock edition' after the Ayrshire town in which it was published. This powerful volume, published a decade before the *Lyrical Ballads*, anticipated and in part underpinned the Lake Poets' later work. Indeed, to a certain extent mid- to late eighteenth-century Scottish poetry, particularly in Burns, but also in the slightly earlier tradition – inspired by James Thomson (1700–48), author of *The Seasons* (1726–30), once generally referred to as a master of 'pre-Romantic verse' – of James Beattie (1735–1803), 'Ossian' (James Macpherson, 1736–96) and Allan Ramsay (1684–1758), was a bedrock of early Romantic poetry, in its indebtedness to the ballad tradition, in its fascination with the experience of the peasantry, and in its shaping of specific regional and national literary identities. Such Scottish poetry emphasised – like much English Romanticism after it – the local, the traditional, the superstitious, the medieval, and the folkloric. Scotland, indeed, has a strong claim to be seen as the cradle of Romantic poetry in Great Britain and Ireland. (The same might also be remarked of periodicals of the period, given the importance of the *Edinburgh Review* (see 'Reviews, Magazines and the Essay').) Even the novel, if we take the national tale and historical fiction as representative of that genre during the Romantic period, can be said to have its roots not in English literary soil but in Sir Walter Scott's influential and vastly popular chronicles of Scottish history in the Waverley novels, and in Maria Edgeworth's and Lady Morgan's narratives of Irish life, notably Edgeworth's *Castle Rackrent* (1800) and Morgan's *The Wild Irish Girl* (1806), a central fiction in the development of the national tale in nineteenth-century Ireland (see 'The Novel').

The most important voice in the emergent tradition of Romantic poetry is that of Burns, his verse in turns idealising, fiercely satirical, and homely; a poetry that is ideologically innovative, learned and canonically allusive in simultaneity. We see in his work many things, but, throughout, a close engagement with Scottish peasant life. Whether in the vivid idiom of his valorisation of cottage ways in 'The Cotter's Saturday Night' ('To you I sing, in simple Scottish lays, / The *lowly train* in life's sequester'd scene'), or in the revival of the political ballad in the Jacobite manner, in such stuff as 'Robert Bruce's March to Bannockburn', popularly known as 'Scots, wha hae', or in songs of romantic sociability, notably that perpetual favourite 'Auld Lang Syne' ('We'll tak a cup o' kindness yet ...'), there is throughout Burns's *oeuvre* an unapologetic revelling in Scottish life and the everyday language of the Scots 'mither tongue'. Simplicity of diction would later define the poetical experiment that was the *Lyrical Ballads*, but it was Burns, over a decade before Wordsworth and Coleridge, who rejected the overelaborate poeticisms of eighteenth-century neoclassicism – what Wordsworth would deride as 'poetic diction' – in favour of a plainer, less adorned idiom.

Take, for instance, Burns's most famous lyric, 'O my Luve's like a red, red rose' (published 1796), a work heavy with the Scots. Before citing it, it should be pointed out that Robert Burns – of all British poets the one most associated with a 'non-standard dialect' – used his Scots as a matter of choice. He could easily write poetry in standard English, as that great poem 'The Cotter's Saturday Night' (1796), which uses both idioms with ease, demonstrates. But in this lyric Burns was writing out his linguistic birthright:

> O my Luve's like a red, red rose,
>   That's newly sprung in June;
> O my Luve's like the melodie
>   That's sweetly play'd in tune. –
>
> As fair art thou, my bonnie lass,
>   So deep in luve am I;
> And I will luve thee still, my Dear,
>   Till a' the seas gang dry.

Setting aside their beauty and power, if we look closely at these lines, one might say that in the poetic tradition of Donne, Shakespeare, and even Pope, which foregrounded witty and striking metaphors (Donne's 'At the round earth's imagin'd corners' and the like), the figurative content of these lines is homely, perhaps to some readers even threadbare. And yet the power of Burns's stanzas lies in their very refusal to work, so to speak, from the copybook of poetic technique. Love, in the poet's account, is so important that self-congratulatory figurative brilliance should give way to good honest metaphor – the real poetic 'language of men', to borrow Wordsworth's famous phrase. Sharp metaphoric formulation – in the Renaissance and Augustan tradition – has yielded to a new Romantic sensibility, which presents itself as true, poignant, and as the very expression of the heart.

Take also, for instance, the aforementioned 'Scots, wha hae' (1794), a poem which relates in a robust vernacular medieval Scotland's struggle to retain its independence. The opening stanza depicts King Robert the Bruce leading the Scottish army against the English at the Battle of Bannockburn in 1314:

> Scots, wha hae wi' WALLACE bled,
> Scots, wham BRUCE has aften led,
> Welcome to your gory bed, –
>   Or to victorie!
>
> Now's the day, and now's the hour;
> See the front o' battle lour;
> See approach proud EDWARD's power,
>   Chains and Slaverie! –

Here, as elsewhere, Burns's idiom is plain, forcefully direct, and affective, a balance of strengths which was manifest in the next few years in Blake's *Songs of Innocence and of Experience* (1794) as well as in the *Lyrical Ballads*. It is also, like its successors, quietly controlled and powerful.

The emotion and simple imagery of Burnsian verse anticipates Wordsworth's use of balladry and his emphasis – the phrase warrants repetition – upon 'the real language of men'. Burns, in turn, had his own take on the Romantic grotesquerie, later found in such works as Coleridge's 'Ancient Mariner' (1798; 1817) and 'Christabel' (1798–1801; 1816), in his 'Tam O' Shanter' (1791), which tells the story of an Ayrshire farmer who has spent the day supping in a warm tavern prior to journeying home alone on his mare. Passing the Kirk at Alloway he sees in the churchyard a frightful vision, conjured by an over-lubricated imagination, of the 'deil's' (devil's) revels. Old Nick himself plays the bagpipes and witches and warlocks dance along to the skirl. Reason and good sense give way to lust as Tam is captivated by the erotic dancing of one diabolically alluring 'winsome wench' in particular. Spotted by the witches, Tam narrowly escapes with his life following a frenetic chase. The poem ends in a tongue-in-cheek moral ('take heed: / When'er to drink you are inclin'd / Or cutty-sarks rin in your mind' ...) that spending time drinking whisky and musing on short skirts will only end in tears.

Ireland and Wales

Stylistically and thematically strong cross-cultural currents link Scottish poetry of the Romantic period to that of Ireland and Wales, represented here by the 'Bard of Erin' Thomas Moore's (1779–1852) *Irish Melodies* (1808–34) and by Felicia Hemans's (1793–1835) *Welsh Melodies* (1822). This intertextual and transnational fluidity is evident in the stress laid in the poetry of all three nations upon the figure of the 'bard' or 'minstrel' as the embodiment or incarnation of the national spirit, and in the idealisation of the 'wild notes' of lyre and song as a marker of national identity. On the other hand, the cheerful bawdiness of Scotland, itself a measure of Scottish selfhood in the ballads of Burns or James Hogg (or, indeed, the picaresque eighteenth-century novels of Tobias Smollett before them), is notably absent from the comparatively sanitised lyrics of Hemans's and Moore's national melodies, which both reach back to the tradition of classical eighteenth-century elegy and to what has been called the 'pre-Romantic' 'Celticism' of Thomas Gray's 'The Bard' (1757), James Beattie's *The Minstrel* (1771) and James Macpherson's 'Ossian' poems (1762/3).

Thomas Moore's *Irish Melodies*

In the figure of Ossian, Macpherson produced a melodramatic blend of idealised bravery and intense sorrow that proved immensely influential on the development of Romantic poetry within the national traditions of Ireland, Scotland, and Wales. The 'Ossian' cycle of poems is a shaping presence on Thomas Moore's *Irish Melodies* and it became a touchstone for antiquarians and poets interested in reclaiming Celtic material, from the Irish scholars Samuel Ferguson and Douglas Hyde through to W. B. Yeats (who in 1889 published his version of the Ossian myth as the title poem of *The Wanderings of Oisin and Other Poems*).

Macpherson provided a sophisticated eighteenth-century audience with a re-creation of the Gaelic past that fused the martial valour of the ancient Celts with fashionable sentimental virtues. In Moore's own lifetime his *Irish Melodies* (published in 10 'numbers' (instalments) between 1808 and 1834), secured him fame as the 'Bard of Erin', Ireland's national poet, a soubriquet that resonated throughout the nineteenth century and much of the twentieth. Heroic sentiment is threaded through the *Irish Melodies*, a series of songs elegiac and martial in which Ireland's warriors are also idealised as lovers, faithful to the last to the memory of the nation's former glories. Consider, for example, the melancholy lyric 'Go Where Glory Waits Thee' (1808):

> Go where glory waits thee,
> But, while fame elates thee,
>   Oh! still remember me.
> When the praise thou meetest
> To thine ear is sweetest,
>   Oh! then remember me.
> Other arms may press thee,
> Dearer friends caress thee,
> All the joys that bless thee,
>   Sweeter far may be;
> But when friends are nearest,
> And when joys are dearest,
>   Oh! then remember me!

The use of evocative, quasi-erotic imagery to advocate the cause of loyalty to Ireland removes the distinction between the personal and political so that loyalty to country is characterised as loyalty to one's beloved. The insistent rhyming of 'thee' and 'me' involves the reader in a shared auditory experience of timeless mutual love between country and patriot.

Moore's musical talent was such that when he was seated at his piano, his songs sometimes reduced his audience to tears. The Irish novelist Lady Morgan recalled that as 'two scrubby-headed and very ill-dressed little girls' she and her sister once heard Moore perform at an informal gathering held at his parents' Dublin home. Her sister's tears, she said, 'dropped like dew – "not touched but rapt, not wakened but inspired"'. Some of Moore's melodies, such as 'The Minstrel Boy' (first published in the fifth instalment, of 1813), which depicts the dead youth as the incarnation of the national patriot-hero, have remained perennially popular (a version by Joe Strummer, of English punk rockers The Clash, provided the soundtrack to the end credits of the 2001 American war movie *Black Hawk Down*, directed by Ridley Scott):

> The Minstrel Boy to the war is gone,
>   In the ranks of death you'll find him;
> His father's sword he has girded on,
>   And his wild harp slung behind him. –
> 'Land of song!' said the warrior-bard,
>   'Though all the world betrays thee,
> *One* sword, at least, thy rights shall guard,
>   *One* faithful harp shall praise thee!'

Song, sword and harp are inseparable in Moore's imagining of Ireland's epic past, captured in the strongly rhythmical beat of the iambic lines and the powerful symbolism of the harp itself. The adjective 'wild', a synonym for the authentic force or passion of the harp, as implicitly contrasted with the febrile excitement of the Regency *bon ton* (in whose drawing rooms the *Melodies* were often performed), places this melody on the primitivist register of the 'Ossian' poems. Moore treats the symbolic harp of Erin as a kind of poetical metaphor for the land and for Ireland's ancient glory.

Felicia Hemans and the *Welsh Melodies*

In similar vein to Moore, Felicia Hemans, who moved to North Wales as a girl aged seven and identified strongly with the Welsh nation, composed lyrics to accompany the volume *A Selection of Welsh Melodies*, published in 1822, for which the airs had been collected and edited by the then renowned Welsh composer John Parry (who wrote music for several volumes of both Welsh and Scottish melodies). Hemans's contribution consisted of some twenty intensely patriotic poems that romanticised 'Cambria's' proud martial history (for example, in 'Owen Glyndwr's War-Song', which honours the fourteenth-century leader of a long – ultimately unsuccessful – rebellion against the perfidious Saxon) and celebrated her bardic culture (in such titles as 'The Harp of Wales' and 'Taliesin's Prophecy').

Hailed by the Welsh societies of the day as a 'poet for Wales', she was made an honorary member of the Royal Cambrian Institution, and in 1822 delivered a poetical address, 'The Meeting of the Bards', to the London Eisteddfod. As with many of Hemans's Welsh poems this address is not represented in modern anthologies of Romanticism, or, indeed, in collections of her verse, in which her Welsh poems tend to be marginalised.

> WHERE met our bards of old? – the glorious throng,
> They of the mountain and the battle-song?
> They met – oh! not in kingly hall or bower,
> But where wild Nature girt herself with power:

The meeting of *Gorseddau*, or bards, occurred in the open air rather than in 'kingly hall or bower'. Here we see Hemans not only identifying herself with the bardic tradition – in her use of the first-person plural possessive pronoun 'our' – but also aligning herself with the martial poetic tradition of heroic resistance to English rule:

> Well might bold Freedom's soul pervade the strains,
> Which startled eagles from their lone domains,
> And, like a breeze, in chainless triumph, went
> Up through the blue resounding firmament!
> Whence came the echoes to those numbers high? –
> 'Twas from the battle-fields of days gone by!
> And from the tombs of heroes, laid to rest
> With their good swords, upon the mountain's breast.

Echoes of Macpherson's 'Ossian' poems and Moore's *Irish Melodies* resound through Hemans's Welsh verses. Unlike Moore and Macpherson, however, Felicia Hemans was not born in the country whose poetry and military heroism she commemorates, and neither was her loyalty exclusive to one nation. The *Welsh Melodies'* celebrations of ancient Welsh culture jockey for attention with her rather more famous verses honouring British victories in the Napoleonic War (both Hemans's husband and her brother were soldiers in Wellington's army), as well with those works commemorating the heroism of the Greek and Spanish armies, in such volumes as *England and Spain; or, Valour and Patriotism* (1808), *Modern Greece* (1817), and *The Siege of Valencia* (1823). This cosmopolitan reach notwithstanding, it was the sentimental poems about English domestic life that established Hemans's popularity in the Victorian age, poems such as the often-anthologised 'Homes of England', which continue (perhaps misleadingly) to define her reputation today.

> The free, fair Homes of England!
>   Long, long, in hut and hall,
> May hearts of native proof be rear'd
>   To guard each hallow'd wall!
> And green for ever be the groves,
>   And bright the flowery sod,
> Where first the child's glad spirit loves
>   Its country and its God!

What are we to make of Hemans's twin allegiances? Hemans's Welsh poetic predecessor Jane Brereton (1685–1740) frequently referred to herself as 'Cambro-Briton' (Welsh-British) and the same could be said of Hemans, who served as the national poet of two nations at once. And it is this duality which makes Hemans so interesting a figure. Hemans's is a nationalism wedded to a cosmopolitan outlook – she is not only linked through the *Welsh Melodies* to the Irish and Scottish traditions, forged in a resistance to English domination, but also to a tradition of what might be called 'transnational' Romanticism. This perhaps signals the existence of a more fluid concept of national identity during the Romantic era than our modern age is often prepared to admit, but to which Byron (born in London, raised in Scotland, and who died in the cause of Greek independence), Hemans, the Anglo-Welsh Briton, and perhaps even Moore, 'Ireland's Minstrel' (who spent most of his adult years in England while writing constantly about Ireland), could testify.

See also Reviews, Magazines and the Essay; The Novel.

Further Reading

Stephen C. Behrendt, *Irish Women Poets of the Romantic Period* (2008).
Katie Gramich and Catherine Brennan (eds), *Welsh Women's Poetry 1460–2001. An Anthology* (2003).
John Kerrigan, *Archipelagic English: Literature, History, and Politics 1603–1707* (2008).
Murray Pittock, *Scottish and Irish Romanticism* (2008).

Medievalism, the Sublime and the Gothic

Medievalism and the 'Gothic Revival'

The Gothic revival of the Victorian period, as manifested in the writings of John Ruskin and Augustus Pugin (and in the neo-Gothic architecture of public buildings such as the rebuilt Houses of Parliament and St Pancras), is well known in English cultural history. However, this upsurge of interest in the art and architecture of the Middle Ages (the word 'Gothic' in its older sense simply means 'medieval') had Romantic-era antecedents, notably in the writings of Sir Walter Scott but also to a certain extent in the medievalism of Robert Burns's 1786 'Kilmarnock edition' and that of the Romantic poets, from Wordsworth and Coleridge's *Lyrical Ballads* of 1798 to Keats's 'La Belle Dame Sans Merci' (1819). These were, in turn, indebted to mid- to late eighteenth-century writings about the Middle Ages. Pugin's *Contrasts: or, A Parallel between the Noble Edifices of the Fourteenth and Fifteenth Centuries and Similar Buildings of the Present Day, Shewing the Present Decay of Taste* (1836), which praised medieval architecture in contradistinction to modern classicism, was the culmination of what has been described as the first Gothic revival, a renaissance of interest which began in the 1750s and which had profound consequences for the architecture, novels and poetry of subsequent decades.

A century before the publication of *Contrasts*, the opinions expressed in Pugin's salute to the 'Christian architecture' of the Middle Ages would have seemed decidedly eccentric in a neoclassical age which valued classical architecture and the literature of Greece and Rome, and tended to consider medieval buildings and works of art as rude and unsophisticated. However, by the early nineteenth century, the art and literature of the Middle Ages had been restored to a measure of critical esteem. This revaluation was not all attributable to the author of *Waverley*. Though Scott, the editor of several volumes of medieval balladry, the author of a number of novels set in the medieval period, and the designer of his own magnificent Gothic pile, Abbotsford near Melrose in the Scottish borders, was the inspiring spirit behind the second Gothic revival, it is important to realise that the author's medievalism had its own, eighteenth-century antecedents. Scott's interest in Border balladry, for example, manifested most particularly in his three-volume collection of *Minstrelsy of the Scottish Border* (1802–3), was heavily influenced by Bishop Percy's highly successful *Reliques of Ancient English Poetry* (1765), an anthology of around two hundred English and Scottish medieval ballads, romances and songs. In his introduction to the *Reliques*, Thomas Percy (1729–1811) made the case for the importance of medieval culture, valorising in particular the concept of chivalry, which he saw as the source of much that was to be lauded in modern manners, whether martial or marital: 'that fondness for going in quest of adventures [and] that respectful complaisance shown to the fair sex … are all of Gothic origin'. (Scott himself concurred. He wrote an 'Essay on Chivalry' in 1818 for the *Encyclopaedia Britannica* and, furthermore, placed these words into the mouth of the eponymous hero of his *Ivanhoe*, published in the following year: 'the pure light of chivalry, which alone distinguishes the noble from the base, the gentle knight from the churl and the savage').

The Reverend Percy was not the first to make such an argument. Five years before the first edition of the bishop's collection, the scholar Richard Hurd (1720–1808) had produced his *Letters on Chivalry and Romance* (1862), a book which portrays the Middle Ages as a period closer to 'nature' than classical times. Hurd views the neoclassical literary standards of the Augustans as unsuitable to explicate the works of art of the Middle Ages, which, he maintains, were composed on different, though equally valid, aesthetic principles. To Hurd the 'Gothic' – 'a world of fine fabling' as he brilliantly puts it – was more poetical than the 'Grecian'. Indeed, Hurd argues that Homer himself would have preferred the Middle Ages to the glory of Greece, on account of 'the improved gallantry of the feudal times and the superior solemnity of their superstitions'.

Late eighteenth-century poetry began to reflect this antiquarian rediscovery of the Middle Ages. The theorist Hurd and the antiquarian Percy were followed by a generation of poets who wrote modern verse indebted in part to medieval balladry: Burns's first collection, *Poems, Chiefly in the Scottish Dialect* (1786; the 'Kilmarnock edition' after the Scottish town in which it was first published), Wordsworth and Coleridge's *Lyrical Ballads* (1798; the 'Rime of the Ancient Mariner' being the most famous post-medieval ballad in

English literature), and Scott's own *The Lay of the Last Minstrel* (1805), which imitates both medieval romance and Scots minstrelsy:

> O Caledonia! Stern and wild,
> Meet nurse for a poetic child!
> Land of brown heath and shaggy wood,
> Land of the mountain and the flood.

The ballads of the Middle Ages gave the poets of the early Romantic period a model of 'simplicity' and of the 'natural' which was ideally suited to their critical repudiation of the over-elaborate nature of contemporary, neoclassical, 'poetic diction' (see 'Literary and Philosophical Key Concepts I: The First Generation Romantic Poets').

Some notable later eighteenth-century poetry actually masqueraded directly as medieval verse. The 'marvellous boy' (Wordsworth's phrase) Thomas Chatterton's 'Rowley poems' (1768–9) purported to be the fifteenth-century verse effusions of the Bristol poet Thomas Rowley – a man who never existed – and James Macpherson's hugely successful 'Ossian' poems (1762/3) fused translations of some elderly Gaelic poetry with much writing of Macpherson's own contrivance. In the year before his death the precocious Chatterton (1752–70), who, beset by worries about debt and failure, committed suicide at the age of seventeen, persuaded Horace Walpole, 4th earl of Orford (1717–97), one of the most notable figures of the mid-eighteenth-century Gothic revival, that a treatise on art which he had written but signed 'bie T. Rowleie' was a genuine medieval document. Walpole, who swiftly disabused himself of this conviction and recognised the hoax (much to Chatterton's bitterness and disappointment), has gone down in history as the father of the 'Gothic novel'. His *The Castle of Otranto. A Gothic Story* (1764), the first effort in that dark genre, is a tale of the supernatural, set, rather imprecisely, somewhere 'between 1095, the era of the first Crusade, and 1243, the date of the last'. This was published four years after Hurd's *magnum opus* and the year before Percy's, and it participates in the same project of re-reading and reinterpreting the Middle – or Gothic – Ages. It was part of the author's decades-long fascination with matters medieval; Walpole was a leading figure in the renaissance of interest in the architecture of the Middle Ages, turning his home at Strawberry Hill in Twickenham into 'a little Gothic castle', and he was also an enthusiastic collector of Gothic artefacts and *objets d'art*.

The word 'Gothic' as it was used in *A Gothic Story*, the subtitle of Walpole's *Otranto*, simply meant 'medieval', the then-conventional sense of the term. However, by the turn of the nineteenth century, the term 'Gothic' was being used by transference to signify the new tales and novels dealing with the fantastic or the macabre and generally set in a threatening past, from Ann Radcliffe's best-selling *The Romance of the Forest* (1791) and *The Italian* (1797) to pot-boilers such as Sarah Scudgell Wilkinson's *The Subterranean Passage; or the Gothic Cell. A Romance* (1803) and the *Priory of St Clair; or, Spectre of the Murdered Nun: A Gothic Tale* (1811). Nowadays, instead of denoting a particular historical setting, the word is used as an adjective which could be applied to novels from the Romantic era and beyond which manifest a claustrophobic air of terror and/or an air of the supernatural, whenever their historical setting, as in James Hogg's *The Private Memoirs and Confessions of a Justified Sinner* (1824), which has an eighteenth-century, northern European (Scottish), Protestant location rather than – as in *Otranto* – a medieval, Roman Catholic, southern European scene. From *The Castle of Otranto* onwards, the Gothic genre enjoyed a considerable vogue in the late eighteenth century, reaching the height of its popularity in the 1790s with the success of Radcliffe's *The Mysteries of Udolpho* (1794) and the scandalous *The Monk. A Romance* (1796) by Matthew Lewis, MP, and, later – during the post-Napoleonic period – that of Mary Shelley's *Frankenstein, or The Modern Prometheus* (1818), John Polidori's 'The Vampyre' (1819) and Hogg's aforementioned *Confessions of a Justified Sinner* (for the recent critical history of the Gothic novel, see 'Gender Criticism', below).

From the sufferings of Isabella and Hippolita in the *Castle of Otranto* onwards, in Gothic fiction there is a frequent emphasis on the emotional responses of the heroes and – more often – the heroines of the tales to the woes which surround them and the dangers that menace them. There are good reasons why this should be so, given the particular antecedents of the Gothic novel. The revival of the Middle Ages apart, the other tributaries flowing into the Gothic novel – and in particular those of 'the mistress of Udolpho' – were the mid-century fictions of Samuel Richardson (notably *Clarissa* (1748–9), which dwell on sexual threat in a manner later highly familiar in the Gothic novel), which informed contemporary novels of senti-ment such as Henry MacKenzie's *The Man of Feeling* (1771), and mid-eighteenth-century aesthetic theories of the sublime, notably those found in Edmund Burke's influential treatise *A Philosophical Enquiry into the Origin of our Ideas of the Sublime and Beautiful* (1757).

Edmund Burke and the Sublime

Burke (1729–97), philosopher, parliamentarian and vigorous opponent of the French Revolution (see 'British Politics 1789–1815'), was an important influence both on Romantic poetry (this encapsulated in William Wordsworth's famous assertion in *The Prelude* (1805) that as a child in the

Lake District he had been 'fostered alike by beauty and by fear') and, indeed, on the Gothic novel. Burke's account of the sublime attends to the psychological effect of the extraordinary, vast and marvellous, grounding the formulation of his aesthetics on a psychological model of pain and pleasure. His work is a kind of early reception theory, inasmuch as he aims to explain the effect of the aesthetic artefact on the reader of a text or the viewer of a painting. However, Burke's central preoccupation is with the impact of natural phenomena on the viewer of a landscape. Burke sees his two central terms as mutually exclusive. The 'beautiful', he maintains, is pleasurable, characterised by those 'qualities in things as induce in us a sense of affection and tenderness'. It is 'small', 'smooth', and – as opposed to the rugged vastness of the sublime – 'an appearance of delicacy, and even of fragility, is almost essential to it'. The 'sublime', on the other hand, whether experienced in the contemplation of a landscape or of a dramatic tragedy, is often painful and threatening. Burke writes:

> Whatever is fitted in any sort to excite the ideas of pain and danger; that is to say, whatever is in any sort terrible, or is conversant about terrible objects, or operates in a manner analogous to terror, is a source of the *sublime*; that is, it is productive of the strongest emotion of which the mind is capable of feeling.

The experience of the sublime, both Burke and Gothic novelists such as Ann Radcliffe were convinced, is necessarily accompanied by fear and terror.

Burke's attention is to nature red in tooth and claw, so to speak, and his concern with the wild 'romantic' landscape – in the eighteenth-century sense of that term – of exotic and immense mountains, waterfalls, and thunderous storms, rather than to the carefully ordered garden evident in the idealised, ordered paradigmatic version of nature available in neoclas- sicism. At the same time, his work has often been judged in gendered terms, with the beautiful seen as feminine and the sublime being viewed as a male, even patriarchal, force. Burke himself associates his notion of beauty directly with the feminine; writing of the 'delicacy' and 'fragility' of the beautiful, he comments that 'This may be remarked alike in plants and in animals, and it is obvious in the case of the fair sex.'

Burke declares in the *Enquiry* that terror is 'productive of the strongest emotion which the mind is capable of feeling'. One does not need to labour the point that the Gothic novel exploits at some level the psychology of the sublime. It aims to inculcate fear and terror in the reader; the Gothic is, in Burke's words, 'conversant about terrible objects'. Theories of the sublime make an association of aesthetics with the terrible, and so does the Gothic novel. Both attend to the psychological effect of the extraordinary and the marvellous. The psychologically-charged landscapes of the Gothic novel

are often dark, vast and gloomy, reflecting the inner turmoil felt by its characters. Writing on the visual arts, Burke characterises the sublime aspects
of landscape as 'great', 'rugged' and 'ever massive'; a grandeur of dimension that threatens an annihilation of the self when it compares its own
littleness with the power of the landscape. This is the threatening landscape
which we often find in the work of Ann Radcliffe. In her *The Romance of the
Forest*, for instance, the novelist at one point portrays the grandeur of the
landscape thus: 'His chateau stood on the borders of a small lake that was
almost environed by mountains of stupendous height, which shooting into
a variety of grotesque forms, composed a scenery singularly solemn and
sublime.' The viewing subject is literally 'stupefied' by the elemental force
of nature (again, this is Burkean; the viewer of the landscape is left in a position of abjection). Radcliffe's descriptions of 'sublime' scenery composed of
'ever-massive' mountains and so on borrows liberally from the discourse of
Burke's *Philosophical Enquiry* (indeed, the *Critical Review*, writing in 1795,
declared that Radcliffe's use of scenery 'raise[s] in the mind the highest
emotion of perfect grandeur or sublimity').

Ann Radcliffe and the Gothic Novel

The Gothic novel, spawned by the revival of interest in the Middle Ages, by
the sentimental novel and by contemporary notions of the sublime, was
described by its progenitor Walpole as an 'attempt to blend the two kinds of
romance: the ancient and the modern'. In other words, Walpole intended a
hybrid of medieval chivalric romance – fantastic and supernatural tales of
chivalry and knighthood featuring the likes of King Arthur – and the modern
romance, that is, the more contemporary novel ('romance' was then a
synonym of the word 'novel'), with its simulated realism, of Daniel Defoe,
Samuel Richardson and others. The early (that is, eighteenth-century)
Gothic novel of Walpole and others frequently invoked the supernatural in
fantastic and macabre stories set amidst picturesque and exotic landscapes, often in southern Europe – principally Spain and Italy – and generally set in some vaguely medieval time. The picturesque settings of these
works often feature a number of conventional scenes – monasteries, grave-
yards, castles, horrid cloisters, subterranean passages, and sinister ruins.
Giants, ghosts, menacing monks and wicked nuns frequently walk the
pages of Gothic novels and alongside all of this 'Gothic machinery' run a
number of stock plot devices: family curses, apparitions, portents and
visions. Here beautiful maidens in distress face patriarchal oppression,
imprisonment, and the threat of violence, sometimes even of sexual viola-
tion. These happenings resound through the Gothic tale in its first decades,
from Walpole's work in the 1760s, to Clara Reeve's in the 1770s (*The*

Champion of Virtue: A Gothic Story (1777; described by its author as a 'literary offspring of The Castle of Otranto', though one which innovates in setting the action in medieval England), which was re-published as *The Old English Baron* in the following year), through to the fiction of Lewis and Radcliffe in the 1790s (which is generally seen as the great decade of conventional Gothic fiction).

The novels of Ann Radcliffe are notable among Romantic-era Gothic novels in manifesting an unwillingness to allow the fictional 'reality' of the supernatural events which provided much of their interest to contemporary readers. Although the novelist employs the post-Walpolean repertoire of preternatural plot devices – spectral appearances, apparitions, and so on – all of these are eventually explained away at the end of her novels of the 1790s, in the manner of the resolution of an episode of *Scooby Doo* (the so-called *surnaturel expliqué* ['supernatural explained'] methodology). Radcliffe raises the spectre of the irrational only to return us firmly, in the final analysis, to the world of rational agency. (Sir Walter Scott noted 'the rule which the author imposes upon herself, that all the circumstances of her narrative, however mysterious, and apparently superhuman, were to be accounted for on natural principles, at the winding up of the story'.) In these morally comforting resolutions, evil is vanquished and Radcliffe's female protagonists – from being imprisoned and menaced by the malign likes of the mysterious monk Schedoni in *The Italian* – are liberated and – like Ellena in that novel – are granted the canonical ending of classical comedy, marriage. Both superstition and excessive passion are ultimately rejected in Radcliffe's rational world view, and the irrational and malevolent, however powerful they once seemed, are eventually seen off.

Matthew 'Monk' Lewis, on the other hand, had no such qualms about the supernatural, and his grotesquerie in *The Monk* is 'real' in its own terms, with his eponymous anti-hero guilty of a catalogue of diabolical wickedness: fornication, matricide, incestuous rape and murder, before Satan himself eventually comes to carry him off to destruction. The heroine of his tale ends up drugged, raped and murdered (by her own brother) in a scene still troubling today. The book disturbed Coleridge, whose review of the volume criticised it strongly on moral grounds; though *The Monk* was the 'offspring of no common genius', it was damaged by its 'libidinous minuteness' and 'impiety' and willingness to portray 'abominations'. Lewisian Gothic – unflinchingly explicit in terms of violence and, indeed, sex, and full of supernatural *diablerie* – has sometimes been referred to as the Gothic 'School of Horror' while that in the Radcliffean manner – more genteel, with its supernatural suggestions, use of tension and ultimate rationalism – has been called the 'School of Terror'. These distinctions are, it might be pointed out, taken from Ann Radcliffe herself. In her essay 'On the

Supernatural in Poetry' (1826), Radcliffe writes that a 'union of grandeur and obscurity' causes the sublime: 'neither Shakspeare nor Milton by their fictions, nor Mr Burke by his reasoning, anywhere looked to positive horror as a source of the sublime, though they all agree that terror is a very high one'. 'Where', she asks, 'lies the great difference between horror and terror, but in the uncertainty and obscurity, that accompany the first?'

To some readers at the time, it seemed as if the widespread taste for Gothic tales raising the spectres of death and horror during the 1790s reflected the turmoil which was then convulsing Europe after the French Revolution. The notorious French nobleman, the novelist and pornographer the Marquis de Sade (1740–1814), wrote in his *Les Crimes de l'Amour* (1800) of 'the new novels, nearly whose whole merit lies in magic and phantasmagoria, with the *Monk* at their head, which are not entirely without merit; they are the fruit of the revolution of which all Europe felt the shock'. *The Monk*'s ill-suppressed delight in riot and preoccupation with crowd violence (notably in its detailed description of an abbess's gruesome death at the hands of an angry mob) supposedly symbolises the threat faced by ancient institutions which was evident throughout Europe after 1789 and, indeed, the socio-political anxieties of a war-torn society. The notion of the supposedly 'escapist' Gothic genre actually offering a profound, if veiled, commentary on European geopolitics has been taken up by more recent critics of the genre such as David Punter (see 'Modern Critical Approaches I: From Deconstruction to Post-colonial and Psychoanalytical Criticism').

In 1794, meditating on what it called the 'Gothick tale', a contributor to the *Anthologia Hibernica* argued that 'to a Briton ... the whole of the Gothic system, with its train of witcheries and magic, has a certain awful obscurity in its nature, that renders it ... peculiarly the fit abode of fiction'. This sentiment is indubitably Burkean, but it is also testimony to contemporary Protestant British perceptions of the Middle Ages as an age of credulity and outdated religion. Gothic fictions often draw an implicit contrast between the past – an age of superstition – and the present – a time of enlightenment. Mediterranean scenes – such as the Italianate settings of much Jacobean and Elizabethan tragedy – are not uncommon in English literature, adding a pleasing exoticism to tales of blood, but there is a certain self-congratulatory aspect to the Gothic novel, a conviction of the superiority of modern British culture over the 'foreign', places which are mired in the past. The last great traditional Gothic novel of the Romantic era, *Melmoth the Wanderer* (1820) by Charles Robert Maturin (1780–1824), a Church of Ireland clergyman, makes the implicit anti-Catholicism of the Gothic novel explicit in its tales of the Spanish Inquisition and soapbox oratory condemning the religious system of Roman Catholicism (Immalee, his 'noble savage' heroine, for instance, when taken to Spain expects to find a 'Christian land', and instead finds 'only Catholics'). (Equally interesting in Maturin's work – and that of M. G. Lewis before him – is its underlying attention to illicit sexuality, notably in its intimations of homosexuality (see 'Gender Criticism').)

In the same period in which Maturin's huge and remarkable book, in the words of Francis Jeffrey in the *Edinburgh Review*, 'rak[ed] in the long-forgotten rubbish of Popery for extinct enormities' ('which he exaggerates as the inevitable result, rather than the casual abuse of the system'), the Gothic was taking new conceptual directions, in both short story and novel, as well as looking backwards at medieval Catholicism. *Blackwood's Edinburgh Magazine*, established in 1817, began to publish its influential series of short Gothic tales which directly influenced the work of Edgar Allan Poe in the 1830s and 1840s. In the same period that monstrous, bloodthirsty figure which still possesses the popular imagination in our day – the vampire – made its first appearance in Gothic fiction, in John Polidori's story 'The Vampyre' (1819) (its central figure, Lord Ruthven, is a thinly-veiled version of Lord Byron, for whom Polidori (1795–1821) – who poisoned himself to death at the age of twenty-five – briefly acted as personal physician).

The Gothic novel was also rapidly mutating into new forms in this period, in James Hogg's meditation on sin and suffering in his religious satire on Calvinism, *The Private Memoirs and Confessions of a Justified Sinner* (1824; see 'Religion and Atheism'), and the 'scientific Gothic' of Mary Shelley's famous *Frankenstein; or The Modern Prometheus* (1818). (It might be pointed out that Shelley's parents had both written fictions which used Gothic elements, notably unjust imprisonment and persecution, though with contemporary settings: William Godwin's *The Adventures of Caleb Williams* (1794), and Mary Wollstonecraft's *The Wrongs of Woman; or, Maria* (1798); for both, see 'The Novel'.) Both Hogg and Shelley emphasise the notions of duality and the Doppelgänger, which were to become so important in Gothic-tinged fictions of the nineteenth century such as R. L. Stevenson's *The Strange Case of Dr Jekyll and Mr Hyde* (1886) and Oscar Wilde's *The Picture of Dorian Gray* (1890). And both of their books deal with matters criminological, in considering how and why people behave – or are driven to behave – in a violent and tyrannical, even murderous manner. The Gothic addresses the important, if time-worn, issue of the origins of evil. The same moral from scripture that Horace Walpole, in the preface to the second edition of his book, considered summed up his *Otranto*: '*that the sins of fathers are visited on their children*', is applicable to the *Confessions* – where Robert's father is a bitter Calvinist who assures him that he is 'a justified person, adopted among the number of God's children', thereby opening his path to madness and murder, and to

Frankenstein, where Victor's rejection of the monster, to some critics a reneging of paternal duty, turns him to the bad ('I was benevolent and good; misery made me a fiend'). Without reaching for the traditional setting in the Middle Ages, Hogg's and Shelley's atmospherics are nonetheless 'Gothic' in their intense and claustrophobic focus on the emotions of paranoia, self-accusation and self-delusion, and guilt.

See also   British History 1789–1815; From Deconstruction to Post-Colonial and Psychoanalytical Criticism; Literary and Philosophical Key Concepts I: The First Generation Romantic Poets; Gender Criticism; Religion and Atheism.

Further Reading

G. J. Barker-Benfield, *The Culture of Sensibility: Sex and Society in Eighteenth-Century Britain* (1992).
Fred Botting, *Gothic* (1996).
E. J. Clery, *The Rise of Supernatural Fiction, 1762–1800* (1995).
Elizabeth A. Fay, *Romantic Medievalism: History and the Romantic Literary Ideal* (2002).
Jerrold Hogle (ed.), *The Cambridge Companion to Gothic Fiction* (2002).
Robert Miles, *Ann Radcliffe, The Great Enchantress* (1995).
Samuel Holt Monk, *The Sublime* (1935).
David Punter (ed.), *Companion to the Gothic* (2000).
David Punter, *The Literature of Terror. A History of Gothic Fictions from 1765 to the Present Day* (1980).
Thomas Weiskel, *The Romantic Sublime: Studies in the Structure and Psychology of Transcendence* (1976).

Millenarianism

Romantic Millenarianism

In 1811, Robert Southey, then soon to be Poet Laureate, met the poet, artist and religious visionary William Blake. According to his friend Henry Crabb Robinson, Southey 'admired both his designs & his poetic talents', but considered Blake a 'decided madman' on the grounds of his conviction that 'Oxford Street is in Jerusalem'. Though this is something of a jesting slant on Blake's beliefs, the notion of a connection between the cities of Jerusalem and London was not uncommon in this period. Though certainly not a 'decided madman', Blake indubitably engaged with some fairly arcane theological beliefs, in his work. Our familiarity with that famous lyric from the preface to his *Milton* (1804–8), 'And did those feet in ancient time' (more popularly known as 'Jerusalem' in the inspirational setting made during the darkest days of the First World War by the British composer Sir Hubert Parry), should not blind us to the sheer oddness of its opening interrogations:

> And did those feet in ancient time
> Walk upon England's mountains green?
> And was the Holy Lamb of God
> On England's pleasant pastures seen?

The most likely answer to both of these questions is a straightforward 'no', of course, but it should be noted that some of Blake's contemporaries amongst the 'British Israelites' really believed that Jesus Christ had visited Albion's shore after his resurrection, and, indeed, many more in the wider Protestant culture were convinced that the saviour was due to return at any moment to usher in a new age of peace in the 'millennium', the thousand-year period of Christian harmony and joy prophesied in the twentieth chapter of the book of Revelation, and establish a paradisal 'New Jerusalem' in the modern-day world ('they shall be priests of God and of Christ', says the Bible, of the redeemed, 'and shall reign with Him a thousand years').

William Blake, like some of his most notable – and most notorious – contemporaries, was a 'millenarian' (the *Oxford English Dictionary* defines such as '[believers] in a future (and typically imminent) thousand-year age of peace and righteousness associated with the Second Coming of Christ'). The conviction spread wide; in his 'Inscription' (1797), Robert Southey himself had looked forward to 'the latter days / When Christ shall come and all things be fulfill'd'. There was a generation of religious thinkers, scientists, poets and lunatics who believed that the chaotic events in France during and after the Revolution of 1789 were apocalyptic; if not quite the seven-year tribulation spoken of in the book of the Apocalypse, then certainly portents of the end of the world and the imminence of the Second Coming. As a young man, Samuel Taylor Coleridge saw the French Revolution as a sign that the last days were nigh. In his long, difficult, visionary poem 'Religious Musings' (1796), Coleridge wrote in rhapsodic manner to implore the imminent appearance – in the material world of the late eighteenth century – of the returned Christ:

> O return! ...
> Return pure Faith! return meek Piety!
> The kingdoms of the world are yours: each heart
> Self-governed, the vast family of Love
> Raised from the common earth by common toil
> Enjoy the equal produce.

The notion of the Son of God arriving through the clouds might strike most people in our modern age as decidedly unlikely. However, it seemed to many in the early part of the Romantic period that the millennium was, indeed, near at hand. In the early 1790s, for instance, the scientist and

Unitarian divine Dr Joseph Priestley (see 'Religion and Atheism') expressed his passionately-held belief to a correspondent that the personal advent of the Messiah would, in his opinion, be manifested in no 'more than twenty years'. After his house was burnt down by a determined crowd of 'Church and King' reactionaries in 1791, Priestley, his family, and some of his followers emigrated to the United States to found a community at Northumberland, Pennsylvania, which, they hoped, would have the equality, peace and harmony that they did not see as being evident in modern British society. What Priestley was doing, in effect, was attempting to hurry along the New Jerusalem, bringing his vision of an ideal society forward in case the personal intervention of Christ should not soon be realised (Priestley's example was swiftly followed by Coleridge and Southey's abortive plans for a 'Pantisocratic' commune on the banks of the Susquehanna in the same state). Romantic-era utopianism was characterised by both a literal anticipation of the millennium (principally in the early 1790s) and an urge to construct a personal version of the ideal world in the here and now – whether in social, poetical or psychological terms (a tendency increasingly evident as the 1790s wore on, and it became obvious that whatever the fruits of the French Revolution might be, Utopia was not going to be one of them).

William Blake himself was raised in a family context of Protestant nonconformity in which millenarianism featured heavily. He had been a member of the London 'New Church', founded in the 1770s by devotees of the Swedish divine Emanuel Swedenborg (1688–1772), who had prophesied that the Last Judgement would take place in 1757, the year of the poet's birth. Blake's early visionary works such as *The French Revolution* (1791) and *America: A Prophecy* (1793) (which begins in eschatological fashion 'The dead brood over Europe, the cloud and vision descends ...') can be seen to be offering a vision of an impending apocalypse. However, as he came to understand – as the decade after the French Revolution wore on – that the new millennium was not literally at hand, Blake's work was transformed. When Blake no longer watched the skies, images of physical apocalypse, violence and rapture were now replaced in his writing by a more psychological vision of possible redemption. Swedenborgian, millenarian mysticism both informed and was mutated into the visionary world of later Blake in those symbolic epics *The Four Zoas* (1797–1804), *Milton* (1804–8), and *Jerusalem: The Emanation of the Giant Albion* (c.1804–20). Indeed, John Beer speaks for many critics in maintaining that the poet 'internalised' his 'sense of apocalypse' after the mid-1790s into a more psychological, mental and internal vision of the New Jerusalem (one other explanation for the complexity of Blake's vision is the possibility that he was seeking to avoid prosecution for his political views by using a veiled idiom known only to the radical Protestant initiate). But that said, Blake old and Blake new had this much in common – a longing for a radically different world from the one they knew at first hand.

In his early work *Descriptive Sketches* (1793), William Wordsworth himself hinted that revolutionary war and violence might be the bloody midwife of a political millennium: 'from the innocuous flames a lovely birth / With its own Virtues springs another earth'. Wordsworth's very words here are couched in biblical phraseology; he urges his reader to 'Look up for sign of Havoc, Fire, and Sword.' In the light of his own disillusionment with the Revolution, Wordsworth, the former revolutionary firebrand, began instead to envisage, in Duncan Wu's fine phrase, a 'millennial Enlightenment' of the mind, especially after his return to the Lake District in 1799 to live in the house we now know as Dove Cottage (with Grasmere being, as Wu puts it, 'a microcosm of the millennial ideal, presided over by a benevolent landscape that literally embraces its inhabitants'). This might be seen as an experiment in living, an attempt, in the words of 'Home at Grasmere' (1800), for Wordsworth and his 'Associates in the joy of purest minds' to live an ideal existence amidst the 'undying life [of] this their mountain sanctuary'. As Morton D. Paley writes, Wordsworth now 'described a millennium only in the microcosm of "Home at Grasmere", not in the larger world'. Gayatri Chakravorty Spivak maintains that Wordsworth came to believe 'that poetry was a better cure for the oppression of mankind than political economy or revolution and that his own life had the preordained purpose of teaching mankind this lesson'. Setting aside the ideological point-scoring here, the notion of a poetic solution to failed hopes and the turn to a form of domestic millennium certainly prevails in Wordsworth's thought at the turn of the nineteenth century. As Jonathan Wordsworth puts it, in 'Home at Grasmere' 'the focus of Wordsworth's concern has shifted ... the millennium is thought of in less excited terms as "the coming of the milder day"'.

Millenarian Prophets

William Blake was familiar with more inflexibly literal-minded millenarians than he eventually proved himself to be. The epoch immediately after the French Revolution was a time of war and geopolitical turmoil and as a consequence – as in the earlier English Revolutionary period – extreme forms of visionary spirituality flourished in Britain: 'Mystics, Muggletonians, Millenaries and a variety of eccentric characters of different denominations', as William Hamilton Reid put it in his splendidly-named *The Rise and Dissolution of the Infidel Societies of this Metropolis* (1800). One of the most remarkable contemporary manifestations of millenarian thought in this period was that of the former naval lieutenant, vegetarian, pacifist and prophet Richard Brothers (1757–1824), 'the Great Prophet of Paddington Street' as he was scornfully described in proto-Southeyan words in *The Times* in 1795. In the manner of the Old Testament prophets, Brothers – a curious mixture of self-delusion, rhetorical inspiration and a kind of careful pedantry – in a series of books and pamphlets predicted the fall of empires, railed at oppressive political power, planned the architecture of the New Jerusalem, lamented the infidelity of the people to God and warned of the dire consequences of the same. After the outbreak of the Revolutionary wars with France in 1793 Brothers imperiously, though unsuccessfully, ordered George III – to his mind a modern Belshazzar – to give up his crown to him. To Brothers the French Revolution was a symbol of divine displeasure and the English monarchy – like the French one before it – was destined for God's wrath. Brothers, like Blake a philosemite, announced himself the 'Prince and Prophet of the Hebrews and Nephew of the Almighty' (this latter honorific the consequence of his supposed descent from James, the brother of Christ).

H. F. Offley, the author of a short apologium for the prophet, *Richard Brothers, Neither a Madman nor an Imposter, with a Few Observations on the Possibility of His Being the Prophet of God* (1795), maintained that Brothers's steadfast foolhardiness (as most would have seen it) in warning the king of his personal danger – in British history people had been executed in highly unpleasant ways for less – indicated that his work betokened the words of a prophet rather than the stuff of a madman's dreams:

> These prophecies have been delivered with a steadiness that little accords with the actions of a Madman; indeed the style of intrepidity with which he has ventured to predict the most fatal disasters to the rulers of nations, seems to spring from something more than an ordinary channel, and to indicate a disdain of danger that is rarely found in common men ... But how dreadful and tremendous are the threats of the Almighty? – and may we not expect that they will be fulfilled, since he [Brothers] is both imprisoned and ill-treated?

The Brotherian zealot ends his proclamation, with a cheery flourish – and in large and small caps – 'THE PEOPLE WILL BE KILLED AND THE CITY SHALL BE DESTROYED!' 'The Prophet of God' would needs be destructive, though after the bloody forces of the apocalypse had visited, the New Jerusalem would be established and it would have been good, to borrow the Biblical words of St Paul, for mankind to have suffered. The thousand-year reign of Christ and the saints would thereby begin (the book of Revelation says the wrath of God will 'destroy the destroyers of the earth'). Brothers would lead the ten 'lost tribes' of the saved to Palestine, the New Jerusalem would be established and the messianic reign of peace would begin (the prophet reckoned these wonders would be achieved by 1798). In 1795, Brothers was committed to an asylum, where he remained for just over a decade.

François Piquet once wrote of 'Blake's affiliation with a plebeian subculture based on overliteralized Biblicism' (and E. P. Thompson's study of the poet, *Witness against the Beast* (1993), pays detailed attention to the 'explosion of anti-rationalism' evident in the London of the 1780s and 1790s in 'illuminism, Masonic rituals [and] millenarianism', reading them in and against the fabric of Blake's work). The poet's talk of a new Jerusalem looks rather less unusual when read in its religious contexts, against the background of a radical nonconformity which could produce the extraordinary likes of Richard Brothers and the contemporary British Israelites, who believed, if not quite that Oxford Street was in Jerusalem, that the British nation descended from the Hebrew Diaspora (testimony to this is Brothers's last book, *A Correct Account of the Invasion and Conquest of this Island by the Saxons* (1822), in which he identified the Saxons with the lost tribes of Israel), and, indeed, in the age in which many yearned to see the arrival of 'Shiloh', the messiah returned. In the early nineteenth century, most notoriously, London thrilled to the spectacular claims of the middle-aged washerwoman prophet Joanna Southcott (1750–1814), the daughter of a farmer and religious zealot, who claimed that she was destined to become the 'Mother of the Second Messiah' (Brothers was not convinced and wrote – from his cell – the *Dissertation on the Fall of Eve* (1802), denying Joanna's status as a prophet). Southcott offered a *Warning*, to give the title of her most significant publication, *To the Whole World, from the Sealed Prophecies of Joanna Southcott, and Other Communications given Since the Writings were Opened on the 12th of January, 1803* (1803). The Anti-Christ was on his way to the world, she warned, a beast – in the words of the book of Revelation – 'with seven heads and ten horns, and seven crowns upon his heads'. This fearsome personage could only be defeated by the birth, again foretold in scripture, of the 'man-child who was to rule all nations'. In 1814, Southcott announced that she was the 'woman clothed with the sun' spoken of in the Bible and that this 'Shiloh' would be born to her – a 64-year-old virgin – in October of that year. No child of wonder ever appeared and poor Southcott died in December of that year of 'ovarian dropsy'.

In the next decade there was another upsurge of millennial feeling centred on the charismatic Scottish preacher the Reverend Edward Irving (1792–1834), briefly a voguish London preacher and the author of *The Last Days: A Discourse on the Evil Character of These Our Times, Proving Them to be The 'Perilous Times' and the 'Last Days'* (1828), in which he declared that Christ would soon return to commence 'the work of destroying all

Antichristian nations, of evangelising the world, and of governing it during the Millennium' ('we are already entered upon the last days', Irving writes, 'and the ordinary life of a man will carry many of us to the end of them'). In the following year, even more dramatically, the arsonist and prophet Jonathan Martin, brother of the great visionary artist John Martin (see 'William Blake and Art'), attempted to burn down York Minster. Martin was convinced that 'the Lord had chosen [him] to destroy the Cathedral' as a consequence of its clerics' corrupt behaviour – as the fire-starter put it – in 'going to plays, cards and such like'. Jonathan's action, indeed, might be seen as an attempt to put the visions of his brother – who had put apocalypse in oils – into practice. That said, though being declared guilty on a charge which carried the death penalty, Martin was spared on account of insanity and committed to Bedlam for life.

Interpretations of Millenarianism

What are we to make of the millenarianism of Blake and Coleridge, and indeed, that of the likes of Brothers and Southcott? E. P. Thompson (1924–93), the Marxist historian, in his great social history *The Making of the English Working Class* (1963), warned against scoffing at the latter visionaries, part of his intention to 'rescue the poor stockinger, the Luddite cropper, the "obsolete" hand-loom weaver, the "utopian" artisan, and even the deluded follower of Joanna Southcott, from the enormous condescension of posterity'. The Luddite's forlorn attempt to turn back 'progress' in destroying industrial machinery (see 'Political Protest and Popular Radicalism') and the prophet Brothers's ordering the king to step down should not be dismissed as mere folly: Thompson writes that 'Their insurrectionary conspiracies may have been foolhardy. But they lived through these times of acute social disturbance, and we did not. Their aspirations were valid in terms of their own experience.'

Though willing to say a word or two in defence of Brothers and Southcott, and many more in favour of Blake, Thompson evinced rather less sympathy for the educated middle-class former millenarians, attacking the 'disappointed Romanticism' of Wordsworth and Coleridge, whom he portrays as 'withdraw[ing] behind their own ramparts of disappointment'. Romantic poetry, Thompson declares, became a 'chiliasm [after the Greek word for the millennium] of despair'. This view, in turn, has been questioned by Seamus Perry, who writes that the Lakers' poetry, after the loss of their millennial hopes, 'reveals a much more interesting, paradoxical, and double-minded predicament: the sense of a teleology without ending, a surviving intuition of the significance or portentousness of objects and events, but without any clear scheme of the providential argument into which they might justly fit'. Either way, this is testimony to millennialism's shaping of Romanticism in both its early and its later days.

See also   William Blake and Romantic-era Art; Religion and Atheism; Political Protest and Popular Radicalism.

Further Reading

John Beer, 'Romantic Apocalypses', in *Romanticism and Millenarianism*, ed. Tim Fulford (2002), 53–70.
J. F. C. Harrison, *The Second Coming: Popular Millenarianism, 1780–1850* (1979).
Morton D. Paley, *Apocalypse and Millennium in English Romantic Poetry* (1999).
Seamus Perry, 'Coleridge's Millennial Embarrassments', *Essays in Criticism*, 50 (2000), 1–22.
François Piquet, 'Shadows of Prophecy. Blake and Millenarian Ideology', *The Yearbook of English Studies*, 19 (1989), 28–35.
Gayatri Chakravorty Spivak, *In Other Worlds: Essays in Cultural Politics* (1987).
E. P. Thompson, *The Making of the English Working Class* (1963).
E. P. Thompson, *Witness against the Beast: William Blake and the Moral Law* (1993).
Jonathan Wordsworth, *William Wordsworth: The Borders of Vision* (1982).
Duncan Wu, *Wordsworth: An Inner Life* (2003).

The Novel

The Development of the 'Realist' Novel and the Gothic Novel

The novel was still a relatively new form in the Romantic era, its roots lying in such groundbreaking works as Aphra Behn's *Oroonoko: or, the Royal Slave* (1688) and Daniel Defoe's *Robinson Crusoe* (1719). The realist novel of Defoe and Samuel Richardson (the author of the best-selling *Pamela, or Virtue Rewarded* (1740)) was joined in the second half of the eighteenth century by the Gothic novel, with its medieval settings and supernatural atmospherics. The first of that genre, Horace Walpole's *The Castle of Otranto* (1764), was described by its author as an 'attempt to blend the two kinds of romance, the ancient [medieval tales of chivalry] and the modern [the realist novel]'. (Sir Walter Scott, in his *Lives of the Novelists* (1821–4), described *Otranto* as 'the first attempt to found a tale of amusing fiction upon the ancient romances of chivalry'.) The Gothic novel, and its relations, the national tale and the historical novel, are key genres within the Romantic- era novel.

The Castle of Otranto, alongside the classic 1790s Gothic novels of Ann Radcliffe, Matthew 'Monk' Lewis and the post-Napoleonic works of Charles Robert Maturin, James Hogg and Mary Shelley, is discussed in 'Medievalism, the Sublime and the Gothic' above, but it is worth tarrying over another, less well known, example here, not least to get a sense of the transgressive potential of the Gothic in the context of the female-authored novel of the period (despite Walter Scott's pre-eminence in the field, women's writing dominates the genre of the Romantic-era novel). Take the case of the notorious *Zofloya, or The Moor* (1806) by 'Rosa Matilda' (Charlotte Dacre, the pseudonym of Charlotte Byrne, *née* King (*c*.1782–1825)), a lurid tale of criminality and sexual misconduct featuring the callous *femme fatale* Victoria and the sexually magnetic and diabolical moor Zofloya, to whom she willingly surrenders her soul. From her aberrant sexuality, murderousness and eventual death at the hands of Satan, Victoria is plainly a female version of Lewis's monk, and Dacre's fiction, in its extremity, challenges the relatively more sedate, Radcliffean form of Gothic. Dacre's anti-heroine is particularly striking: tall, statuesque and possessed of 'bold masculine features', she is uncontrollably jealous of her love rival, the small, dainty and conventionally beautiful Lilla, whom she wounds mortally in what seems to be a direct attack on the girl's physical femininity: 'With her poignard she stabbed her in the bosom, in the shoulder, and other parts.'

The *Annual Review* was not impressed with the novel: 'The principal personages in these wild pages are courtezans of the lewdest class, and murderers of the deepest dye.' It rightly, if sarcastically, acknowledged that 'the style and the story of *Zofloya*, are formed on the *chaste* model of Mr Lewis's "Monk"'. The performance is dismissed as 'an exhibition of wantonness of harlotry, which we should have hoped, that the delicacy of a female mind, would have been shocked to imagine'. The spectacular taboo-breaking of Dacre's novel in its depiction of murder, lust and transracial sexual desire (Victoria's taste for the exoticised and eroticised black) may not have had a direct politically radical agenda, but it was a bold step for a woman novelist writing in the early 1800s given the reactionary backlash against revolutionary feminism and feminine outspokenness prompted by the recent disgrace of Mary Wollstonecraft, following William Godwin's posthumous *Memoirs of the Author of A Vindication of the Rights of Woman* (1798), his candid (if seriously ill-judged) account of Wollstonecraft's unconventional sexual history (her death as a consequence of childbirth seemed to some of her harsher detractors to be a fitting end to a life ill led).

The National Tale

Contemporaneous with the emergence of the Gothic novel was the first appearance of what quickly became known as the 'national tale', in such works as Thomas Leland's now little-read *Longsword, Earl of Salisbury: An Historical Romance* (1762), and Clara Reeve's *The Old English Baron* (1778) (this latter perhaps best described as a fusion of the Gothic and the national tale). Notwithstanding these efforts by English authors, the national tale was particularly significant in terms of the Irish and Scottish traditions, especially given its purpose of proselytising, however implicitly, for nationalist causes, notably in pointing out historical wrongs or peddling narratives (or myths, depending on one's perspective) of a lost golden age. Many of Scott's fictions (to which we will return) suit this template (though the author was, it should be pointed out, a romantic nationalist who supported the Act of Union rather than an advocate of Scottish independence), as do some of the novels of the indefatigable Lady Morgan, *née* Sydney Owenson (1776–1859), poet, travel writer, memoirist and author of nine sizeable novels, of which her influential contribution to the genre of the national tale, *The Wild Irish Girl* (1806), became the most well known.

The Wild Irish Girl, which was the first fiction to use the subtitle 'A National Tale', is an epistolary love story set in former times that weaves its national concern – the plight of the Irish people – into the romance between the wild Irish girl of the novel's title, Glorvina, a Gaelic princess of ancient lineage, and the English narrator, Horatio Mortimer, son of an absentee landlord whose ancestors were granted the land belonging to Glorvina's noble family during the Cromwellian wars. In an act of reconciliation and justice, Mortimer sets out to learn the Irish language and history in order to understand (and judge) the sister nation. He also restores the property and titles originally belonging to Glorvina's ancient family line by marrying into it, a union that concludes the novel's national love plot (this notwithstanding the revelation at the altar that Mortimer and his father are descendants of the Cromwellian robber-barons who murdered Glorvina's ancestors).

The Wild Irish Girl appeared just five years after the Act of Union that bound Ireland legislatively to Westminster took effect and is generally understood in the light of that circumstance as a political allegory of colonial relations in Ireland. The romantic union of Glorvina and Mortimer is prefigured earlier in the novel by Glorvina's translations of Gaelic bardic poems into English, which she gives Mortimer to read, although the aspirant scholar of Irish history fails to understand their allegorical significance, his ignorance highlighting Morgan's own hostility towards the recent union of Ireland and Great Britain but also, perhaps, a pragmatic acceptance of the necessity of forgiveness and, possibly, even eventual reconciliation to the union itself, signalled to some by the clemency Glorvina extends to Mortimer's family through her marriage. A notice in the *Monthly Review* said of Lady Morgan's novel that 'it speaks many a good word for Ireland'. Indeed, the author herself was candid about the ideological purpose of the national tale: 'A novel is especially adapted to enable the advocate of any cause to steal upon the public, through the by-ways of the imagination, and to win from its sympathies what its reason so often refuses to yield to undeniable demonstration.'

Notwithstanding Morgan's importance in the national tale, it is another Irish woman writer, Maria Edgeworth, who has sometimes been credited with initiating the first truly historical – and regional – novel in English in her idiosyncratic and brilliant *Castle Rackrent, an Hibernian Tale* (1800). Set 'before the year 1782', this short experimental novel – which uses the device of an unreliable narrator (previously deployed by her compatriot Laurence Sterne) to keen ironic effect – is a satire on Anglo-Irish landowners which tells the story of the mismanagement of Castle Rackrent by four generations of avaricious heirs. The system of 'rack-renting' invoked in the novel's title refers to the system of inefficient estate management common in Edgeworth's day by middlemen appointed in lieu of (absentee) landlords, whose sole motivation was to extract as much profit from the rents as possible, mainly by sub-letting the land to tenant farmers.

A satiric protest at the abuses of rack-renting in particular, and more broadly at the system of absentee landlordism prevalent in the Anglo-Irish landowning class to which Edgeworth belonged, *Castle Rackrent*, like Lady Morgan's *Wild Irish Girl*, is distinguished by having a political purpose, namely to draw attention to the corrosive consequences for the Irish peasantry of (Anglo-Irish) absenteeism. The rickety nature of the Irish estates is symbolic of the corrupt and ramshackle nature of English rule in Ireland. National union has been built on poor and unreliable foundations.

The 'Jacobin' Novel

The novel was informed by ideology throughout the Romantic period. This was true of Great Britain as well as of Ireland. Much British fiction published in the 1790s was explicitly radical in its politics, unsurprisingly given the momentous events of 1789 and the impact they had on British society. This body of writing has come to be known as the 'Jacobin novel' ('Jacobin' – the party of Robespierre – was the insult thrown at British radicals by conservatives). It did not seek to offer escapist entertainment. By the 1800s the *Monthly Review* could write: 'novels were formerly written to make old women sleep, and to keep young women awake. They interfered not with the serious affairs of the world ... they amused the mind, and banished *ennui.* – Now however, they are frequently made the vehicles of the most marked and serious instruction.'

Not merely a form of cultural diversion, the Jacobin novel was what the Germans call a *tendenzroman*, which is to say a novel with a moral tendency or political purpose. A foremost example of the genre is William Godwin's *Things as They Are; or, The Adventures of Caleb Williams* (1794), a novel of crime and detection and a propagandising psychological study which was also designed, in Godwin's words, 'to show the tyranny and perfidiousness exercised by the powerful members of the community against those who are less privileged than themselves'. The work deals with the persecution of Caleb Williams, a self-taught man of humble origins, who pries too deeply into his master Falkland's dark secrets. For this, he is pursued and hounded by Falkland and his agents, with this persecution clearly a metaphor for the trial and imprisonment of various members of the London Corresponding Society in the London treason trials of 1793 (see 'British Politics 1789–1815'). Godwin attacks the system of political surveillance, spying and attempts to restrict political enquiry which are evident both in a national and a domestic context, examining allegorically how, as he put it, 'the spirit and character of the government intrudes itself into every rank of society'.

A fellow traveller on the Jacobin road, Robert Bage (1730–1801), entrepreneurial paper manufacturer and one-time business partner of the poet and scientist Erasmus Darwin (see 'Medicine and Science'), had a relatively late career as a radical novelist in his early fifties. Brought up as a Quaker, Bage had a strong sense of social duty (he always paid his bills on time, and encouraged others to do likewise). The French Revolution drew him into wider public debate and his first Jacobin novel, *Man as He Is* (1792), features a young baronet who is reformed from a rakish life of fashionable aristocratic vice both through the love of a virtuous woman and by his association in France with the moderate wing of the Revolutionary leadership.

In contrast to some of his radical political caste (the names Godwin and Wollstonecraft spring to mind), Bage was no po-faced supporter of the Revolutionary social contract, demonstrating a wit evidenced by his best known fiction-for-the-cause, *Hermsprong; or, Man as He Is Not* (1796), a good-humoured satire which utilises the Rousseauian figure of the child of nature, the so-called 'noble savage', to point moral lessons for British society. Hermsprong, raised in North America by what we now describe as Native Americans, is a 'natural man', in a phrase inspired by Rousseau, who, on his arrival in England, questions orthodox social views, especially those concerning religion, morality and politics. Daringly, he walks rather than taking a coach-and-four and maintains that he could never 'suppress the sentiments of a free-born mind from any fear, religious or political'. Bage's comic novel both served a moral and political purpose and entertained; indeed, the ideologically sympathetic *Monthly Magazine* write that the author had 'probably diffused more liberal, and more just moral ideas, than could, in the same space of time, have been inculcated upon the public by a thousand sermons, or by as many dry political disquisitions'.

Bage was considered a subversive writer by many of his contemporaries; Anna Laetitia Barbauld once wrote that *Hermsprong* was 'democratical in its tendency. It was published at a time when sentiments of that nature were prevalent with a large class of people, and it was much read.' Another eminent reader, Sir Walter Scott, highly rated Bage's novelistic skills but publicly decried his politics, his theology, and, not least, what seemed to Scott to be Bage's 'sport with the ties of marriage'. The bold yet delightful character of the resolutely unmarried Miss Fluart inspired the latter charge, her subversive wit echoing Mary Wollstonecraft's notion that a woman in the married state is little better than a slave. Unlike the caricature of independent women as dour and joyless evident in conservative satire of the time, Miss Fluart has a lively sense of humour and, indeed (as her name hints), a touch of the flirt about her (accosted in one instance by an over-amorous peer, she retorts playfully: 'A kiss! Lord bless me, I thought your lordship ... had wanted to undress me!'). In *Hermsprong*, Bage created a comic and genuinely good-hearted Jacobin novel, to complement radical works of moral instruction and political jeremiads.

Wollstonecraft herself enjoyed success (and some posthumous notoriety) as a politically sententious novelist (for her contemporary Mary Hay's work, see 'Sexualities'). However, she deliberately eschewed the term 'novel', and decried the 'reveries of stupid novelists' – to use a phrase from *Vindication of the Rights of Woman* – who 'work up stale tales and describe meretricious scenes', in favour of 'fiction', thereby signalling her distance from the novelistic tradition. In its title and its preface, *Mary. A Fiction* (1788), the first of Wollstonecraft's two attempts at fictional prose, rejects the term novel, a literary form criticised for its slavish adherence to 'prescribed rules of art'. Instead, Wollstonecraft aimed to produce 'an artless tale', as she puts it, that is, a tale drawn from life, in which 'the mind of a woman who has thinking powers is displayed'. Neither particularly virtuous nor pretty, the eponymous character Mary is Wollstonecraft's feminist counterblast to the popular male-authored idealisations of femininity of her age, on the one hand Samuel Richardson's incomparable Clarissa, the all-too-too perfect heroine of his eighteenth-century blockbuster *Clarissa* (1748–9), and on the other, Jean-Jacques Rousseau's Sophie, the sexy young playmate of the boy-hero of his novel of education, *Émile* (1762).

Wollstonecraft's second (and still more radical) fiction, *The Wrongs of Woman: or, Maria. A Fragment*, lay unfinished at her death. Included by her bereaved husband Godwin in his *Posthumous Works of the Author of A Vindication of the Rights of Woman* (1798), it recounts the fate of a woman of intelligence, who discovers that the husband she has come to detest married her only for her money and prefers the company of drink and 'debauched' women to that of his wife and infant daughter. Following an attempt by her husband to prostitute to her one of his male friends, Maria tries to flee to France with her baby girl. She is thwarted in this endeavour by her husband who, fearful of losing his 'property', has her committed to an asylum where she meets and falls in love with a fellow inmate, Darnford. Maria's husband subsequently brings an action against Darnford for adultery whereupon she writes a letter to the court stating her right to leave a dissolute husband, take a new lover, and sue for divorce. The judge does not agree and the story closes (in one of the novel's several draft endings) with Maria deciding not to take her life (after Darnford abandons her) and choosing instead to live for the sake of her child together with Jemima, her warder at the lunatic asylum (a woman brutalised by misogyny and class prejudice), whom Maria transforms by the example of her own sensibility from an unsympathetic figure into a caring nurse and companion. Wollstonecraft's daring criticism of contemporary society's treatment of women is damning and comprehensive, with its attacks on the sexual double standards of the day, on the law, and on marriage as currently constituted.

Female Poets as Novelists – Charlotte Smith and Mary Robinson

The poets Charlotte Smith and Mary Robinson also enjoyed fame as novelists. Indeed, in the case of Smith (*née* Turner, 1749–1806), her novels (she published eleven between 1788 and 1802) were decidedly more successful than her poetry in commercial terms and provided her with a necessary means of subsistence. (Deserted by a feckless husband, she was left to provide for her large family alone.) In contrast to the overwhelming melancholy of Smith's poetry (see 'Literary and Philosophical Key Concepts I'), her novels, according to *The Oxford Companion to English Literature*, are 'brisk, ironic, and confident'. Her early fictions are unafraid of raising explicitly political issues. A striking illustration of that confidence is *Desmond* (1792), in which the eponymous hero travels to Revolutionary France and sees – and approves of – the Revolution at first hand, with the clear implication that Britain required root-and-branch political reform as well. The novel also defends a woman's right to be interested in politics in its portrayal of Geraldine Verney, the long-suffering wife who is eventually freed from her tyrannical and profligate husband (recalling the situation of Wollstonecraft's heroine Maria). Smith, who was estranged from her own profligate, and possibly violent, husband, expands autobiographical material into general political critique. Indeed, a key argument of the book is that women's domestic mission and domestic circumstances should actually guarantee their participation in political debate, as Smith's preface makes clear:

Women it is said have no business with politics – Why not? – Have they no interest in the scenes that are acting around them in which they have fathers, brothers, husbands, sons, or friends engaged? – Even in the commonest course of female education, they are expected to acquire some knowledge of history; and yet, if they are to have no opinion of what *is* passing, it avails little that they should be informed of what *has passed*, in a world where they are subject to such mental degradation; where they are censured as affecting masculine knowledge if they happen to have any understanding; or despised as insignificant triflers if they have none.

This passage would have sat easily in the *Vindication of the Rights of Woman*, and in the preface to her later novel, *The Young Philosopher* (1798), Smith openly expresses her admiration for Wollstonecraft; she speaks out, in the voice of one of the novel's characters, Mrs Glenmorris, against the herd mentality that restricts women's freedom of thought and expression:

If it be romantic to dare to have an opinion of one's own, and not to follow one formal tract, wrong or right, pleasant or irksome, because our grandmothers and aunts have followed it before; if not to be romantic one must go through the world with prudery, carefully settling our blinkers at every step, as a cautious coachman hoodwinks his horses' heads; if a woman, because she is a woman, must resign all pretensions to being a *reasoning* being and dares neither look to the right nor to the left, oh!

Testimony to the political disappointment that Smith felt by this period with both France and Britain is the resolution of this novel in which George Delmont, the young philosopher, leaves for a new life in the United States despairing of the reception in Great Britain of any 'whose opinions differed from those of the common world'.

Smith's feminist sentiments were something with which her celebrated contemporary Mary Robinson (*née* Derby, 1758–1800) would have concurred. Robinson published a feminist treatise, *A Letter to the Women of England on the Injustice of Mental Subordination* (1799), under the name of Anne Francis Randall, which continues the argument of Wollstonecraft's *Vindication* (see 'Sexualities'), and was a member of the Wollstonecraft and Godwin circle who defied the bounds of marital propriety in her own life by becoming the mistress of the Prince of Wales in the late 1770s (see 'Literary and Philosophical Key Concepts I').

Robinson's affair with the Prince granted her instant fame – as well as a good measure of notoriety (the satirists and caricaturists had a field day and she was mercilessly ridiculed as a money-grabbing starlet (see 'Satire')). Even so, such notoriety proved good publicity for the novels which were her principal means of support in the 1790s. The plight of the virtuous but oppressed woman which preoccupied Wollstonecraft and, to a lesser extent, Smith was evident in Robinson's third novel *Angelina* (1796), which echoes Wollstonecraft's radical view of the institution of marriage as a form of legalised prostitution and, indeed, was highly praised by the philosopher (the influence of the *Vindication of the Rights of Woman* is further apparent in Robinson's fifth novel, *Walsingham; or, The Pupil of Nature* (1797), a work that advocates women's right to inherit property and urges the importance of education for both sexes).

The *Analytical Review* (in the shape of an unsigned review by Wollstonecraft herself) wrote that the 'principal object' of the three volumes of *Angelina* 'is to expose the folly and the iniquity of those parents who attempt to compel the inclinations of their children into whatever conjugal connections their mercenary spirit may choose to prescribe, and to hold forth to just detestation the cruelty of those, who scruple not to barter a daughter's happiness, perhaps through life, for a sounding title or a glittering coronet'. Young society women are compared to African slaves, sold in golden metaphorical chains as the chattels of their fathers, notably in the figure of the unpleasant patriarch Sir Edward Clarendon, 'a perfect picture of gothic ignorance and barbarity', as the *Analytical* put it, who views his daughter Sophia as no more than a 'piece of ... merchandise'. The lively social melodrama, elopements and fainting fits of the novel are complemented by some serious proto-feminist polemic against 'legal prostitution' and for female education. Wollstonecraft argued that Robinson's fiction 'breathe[s] a spirit if independence'; for her, 'The sentiments contained in these volumes are just, animated, and rational.'

Sir Walter Scott

One of the publishing sensations of the Romantic age was the series of historical novels by Sir Walter Scott (1771–1832) initiated by the appearance of his tale of the 1745 Jacobite uprising *Waverley, or 'Tis Sixty Years Since* in 1814, published by Archibald Constable. (The second Jacobite Rebellion, or 'The Forty-Five', is the name given to the attempts of the rebel Scottish army, led by Charles Edward Stuart – Bonnie Prince Charlie as he was known – to unseat the Hanoverian rule over England and Scotland and to restore a Stuart monarchy.) Scott, already famous as a poet, initially published his novels anonymously and from the publication of *Waverley* onwards – succeeding novels were attributed to 'the author of Waverley' – the identity of 'the Great Unknown' became a subject of gossip and speculation until Scott confirmed the badly kept secret of his authorship in 1827.

The best of Scott's fiction is set in his native Scotland, notably the tales focused around Jacobite rebellion such as *Rob Roy* (1817), the aforementioned *Waverley*, and *Redgauntlet* (1824). However, he also used English settings, as in the successful *Ivanhoe* (1820; a tale of Richard the Lionheart) and *Kenilworth* (1821; set amidst the glories and treachery of the reign of Elizabeth I). Though by no means the first historical novelist, Scott is generally seen as the first major British adept of the form and he endowed his historical writing with a serious purpose not immediately evident in such Gothic fictions as Walpole's *Otranto*. Scott attempted a truth to nature in his construction of character and dialogue, a verisimilitude of plot and incident – both on the national and the local scale – which he saw as absent in the fantastic or implausible works of Gothic authors such as Radcliffe and in the earnest eagerness to instruct in the case of some of the Jacobin novelists and authors of previous national tales.

In his 'Essay on Romance' (1824), Scott defined the novel as 'a fictitious narrative, differing from the Romance, because the events are accommodated to the ordinary train of human events, and the modern state of society', an indication of what he himself brought to the novel form – an 'unmatched combination of common sense with poetic imagination', in the words of George Saintsbury. Though generals, princes and warlords feature in Scott's fictions, his heroes, as Georg Lukács observed in *The Historical Novel* (1937), are often minor figures – the foot soldiers of the narrative, so to speak – and it is they who invest the plot with meaning and incident. Scott communicates the heroic ideals of nationalism through everyday characters ('more or less mediocre, average English gentlem[e]n', as Lukács puts it) caught up in extraordinary incidents, anchoring his fictions in the life of the mass of the people against the dramatic and gripping backdrop of national conflict. Lukács saw him as a great realist rather than a fabulist in the tradition of the 'third-rate writers (Radcliffe, etc) who were supposed to be important literary forerunners of his'.

Take *Waverley*, for example, which has as its hero Edward Waverley, a young Englishman and army officer who is posted to Scotland in 1745. Neglected by his pro-Hanoverian father, Edward is much taken with his elderly uncle, a Jacobite sympathiser, and a large part of the power of the narrative resides in following Edward's own increasing enthusiasm for the Jacobite cause even though his reason tells him it is doomed to failure. Introduced to Bonnie Prince Charlie, Edward is won over by his personal charm (as much as by his political ideals), just as he is also persuaded by the enthusiasm and beauty of Flora MacIvor, sister to a young Highland chieftain and ardent Jacobite Fergus MacIvor. With the failure of the rebellion Fergus is condemned and Edward, who is rejected by Flora, marries the less glamorous Rose Bradwardine, whose placidity contrasts with Flora's enthusiasm and represents the path of political moderation. In settling for

Rose over Flora, Edward finally identifies with the realistic present of post-Union Scotland as opposed to the passionate nationalism represented by Flora. A nationalist but not a rebel – and no unthinking reactionary either – Scott suggests in his novels the need to keep the status quo and work for improvement and historical understanding within the existing order of things.

The first edition of *Waverley* sold its one thousand copies within two days of publication and established Scott as a novelist with an international reputation. An exceptionally laudatory review came from the pen of the *Edinburgh*'s Francis Jeffrey, best remembered today as the foremost antipathetic critic of William Wordsworth (see 'Reviews, Magazines and the Essay'). Even in what he called 'the marvellous parts of the story' Jeffrey identified a truth to nature in Scott's work which cast 'the whole tribe of ordinary novels into the shade'. The term 'marvellous' is suggestive here. Scott's fiction, whatever Lukács thought, owed something to the Gothic in its preoccupation with the turmoil of the past; the Waverley novels, wrote William Hazlitt, another great contemporary reviewer of Scott, 'carry us back to the feuds, the heart-burnings, the havoc, the dismay, the wrongs and the revenge of a barbarous age'. Indeed, for the essayist, reading Scott involved the modern, 'civilised' reader giving way to 'lawless, unrestrained impulses' (the release of the id, as Freudians would call it): 'as we read we throw aside the trammels of civilisation, the flimsy veil of humanity'.

Notwithstanding such contemporary critical and popular recognition of Scott's innovative genius, the author, as Edmund Blunden remarked in 1961, ultimately suffered a 'tragic enslavement' to 'the merciless machine of commercial publishing'. From the first decade of the nineteenth century Scott was among the most prolific writers of his age (between 1814 and his death in 1832 Scott published 23 works of fiction in addition to his poetry, his dramatic works and numerous reviews, essays and biographies, notably in the *Lives of the Novelists*, 1821–4). However, the banking disaster of 1826, which resulted in him being held responsible (as a partner in the printer and publisher James Ballantyne & Co.) for the collapse of Constable's company and liable for a debt of £114,000, forced him to even greater gargantuan feats of productivity, arguably shortening his life, in order to pay off his creditors, who were recompensed in full after his death in 1832. (Jane Austen did not know what was to befall Scott financially when she wrote mock-petulantly in 1814: 'Walter Scott has no business to write novels, especially good ones. – It is not fair. He has Fame and Profit enough as a Poet, and should not be taking the bread out of other people's mouths. – I do not like him, & do not mean to like *Waverley* if I can help it – but fear I must.')

Jane Austen

In a journal entry for 14 March 1826, Sir Walter Scott wrote of Jane Austen (1775–1817) that this 'young lady had a talent for describing the involvements and feelings and characters of ordinary life, which is to me the most wonderful I ever met with. The big Bow-Wow strain I can do myself like any now going; but the exquisite touch which renders ordinary commonplace things interesting from the truth of the description and the sentiment is denied to me! What a pity such a gifted creature died so early!' Like Scott the realist, Austen valued the 'truth of description' in her fiction, and she – also like the author of Waverley – was Tory in her politics, 'a conservative Christian moralist', as Marilyn Butler calls her.

Another thing Austen and Scott had in common was being well-versed in a Gothic novel which they both aimed to transcend. Her first significant fiction, *Northanger Abbey* (written 1798–1803 but not published until 1818), contains much brilliant parody and satire on Gothic fiction of the Radcliffean school. Diverting though the works of Anne Radcliffe might be, Austen's position was that the best fiction dealt with 'human nature' and, as her narrator puts it, 'Charming as were all Mrs Radcliffe's works, and charming even as were the works of all her imitators, it was not in them ... that human nature, at least in the midland counties of England, was to be looked for.' Apart from the gentle but incisive mockery of the Gothic, the book also famously contains an eloquent, indeed, a prophetic, plea for the kind of novels which Austen admired – by Maria Edgeworth and Frances Burney most particularly – to be respected as serious works of literature, in the famous peroration where Austen's narrative voice mounts the critical soapbox:

> 'I am no novel reader – I seldom look into novels – It is really very well for a novel.' – Such is the common cant. – 'And what are you reading, Miss—?' 'Oh! it is only a novel!' replies the young lady; while she lays down her book with affected indifference, or momentary shame ... only some work in which the greatest powers of the mind are displayed, in which the most thorough knowledge of human nature, the happiest delineation of its varieties, the liveliest effusions of wit and humour are conveyed to the world in the best-chosen language.

Only a fool would look down on the novel, which is sustenance for the heart and mind. *Northanger Abbey*'s hero Henry Tilney tells the astonished Catherine Morland that men 'read nearly as many [novels] as women'; the telling exception being the story's idiotic boy racer John Thorpe who has read only two, the morally spotty *Tom Jones* (1749) and Matthew Lewis's near-pornographic *The Monk* (1796).

Without the contemporary success of Scott, and with a mere handful of novels (*Sense and Sensibility* (1811), *Pride and Prejudice* (1813), *Mansfield Park* (1814), *Emma* (1816), *Persuasion* and *Northanger Abbey* (published posthumously in 1818)), Austen revolutionised the English realist novel as surely as her great contemporary. Impatient with the restrictions of the eighteenth-century epistolary form, which confined a reader's understanding of a character and 'knowledge of human nature' to what he or she could say in a letter or a journal, Austen's use of narrative irony, free indirect speech (a fusion of first and third person narrative which permitted a new interiority in the English novel) and an omniscient narrator who could position characters on the novel's moral compass and tell the reader more about them than they could themselves, facilitated the development of the nineteenth-century novel in the shape of the sisters Brontë, George Eliot and Thomas Hardy. Butler writes that after Austen, 'The great nineteenth-century novelists changed the reader's relationship to the consciousness of the central character, so that we are trained to involve ourselves more sympathetically than critically in the inward experience a novel has to offer.'

Austen did not attempt the historical sweep of her admirer Scott's epic treatment of the great social and historical forces determining the moral lives and choices of individuals. Indeed, she portrayed herself as a woman writer closeted from the wider public world with her tools of representation narrow (she compares herself to an artistic miniaturist, writing of 'the little bit (two Inches wide) of Ivory on which I work with so fine a Brush'). However, this does not mean that her novels are uninterested in politics on the micro scale, so to speak. Her novels yield a satirical and, one might say, worldly ethical vision, of the moral behaviour of the English classes in their domestic environment. Butler challenges the image of Austen as writing at one remove from the wider world in her *Jane Austen and the War of Ideas* (1975), the first study properly to acknowledge Austen's relationship to the literature of ideas and to place her novels in the political and intellectual context of post-Revolutionary Britain. While not denying that the novels' primary focus is on character and romance, Butler sees the impact of huge issues such as the French Revolution, industrialisation and the slave trade informing Austen's genteel world, and has significantly reshaped our understanding of the author's involvement with the public world.

Thomas Love Peacock

Austen apart, the other great satirical novelist of the Regency period was Thomas Love Peacock (1785–1866), the novelist, poet and essayist (notably of 'The Four Ages of Poetry' (1820), which prompted his friend

Shelley to pen his great polemical reply 'A Defence of Poetry' (1820; see 'Literary and Philosophical Key Concepts II')). Peacock wrote a series of brilliant prose satires during the Regency, notably – and in quick succession – *Headlong Hall* (1816), *Melincourt* (1817), and *Nightmare Abbey* (1818). These works eschew the realism of Austen in their use of Socratic dialogue (in featuring long, hilarious conversations, often over drink and dinner). They also – and again unlike the author of *Pride and Prejudice* – do not manifest a conservative politics. However, the radical friend of Shelley shared Austen's sceptical eye and his satires on contemporary poetry, politics and philosophy offer a sharp critique of what we now refer to as Romanic poetry.

Nightmare Abbey, a *roman à clef* satirising some of the major poets of the day, mocks what it implies are Byron's (Mr Cypress's) dark self-preoccupations, Shelley's (Scythrop Glowry's) esoteric enthusiasms, and Coleridge's (Mr Flosky's) gloomy Germanic transcendentalism (even Scythrop's tiggerish energy cannot rouse the residents and house guests of the abbey from their immersion in the 'blue devils'). Byron is perhaps the principal target; Peacock declared that he thought 'it necessary to "make a stand" against the "encroachments" of black bile' in 'Byronism' (see 'Literary and Philosophical Key Concepts II'). 'The fourth canto of "Childe Harold"', Peacock maintained, 'is really too bad. I cannot consent to be *auditor tantum* [a listener only] of this systematic "poisoning" of the "mind" of the "reading public".' Peacock skewers his lordship in Mr Cypress's misanthropic effusions, some of which are verbatim parody of the first canto of *Childe Harold's Pilgrimage* (1812). For instance, Byron writes in the following manner in that poem:

> Our life is a false Nature – 'tis not in
> The harmony of things – this hard decree,
> This uneradicable taint of Sin,
> This boundless Upas ...

In Peacock's prose parody, what the novelist saw as Byron's relish for attitudinising and morally pernicious angst-ridden misanthropy (symbolised by the image of the poisonous Upas tree), is transformed thus:

> I have no hope for myself or for others. Our life is a false nature; it is not in the harmony of things; it is an all-blasting upas, whose root is earth, and whose leaves are the skies which rain their poison-dews upon mankind. We wither from our youth; we gasp with unslaked thirst for unattainable good; lured from the first to the last by phantoms – love, fame, ambition, avarice – all idle, and all ill – one meteor of many names, that vanishes in the smoke of death.

Nightmare Abbey's satire on contemporary literary miserabilism and the fashionable cant of and relish for unhappiness is captured best in Scythrop's singing of Peacock's brilliantly gloomy Byronic parody, 'There is a fever of the Spirit', and the comic dialogue which precedes it:

The Honourable Mr Listless.
How can we be cheerful when our nerves are shattered?
Mr Flosky.
How can we be cheerful when we are surrounded by a *reading public*, that is growing too wise for its betters?
Scythrop.
How can we be cheerful when our great general designs are crossed every moment by our little particular passions?
Mr Cypress.
How can we be cheerful in the midst of disappointment and despair?
Mr Glowry.
Let us all be unhappy together.
...
All.
A song from Mr Cypress.
Mr Cypress *sung* –

> There is a fever of the spirit,
> The brand of Cain's unresting doom,
> Which in the lone dark souls that bear it
> Glows like the lamp in Tullia's tomb:
> Unlike that lamp, its subtle fire
> Burns, blasts, consumes its cell, the heart,
> Till, one by one, hope, joy, desire,
> Like dreams of shadowy smoke depart.

...
Mr Glowry
Admirable. Let us all be unhappy together.

See also   Irish, Scottish and Welsh Poetry; Medicine and Science; Satire

Further Reading

Marilyn Butler, *Maria Edgeworth: A Literary Biography* (1972).
Marilyn Butler, *Jane Austen and the War of Ideas* (1975).
Marilyn Butler, *Peacock Displayed – A Satirist in His Context* (1979).
Ina Ferris, *The Romantic National Tale and the Question of Ireland* (2002).
Gary Kelly, *The English Jacobin Novel, 1780–1805* (1976).
Georg Lukács, *The Historical Novel* (1937).
Julia M. Wright, *Ireland, India, and Nationalism in Nineteenth-Century Literature* (2007).

'Peasant' or Labouring-class Poets

Ann Yearsley and *The Rural Lyre*

The figure of the so-called 'peasant poet' (to use the contemporary label applied to such poets as John Clare, 1793–1864) or 'labouring-class poet' (the term more commonly used today) features prominently in the landscape of British Romanticism. Both usages refer to those members of what was then unsubtly termed 'the lower orders' who transcended relatively underprivileged backgrounds to make a stir in the literary world. The phenomenal success of the Scottish poet Robert Burns (1759–96) was the most remarkable of these literary achievements but there were also less well known poets such as the 'Bristol milk woman' Ann Yearsley (*c.*1753–1806; Yearsley also used the more elevated pseudonym 'Lactilla'), the daughter of a milkmaid who initially followed her mother's trade before achieving a modicum of poetical success with her volumes *Poems, on Several Occasions* (1785), *Poems on Various Subjects* (1787) and *The Rural Lyre* (1796). As a result of Hannah More's patronage, Yearsley's poetical talents came to the attention of the literary *bon ton* (high society), her first published collection eliciting over a thousand subscribers, several duchesses and countesses among them, as well as notable literary figures such as Sir Joshua Reynolds, Horace Walpole, Frances Burney, and a good number of the Bluestocking set.

In 1784 an anonymous letter from a fellow Bristolian praising Yearsley's natural poetic gifts appeared in the *Gentleman's Magazine* (an eighteenth-century miscellaneous periodical), voicing what became the commonplace assumption about Yearsley, that she was a natural genius, an unlettered Calliope – the muse of heroic poetry – warbling her 'wild notes' in simple verses. It should be noted that Yearsley was complicit in this self-image notwithstanding the fact that much of her verse evidences her learning and her involvement in the wider public political sphere. 'A Poem on the Inhumanity of the Slave-Trade' (1788), for example, provides a striking example of Lactilla's poetic erudition, her skill in fashionable sentimental verse, and, simultaneously, her successful deployment of the milkmaid persona as a guarantee of the heartfelt sincerity and, hence, the legitimacy of her public statements. Yearsley composed the poem, a powerful sentimental indictment of slavery's 'inhumanity', in anticipation of the passing of Sir William Dolben's Bill, a first step towards abolition which aimed to restrict the number of slaves who could be shipped from West Africa to Britain's colonies in the West Indies. It was published at the same time as her mentor Hannah More's poem 'Slavery' (see 'Slavery, Abolition and African-British Literature'), also inspired by the Dolben Act, and it firmly situates Yearsley with More in the eighteenth-century sentimental tradition of humanitarian poetry. The first blank-verse paragraph opens thus:

Bristol, thine heart hath throbbed to glory: slaves,
E'en Christian slaves, have shook their chains, and gazed
With wonder and amazement on thee. Hence,
Ye grov'ling souls, who think the term I give
Of Christian slave, a paradox! To *you*
I do not turn, but leave you to conception
Narrow; with that be blessed, nor dare to stretch
Your shackled souls along the course of freedom.
    Yet Bristol, list! nor deem Lactilla's soul
Lessened by distance; snatch her rustic thought,
Her crude ideas, from their panting state,
And let them fly in wide expansion.

This is verse far from the simple strains of an untutored songbird. In measured tones, Yearsley constructs a complex rhetorical response that works through a series of ironic contrasts and juxtapositions: the image, for example, of the Bristolian slave traders being 'blessed' with 'conception narrow'.

Elizabeth Hands

The contradiction that we see in the case of Yearsley between the persona (of the simple milkwoman) and the quality of the verse she produced – which of course was a special selling point – also informs the work and reputation of another contemporary female versifier from what used to be called the lower orders, the poetical serving maid and satirist Elizabeth Hands (c.1746–1815). While documentary records of her life are incomplete, we do know that Hands worked as a domestic servant for the Huddesford family of the village of Allesley, near Coventry, and was thus ideally placed to observe the upper classes in their natural habitat. Following the publication of several of her poems in the *Coventry Mercury*, under the pastoral pseudonym 'Daphne', Hands published – by subscription and with the encouragement of her employers – her poetical volume *The Death of Amnon* (1789), which brought her moderate fame.

This collection includes poetic forms – pastoral, blank verse, mock heroic and satire – fashionable with educated readers of the late century but generally considered beyond the ken of serving maids such as Hands. In two remarkable satires, which wittily anticipate the reception of her work among the Coventry gentry, Hands ridicules the pretensions to learning and gentility of her employers. 'A Poem, On the Supposition of an Advertisement Appearing in a Morning Paper, of the Publication of a Volume of Poems, by a Servant Maid' and its companion piece 'A Poem, On the Supposition of the Book Having Been Published and Read' gently mock the assumption that a serving maid's thoughts could ever rise above the downstairs world of mops and brushes:

> A servant write verses! Says Madam du Bloom;
> Pray what is the subject? – a Mop, or a Broom?

A stronger line of critique comes, however, in the satirical assault on upper-class arrogance and ignorance. Hands mocks the unthinking prejudices of her 'betters' who assume that a serving girl could only write doggerel ('A stile elevated you cannot expect') and turns their narrow mindedness back on themselves through the application of stock names and stereotypes familiar from the Restoration stage; as Nichols Mason has written: 'the traditional rake (Captain Bonair), the superannuated beauty (Madam du Bloom) ... the prude (Mrs Consequence) ... the coquette (Miss Coquettella, Miss Gaiety, Miss Belle)', and so on. Of the many faults of the group, it is their biblical knowledge (or lack of it) as they struggle to decipher the biblical allusion in the title of Hands's volume *The Death of Amnon* that reveals their moral ignorance.

> Of Amnon, of Amnon, Miss Rhymer, who's he?
> His name, says Miss Gaiety's quite new to me: –

Perhaps, 'most damningly', as Mason has pointed out, 'Hands makes the central joke of her second poem the fact that very few participants in the supposedly learned debate over the merits' of her book 'have actually bothered to *read* the poems being discussed':

> Says Sir Timothy Turtle, my daughters ne'er look
> In any thing else but a cookery book:
> The properest study for women design'd;
>
> ...
> Says, Lady Jane Rational, the bill of fare
> Is th' utmost extent of my cookery care:
> Most servants can cook for the palate I find,
> But very few of them can cook for the mind.

Whatever their aspirations, Yearsley and Hands' reception and poetic reputation were dominated by their peasant persona. Why this image of the pastoral poetess gripped the attention of the reading public when her poetry was in actuality far from rustic or unlearned needs to be explained in terms of the increasing sway held by various Romantic-era concepts of original genius. The age itself was characterised, in part, by the notions of the 'child of nature' (whether in the work of Rousseau or that of Wordsworth and Coleridge) and of the 'noble savage' (the tradition of the native uncorrupted by society exemplified in Saint-Pierre's 1787 novel *Paul et Virginie*). Small wonder that the idea of the peasant poet, the unlettered and untutored songbird possessed of innate genius and untainted by book learning – a poet of God's creation rather than of the university or the public school – had great resonance. This was particularly the case after the wild success of Robert Burns, a man humbly born who was working as a farm labourer at the age of fifteen, but someone who, after his death, became one of the best-selling poets of the day. Burns was posthumously romanticised as the handsome son of the soil, passionate, intuitively gifted and doomed to die young. In Wordsworth's phrase a man 'who walk'd in glory and in joy / Behind his plough' ('Resolution and Independence'), Burns was frequently portrayed both in terms of his social class and as someone who transcended it in his courting of the muse of poetry.

'Peasant' Poetry

One important thing to register about labouring-class poetry of the late eighteenth and early nineteenth century is the sheer number of significant poets who emerged from the so-called 'lower orders', from the work of Burns and his Scottish contemporaries James Hogg (1770–1835), poet, satirist and novelist – whose nickname the 'Ettrick Shepherd' reinforces his status as a countryman – and the poet and folklorist Allan Cunningham (1784–1842), to that of women poets – notably the aforementioned Ann Yearsley, the 'Bristol milk woman', and Elizabeth Hands, the poetical serving maid – to the poets of humble rural stock Robert Bloomfield (1766–1823), the Suffolk 'Farmer's Boy', the Tory satirist and editor of the *Anti-Jacobin* and the *Quarterly Review* William Gifford (1756–1826), a former cobbler, and finally the man who might be seen as Bloomfield's great successor, the 'Northamptonshire Peasant Poet', John Clare, who after a brief success descended into poverty and madness but is now recognised as one of the greatest of Romantic-era poets. The reader will notice the predominance of rural poets here – the terms 'peasant poet' and 'labourer-class poet' are rarely applied to metropolitan artisans such as William Blake, the son of a hosier.

In truth, however, the commercial success of the peasant poet was to a significant degree dependent upon marketing. Poets from humble backgrounds were skilfully promoted by the contemporary book industry. Publishers emphasised the poets' quondam professions in announcing a crowd of versifying ploughboys, milkmaids, shepherds and so on, with the metonymical trades sometimes seeming more important than the names of the actual authors, as demonstrated by the case of Ann Yearsley above. The same is in evidence in the career of John Clare, whose image of 'peasant poet' was to a degree the brainchild of his publisher John Taylor, who saw a marketing opportunity in presenting Clare as the 'Northamptonshire Peasant'. Accordingly, his first volume, *Poems Descriptive of Rural Life and Scenery* (1820), was successfully advertised as 'by John Clare, A Northamptonshire Peasant'. Taylor's skilful publicity methods helped to make Clare a literary celebrity. These mythologising processes also helped to avoid the subject of the underlying politics of the poet should he or she prove regrettably anti-establishment. For example, when the boozy and womanising Burns, initially a political radical and enthusiast for the French Revolution, was safely dead he could be misleadingly portrayed as a politically quietist versifier, rooted in traditional custom and folklore with little concern for the broader Revolutionary politics of the age.

Not uncommonly, those elected to the role of 'peasant poet', either by upper-class mentors and patrons (Hannah More in the case of Yearsley) or by their market-savvy publishers (Taylor in Clare's case and Vernon and Hood in Robert Bloomfield's), grew to resent the way in which their reputations were manipulated and limited to the role of the rustic or artisan poet at the expense of the subtlety, range and power of their writing. Robert Bloomfield certainly begrudged the manner in which his first publishers stressed the supposedly miraculous notion of a boy born into poverty writing poetry over the innate quality of his verse, the implication on the part of the publishers being that there was something freakish about a successful poet from the lower orders. But in commercial terms, the publishers were right – in advertising the work of labourer-class poets, the more disadvantaged their background could be made to appear the more the public marvelled, as they would if a horse started dancing a jig – for the very fact rather than for the quality of the dance.

Robert Burns

Much of the work of labourer-class poets is characterised by a heightened interest in the incidents of common life and what Wordsworth called in his 'Preface' to the 1800 edition of *Lyrical Ballads* 'the real language of men'. Burns, who published his *Poems, Chiefly in the Scottish Dialect* in 1786, more than ten years before the publication of *Lyrical Ballads* in 1798, has a real claim to have ushered in, or at least anticipated, the dawn of literary Romanticism with its heightened interest in the real language of men and the incidents of common life. Burns, like Wordsworth and Coleridge after him, valorised the experience of the rural poor in a way unheard of in British poetry before the late eighteenth century. Whether in the vivid idiom of his valorisation of cottage ways in 'The Cotter's Saturday Night' ('To you I sing, in simple Scottish lays, / The *lowly train* in life's sequester'd scene'), or in the revival of the political ballad in the Jacobite manner, in such stuff as 'Scots, Wha Hae wi' Wallace bled', or in songs of romantic sociability, notably that timeworn favourite 'Auld Lang Syne' ('We'll tak a cup o' kindness yet ...'), there is throughout Burns's *oeuvre* an unapologetic revelling in Scottish life and the everyday language of the Scots 'mither tongue' (see also 'Irish, Scottish and Welsh Poetry').

Sentimental and satirical, bawdy and romantic by turn, Burns captured the earthy sexuality and superstitious mentality of his country folk, notably in the comic grotesquery of his famous poem 'Tam O' Shanter'. The eponymous Tam, rather than chastened by his drunken encounter with the supernatural (he stumbles upon the bawdy night-time revelling of 'Warlocks and witches in a dance'), splendidly defies the rationality of the poem's moral not to spend time drinking whisky and musing on short skirts ('take heed: / When'er to drink you are inclined / Or cutty sarks rin in your mind'). Indeed, his only spoken words in the poem, 'Weel done, Cutty Sark!', a challenge to respectability and sententiousness, have been presented as a joyous cry of national liberty, roared out as it is in local dialect, as contrasted with the orthodox Anglo-Scots voice of the narrator.

Robert Bloomfield

Three years after Burns's early death, appeared a poet who was consciously marketed as an English version of Burns. This was Robert Bloomfield, famous for *The Farmer's Boy* (1800). In heroic couplets heavily indebted to Pope, Bloomfield's *Farmer's Boy* poeticised the life of Giles, a farm worker and an orphan, but also someone with a heightened appreciation of nature:

> 'Twas thus with GILES, meek, fatherless, and poor
> Labour his portion, but he felt no more
> No stripes, no tyranny, his steps persu'd
> His life was constant, chearful servitude:
> Strange to the world, he wore a bashful look
> The Fields his study, Nature was his book,
> And, as revolving SEASONS chang'd the scene
> From heat to cold, tempestuous to serene,
> Though every change still varied his employ,
> Yet each new duty brought its share of joy.

Bloomfield's poem, published in the same year as the 'Preface' to the *Lyrical Ballads*, was praised in unwittingly Wordsworthian terms for its 'primitive simplicity' by the *New London Review*. The *Monthly Mirror* described the poet as 'this favoured child of genius and the Muse, who, with no adscititious [inherent] advantages of birth, fortune, education or connexion, has produced a poem which may be read with delight'.

'*The Farmer's Boy* may be looked on as a new model of genuine pastoral', wrote the *New London* of Bloomfield. In a language often characterised by poetic realism, Bloomfield overturns the idealised images of country life familiar from the pastoral literary tradition of the eighteenth century. Take, for instance, the portrayal in 'Spring' of the 'clatt'ring Dairy-Maid immers'd in steam, / Singing and scrubbing midst her milk and cream' who 'Bawls out, "Go fetch the Cows!"' (ll. 165–7). The maid's cacophonous clattering and discordant bawling breaks through any anticipated air of pastoral tranquillity and it is lines such as these that led John Clare – Bloomfield's junior by over twenty years – to name the elder poet 'the English Theocritus'. (The Greek poet Theocritus (early third century BC) was the first pastoral poet to maintain a balance between realism and idealism in his attempt to tell the truth of rural life.)

John Clare

Following in Bloomfield's footsteps was Clare, the ill-starred 'Northamptonshire Peasant Poet', who, though destined to insanity, captured the public imagination in the 1820s with poetry celebrating in minute detail the unsung grandeur of his local environs. Born and raised in the village of Helpstone, Clare describes in unflinching detail rural customs – the habitat of the local wildfowl, however mean ('To the Snipe') – and rural sports, however brutal, such as badger baiting (in the 'Badger' sonnets), all recorded in both standard English and local dialect. Clare, in fact, was reluctant to travel even three miles beyond the village of his birth, and in 1832 he suffered profound mental disturbance as a consequence of moving the short distance to Northborough to live in a cottage supplied by a wealthy patron. His acute sense of displacement and homesickness is recorded with simple if affecting honesty in 'The Flitting':

> Ive left my own old home of homes
> Green fields and every pleasant place
> The summer like a stranger comes
> I pause and hardly know her face
> I miss the hazels happy green
> The blue bells quiet hanging blooms
> Where envys sneer was never seen
> Where staring malice never comes

Clare's vernacular commemorates nature in a plain yet fresh and vivid idiom which recalls Wordsworth's desire to write in the 'real language of men'. 'To the Snipe', 'Little Trotty Wagtail' and the *sui generis* badger sonnets are among Clare's best known poems, which celebrate the rich diversity of the natural world of his immediate surroundings from an acutely personal perspective (the first-person pronoun abounds in his verse). This said, Clare is excluded from what Seamus Perry terms the 'colossal imaginative egotism' of Wordsworthian Romanticism. Writing in 2005, Perry cites Jonathan Bate, whose study *The Song of the Earth* (2000) eloquently argues the case for John Clare as a poet of '"thing-experience" who bucks the expectations of the egotistical sublime'. Clare, it might be argued, refused to fetishise in nature poetry the life of the mind, but rather combined what Coleridge, in 'Dejection. An Ode', calls 'My shaping spirit of imagination' with an unsentimental descriptive realism, what Jonathan Bate labels the poet's 'dirty realism'. Bate writes:

> Though Clare always looked back with longing upon his childhood, once he grew in confidence as a writer he refused to poeticise the life of the village. He rein- vented the pastoral tradition of poetry in a mode of dirty realism.

The horny-handed colloquialisms of the badger sonnets demonstrate the point. Here is the fourth sonnet in the series, which portrays the animal's futile attempt to outrun his tormentors:

> The frighted woman takes the boys away
> The blackguard laughs and hurrys on the fray
> He trys to reach the woods a awkward race
> But sticks and cudgels quickly stop the chace
> He turns agen and drives the noisey crowd
> And beats the many dogs in noises loud
> He drives away and beats them every one
> And then they loose them all and set them on
> He falls as dead and kicked by boys and men
> Then starts and grins and drives the crowd agen
> Till kicked and torn and beaten out he lies
> And leaves his hold and cackles groans and dies.

Clare neither sentimentalises the creature's plight nor refines the role of the baiters and their dogs in bringing about his eventual demise after a prolonged game of cunning during which the badger 'falls as dead'. This is rural life stripped bare of pastoral sweetness, the somewhat macabre humour of the grinning animal heightening Clare's 'dirty realism'. It was to prove, however, an evanescent mode that did not appeal to the refined sensibilities of the pre-Victorian reader, and the second half of the nineteenth century witnessed a severe falling off of Clare's popularity.

Finally, it is true to say that not all poets in the peasant and labouring-class tradition fit the description of peasant poetry as primarily concerned with nature and country living. The shoe-maker poet William Gifford's vitriolic attacks on the Della Cruscans and the so-called 'Cockney School' (in his role of editor of the ultra-Tory *Quarterly Review* Gifford bitterly criticised Leigh Hunt's work and he also readily published John Wilson Croker's acidulous review of Keats's *Endymion*, which went down in legend as a cause of the latter poet's premature death) are not contributions to modern 'neo-pastoralism' of the type innovated by Bloomfield and Clare. Neither does the term fit with all female labouring-class poets; most particularly the tradition excludes the sentimentalism and political commentary of Yearsley and the social satire of Hands, both of whom stand a degree closer to Blake and the tradition of urban artisan poetry than to that of Wordsworth and his followers of nature.

Further Reading

Jonathan Bate, *The Song of the Earth* (2000).
Jonathan Bate, *John Clare: A Biography* (2003).
John Goodridge and Simon Kövesi (eds), *John Clare: New Approaches* (2000).
Nicholas Mason, *Collected Satires I*, vol. 1 of *British Satire 1785–1840*, gen. ed. John Strachan, 5 vols (2003).
David Perkins, *Romanticism and Animal Rights* (2003).
Seamus Perry, 'Literary Criticism and Theory', *Romanticism: An Oxford Guide*, ed. Nicholas Roe (2005), 593–606.

Reviews, Magazines and the Essay

The New Reviews: *The Edinburgh* and the *Quarterly*

Historically, in times of conflict the British rush to the printing press. During the civil wars of the seventeenth century the Royalists and the Puritans fought their opponents both in terms of pitched battle and in polemical print: in pamphlet, broadsheet and journal. Print culture became an echo of war as both parties realised the potency of the written word; if not quite more powerful than the sword, the pen was irredeemably linked to it. After the civil strife of the 1640s and early 1650s and the 'Glorious Revolution' of 1688, the next great epoch of social turmoil in Great Britain was the period after the French Revolution of 1789 (see 'British Politics 1789–1815') in which 'Jacobin' advocates of radical British reform, even revolution, met with sternly repressive measures from the Tory government of William Pitt the Younger. Small wonder, then, that partisan politics prompted literary debate. The arguments between the ruling Tories and the oppositionalist Whigs and Radicals in this period were reflected in the 'Revolutionary Controversy' of the 1790s, in which the opposing parties articulated their positions in books, pamphlets and the public prints (again, see 'British Politics 1789–1815' for this aspect of Romantic-period print culture). Similarly, in the period of political turmoil in Great Britain which followed the defeat of Napoleon at the Battle of Waterloo in 1815, political journals became a vital site for articulating reformist ideology (for discussion of William Cobbett's periodicals, T. J. Wooler's *Black Dwarf*, and 'unstamped' newspapers, see 'Political Protest and Popular Radicalism').

The most memorable Tory periodical of the post-Revolutionary decade was the *Anti-Jacobin* (1797–8), the politically combative satirical journal which berated what it saw as the politically subversive literary friends of the French Revolution using both parody and more orthodox critical writing (see 'Satire' for fuller treatment of the *Anti-Jacobin*). This journal, though a weekly newspaper, is of more than passing interest to the present topic. The *Anti-Jacobin*, in making a clear association between literature and politics – and in its wit, combative temper and ferociously partisan politics – set the tone for much of the reviewing culture of the Romantic era, notably in the two important journals which followed soon after it, the *Edinburgh Review* and the *Quarterly Review*. These, like the *Anti-Jacobin*, were party political, the first generally Whiggish in tone (its covers were draped in the blue-and-buff colours of the Whig party) and the second staunchly allied to the 'Church-and-King' Tory interest.

Before the *Edinburgh*, founded in 1802, the established reviews, the *Monthly Review* (1749–1845) and the *Critical Review* (1756–1817), featured a large number of short summary notices, generally consisting of extensive quotations from the volumes under discussion. The *Edinburgh*, on the other hand, had fewer (generally around eight to ten) and longer reviews per number, offering in-depth and highly opinionated coverage. It shared the *Anti-Jacobin*'s delight in vituperation; the journal's brilliant founding editor, the Scottish lawyer and critic Francis, later Lord, Jeffrey (1773–1850), believed that a 'stinger', an entertainingly bilious character assassination or hatchet job, was what most readers appreciated, and many of the numbers of the journal contained at least one effort in this vein (reviews in these days were not signed and intemperate contributors could shelter behind anonymity). To this end he and his early coadjutors, notably Henry, later Baron, Brougham (1778–1868) (author of a ferocious, if not unfair, assault in the *Edinburgh* on Byron's 'prentice work *Hours of Idleness* (1807) as 'so much stagnant water', which prompted the poet to compose his first book-length satire, *English Bards and Scotch Reviewers* (1809), in response), set about their political and literary opponents. This was done out of conviction certainly, but also in the knowledge that controversy rarely damages a periodical's circulation.

Jeffrey's most notable target was the 'Lake School', and he dogmatised on the inanity of Wordsworth in particular, and at length. Though he was capable of admiring at least one of the contemporary poetic avant-garde, John Keats (whose *Lamia, Isabella, The Eve of St Agnes and Other Poems* (1820) he welcomed in a notice of August 1820), Jeffrey generally had no time for the poetic experimentations of the new school, which he considered, in large part, a fatuous waste of God-given talent. He scoffed at many of Wordsworth's *Poems in Two Volumes* (1807) as ludicrous and infantile drivellings and famously began his notice of the poet's *The Excursion* (1814) with the words 'This will never do' (for further discussion of Jeffrey's criticism of Wordsworth, see 'Contemporary and Victorian Reception').

This all said, the *Edinburgh* excelled at more than entertaining *ad hominem* diatribe and the nay-saying of early Romanticism. It featured a remarkable list of contributors during its first three decades, Jeffrey and Brougham apart, that included Thomas Carlyle, William Hazlitt, Thomas Babington Macaulay and Sydney Smith. The scope of the *Edinburgh* was not confined to literature; it also covered a wide range of other topics in its reviews – fine arts, travel writing, political economy, science, religion and so on. Its circulation was large by the standards of the time (12,000 in 1818, several thousand more than the daily circulation of upmarket newspapers such as *The Times*, for instance). Though generally conservative in literary matters, the *Edinburgh* was progressive in terms of its attitudes to politics and economics, becoming the *de facto* organ of the Whig party. Indeed, such was the journal's authority in liberal circles that the aforesaid Carlyle labelled it 'a kind of Delphic oracle'.

The *Edinburgh Review* continued publication for exactly one hundred years after Jeffrey's resignation as editor in 1829. The periodical was eventually superseded in longevity, however, by its near contemporary the *Quarterly Review*, which was founded in 1809 and continued until 1967. The *Quarterly* was established as a London-based, Tory competitor to the *Edinburgh* by that renowned publisher the second John Murray (1778–1843), who installed William Gifford (1756–1826), the former editor of the *Anti-Jacobin*, as its first editor after Walter Scott had turned down the offer of the chair. Despite this refusal, the vigorously Tory Scott, who had received some rough handling from the *Edinburgh*, nonetheless contributed a number of articles to the journal (notably his highly positive review of Jane Austen's *Emma* (1816)), as did Robert Southey, both before and after he became Poet Laureate in 1813, and, indeed, Charles Lamb, in his defence of the *Edinburgh*-chastened *Excursion* (though he complained of Gifford 'mangling' his copy). Gifford also employed two of the principals of the *Anti-Jacobin* as contributors, George Canning (1770–1827), later Tory Prime Minister, and John Hookham Frere (1769–1846).

The *Quarterly*, which quickly achieved a higher circulation than the *Edinburgh* (it sold 14,000 copies per issue in 1818, for instance, 2,000 more than the latter), was as wide-ranging as its northern rival. It could also, again like the *Edinburgh*, be both magisterial and venomous in turn (though the former tone tended to prevail after 1825, when J. G. Lockhart (1794–1854) succeeded Gifford as editor). Unlike Jeffrey's *Edinburgh*, the *Quarterly* – with Southey as a contributor – tended to support the Lake Poets (fellow Tories by this stage), and despite his radical politics Lord Byron generally escaped the lash (the fact that he was published by John Murray, it might be pointed out, may have helped in this regard). The *Quarterly* was less keen on what it described as 'Cockney' poetry, notably the 'insane' – John Wilson Croker's description – writings of Leigh Hunt and John Keats, or on Cockney prose such as that of Hazlitt, a critic described by the editor in one number as 'a death's head hawk moth' with a 'startling' and 'disagreeable' appearance whose work was spiteful, poisonous and malevolent. Indeed, the *Quarterly* it was, in the shape of Croker's notorious demolition of Keats's 'unintelligible ... tiresome and absurd' 1818 poem *Endymion*, that was responsible for the notice which many of the poet's contemporaries, including Shelley and Byron, erroneously saw as responsible for Keats's premature death (Keats, wrote Byron, was 'snuffed out by an Article') (see 'Contemporary and Victorian Reception' for discussion of this attack). Keats and Hunt were in good company. In its first four decades the *Quarterly* also published denunciations of Shelley, Lady Morgan, C. R. Maturin, and, later, the young Charles Dickens, Tennyson and the sisters Brontë.

Literary Magazines

In the 1810s the reviews were joined by what we now refer to as literary magazines. In contrast to the likes of the *Quarterly*, these had something of the miscellany – in the manner of the long-established hotchpotch the *Gentleman's Magazine* (1731–1907) – about them. Alongside notices of books, they also featured what one might call creative writing – poetry, short stories and imaginary dialogues – as well as 'familiar' essays (couched in informal, discursive prose) and so on. Novels, travelogues and sketches were serialised before their first publication in book form, and a series of pseudonymous essayists introduced themselves, from 'Elia' (Charles Lamb of the *London Magazine*), 'Harry Honeycomb' (Leigh Hunt's *New Monthly* alias), and 'Janus Weathercock' (the essayist and poisoner Thomas Griffiths Wainewright (1794–1847) of the *London* and later of Botany Bay, who also used the less felicitous name 'Cornelius van

Vinkbooms'), in a tradition which culminated in the work of 'Boz' (Charles Dickens) in the early 1830s.

That repository of book reviews, verse, comic whimsy, essays and stories, the *New Monthly Magazine* (1814–84) is generally seen as the exemplar of the late Georgian fashionable miscellany (though it is testimony to the partisan nature of contemporary letters that even this journal originally began as a Tory and determinedly anti-Radical review before being recast as a less overtly ideological organ when sales were initially low). The refocused *New Monthly* was consciously designed to attract a higher percentage of female readers than bothered with the sometimes-ponderous *Quarterly*. Indeed, the magazine owed something to the mixed literary content of journals intended solely for women such as the *Lady's Magazine*, the female counterpart of the *Gentleman's* (1770–1837; also known as the *Entertaining Companion for the Fair Sex, Appropriated Solely to Their Use and Amusement*), and *La Belle Assemblée* (1806–68; *A Fashionable Magazine Addressed Particularly to the Ladies*, in the words of its own elephantine subtitle).

The *New Monthly* was established by the fashionable, unscrupulous and highly successful society publisher Henry Colburn (*c*.1784–1855). To give the journal literary kudos Colburn installed the then highly esteemed Scottish poet Thomas Campbell (1777–1844) as nominal editor in 1821 (though much of the actual day-to-day editorial work was done by his assistants, notably Cyrus Redding (1785–1870)). Colburn was willing to pay decent sums for talented contributors to his journal, and many of the literary notables of the 1820s and beyond wrote for the periodical: Thomas Hood, Leigh Hunt, Lady Morgan, Mary Shelley, James and Horace Smith and others.

Colburn also founded the *Literary Gazette*, which he established in 1817. This was a highly successful weekly review in the old-fashioned cheap-to-produce manner, with analytical commentary greatly outweighed by long quotations. Nonetheless, the *Gazette* published some significant contemporary writers in its pages. Alongside George Crabbe (1754–1832) and 'Barry Cornwall' (Bryan Waller Proctor (1787–1874)), its editor William Jerdan also published important female contributors, notably Mary Russell Mitford (1787–1855; later to achieve fame at the *Lady's Magazine* for her series of sketches *Our Village* (1824–32)), and the poet Letitia Elizabeth Landon (who was, according to some accounts, Jerdan's mistress) who published a large number of poems and reviews in the journal. (While some thought the *Edinburgh* and the *Quarterly* damaged by their partisan flavour, the *Gazette* faced a different threat to its reputation; the practice of 'puffing', Colburn's notorious habit of having his journals salute the books published elsewhere in his literary empire.)

William Hazlitt

Perhaps the most notable thoroughbred in Colburn's stable to the modern eye, however, was William Hazlitt, whose great essay 'The Fight', an account of the championship boxing match between Bill Neat and Tom Hickman, the 'Gasman', was published in the *New Monthly* in February 1822. Several of Hazlitt's famous *Table Talk* essays (from 1821 onwards), and, indeed, that great series of literary-biographical sketches *The Spirit of the Age* (published in book form in 1825), also first saw the light of day in Colburn's journal.

Hazlitt, of the *New Monthly Magazine* – and indeed, of the *London Magazine*, the *Black Dwarf*, the *Edinburgh*, and elsewhere – was one of the most acute critics and essayists of the Romantic era, at home in the criticism of literature – poetry, prose and the drama (for his theatrical criticism, see 'Drama') – and, indeed, in the analysis of popular culture – sport, tightrope walkers and Indian jugglers. Hazlitt also published a large number of philosophical essays (his first book was a work of metaphysics, *An Essay on the Principles of Human Action*, published in 1805) such as 'On the Fear of Death', 'On Conduct of Life', and 'On Reason and Imagination'. The 'death's head hawk moth' of William Gifford's imagination could certainly match the editor of the *Quarterly* for vituperation (indeed, he once described Gifford's work in print as 'dung'), and proudly described himself as a 'great hater'. ('Hazlitt smiled upon no man', wrote his Tory rival Thomas De Quincey in a fine but exaggerated phrase.) His attacks on Coleridge and Wordsworth, the Lake Poets whom he had idolised as a young man, are well known, as are his feuds with the Tory journals the *Quarterly* and *Blackwood's*. Both of the latter jeered gleefully at the publication of his most controversial work, *Liber Amoris*, the barely-fictionalised story of Hazlitt's doomed obsession with a London serving wench Sarah Walker, which appeared in 1823 (the account of 'a sordid love affair' scoffed *Blackwood's*, which was always keen to mock a man it designated, with its usual sense of cruel fun, 'pimpled Hazlitt').

It is as a master of English prose, however, rather than for score-settling for which Hazlitt is best remembered today. Take the aforesaid *New Monthly* piece, 'The Fight', the essayist's account of seeing his first boxing match near Hungerford in Berkshire in December 1821. This begins in jovial and self-deprecating mode, a light-hearted form of confessional prose in which Hazlitt describes his misadventures to the 'lady' readers, to whom the essay is directly addressed, as he travels uncertainly towards the fight. The contest begins, and the nature of the prose changes, becoming sublimised, as Hazlitt describes the knock-out blow as Hickman falls to the ground, broken and bloody. It is as if Valhalla had come to Berkshire:

I never saw anything more terrific than his aspect just before he fell. All traces of life, of natural expression, were gone from him. His face was like a human skull, a death's head, spouting blood. The eyes were filled with blood, the nose streamed with blood, the mouth gaped blood. He was not like an actual man, but like a preternatural, spectral appearance, or like one of the figures in Dante's 'Inferno'.

Leigh Hunt

Leigh Hunt, who contributed a number of articles to Colburn's *New Monthly*, himself established a number of generally short-lived literary magazines, such the *Indicator* (1819–21), the *Literary Examiner* (1823), the *Companion* (1828), and *Leigh Hunt's London Journal* (1834–5). Of these, perhaps most important was the weekly *Indicator*, which featured the editor's familiar essays, original poetry by himself and eminent friends (including the earliest version of Keats's 'La Belle Dame sans Merci', published in May 1820), and translations from foreign literature. Charles Lamb said of it in doggerel verse: 'Wit, poet, prose-man, translator – / H-, your best title yet is the Indicator'), and Hazlitt declared that the conversational style of the journal's essays reflected the renowned conversationalist in full flow: 'The reader may, if he pleases, get a very good idea of L. H-'s conversation from a very agreeable paper he has lately published, called the *Indicator*'. In his *Autobiography* (1850), Hunt recalled that Keats's favourite paper in the journal was 'A "Now"', an essay in which every sentence in the first few pages begins with that adverb:

Now the mower begins to make his sweeping cuts more slowly, and resorts oftener to the beer. Now the carter sleeps a-top of his load of hay ... looking out with eyes winking under his shading hat, and with a hitch upward of one side of his mouth. Now the little girl at her grandmother's cottage-door watches the coaches that go by, with her hand held up over her sunny forehead. Now labourers look well resting in their white shirts at the doors of rural alehouses. Now an elm is fine there, with a seat under it; and horses drink out of the trough, stretching their yearning necks with loosened collars ... Now cattle stand in water, and ducks are envied ... Now the bee, as he hums along, seems to be talking heavily of the heat. ... Now a green lane ... thickset with hedge-row elms, and having the noise of a brook 'rumbling in pebble-stone', is one of the pleasantest things in the world.

Small wonder that the author of 'To Autumn' should enjoy Hunt's well-crafted prose pastoral (Hunt's familiar style might give the impression of casual conversation, but it is, of course, carefully crafted).

The *Indicator* was, in the main, literary and non-political ('a retreat from public cares', its editor called it), but this should not be seen as betokening a lack of ideological commitment on Hunt's part. Leigh Hunt was best known in his day as the editor of the weekly newspaper *The Examiner*, established in 1808, the mouthpiece of middle-class radicalism, for the free-dom-of-the-press heroics which had landed him with a £5,000 fine in 1813 and two years in gaol for daring to suggest that the Prince Regent was a gluttonous, womanising spendthrift (see 'Satire') and for his innovative and controversial poetry, notably his long narrative poem *The Story of Rimini* (1816) about the adulterous love of Francesca di Rimini and her brother-in-law which earned the politically-motivated scorn of *Blackwood's*, which dubbed it his attempt at 'trying his hand at a tale of incest'.

Blackwood's Edinburgh Magazine

In the pages of the *Examiner* Leigh Hunt – a remarkable literary talent spot-ter – patronised and published Shelley, Keats, and J. H. Reynolds (the 'Young Poets', as he called them in an article of December 1816), and printed and patronised both Lamb and Hazlitt. Hunt's radical politics and his associa-tion with Keats led the *Quarterly Review* in its April 1818 notice of the latter's *Endymion* to label their work 'Cockney' poetry, implying that the poets were a bunch of vulgar, ignorant, and ill-educated Londoners. This notion was enthusiastically taken up by that most entertaining, brilliant and troubling late Georgian Tory literary magazine, *Blackwood's Edinburgh Magazine* (1817–1980). The three principal early contributors to the journal, John Wilson (1785–1854), John Gibson Lockhart (1794–1854) and William Maginn (1794–1842), attacked what the magazine christened in memo-rable, if unfair, phrase the 'Cockney School of Poetry' of Hunt, Keats, and others less notable. Lockhart, for instance, writing as 'Z' in August 1818, condemned the 'calm, settled, imperturbable drivelling idiocy' of *Endymion* and dismissed the author of *Rimini* as 'the meanest, the filthiest, and the most vulgar of Cockney poetasters'. Such fellows, the magazine implied, who lack the classical education appropriate to a gentleman, would be better off taking up some more appropriate vocation than that of poet (the trade of 'man-milliner' is suggested for Hunt). Lockhart urged Keats to return to his old calling of apothecary ('back to the shop Mr John, back to "plasters, pills, and ointment boxes", &c'), though adding waspishly that, if he did so, then the poet should 'be a little more sparing of extenuatives and soporifics in [his] practice than [he had] been in [his] poetry'.

   Blackwood's, which never deviated from its ultra-Tory politics, was indebted to both Whig and Tory journals, owing something of its verve, venom and vigour to the *Anti-Jacobin*, the *Quarterly*, the *Edinburgh* and, indeed, to the *Examiner*, the weekly newspaper edited by the man that 'Maga' loved to hate. Founded in April 1817, it was initially unsuccessful, and as a consequence was spectacularly relaunched in October of that year in a number which included the notorious Biblical parody the 'Chaldee manuscript', a thinly-veiled assault on Whig political and literary Edinburgh, together with an attack on Coleridge's *Biographia Literaria* so fierce that the poet considered legal action, and severe strictures on the *Edinburgh Review*. The magazine was miscellaneous, featuring reviews, essays, poems, short fiction, parodies and satires. It could veer widely in critical stance, for instance in both ridiculing and – more often – praising the Lake Poets, it early recognised the genius of both Byron and Shelley (despite what were to the magazine their regrettable politics), and published an influential series of 'tales of terror' (short Gothic fictions) from its very early days. A series of fictional contributors echo through its pages ('Christopher North', 'Ensign Odoherty' and so on) both as supposed contributors and as characters in the pages of the remarkable series of imaginary tavern conversations, mostly by Wilson, the *Noctes Ambrosianae* (1822–35; the 'Ambrosian Nights', set in Ambrose's hostelry in Edinburgh), alongside the 'Ettrick Shepherd' (an exaggerated version of James Hogg) and the 'Opium Eater' (an exaggerated version of Thomas De Quincey).

Though a supporter of the national, Tory British government, *Blackwood's* saw itself in Scottish – specifically Edinburgh – terms, as an oppositionalist journal, one which set its face against the Whig hegemony of that city and, indeed, the journal named after it. It copied – and outstripped – the *Edinburgh's* acerbic style, for example in taking *ad hominem* verse satire to new heights of venom (depths some would say) in Maginn's 'Elegy on my Tom Cat' (1821), the Irishman's parody of P. B. Shelley's elegy to John Keats, *Adonais*. Where Shelley begins 'I weep for Adonais – he is dead', Maginn's ignoble spoof likens Keats's demise to the death of an alley cat. The first three lines will suffice:

> Weep for my Tomcat! all ye Tabbies weep.
> For he is gone at last! Not dead alone.
> In flowery beauty sleepeth he no sleep.

Thomas De Quincey

The 'Opium Eater', Thomas De Quincey, was one of *Blackwood's* most notable contributors. Though 'diminutive' – Dorothy Wordsworth's description – in size, De Quincey stands very tall in terms of the Romantic-era essay. His life was remarkable, and characterised, in his own account, by suffering and trauma. A remarkably brilliant child, he was deeply affected by the death in youth of his sister and by the loss of 'Ann of Oxford Street' (see 'Sexualities'), the young prostitute who helped the boy Tom in his misery during his time as a runaway, homeless teenager in London ('This child has been in Hell', said Thomas Carlyle of De Quincey).

Addicted to laudanum (alcoholic tincture of opium) for much of his adult life, De Quincey was a spendthrift who ran through a sizeable inheritance and had to leave the Lake District he adored (he was tenant of Dove Cottage from 1809 to 1830, far longer than William Wordsworth before him) to live in Edinburgh to escape his debtors. In Scotland's capital he found the *Blackwood's* crew congenial company and contributed dozens of articles to the magazine, including some of his most renowned works: 'On Murder Considered as One of the Fine Arts' (1827), 'Suspiria de Profundis: Being a Sequel to the Confessions of an English Opium-Eater' (1845), and 'The English Mail-Coach, or the Glory of Motion' (1849). His finest achievement in *Blackwood's* was the 'Suspiria' (for this essay's magnificent prose aria on childhood see 'Key Literary and Philosophical Concepts I'), which contains several remarkable set-piece Romantic meditations such as its famous digression on the mind and the human memory, which De Quincey compares to a 'palimpsest' (a medieval manuscript which has been erased and used again) upon which, paradoxically, nothing is ever lost:

> What else than a natural and mighty palimpsest is the human brain? Such a palimpsest is my brain; such a palimpsest, O reader! is yours. Everlasting layers of ideas, images, feelings, have fallen upon your brain softly as light. Each succession has seemed to bury all that went before. And yet in reality not one has been extinguished.

De Quincey and the *London Magazine*

His connection to 'Maga' notwithstanding, it was in the *London Magazine* (1820–9) that Thomas De Quincey first made his name, with the 1821 publication of the *Confessions of an English Opium Eater*. These meditated on his own addiction and the way in which opium – here analogous to the Wordsworthian imagination – informed De Quincey's dreams and nightmares in the author's grimly inevitable progress from the 'pleasures' to the 'pains of opium'. The apostrophe to opium at the end of the 'Pleasures of Opium' section – before the descent into Hell – is testimony to De Quincey's elaborate prose cadences:

> Oh! just, subtle, and mighty opium! that to the hearts of poor and rich alike, for the wounds that will never heal, and for the 'pangs that tempt the spirit to rebel', bringest an assuaging balm; eloquent opium! that with thy potent rhetoric stealest away the purposes of wrath; and to the guilty man, for one night, givest back the hopes of his youth, and hands washed pure from blood ... thou buildest upon the bosom of darkness, out of the fantastic imagery of the brain, cities and temples

beyond the art of Phidias or Praxiteles, – beyond the splendour of Babylon and Hecatompylos; and 'from the anarchy of dreaming sleep' callest into sunny light the faces of long buried beauties, and the blessed household countenances, cleansed from the 'dishonours of the grave'. Thou only givest these gifts to man; and thou hast the keys of paradise, Oh! just, subtle, and mighty opium!

The two 'Confessions' essays were originally promised to *Blackwood's Edinburgh Magazine* but appeared instead in the *London*. This is telling. The *London* was engaged in Oedipal strife with *Blackwood's*. Just as the *Quarterly* followed the example of the *Edinburgh*, so the *London Magazine* walked in the footsteps of a Scots predecessor, in its case *Blackwood's*. The *London* was a metropolitan, Whiggish version of 'Maga'; its editor, the Scottish travel writer and journalist John Scott (1784–1821), aimed to inculcate what he described as the 'spirit of life' evident in *Blackwood's* in his own journal (Simon P. Hull has called the magazine 'a quintessentially, consciously metropolitan, periodical dedicated to translating into a lively miscellany the dynamism and hurly-burly of London life'). De Quincey apart, its contributors included Hazlitt, Lamb, Wainewright and the young Thomas Hood (who had an editorial role at the journal as well as contributing much poetry and comic whimsy in prose).

The *London* is, however, forever associated with one of the most notorious episodes in Romantic-era literary life. The literary violence which underpinned what one might call the magazine wars of the Romantic period was made explicit in early 1821 when Scott was killed in a duel with J. G. Lockhart's friend Jonathan Henry Christie (d. 1876) as a result of a literary spat in the pages of the two periodicals. After initially admiring the 'merry ruffianism' of *Blackwood's*, towards the end of 1820 Scott had changed tack and begun attacking his northern rival, charging Lockhart in personal terms as guilty of 'a felon conspiracy against the dignity of literature'. After much in the way of threats and bluster, Christie fought with the hapless Scott and the symbolical literary and political blood-letting of contemporary magazine culture gave way to the physical reality (Mark Parker calls the incident a manifestation of a 'sickly and depraved literary scene').

Charles Lamb ('Elia')

Alongside De Quincey, a central contributor to the *London Magazine* was the essayist, dramatist, poet, and critic Charles Lamb ('Our ELIA ... the pride of our magazine', as the *London* called him), who, like Hunt, was a master of the contemporary familiar essay. This author had a gift for friendship and was close to both Wordsworth and Coleridge among many others. He spent over thirty years toiling as a clerk at the East India House in London (the East India Company was responsible for the administration of much of British India). Lamb, after failing in the theatre (see 'Drama'), contributed verse and prose to Hunt's *Examiner*, notably his famous skit on bad Prince George's obesity, loose morals and political tergiversation (in turning his back on the Whigs) 'The Triumph of the Whale' (1812; see 'Satire'), and book reviews to the *Quarterly*, notably in speaking up for Wordsworth's *Excursion* in its October 1814 number. Lamb was also known for the *Tales from Shakespear* (1807), his successful collaboration with his sister Mary (1764–1847), 'the portal by which most children enter the magic realm of Shakespeare', as a Regency book advertisement put it (Miss Lamb, who killed their mother in a fit of insanity in 1796, was responsible for the major crisis in Charles's life). However, Lamb came into his own in literary terms in his brilliant correspondence and in the 'Elia' essays for the *London*, which were collected in the *Essays of Elia* (1823) (the *Last Essays of Elia* followed ten years later).

Many of the 'Elia' essays (the name, pronounced 'Ellia', according to Lamb was borrowed from that of an Italian clerk at the India House) are based on personal reminiscence, though it would be most unwise to regard them as unclouded autobiography. The cast of characters and list of places which populate the essays (Elia's cousin Bridget, the card-playing Mrs Battle, the Old Margate Hoy, Mackery End, the South Sea House) became very familiar in the nineteenth and early twentieth centuries, when there was an appetite for Lamb's works which is little evident today. The Elian sense of nostalgia and gentle whimsy, Lamb's status as a devotee of old books, and his preoccupation with the old-fashioned (this also evident in the conscious archaisms of its language) are manifest in essays such as 'Oxford in the Vacation':

> Above all thy rarities, old Oxenford, what do most arride and solace me, are thy repositories of mouldering learning, thy shelves –

> What a place to be in is an old library! It seems as though all the souls of all the writers, that have bequeathed their labours to these Bodleians, were reposing here, as in some dormitory or middle state. I do not want to handle, to profane the leaves, their winding-sheets. I could as soon dislodge a shade. I seem to inhale learning, walking amid their foliage; and the odour of the old moth-scented coverings, is fragrant as the first bloom of those sciential apples which grew amid the happy orchard.

In the *Spirit of the Age*, Hazlitt, rightly or wrongly, sees Elia as a counter-intuitive voice set against modernity: Lamb 'has raked among the dust and cobwebs of a more remote period ... for the benefit of the more inquisitive and discerning part of the public. ... [Elia] has succeeded, not by conforming to the Spirit of the Age, but in opposition to it. He does not march boldly along with the crowd, but steals off the pavement to pick his way in the contrary direction.'

'The Elian spirit of friendliness and humour' (these words from the motto of the modern-day Charles Lamb Society) is certainly manifested in the generosity of spirit evident in Lamb's work. Nonetheless, from the first *London* essays ('The South-Sea House' and 'Oxford in the Vacation') onwards, alongside 'a serious joy' the Elia lucubrations (meditations) also manifest – in Lamb's friend P. G. Patmore's description – 'a still more serious melancholy' (as Duncan Wu has written, 'the Elian manner is typically elegiac'). Lamb's seriousness is often the very seriousness of high Romantic argument. Take, for example, the Elia essay 'Witches, and Other Night Fears', in which Lamb, like De Quincey, talks of his dreams drifting towards his own personal place of demons. Though 'My night-fancies [nightmares] have long ceased to be afflictive', writes Lamb (as they were when he was a child), they still have power and resonance:

> I confess an occasional night-mare; but I do not, as in early youth, keep a study of them. Fiendish faces, with the extinguished taper, will come and look at me; but I know them for mockeries, even while I cannot elude their presence, and I fight and grapple with them.

This essay of Elia was published in the *London Magazine* in October 1821, in the very same number as the concluding, second, part of De Quincey's *Confessions*, with its dark account of the 'Pains of Opium'. Charles Lamb deserves his place with the Romantic poets and essayists; alongside the puns and whimsicalities, he, too, could peer into the inner world of the imagination.

In its meditation on fear and dreaming, 'Witches' also quotes extensively from 'The Rime of the Ancient Mariner'. Lamb was not S. T. Coleridge and William Wordsworth's close friend for nothing; their work directly informs his meditation upon the nature of mind and memory. Elia envisages the child on his 'little midnight pillow' tormented by anxieties somehow innate to his soul and 'unborrowed from tradition':

> 'Gorgons, and Hydras, and Chimaeras dire' – stories of Celaeno and the Harpies – may reproduce themselves in the brain of superstition – but they were there before. They are transcripts, types – the archetypes are in us, and eternal. How else should the recital of that, which we know in a waking sense to be false, come to affect us at all?

Such fears do not come from books or elderly nurses' stories; like Wordsworth's 'Immortality Ode', Lamb suggests that our very souls and imagination owe something to a mysterious, elevated form of pre-existence. As Wu writes, 'Lamb follows Wordsworth also in regarding everything that follows childhood as decline; he is in dialogue with a pre-natal past, the source of those clouds of glory the fading glow of which illu-minates the ideal Romantic childhood':

> That the kind of fear here treated of is purely spiritual – that it is strong in propor-tion as it is objectless upon earth – that it predominates in the period of sinless infancy – are difficulties, the solution of which might afford some probable insight into our ante-mundane condition, and a peep at least into the shadow-land of pre-existence.

See also   British Politics 1789–1815; British Politics 1815–1832; Contemporary and Victorian Reception; Satire; Sexualities.

Further Reading

David Higgins, *Romantic Genius and the Literary Magazine: Biography, Celebrity, Politics* (2005).
Simon P. Hull, *Charles Lamb, Elia and the London Magazine: Metropolitan Muse* (2010).
Robert Morrison, *The English Opium Eater: A Biography of Thomas De Quincey* (2009).
Mark Parker, *Literary Magazines and British Romanticism* (2000).
Nicholas Roe, *Fiery Heart: The First Life of Leigh Hunt* (2005).
Kim Wheatley (ed.), *Romantic Periodicals and Print* (2003).
Duncan Wu, 'Charles Lamb: *Elia*', in *A Companion to Romanticism*, ed. Duncan Wu (1999), 277–82.
Duncan Wu, *William Hazlitt: The First Modern Man* (2008).

Satire

Romantic-era Verse Satire

Satire it was, in the form of the *Anti-Jacobin* newspaper's 1797 attack on Coleridge and Southey's 'New School' of Poetry, that first identified the liter-ary movement which we now label 'Romanticism', and satire we have met several times before in this book: in Robert Burns's verse satire on Calvinism 'Holy Willie's Prayer' (published 1799), James Hogg's prose satire on the same in the *Private Memoirs and Confessions of a Justified Sinner* (1824), Lord Byron's mockery of the poet Wordsworth in *Don Juan* (1819–24) and elsewhere, his lordship's friend Thomas Moore's scorn for vulgar *nouveau riche* travellers in *The Fudge Family in Paris* (1818), the London Corresponding Society luminary Thomas Spence's scornful dismissal of '[Edmund] Burke's Address to the Swinish Multitude' (1793), James Gillray's more positive treatment, on the other hand, of the great Irish parliamentar-ian in 'Smelling out a Rat' (1790), and last, though certainly not least, in William Cowper's attack on the blood-stained products of the slave trade in 'Pity for the Poor Africans' (1788).

There was a vein of powerful and clamorous satire in the Romantic period, which was manifested both in poetry and prose. And yet this state of affairs was not always recognised in critical scholarship. The satirical aspects of the Regency novels of Jane Austen and Thomas Love Peacock have long been cherished but, until fairly recently, the common critical perception was that though the late Georgian period was undoubtedly an age of great graphic satire (notably in the work of that ferocious personage Gillray, of the brothers Cruikshank (Isaac and the more famous George) and of Thomas Rowlandson), it was not a period in which there was much to remember in terms of poetic satire, the monumental figure of Byron excepted. Indeed, his lordship's affection for the Augustan satire of Dryden and Pope and frequent use of satire, from *English Bards and Scotch Reviewers* (1809) to *Don Juan* (1819–24), a poem left incomplete at his death in 1824, was sometimes seen as having something attitudinising about it. Fondness for the Augustan masters was seen as another way in which Byron could set himself apart from his peers, a conscious archaism which repudiated the anti-Popean critique of neoclassicism made by Wordsworth, Coleridge and others (see 'Literary and Philosophical Key Concepts I'). Apart from his cele-bration of Pope in *Don Juan*, Byron also wrote a brace of prose pamphlets defending 'The Life and Writings of Pope' in 1821 from the strictures of the poet and clergyman the Reverend William Lisle Bowles (1762–1850).

Though the fact is not evident in many twentieth-century literary histo-ries published before the 1990s, satire was a principal literary form of the Romantic period and Byron's work was but the sharpest tip of an iceberg large in size. Over the last two decades or so, scholars of Romanticism have made a remarkable rediscovery; that the late Georgian age was a period in which verse satire – previously thought of as a faded poetic fashion and as the literary province of the Augustans – thrived and prospered. As Marilyn Butler dryly remarked in 1984, 'The so-called Romantics did not know at the time that they were supposed to do without satire' (her hint prompted renewed critical attention to Romantic-era satire in terms of both scholarly monographs and editions; see 'Further Reading'). But all of the canonical literary figures of the period, Wordsworth included, wrote satire, and, in Byron, even the most restrictive canon of Romantic poetry – the so-called 'Big Six' – includes a figure of the greatest satirical virtuosity.

Though he had little time for 'personal and occasional satire' (that writ-ten for a particular moment or 'ad hominem' against a particular person), which he saw as ephemeral and not worth the 'name of poetry', Wordsworth praised 'philosophical satire, like that of Horace and Juvenal' in the 'Preface' to his 1815 *Poems*. Indeed, he composed an 'Imitation of Juvenal' in 1795, the near regicidal 'Ye kings, in wisdom, sense and power' ('These freaks are worse than any sick man's dream ...'). Coleridge wrote a number of newspaper squibs on contemporary politics in the ideological heat of the 1790s, all written from the radical viewpoint, such as the once notorious 'Fire, Famine, and Slaughter', a satire on the policies of William Pitt's administration which appeared in the *Morning Post* in 1798. A collaboration with Southey, published in the same paper in the following year, produced 'The Devil's Thoughts', which portrays Britain as a corrupt, even diabolical, nation. Blake satirised priestcraft, Swedenborgianism and much else in *The Marriage of Heaven and Hell* (*c*.1790–3). Of Byron we have already heard, but Keats and Shelley also courted the satirical muse.

Although Keats wrote in 1818 that 'We hate poetry that has a palpable design upon us', the poet was not always faithful to such principles, and even he worked in the designing literary art of satire, from weaving in *en passant* satire on the greed of Isabella's 'money-bags' brothers in 'Isabella, or The Pot of Basil' (published 1820) to the sustained if unfinished allegorical satire *The Cap and Bells* (1820). Shelley's most overt satire is found in his lampoon of Wordsworth in *Peter Bell the Third* (1819), which caricatured Wordsworth as a political turncoat and as a poet with as much 'imagination as a pint pot'. That said, Steven E. Jones's 1994 study of Shelley's satire sees ambivalence here; given that 'the basis of Shelley's satire is in violence rather than laughter', the poet fretted about its compatibility with his 'social mission', 'whether the violent medicine (or poison) of satire can ever contribute to that responsibility'.

Political Satire

The 'Big Six' apart, the wider print culture of the Romantic period was saturated in satire. The political, social and literary issues of the day resound through the age's satirical writing. Caricaturists, satirical pamphleteers, and broadsheet balladeers fed the taste for satire, and anonymous lampoonery and personal invective, from the left and the right, became a staple of daily newspapers. Broadsheet, handbill and radical journals also brought satire to the working classes in periodicals such as Wooler's *Black Dwarf* (see 'Political Protest and Popular Radicalism'), which frequently used satire. The likes of Thomas Moore and Leigh Hunt developed reputations as feared newspaper satirists, and it did not seem beneath their dignity for S. T. Coleridge, Charles Lamb, Mary Robinson, P. B. Shelley and Lord Byron to contribute satirical verse to daily and weekly newspapers.

Lamb, for instance, published 'The Triumph of the Whale' in Hunt's *Examiner* in March 1812, an occasional satire on the Prince of Wales, who after being made Prince Regent on the second, and final, lapse of his father into insanity, had maintained the Tories in power, much to the rage and disappointment of his former Whig allies (see 'British Politics 1789–1815'), and, overnight, had been transformed in oppositional opinion from bold champion of liberty to obese, treacherous libertine. Lamb plays on the obvious pun 'Wales'/'whales' in portraying the famously overweight Prince George as a huge blubbering weight (and slips in a reference to the fellow's well-known fondness for strong drink for good measure – the Prince was what the late Georgians called a 'five-bottle man'):

> Not a mightier Whale than this
> In the vast Atlantic is;
> Not a fatter fish than he
> Flounders round the polar sea.
> See his blubbers – at his gills
> What a world of drink he swills.

The Prince Regent is surrounded by malign Tory counsellors, mistresses (his royal highness was not only corpulent, but also a corpulent womaniser), and fawning toadies says Lamb, though not, of course, in quite those words:

> But about his presence keep
> All the Monsters of the Deep;
> Mermaids, with their tails and singing
> His delighted fancy stinging;
> Crooked Dolphins, they surround him,
> Dog-like Seals they fawn around him.

The poem ends in a flourish by posing – and answering – the following pointed question:

> Name or title, what has he?
> Is he Regent of the Sea?
> …
> By his bulk and by his size,
> By his oily qualities,
> This (or else my eyesight fails),
> This should be the Prince of Whales.

To radicals and Whigs, the codified nature of satire such as this allowed a measure of outspokenness in a society where free speech was severely restricted (the failed trial of the radical satirist William Hone in 1817 for a liturgical parody which contained a veiled attack on the government demonstrated that it was notoriously difficult to prosecute for the publication of a satire). It is not insignificant that Leigh Hunt was imprisoned in 1813 for seditious libel on account of an outspoken leading article on the Prince Regent (which dismissed him as 'a corpulent gentleman of fifty … a

252 Texts: Themes, Issues, Concepts

violator of his word, a libertine, over head and ears in debt and disgrace [and] a despiser of domestic ties') rather than for publishing Lamb's 'The Triumph of the Whale', which makes the same points in satirical verse (Hunt himself, on his release from prison, felt able to lampoon the Regent, later King George IV, in a stream of verse satires published in the *Examiner* over the decade after his release from gaol).

From the start of the Romantic period, as Gillray's 'Smelling out a Rat', a pointed mockery on Dr Richard Price's radical 'Nunc Dimittis' sermon of 1789 (fig. 4 on p. 101), demonstrates, satire – comedy with a moral purpose – was a key part of the political and literary quarrels of the day. There are good reasons why this should be so. The late Georgian satirist James Harley portrayed satire as an ethically corrective force in *The Press* (1822), asking 'But who now listens to a sermonic discourse?' 'No-one' is the implied answer here; instead, satire will point moral lessons, sugaring the pill of instruction with wit:

> Satire has always shone among the rest,
> And is the boldest way, if not the best,
> To tell men freely of their foulest faults.

Some of the 'boldest' and most successful satirists of the 1790s are now unknown amongst general readers. The Tory satirist William Gifford – whom Lord Byron considered the first satirist of the age – was most famous for *The Baviad* (1791), which railed against the sentimental, mutually congratulatory and ornamental verse of the Della Cruscan school of poetry, led by Robert Merry (who used the pseudonym 'Della Crusca'; 1755–98) and Hannah Cowley ('Anna Matilda' in Della Cruscan taxonomy; 1743–1809). His Whig counterpart was John Wolcot (1738–1819), Gifford's bitter enemy – the two had a public brawl in a Piccadilly bookshop in 1800 – who went by the pseudonym 'Peter Pindar'. Wolcot's principal satirical targets were the Royal Academy, the biographers of Dr Johnson and, in particular, George III, who was ridiculed in Pindar's mock-heroic poem *The Lousiad*, published in five cantos between 1785 and 1795, and various other satires.

Satire on Women and by Women

In the Romantic period, satire on the bluestockings – in the time-worn manner of Pope – continued apace, sometimes wry and affectionate (Leigh Hunt's *Blue-Stocking Revels* (1837)), and sometimes vitriolic (Gifford's ferocious handling of Hannah Cowley and, especially, Mary Robinson in *The Baviad*). And the emergence in the 1790s of the radical female 'Jacobin' author – Mary Wollstonecraft the most significant – provoked a good deal of rancorous Tory satire such as Richard Polwhele's *The Unsex'd Females. A Poem* (1798), much of which fastened delightedly on William Godwin's unfortunately over-candid memoir of his late wife, *Memoirs of the Author of A Vindication of the Rights of Woman* (1798). Here is Dr Polwhele:

> See Wollstonecraft, whom no decorum checks,
> Arise, the intrepid champion of her sex;
> O'er humbled man assert the sovereign claim,
> And slight the timid blush of virgin fame.

Women were not just the recipients of such caustic satire. There were also significant satirical writings by female authors, the likes of Anna Laetitia Barbauld, Anna Dodsworth, Lady Ann Hamilton, Elizabeth Hands, Mary Robinson, and others. The last named, for instance, was a keen social critic of the high society with which she was once so familiar in her days as an actress and as 'Perdita', mistress of the Prince of Wales. In both her fictions and her poetry, Robinson attacked corruption in high places, empty fashion, vulgarity and vain display. The prose satire evident in her novels such as *Walsingham; or, The Pupil of Nature* (1797) is also present in her satirical verse, for instance *Modern Manners* (1793), which was published under the exalted pseudonym 'Horace Juvenal' ('Horatian' satire, after the Roman poet Horace, attacks human folly; 'Juvenalian' satire, after his successor Juvenal, condemns vice).

As well as taking revenge on the 'lesser Dunce' Gifford in the Juvenalian manner of Pope's *The Dunciad* (1728–43) (one of 'the calm assassins of *poetic* worth', she calls him, fit only for 'flatt'ring fools and running Genius down'), Robinson attacks, in the Horatian manner of Pope's *The Rape of the Lock* (1714), the foolishness of high society: she mocks its devotion to gossip, liquor and clothes, to – italicising these words for moral emphasis – '*slander*', '*scandal*', '*fashion*', '*folly*', and '*dissipation*':

> Preposterous Fashion! Imp of dangerous art,
> Who bids Philanthropy forsake the heart;
> Insidious monster, of infernal birth,
> That leads to ruin half the tribes of Earth!

Robinson's pseudonym 'Horace Juvenal' is apt, given that the poet moves from satire on folly to that of vice. Take her handling of fashion. On the one hand, Robinson could mock an obsession with finery as mere foolishness; on the other she could see some of its manifestations as morally pernicious in claiming, for example, that wearing French fashion was politically reprehensible. Though she had enthusiastically welcomed the French Revolution in 1789 (her *Ainsi va le Monde* (1790) is one of the earliest poetical salutes to the events of 1789), Robinson turned against it (rather sooner than her male peers Wordsworth and Coleridge), principally as a consequence of the execution of Louis XVI and the Terror. She argues that Francophile Englishwomen who buy French finery are guilty of a betrayal of their country:

> Ye beauteous Dames! the boast of modern times,
> Who *ape* the French, – yet *shudder* at their crimes;
> …
> Why mourn a murder'd M—h's dire disgrace,
> In Paris *linon* trimm'd with Paris *lace*?
> …
> Why deck your brows with *flow'rs* from *Gallia*'s shore,
> When Gallia's lily withers – drench'd in gore?

Socio-political Satire: Mary Robinson and William Hone

In verse and prose Mary Robinson's socio-political satire attacks snobbery, gaming, bitchiness and dressing in ludicrous and affected clothes. She was not alone in social satire on the latter extravagances. The fashions of the day were frequently viewed in scandalous terms in satire as the very height of foolishness. Fig. 13 gives an example in graphic satire from George

Monstrosities of 1822 —

Fig. 13   George Cruikshank, 'Monstrosities of 1822' (1822)

Cruikshank's 'Monstrosities' series (1816–28) which lampoons the newly fashionable trousers – here hugely-exaggerated and billowing – elaborate coiffures – the hats as high as Nelson's Column – and the move back to steel corsetry. Often these attacks on the thoughtless foppery of the rich had a political tinge about them, as in Robinson's attack on Francophile women. Indeed, the attacks on the Prince Regent which stressed Prince George's corpulence and unloveliness also focused on his obsession with his appearance (the Prince used elaborate corsetry to hold in his o'erbrimming figure and treated his body with hugely expensive oils and perfumes).

Toward the end of the Regency, the best-selling radical satirist William Hone's brilliant satire on the Tory establishment *The Political House that Jack Built* (1819), a collaboration with Cruikshank which was highly successful, going through over fifty editions, made the same point as Lamb's 'Triumph', portraying the Prince as a fat 'Dandy of Sixty' on account of his inappropriate vanity, well-known preoccupation with fine ladies, and lavish dress. While portions of the British populace starved, the Nero-like Prince took no notice of their sufferings, in his obsession with clothes, food and drink:

The Dandy of Sixty

Fig. 14 George Cruikshank, 'The Dandy of Sixty' (1819). Illustration for William Hone and George Cruikshank's *The Political House that Jack Built*

THE DANDY OF SIXTY, who bows with a grace,
And has taste in wigs, collars, cuirasses and lace;
Who, to tricksters and fools, leaves the State and its treasure,
And, when Britain's in tears, sails about at his pleasure.

The *Anti-Jacobin* and Tory Satire

The most important satirical journal of the 1790s, the era of Gifford, Pindar
and Robinson – and much more satire besides – was the aforesaid Tory
journal the *Anti-Jacobin* (1797–8), which was directly sponsored by the
government of William Pitt the Younger. This combined parody and satire
with more orthodox critical writing in the paper's campaign against the
British friends of liberty, whom it labelled 'Jacobins', after the extreme
French Revolutionary party of Maximilien Robespierre. As Jonathan
Wordsworth has written, the *Anti-Jacobin* was 'Burkean in its standards'
and devoted to 'attacking all that can be labelled radical or French, defending all that is decent and established within the fabric of English society'.
The journal's principal parodist was George Canning (1770–1827), the brilliant young Tory MP (and later Prime Minister), a former Whig who had
joined the Tories under the influence of Burke's *Reflections on the
Revolution in France* (1790). In the 'Prospectus' to the journal, Canning
writes that 'in one word, of JACOBINISM in all its shapes, and in all its
degrees, political and moral, public and private, whether as it openly
threatens the subversion of States, or gradually saps the foundations of
domestic happiness, we are the avowed, determined and irreconcilable
enemies'.

Alongside its prose attacks on what it called the 'Mistakes,
Misrepresentations, and Lies' of the Whig and radical press, the *Anti-
Jacobin*, like many politically partisan journals after it (*Blackwood's
Edinburgh Magazine* most importantly – for *Blackwood's* satire, see
'Reviews, Magazines and the Essay'), was engaged in a kind of literary
pincer movement with combative parody and satire making the same
points as its more orthodox critical writing. In the very first number Canning
parodied a politically incendiary sonnet by Robert Southey, one of a series
of 'Inscriptions' on several places, some of which were highly evocative to
a radical audience ('For a Column in Smithfield where Wat Tyler was Killed',
for instance). The most extreme was a hymn to the regicide Henry Marten
(1602–80), one of those who sat in judgment on Charles I, which commemorates the cell in Chepstow castle in which he had been incarcerated for
nearly two decades (the poet exaggerates: 'For thirty years secluded from
mankind / Here Marten linger'd ...'). Southey concludes his poem with the
following question and answer:

> Dost thou ask his crime?
> He had rebell'd against the King, and sat
> In judgment on him; for his ardent mind
> Shap'd goodliest plans of happiness on earth,
> And Peace and Liberty. Wild dreams! but such
> As Plato lov'd; such as with holy zeal
> Our Milton worshipp'd. Blessed hopes! awhile
> From man with-held, even to the latter days
> When Christ shall come, and all things be fulfill'd.

Southey's sonnet is millenarian, idealist, republican, an able piece of Jacobin martyrology. Canning takes Southey's sentiments and debunks them, achieving this by replacing Marten with the repellent figure of the murderer Elizabeth Brownrigg (1720–67), a villain familiar to the eighteenth-century reader from the *Newgate Calendar*, awaiting her execution for killing two of her domestic servants, cursing and screaming for strong drink, before 'in slow-drawn cart she went / To execution':

> Dost thou ask her crime?
> She whipp'd two female 'prentices to death,
> And hid them in the coal-hole. For her mind
> Shap'd strictest plans of discipline. Sage schemes!
> Such as Lycurgus taught, when at the shrine
> Of the Orthyan Goddess he bade flog
> The little Spartans; such as erst chastised
> Our Milton when at College. For this act
> Did Brownrigg swing. Harsh laws; but time shall come,
> When France shall reign, and laws be all repeal'd!

Through the idealisation of the infamous Brownrigg, Southey's liberal criminology is made to appear morally repellent and his millenarianism an endorsement of lawless anarchy.

Satire on the 'Lake Poets'

Satire and parody, as the *Anti-Jacobin* well knew, are forms of critical discourse and can usefully be seen as an alternative mode of literary criticism. The journal's methods were certainly evident – consciously or unconsciously – in the reception of William Wordsworth. The critical broadsides that the poet received were echoed in the chorus of satirical writing which greeted his work. Francis Jeffrey's famously stinging reviews of *Poems in Two Volumes* (1807) and *The Excursion* (1814) were followed by satirical versions of the same charge. Whereas Jeffrey attacked the Lakers for 'furnishing themselves from vulgar ballads and plebeian nurseries', 'The Baby's Debut', one of James and Horace Smith's famous collection of parodies *Rejected Addresses* (1812), makes the same charge in metre ('we pounced on his popular ballads', they wrote in the eighteenth edition of the book in 1833, 'and exerted ourselves to push their simplicity into puerility and silliness') in its portrayal of the infantile babbling of the verbally incontinent Nancy Lake, 'a girl eight years of age':

> My brother Jack was nine in May,
> And I was eight on New Year's Day;
> So in Kate Wilson's shop
> Papa (he's my papa and Jack's)
> Bought me, last week, a doll of wax,
> And brother Jack a top.

And so it goes on. To complete the circle Jeffrey reviewed the brothers Smith's book in the *Edinburgh* and declared that the authors had 'succeeded perfectly in the imitation of [Wordsworth's] maukish [*sic*] affectations of childish simplicity and nursery stammering'.

The editor of the *Edinburgh* scoffed at what he saw as Wordsworth's habit of attaching metaphysical significance to trifles – a friend's shovel, the drivellings of a travelling tinker, a little girl's duffle coat – and James Hogg made the same point in parodic shape in *The Poetic Mirror* (1821), his brilliant collection of parodies of the likes of Wordsworth, Coleridge, and Byron. In 'The Flying Tailor', a blank-verse parody of Wordsworth's *Excursion*, Hogg makes sport with the Wordsworthian aesthetic of inwardness and transcendence, gently mocking the notion that solitude and closeness to nature, rather than society, produces a higher, more moral form of poetry. In Hogg's parody the contemplative, inward-looking poet finds a source of wonderment and profound mystery in a mere pair of breeches.

> A pair
> Of breeches to his philosophic eye
> Were not what unto other folks they seem,
> Mere simple breeches, but in them he saw
> The symbol of the soul – mysterious, high
> Hieroglyphics! such as Egypt's Priest
> Adored upon the holy Pyramid,
> Vainly imagined tomb of monarchs old,
> But raised by wise philosophy, that sought
> By darkness to illumine, and to spread
> Knowledge by dim concealment – process high
> Of man's imaginative, deathless soul.

Here the parody mocks the high Romantic tendency to freight the quotidian with a symbolic resonance it does not, to the plainer mind, deserve.

That other great satirist/critic Lord Byron began his long and generally antipathetic engagement with the Lake School in an 1808 notice of the *Poems in Two Volumes* which briskly dismisses Wordsworth's poetic experimentation as being couched in 'language not simple, but puerile'. In Byron's first published satire, *English Bards and Scotch Reviewers* (1809), he similarly lampoons that 'apostate from poetic rule, / The simple Wordsworth', mocking him as a prosaic waffler, and identifying the simpleton Johnny Foy – 'The Idiot Boy' of the *Lyrical Ballads*' poem of that name – with his creator:

> Who, both by precept and example, shows
> That prose is verse, and verse is merely prose;
> ...
> Thus, when he tells the tale of Betty Foy,
> The idiot mother of 'an idiot boy';
> ...
> That all who view the 'idiot in his glory'
> Conceive the bard the hero of the story.

'Gentle Coleridge' scarcely fares better. He is also dismissed as a bore (being guilty of both 'turgid ode and tumid stanza') and as someone guilty of an absence of literary brainwork. The author of the 'Effusion To a Young Ass' (1794) – not the happiest title it must be said – in which he democratically informs the animal 'I hail thee BROTHER' – is himself portrayed as a kind of poetic donkey:

> Yet none in lofty numbers can surpass
> The bard who soars to elegise an ass.
> So well the subject suits his noble mind,
> He brays the laureat of the long-ear'd kind.

Lord Byron's Satire

Though it might be tempting to regard satire as a kind of literary Jolly Roger crewed with parodical pirates and burlesque buccaneers all aiming to hole the side of the good ship Romanticism, there is much more to late Georgian period satire than the simple reactionary. Thomas Moore's satirical travelogue *The Fudge Family in Paris* (see 'Empire and Travel') has arguably more power and vigour than his *Irish Melodies* (see 'Irish, Scottish and Welsh Poetry'), Austen's and Peacock's achievements in prose need no commendation and Moore's friend Lord Byron's most creative, and indeed, imaginative work is in satire, particularly after he abandoned the Popean heroic couplet and borrowed John Hookham Frere's English version of the Italian eight-line *ottava rima* stanza in *Beppo* (1818) and *Don Juan* (1819–24). The latter has generally been seen as his undisputed masterpiece. Indeed, the editor of the standard scholarly edition of Byron's work, Jerome J. McGann, declares that *Don Juan* is 'the most important poem published in England between 1667 (when *Paradise Lost* was issued) and 1850 (when *The Prelude* finally appeared in print)'.

In the 'Dedication' to *Don Juan*, Byron returns to the mockery of the Lake Poets with which he had begun his satirical career, tartly commenting that a reader capable of understanding Wordsworth's *Excursion* 'would be able / To add a story to the Tower of Babel'. Similarly, Byron says mock-ruefully of the *Biographia Literaria*, in which Coleridge had recently been 'explaining metaphysics to the nation', that 'I wish he would explain his explanation'. In the first canto of the poem, Byron sets out his famous satirical 'poetical commandments':

> Thou shalt believe in Milton, Dryden, Pope;
> Thou shalt not set up Wordsworth, Coleridge, Southey;
> Because the first is craz'd beyond all hope,
> The second drunk, the third so quaint and mouthy.

Byron charges the Wordsworth gang with solipsism, of residing in the Lake District contemplating their poetical navels and paying no mind to the sufferings of the poor or the wider European geopolitical context with which the cosmopolitan Byron was so familiar:

> You – Gentlemen! by dint of long seclusion
> From better company, have kept your own
> At Keswick, and, through still continu'd fusion
> Of one another's minds, at last have grown
> To deem as a most logical conclusion,
> That Poesy has wreaths for you alone:
> There is a narrowness in such a notion,
> Which makes me wish you'd change your lakes for Ocean.

This ill suits, Byron maintains, a poet such as Wordsworth, who once 'season'd his Pedlar Poems with democracy'.

The poem, left unfinished at its author's death, tells the story of a young Spanish nobleman forced to leave Spain after a sexual intrigue with an older woman, and his European wanderings, to Greece, Russia and eventually to England. 'I *have* no plan' wrote Byron of his poem; 'the Soul of such writing is its licence'. Byron's estranged wife once said of her errant husband that 'He is the absolute monarch of words,' and the capacious wandering structure of *Don Juan* allowed Byron to feign the role of improvisator, facilitating his commentary upon political, literary, social and sexual matters. The poem, he wrote to his publisher John Murray, was 'a satire on the abuses of the present state of society'. As well as the famous literary satire on the Lake Poets, Byron also included acerbic Juvenalian political satire, as in his savage attack on the hated Foreign Secretary, the 'intellectual eunuch Castlereagh' and his pitiless treatment of Ireland ('Erin'):

> Cold-blooded, smooth-fac'd, placid miscreant!
> Dabbling its sleek young hands in Erin's gore,
> And thus for wider carnage taught to pant,
> Transferr'd to gorge upon a sister shore,
> The vulgarest tool that Tyranny could want,
> With just enough of talent, and no more,
> To lengthen fetters by another fix'd,
> And offer poison long already mix'd.

The more expansive metre of *ottava rima* in *Don Juan* does not mean that Byron loses the epigrammatic force of the Popean couplet (each eight-line stanza concludes with a couplet). Indeed, Byron uses a large number of audaciously inventive double and triple rhymes in his famous and ingenious closing couplets here:

> But – Oh! ye lords of ladies intellectual,
> Inform us truly, have they not hen-pecked you all?
> …
> Christians have burnt each other, quite persuaded
> That all the Apostles would have done as they did.
> …
> Let us have wine and women, mirth and laughter,
> Sermons and soda-water the day after.

The poet declared in 1823 that 'there are but two sentiments to which I am constant – a strong love of liberty, and a detestation of cant', and he, like so many Romantic-era authors before him, used satire to articulate his political, moral and literary convictions.

See also   Ireland and the 'Catholic Question'; Literary and Philosophical Key Concepts I: The First Generation Romantic Poets; Literary and Philosophical Key Concepts II: The Second Generation Romantic Poets; Reviews, Magazines and the Essay.

Further Reading

Marilyn Butler, 'Satire and the Images of the Self in the Romantic Period', in *English Satire and the Satiric Tradition*, ed. Claude Rawson (1984), 209–25.

Gary Dyer, *British Satire and the Politics of Style, 1789–1832* (1997).

Steven E. Jones, *Shelley's Satire: Violence, Exhortation, and Authority* (1994).

Steven E. Jones, *Satire and Romanticism* (2000).

Steven E. Jones (ed.), *The Satiric Eye: Forms of Satire in the Romantic Period* (2003).

Graeme Stones and John Strachan (eds), *Parodies of the Romantic Age*, 5 vols (1999).

John Strachan (gen. ed.), *British Satire, 1785–1840*, 5 vols (2003).

John Strachan, *Advertising and Satirical Culture in the Romantic Period* (2007).

Marcus Wood, *Radical Satire and Print Culture 1790–1822* (1994).

Jonathan Wordsworth, *Visionary Gleam: Forty Books from the Romantic Period* (1993).

3 Criticism: Approaches, Theory, Practice

Contemporary and Victorian Reception

Contemporary Controversies

Though we now think of the Romantic poets as among the established, canonical greats of English literature, part of a tradition that stretches from Geoffrey Chaucer to the present day, their reception in the late eighteenth and early nineteenth centuries was by no means unequivocally positive. Wordsworth and Coleridge were, it should be remembered, part of a conscious *avant garde* which deliberately positioned itself against the conventions of eighteenth-century poetry, bold young men who implicitly asserted the superiority of their work over the likes of Alexander Pope and Thomas Gray and who were also, scandalously, associated with the 'Jacobin' supporters of the French Revolution. Small wonder that it took time for their work to establish itself. In his polemical 'Essay, Supplementary to the Preface' [to the 1800 *Lyrical Ballads*] (1815), Wordsworth recalled Coleridge telling him that 'every author, as far as he is great and at the same time original, has had the task of creating the taste by which he is to be enjoyed'. This was certainly true for the Lake Poets, and for William Wordsworth in particular. As Thomas De Quincey wrote in 1835, Wordsworth took time to be 'enjoyed': 'Up to 1820 the name of Wordsworth was trampled underfoot; from 1820 to 1830 it was militant; from 1830 to 1835 it has been triumphant.' Triumphant indeed; by 1843, Wordsworth was Queen Victoria's first appointment as Poet Laureate and the unquestioned patriarch of contemporary English poetry. The 'Bard of Rydal Mount' had iconic status in the Victorian era and, indeed, shaped English literature in that period and beyond.

The contentious initial reception of the Romantics is fascinating, and notable for the fact that from its earliest appearance their work provoked controversy. The first critical identification of what we now think of as the Lake Poets was made as early as 1797, and was antipathetic on both artistic and ideological grounds (it is important to realise that criticism and political bias were closely aligned in late Georgian letters). In October of that year, the satirical Tory weekly newspaper the *Anti-Jacobin* scoffed at what it called the 'NEW SCHOOL' of poetry, of 'Coleridge, Southey, [Charles] Lloyd, [Charles] Lamb and co.', and berated it as dangerously pro-French. Such revolutionary verse, it declared, 'openly threatens the subversion of States'. The *Anti-Jacobin* repeatedly lampooned Coleridge and Southey, parodying their work as a mixture of radicalism and gibberish:

> Reason, philosophy, 'fiddledum diddledum',
> Peace and Fraternity, 'higgledy piggledy'.
> Higgledy piggledy, fiddledum diddledum.
> *Et caetera, et caetera, et caetera.*

After the publication of the two volumes of the *Lyrical Ballads* (1798; 1800), Wordsworth himself began to receive critical attention, much of it adverse. One 1804 notice dismissed his attempts to use a simpler form of language in verse than the 'poetic diction' of the neoclassical poets as no more than 'an affectation of simplicity, and a reality of silliness', and – most notably – the *Anti-Jacobin*'s nose-thumbing of the new liberals was followed by Francis Jeffrey's attempt to trample Wordsworth underfoot, to borrow De Quincey's vivid phrase. Lord Jeffrey (1773–1850), the editor of the influential Whig journal the *Edinburgh Review*, famously reviewed Wordsworth's book-length blank-verse poem *The Excursion* (1814), in a poisonous notice which began with the forthright words 'This will never do.' Jeffrey was conservative in critical terms, his poetic models the Elizabethan poet-dramatists, and he attacked the Lake School as '*dissenters* from the established systems in poetry and criticism'. He found the new poetic tone all the more pernicious because it represented to him the misapplication of undeniable talent, inasmuch as 'the perverseness and bad taste of this new school was combined with a great deal of genius and of laudable feeling'.

Interestingly, what we now tend to see as the central preoccupation of Romanticism in such works as 'Tintern Abbey' and the 'Preface' to the *Lyrical Ballads*, the importance of the creative imagination, is nowhere mentioned in Jeffrey's criticism. Instead, it was the Preface's attention to the 'real language of men', Wordsworth's endorsement of the ancient ballad tradition, and his preoccupation with rustic life – pedlars, leech-gatherers, female vagrants and the like – that provoked Jeffrey's ire. Wordsworth wrote in the original 'Preface' to the *Lyrical Ballads* that 'The principal object, then ... was to choose incidents and situations from common life, and to relate or *describe* them.' From Francis Jeffrey's perspective, this was no more than a foolish misapplication of the muse's lyre. Wordsworth and

Coleridge's use of the ballad tradition and their valorisation of the experience of the rural poor were dismissed as low posturing and the authors of the *Lyrical Ballads* censured for 'furnishing themselves from vulgar ballads and plebeian nurseries'.

Jeffrey's stinging review of Wordsworth's *Poems in Two Volumes* (1807), a collection which includes the 'Immortality Ode', 'I Wandered Lonely as a Cloud', the sonnet 'Composed Upon Westminster Bridge', 'We are Seven' and many other remarkable poems, condemned their author for wasting his talent by dwelling on subjects unsuitable for the muse of poetry – daffodils, a little girl's duffle coat, a kitten chasing falling leaves – in 'connecting his most lofty, tender, or impassioned conceptions, with objects and incidents, which the greater part of his readers will probably persist in thinking low, silly, or uninteresting':

> It is possible enough, we allow, that the sight of a friend's garden spade, or a sparrow's nest, or a man gathering leeches, might really have suggested to such a mind a train of powerful impressions and interesting reflections; but it is certain, that, to most minds, such associations will always appear forced, strained, and unnatural; and that the composition in which it is attempted to exhibit them, will always have the air of parody, or ludicrous and affected singularity.

This notion of Wordsworth's supposed foolishness or childishness was a fairly widespread critical perception in the first days of Romanticism. That fine satirist/critic Lord Byron (whose own critical reception is examined in the discussion of 'Byronism' in 'Key Literary Concepts II: The Second Generation Romantics', above), in the very first review of the *Poems in Two Volumes* – written when he was a schoolboy at Harrow – dismissed Wordsworth's poetry as 'language not simple, but puerile', and Byron's extended satirical poem *English Bards and Scots Reviewers* (1809) similarly mocked 'That mild apostate from poetic rule, / The simple Wordsworth'. However, both Jeffrey and Byron changed their tune – though not in a positive way – in the light of the publication in 1814 of Wordsworth's long blank-verse philosophical poem *The Excursion*. Jeffrey condemned the 'profuse and irrepressible wordiness' of the poem, and Byron's *Don Juan* portrayed it as long-winded obscurantism:

> And Wordsworth, in a rather long 'Excursion'
> (I think the quarto holds five hundred pages),
> Has given a sample from the vasty version
> Of his new system to perplex the sages;
> ...
> And he who understands it would be able
> To add a story to the Tower of Babel.

Wordsworth had moved, in such critical accounts, from a purveyor of infantile inanities into a verbose and incomprehensible babbler.

Our sense of what constituted the major poets of the Romantic period was not that of the late Georgian era, where the now little-read poetry of Sir Walter Scott sold in huge quantities and where Thomas Campbell (1774–1844), author of *The Pleasures of Hope* (1799), and Samuel Rogers (1763–1855), author of *The Pleasures of Memory* (1792), were amongst the most popular poets of the day. Certainly Lord Byron was a success all over Europe, but his friend P. B. Shelley died fearing that he would become an 'inheritor of unfulfilled renown' (his own opinion of John Keats in his elegy for that poet *Adonais* (1821)). The people of England had not responded to Shelley's incendiary political poems and though he had received a modicum of critical esteem (Leigh Hunt had consistently praised Shelley's verse in the pages of his various journals and *Blackwood's* acknowledged his talent whilst being appalled by his radicalism), his work was generally unnoticed by middle-class readers. Blake's critical reputation, it might also be pointed out, is a thing of the later nineteenth and early twentieth centuries. His books were self-published in a tiny number of copies, and excepting a few remarks in then unpublished sources – letters and journals and so on – he left little trace in the criticism of the time.

John Keats's work, on the other hand, certainly caused a stir in the critical magazines of the day, though not always in a manner from which the poet took any pleasure. Most of the sharp critical comment that Keats received was politically motivated, as Tory journals associated him closely with his early mentor, the radical journalist and poetical innovator Leigh Hunt. In the five short years before his death in 1821, Keats, whose earliest published work, 'On First Looking into Chapman's Homer', appeared in the *Examiner* in December 1816, was much praised and sponsored by Hunt, the first critic to recognise his talent. Unfortunately for Keats this led him to be caught in the crossfire between 'Mr Examiner Hunt' and his ideological opponents. John Wilson Croker, in his 1818 *Quarterly Review* notice of Keats's second volume of verse, the mythological romance *Endymion* (1818), dismissed the book as a piece of poetical 'insanity' which had itself been infected by 'Mr Leigh Hunt's insane criticism':

> It is not that Mr Keats ... has not powers of language, rays of fancy, and gleams of genius – he has all these; but he is unhappily a disciple of the new school of what has been somewhere called 'Cockney Poetry'; which may be defined to consist of the most incongruous ideas in the most uncouth language. [He] ... is a copyist of Mr Hunt; but he is more unintelligible ... and ten times more tiresome and absurd than his prototype.

(Both Byron and Shelley peddled the myth that this review brought on Keats's final illness, that he was, in Byron's unfortunate phrase, 'snuffed out by an Article'.)

Keats was similarly attacked by the Tory wits of *Blackwood's Edinburgh Magazine* in their entertaining if malodorous attacks on Hunt and his so-called 'Cockney School of Poetry'. J. G. Lockhart gleefully attacked the 'calm, settled, imperturbable drivelling idiocy' of *Endymion*, and the waspish conclusion to his review snobbishly urged the poet to return to his previous trade of apothecary:

> We venture to make one small prophecy, that his bookseller will not a second time venture £50 upon any thing he can write. It is a better and a wiser thing to be a starved apothecary than a starved poet; so back to the shop Mr John, back to 'plasters, pills, and ointment boxes', &c. But, for Heaven's sake ... be a little more sparing of extenuatives and soporifics in your practice than you have been in your poetry.

In the 1820s, as, indeed, since the 1790s, the Romantic poets' reputations were by no means critically certain. However, this was about to change.

Victorian Responses

When John Keats's friend, the painter Joseph Severn – who had tended to the poet as he writhed in his tubercular death-throes – returned to England in 1838 after an absence of some seventeen years, he noted with pleasure and surprise that the fame of his own 'dear Keats' was 'not only well established, but was increasing from day to day'. Undeniably, some of this posthumous renown was the consequence of the poet's moving biography, the narrative of the prodigious, doomed, love-lorn talent – the 'pale flower by some sad maiden cherished' in Shelley's phrase – cut down in his early manhood (for Matthew Arnold, writing in 1853, Keats was 'one whose exquisite genius and pathetic death render him for ever interesting'). Nonetheless, Severn's words are testimony to the Victorian sense of the 'exquisite genius' of the poets of the earlier nineteenth century evident from the 1830s onwards. Indeed, by the mid-nineteenth century, the notion of Wordsworth as a puerile driveller or Keats as an ignorant Cockney upstart were already seen as the partisan and eccentric views of a bygone factional age. In 1859, for instance, a contributor to *Harper's New Monthly Magazine* wrote of Wordsworth as 'a great name built up amidst ridicule and scoffing': 'what a droll idea it gives of the state of the English mind forty and fifty years ago, to know that reviews which laughed at Wordsworth as an old woman were feared and respected as literary authorities!'

The Romantic poets, it seemed, had 'creat[ed] the taste by which [they were] to be enjoyed', in the words of Wordsworth's 'Essay, Supplementary'. Indeed, a notice of the laureate's nephew Christopher Wordsworth's *Memoirs of William Wordsworth*, published in 1851, wrote of that recently deceased author that 'As a poet his genius is now as unquestioned as it ever really was unquestionable.' Wordsworth began to be seen by Victorian critics as the poetic master spirit of the literature of the late eighteenth and early nineteenth centuries, then newly christened the age of 'Romanticism'. That said, in his pomp the author never knew he was a 'Romantic' poet, and nor did his great contemporaries, for to use the term 'Romanticism' to encapsulate the thematic concerns of late Georgian poetry was a Victorian critical conceit borrowed – like much else in mid-nineteenth-century thought – from Germany, where controversies had raged between 'classical' and 'Romantic' writers from the late 1790s onwards (see 'What is Romanticism?' for an account of this phenomenon).

Romanticism in a British context is a mid-nineteenth-century term, used as the poets and critics of the second half of the century looked back at its first decades. And what many of the most significant figures within Victorian letters – Matthew Arnold, John Stuart Mill, Walter Pater, John Ruskin, and the pre-Raphaelites – valued in the literature of that period was Wordsworth, and to a slightly lesser extent the poets Coleridge, Keats and Shelley (Byron's somewhat sulphurous reputation and extensive use of satire did not suit many Victorians, and Blake's stock, as we have seen, was slow to rise). Similarly, the most notable canonical poets of the Victorian period were influenced by the Romantics, being post-Wordsworthian in the work of Arnold, Elizabeth Barrett Browning and Alfred, Lord Tennyson (a poet also hugely indebted to Keats), and arguably manifesting a post-Shelleyan vision in that of Robert Browning and Arthur Hugh Clough. In 1880, just sixty years after Lockhart's animadversions in *Blackwood's*, Matthew Arnold could call Keats 'one of the very greatest of English Poets', and by the 1920s, few would have thought it unusual that John Middleton Murry could write a book entitled *Keats and Shakespeare*. A hundred years previously, the very name of this volume would have struck John Gibson Lockhart as risible but it is emblematic of the posthumous triumph of the Romantics, who enjoyed critical esteem from such as Arnold alongside the contemporaneous, rather saccharine Victorian idealisation of the likes of Shelley and Keats as unchallenging poetic pet-lambs, even as unworldly and ethereal creatures, the latter attitude exemplified in William Howlitt's *Homes and Haunts of the Most Eminent British Poets* (1847), which breathlessly declared that 'Keats was one of those sweet and glorious spirits who descend like the angel messengers of old ... neither ours nor any other history can furnish a specimen more beautiful than John Keats. He was of feeling and "imagination all compact". His nature was one pure mass of the living light of poetry.'

The canonisation of the Romantic poets coincided with what might be called the pedagogical institutionalisation of English Literature in a plethora of Victorian popular critical histories and anthologies from the much-reprinted *Chambers' Cyclopedia of English Literature* (1842–4) through to late nineteenth- and early twentieth-century literary criticism aimed at a general audience by the likes of Oliver Elton, Émile Legouis, and George Saintsbury, but also – and in the end more significantly – in the rise of English Literature in nineteenth-century universities after the establishment of the University of London in the 1820s. University College, London, founded as a non-denominational alternative to the medieval universities, taught English literature from its commencement. The Revd Thomas Dale was appointed its first Professor of English Literature in 1826, and he was followed soon after, in 1829, by King's College, London's founding Professor of English Literature, the Revd J. S. Brewer. Provincial colleges and higher education institutions in the Empire copied these examples, and were eventually succeeded by the older universities (Oxford's English faculty was founded in 1894, Cambridge's as late as 1919). In the United States there were professors of English Literature in some of the most important schools by 1860 (Brown, Columbia, Pennsylvania, Rutgers, and Yale among them).

'When we read and study Wordsworth we always do so within a certain institutional framework,' wrote Jerome J. McGann in his famous polemic *The Romantic Ideology* (1985), and the dominance of (male) high Romantic argument was certainly felt in the fashioning of the first university courses in English Literature. 'Romanticism,' writes Ian Reid in his important study *Wordsworth and the Formation of English Studies* (2004), 'a powerful and pervasive discursive formation, shaped the main features of modern education systems in the English-speaking world, and especially of literary studies'. The centrality of the Romantic poets – and what the Byronist McGann labels the Romantic ideology – was ingrained in the early English departments and faculties established in both the United States and the United Kingdom, leaving little time for the study of the likes of Felicia Hemans's nationalistic verse and domestic narratives, the baronet Scott's tales of heroism and military derring-do, and, indeed, Lord Byron's satirical verse. The Lake Poets, and Leigh Hunt's confreres Keats and Shelley, had won their battle over the nay-sayers in the most resounding manner.

Twentieth-century Criticism from Modernism to the New Criticism

Modernism

The critic Edmund Gosse, writing in 1900 – the final full year of Queen Victoria's long reign, which had spanned eight decades – declared that the Victorian period had seen 'the maintenance, without radical change of any kind, of the original Romantic system, now just one hundred years old'. 'Poetry in England', Gosse maintained, 'is still what it became when Wordsworth and Coleridge remodelled it in 1797.' In such accounts, late Victorian poetry, especially in its crepuscular lingering into the twentieth century, was little more than an exhausted vein of Romanticism. In the 1820s the Romantics were contentious; in the 1900s they were old masters, so to speak – and, undeniably, to the point of tedium to some.

The state of affairs described by Gosse was hardly likely to last indefinitely; the critic clearly – and rightly – implies that the literary world was ready for something new, for another literary movement to establish itself by critical repudiation of its forebears, just as the Wordsworthian crowd had done decades before. When it came, the backlash against nineteenth-century poetry and, it might be pointed out, European high culture in general, was extreme. Indeed, the 'Modernist' rejection of the past in the first decades of the twentieth century spread rather more widely than a straightforward shaking off of a tired Romanticism. Herbert Read famously declared in 1933 that Modernism was 'an abrupt break with all tradition ... The aim of five centuries of European effort is openly abandoned.' This was a thoroughgoing assault on all of the principal European art forms. Modernism rejected the cultivation of realism in the novel, scoffed at what it saw as the sentimentality and untrammelled Romanticism of nineteenth-century art and music, and jettisoned the constraints of metre, rhyme and regular syllabic counts in its free verse, notably – in terms of English literature – in the work of the two American authors who shook poetry warmly by the throat in the 1910s and 1920s, T. S. Eliot and Ezra Pound.

One of the earliest and most influential British Modernist broadsides against Romantic poetry and its values came from the critic, poet and philosopher T. E. Hulme (1883–1917), later to die in action during the First World War, who dismissed the nineteenth-century tradition in his forthright essay 'Romanticism and Classicism' (1913–14) as no more than 'spilt religion', and called instead for a new 'dry and sophisticated' poetry:

> I object even to the best of the Romantics ... I object to the sloppiness which does-
> n't consider that a poem is a poem unless it is moaning or whining about some-
> thing or other ... The thing has got so bad now that a poem which is all dry and

hard, a properly classical poem, would not be considered poetry at all. [People] cannot see that accurate description is a legitimate object of verse. Verse to them always means a bringing in of some of the emotions ... The great aim is accurate, precise, and definite description.

Hulme, the unyieldingly anti-Romantic, short-lived polemicist, was a key influence on the (Missouri-born) father of British Modernist poetry, Thomas Stearns Eliot (1888–1965), who admired the author greatly, describing him – in Eliotesque paradox – as a 'classical, reactionary and revolutionary' figure in simultaneity. Certainly Eliot's early poetry is highly 'sophisticated' and – in a tonal and thematic sense – it might be described as self-consciously 'dry'. Whereas Wordsworth aspired to a poetry which would reach 'far into the heart', Eliot cultivated a studied detachment; poetry, he declared, was 'not a turning loose of emotion but an escape from emotion'.

In place of the clear sense of poetic selfhood evident in Wordsworth and Coleridge's verse, in Eliot's work there is a post-Freudian attention to what might be seen as the fractured modern psyche, especially in the aftermath of the First World War, as demonstrated in what is generally seen as his masterpiece, *The Waste Land* (1922). Eliot dismissed what he saw as a cult of 'personality' in Romanticism, arguing instead for a 'dissociation of sensibility' which would get beyond the egotistical sublime (to borrow a phrase from previous critics of Wordsworth). Though influenced by *fin de siècle* European avant gardists and the Renaissance poet Dante, Eliot also drew up his own personal canon within British poetry, in which the Romantics, so to speak, did not trouble the scorers: Elizabethan and Jacobean verse drama (like the anti-Romantic Jeffrey before him), Donne, Marvell and the Metaphysical poets.

The poet-critic Eliot's leeriness of Romanticism had its contemporary academic equivalents, notably in the work of his old tutor Irving Babbitt (1865–1933), a professor of English at Eliot's alma mater, Harvard University. Babbitt proselytised for what he called a 'New Humanism' in the post-War period, attacking Romanticism in his influential *Rousseau and Romanticism* (1919) as a 'revulsion from the rational'. Anti-rationalist, Romantic nationalism had, in this account, led to the First World War; instead, Babbitt endorsed an emphasis on the value of reason, restraint and pragmatism (in the early 1920s, Eliot described himself as a 'disciple' of Babbitt, though later in the decade he dismissed Babbitt's humanism (in the godless sense) as the poet turned towards Anglicanism). Babbitt's ideas as to the potential dangers of Romanticism were later echoed by the British poet and critic F. L. Lucas (1894–1967), author of *The Decline and Fall of the Romantic Ideal* (1936), one of the earliest psychoanalytical accounts of Romanticism. 'The advantage of the Freudian viewpoint', writes Lucas, 'is that it links together *various* characteristics of Romanticism, some healthy, some morbid.' For Lucas, the morbid side of Romanticism, in a Europe where Hitler and his felonious cohorts were in charge of Germany, was coming to the fore: 'Romanticism is not, in Goethe's phrase "disease". It is intoxicated dreaming. But it is easy to see, and we shall see, that such auto-intoxication can often become the reverse of healthy.' In a 1963 reissue of the book, Lucas lamented that his predictions as to 'the destructiveness of a Romanticism gone rotten' had proved all too accurate: 'Hitler, though he might pride himself on ruthless realism, remained, still more, a perverted Romantic.'

T. S. Eliot himself ventured into print with his opinions of the second-generation Romantics in his essay 'Shelley and Keats' (1933). Though he admired Keats as 'a great poet ... occupied only by the highest use of poetry', Eliot poured ire on the life and work of P. B. Shelley. One literary magpie writing about another, Eliot dismissed his predecessor, not because 'he borrowed ideas – which ... is perfectly legitimate – but [because] he borrowed shabby ones'. The conservative Eliot did not much care for the radical Shelley: 'I find his ideas repellent.' Eliot does not specify which particular ideas he found so unappealing but Shelley's atheism, republican-ism and sexual libertarianism were hardly likely to appeal to someone of his particular cast of mind. Curiously for someone closely associated with an impersonal notion of poetry, Eliot conflates the work with the man, with both awarded black marks from teacher: 'the biographical interest which Shelley has always excited makes it difficult to read the poetry without remembering the man: and the man was humourless, pedantic, self-centred and sometimes even a blackguard'.

F. R. Leavis and I. A. Richards

Eliot's position on the demerits of Shelley was shared by F. R. Leavis (1895–1978), the brilliant, spiky and quarrelsome Cambridge critic whom he influenced greatly and who became a central, if highly contentious, figure in mid-twentieth-century British criticism. Leavis propagandised for Eliot and Pound, seeing them as a breath of fresh air which had dispelled the fug of 'late Victorian poetastry' – this including Tennyson and Swinburne – and, like the author of *The Waste Land*, attempted to dethrone the Romantics. Leavis, who was given to rewriting canons to his own satis-faction, as in his study of the English novel *The Great Tradition* (1948), valued the work of Donne and the Metaphysical poets (with Eliot), that of Pope and Dr Johnson, and later, G. M. Hopkins and Eliot himself. This is a poetic tradition where the Romantics are no longer central (Leavis also tilted at those not inconsiderable windmills Milton and Spenser). In his book *Revaluation* (1936), Leavis bluntly maintained that Shelley's philo-sophical poetry demonstrates a 'bewildered confusion'. Shelley is dismissed as muddled and prosy, offering 'nothing but wordy emotional generality [which] does not grasp and present anything'. As Eliot had done three years previously, Leavis uses Keats as a stick to beat Shelley, the former being commended for possessing 'a general concrete vigour [and a] strong grasp upon actualities', unlike the latter. What 'makes Keats so different from Shelley', writes Leavis, is his 'firm sense of the solid world', the latter's head being full of pie-in-the-sky notions of democracy, univer-sal brotherhood and philanthropy (the *Anti-Jacobin*'s critique of Coleridge and Southey springs to mind here).

Leavis's Cambridge colleague and former tutor I. A. Richards (1893–1979), who pioneered a form of close reading known as 'Practical Criticism' which (instead of the historical, narrative and philological forms of literary analysis then widespread in contemporary English departments) concentrated on addressing a poem as 'a thing in itself' rather than addressing its contextual 'extraneous' significance, was more charitable to the Romantics than his contemporary. In his *Coleridge on Imagination* (1934), Richards sets out an interesting fusion of rationalism and Romanticism, endorsing both reason and the creative power of the imagi-nation. In the year after Adolf Hitler had become Chancellor of Germany, Richards lamented 'the general revolt against reason, which shows itself most flagrantly in mid-European politics', and consciously sought to get beyond the distinction which had divided European literature since the work of the Schlegels in the 1790s: 'I don't really want to touch any such question of Classicism and Romanticism … or any historical questions.'

New Criticism

Richards is often, though not uncontentiously, seen as the father of the New Criticism, a form of close reading which flourished in the United States and beyond from the mid-1930s to the 1960s. The leading lights of the move-ment, named after John Crowe Ransom's book *The New Criticism* (1941), were Southerners: Ransom (1888–1974), his former student Allen Tate (1899–1979), Robert Penn Warren (1905–89), and Cleanth Brooks (1906–94). Drawing on the critical ideas of Eliot and Richards (and those of the latter's pupil Sir William Empson (1906–84)), the New Critics maintained that it was not the business of criticism to waffle in paraphrasical manner about the 'content' of a poem or, indeed, to be primarily focused upon its biographical or historical origins. Instead of extrinsic matters – political, psychological, or social – the critic should address a poem as a complex matter of language in an attention to 'intrinsic' meaning and a preoccupation with the actual 'words on the page'. Though setting aside the contextual resonance of Romanticism (its attitudes to the French Revolution, slavery or the Industrial Revolution, for instance), the New Critics were more favourable to the Romantic poets than the likes of Eliot (though Tate gave Shelley some more harsh words). Penn Warren was an important Coleridgean and Brooks's most celebrated essay, re-published in his book *The Well Wrought Urn* (1947), is on John Keats's 'Ode on a Grecian Urn'. Keats, remember, addresses the urn as a 'Sylvan historian' which, to use Brooks's terminology, 'will recite its history to other generations'. 'What will it say to them?' asks Brooks, and then answers his own question: that 'imaginative insight embodies the basic and fundamental perception of man and nature' (this internalisation of Romanticism's own preoccupation, as we will see, is the kind of thing that was to be heavily criticised by the New Historicists).

In the New Criticism, the poet is seen as creating principally from the imagination, matters of 'extrinsic' outside reality being outwith the proper business of literary enquiry. In *Coleridge on Imagination*, Richards had renounced 'historical questions', a manoeuvre of which the New Criticism strongly approved. That said, Brooks did see Keats's work as addressing history of a particular kind; the 'Sylvan historian ... takes a few details and so orders them that we have not only beauty but insight into essential truth. Its "history", in short, is a history without footnotes. It has the validity of myth – not myth as pretty but irrelevant make-believe, and idle fancy, but myth as a valid perception into validity.' Brooks sees the text as creating and fashioning an imaginative truth of its own rather than merely reflecting the extra-textual context in which it was written (the notion of an absence of footnotes in reading Keats and by extension of de-emphasising the socio-political resonance of his work has been much challenged in the last three decades by Romanticists such as Nicholas Roe in his *John Keats and the Culture of Dissent* (1999)).

The New Criticism inspired some of the best traditional twentieth-century mainstream formalist criticism, and its legacy is arguably felt in *tour de force* close readings of the Romantics in such works as Geoffrey H. Hartman's *Wordsworth's Poetry 1787–1814* (1964), Christopher Ricks's *Keats and Embarrassment* (1974) and Helen Vendler's *The Odes of John Keats* (1983). Though it no longer provokes controversy – in the manner in which Richards's early work did – close reading never goes away, of course, and excellent formal criticism of the Romantics co-exists with recent theoretical fashions such as the New Historicism in such studies as Thomas McFarland's *The Mask of Keats* (2000), Michael O'Neill's *Romanticism and the Self-Conscious Poem* (1997), and Seamus Perry's *Coleridge and the Uses of Division* (1999). At the same time, there has also been a 'new formalism', associated with Susan J. Wolfson's *Formal Charges: The Shaping of Poetry in British Romanticism* (1997), which aims to reconnect formal with historical analysis.

M. H. Abrams

The New Criticism also shaped and informed the work of the critic M. H. Abrams (born 1912), generally considered – for better or worse – one of the most significant twentieth-century critics of Romanticism. I. A. Richards inspired the New Criticism from afar, but taught and directly influenced Abrams, who went from Harvard to Cambridge as a postgraduate student. One of the most eloquent of liberal humanist apologists for literature, Abrams idealistically maintained that a poem is 'one of the most nuanced of the arts in expressing what is human'. And, for him, the most 'human' form of English literature was that of Romanticism. Before the First World War, T. E. Hulme had jeered at Romanticism as 'spilt religion'; Abrams agrees but sees this as critically fruitful rather than as a negative. In his *Natural Supernaturalism* (1971) Abrams argued that at the centre of Romantic verse there was a quest narrative, a sense and hope that poetry can take one on a road back to 'a lost paradise'. Disappointed by the French Revolution, he maintains, Wordsworth put aside 'militancy of overt political action' and moved from 'revolution' to 'evolution' in a 'shift to a spiritual and moral revolution which will transform our experience of the old world'.

In Abrams's account, 'faith in an apocalypse by revolution ... gave way to faith in apocalypse by imagination or cognition'. This principle he sees as evident not just in the work of Wordsworth, being 'also the argument of a number of later writings by Blake, Coleridge and Shelley' (Byron does not fit the thematic template, and his 'ironic counter-voice' – which consciously mocked 'the vatic [prophetic] stance of his contemporaries' – is deliberately excluded from the book). The redemptive poetics evident in Wordsworth is also found, for example, in Shelley's *Prometheus Unbound*, that 'most detailed and successful' examination of the 'theme of the human need for love to fulfill what is incomplete and to reintegrate what has been divided'. This being Shelley, this reformation is both psychological and political, manifested 'both in the individual psyche and in the social order'.

Northrop Frye

Whereas Abrams was shaped by the New Criticism, his exact contemporary, the Canadian scholar Northrop Frye (1912–91), is generally seen as having repudiated it. Frye initially made his name by his monograph on Blake, *Fearful Symmetry* (1947), a study of the poet's use of allegory. The systematic allegory available in Blake suited the similarly systematic nature of the critic's thought, which came to full theoretical fruition in his most notable book, *Anatomy of Criticism* (1957), which attempted to reorient interpretation away from 'close reading' in the New Critical manner towards criticism on an epic scale in the study of genre, literary modes and what Frye, borrowing from the thought of the psychologist Carl Jung, called 'archetypes'. Frye traced a schematic pattern of 'generic structures' which, he maintained, were evident throughout the history of Western literature from Homer onwards. Where Jung discerned a universal symbolic language of dreams, the Romanticist Frye saw something similar occurring in the history of literature – what suited the interpretation of Blake could be writ large in Frye's all-embracing taxonomic account of literature. Frye's criticism, like the New Criticism itself, was ahistorical, and, indeed, he went further in repudiating what had previously been seen as the duty of critical evaluation, in arguing for a form of scientific, value-judgement-free literary criticism. Frye's work arguably anticipated the continental structuralism of Roland Barthes and Tzvetan Todorov, itself an effort to codify literature and a key part of a European literary theory which was soon to revolutionise the study of Romanticism in the United States and Great Britain.

Modern Critical Approaches I: From Deconstruction to Psychoanalytical Criticism

Deconstruction

In its critical sophistication, brilliance in critical analysis and, indeed – as some of its critics have had it – relative inattention to matters of history, American literary deconstruction, which thrived in the 1970s and 1980s, was a methodological descendant of the mid-century New Criticism. Certainly it was directly influenced by New Critical close reading techniques, deploying them alongside a joy in hermeneutical complexity which was inspired by the French post-structuralism associated with Roland Barthes (1915–80), which stressed the open, multiple meanings of literary texts and declared itself possessed of a near sexual pleasure – *jouissance* – in the activity of reading ('the pleasure of the text', as Barthes memorably called it).

The deconstructionist Paul de Man rightly called the method a fusion of the 'enlightened formalism of the new criticism [with] the recent and highly promising rapprochement of European and American criticism'. Its principal begetter was the French philosopher Jacques Derrida (1930–2004), who developed post-structuralism into what was denominated 'deconstruction' in two subtle, highly influential and formidably difficult treatises published in 1967, *De la Grammatologie* (*Of Grammatology*) and *L'Écriture et la Différence* (*Writing and Difference*). Like Barthes, Derrida insisted upon the multiplicity of possible meanings available from a given literary text or work of philosophy. Indeed, he argued further that the notion of a definitive meaning was nigh on impossible, being endlessly 'deferred' as a consequence of the instability and perplexing nature of language itself. Western philosophy, in his account – and by implication the whole history of European poetry – though aspiring to the noble purpose of arriving at fixed eternal verities – 'transcendental signifiers' – was constantly thwarted in this aim by the slippery nature of language, which (borrowing the arguments of the linguistician Ferdinand de Saussure (1857–1913)) was a system of arbitrary signs 'without positive terms' and thus unable to deliver 'full meaning'. At the very moment when philosophy – or poetry – attempts to posit truth, the nature of language itself will create an 'aporia', a critical impasse in which one cannot decide between a range of possible meanings, and the possibility of unitary truth slips away.

Derrida was a visiting professor at Yale University in the 1970s and inspired a group of the school's English and Comparative Literature faculty – Geoffrey Hartman, Harold Bloom, Paul de Man, and J. Hillis Miller – to write criticism influenced by his methodology. Their critical positions were set out in the 1979 essay collection *Deconstruction and Criticism*, which gave rise to the notion of the so-called 'Yale School' and proselytised for the potential of deconstruction as a method of literary interpretation. That said, in its preface, Hartman argued that he and Bloom were 'barely' deconstructionists and were capable of writing 'against it', though the other contributors, Hillis Miller, de Man and Jacques himself, are described as 'boa deconstructionists, merciless and consequent'; and all were ready to find their prey in the Romantic grasslands. It is not hard to see why Romanticism, with its idealisms and heavily philosophical preoccupations, suited the agenda of the more serpentine deconstructionists, who focused on the manner in which that poetry's claims to truth always seem to be disappointed in the final analysis, leaving us with – in Wordsworth's wonderful, strangely proto-deconstructionist words from *The Prelude* – 'Effort, and expectation, and desire / And something evermore about to be', a sense that the arrival of full philosophical meaning is eternally deferred. In deconstructionist accounts, in high Romantic poetry (Wordsworth's *Prelude*, Keats's Odes or Shelley's 'The Triumph of Life', for instance), in the very moment in which that poetry seemed to be achieving its highest aspirations, the incapacity of language to represent truth undid its arguments.

Paul de Man

Perhaps the most influential of the Yale school was the gifted Belgian-American critic Paul de Man (1919–83), John the Baptist to Derrida's Christ in North America, a man who made the study of Romantic poetry appealing to a new generation of theory-minded college students and professors alike with his imperturbably difficult form of prose and his distinctive brand of deconstructive formalism, notably in *Allegories of Reading* (1979). De Man challenged the conventional notion that Romantic poetry unites the human imagination with nature, arguing that it actually demonstrates the impossibility of such an idealistic reconciliation. In the posthumously published *The Rhetoric of Romanticism* (1984), for instance, de Man identified what he saw as a gulf between language and meaning which thwarted 'the autonomous will to power of the self'. Though 'the interpretation of Romanticism remains for us the most difficult and at the same time most necessary of tasks', Romanticism 'seems continually to resist interpretation'. De Man's most famous essay on Romantic poetry is arguably 'Shelley Disfigured', published in both *Deconstruction and Criticism* and *The Rhetoric of Romanticism*, a piece which asks some big questions: 'What is the meaning of *The Triumph of Life*, and of Shelley, and of Romanticism?' To these enquiries, de Man concludes that there are no final answers, and no reply to the narrative voice of the poem, which asks, insistently, 'And what is this?' There can be no univocal 'clear answer' to the poem's incessant interrogations: 'They always lead back to a new science of questioning which repeats the quest and recedes in infinite regress.'

Deconstruction became highly influential in American and British literary criticism in the 1980s, and in the United Kingdom it sparked what has been called a 'theory war', a brief but highly vitriolic quarrel as academic supporters of high theory quarrelled with adherents of more traditional forms of literary criticism, who saw deconstruction as an arcane and unnecessary import from French philosophy which was of little value to English studies (in the mid-1980s, opponents of deconstruction gleefully greeted the news that Professor de Man had contributed to a malodorous collaborative journal in Belgium during the Second World War, penning at least one piece manifesting anti-Semitic views).

Harold Bloom

De Man's colleague Harold Bloom (born 1930) is also a career-long Romanticist, being a critic much preoccupied with both the Romantic and post-Romantic canon (he is the author of *Shelley's Myth-Making* (1959), *Yeats* (1970), and *Wallace Stevens* (1977)). Bloom made his name with a study of the Romantic poets, *The Visionary Company* (1961), a work New Critical in its close reading methods but also one self-consciously positioned against Eliot and Leavis's critical hegemony and their sense of the canon (as was Bloom's previous eloquent apologium for Shelley). The volume also owed something to Northrop Frye's book on Blake, which, Bloom once declared, 'ravished my heart away'. In the early 1950s, Frederick A. Pottle, who taught Bloom at Yale, wrote an essay, 'The Case of Shelley', in which he repudiated the post-Eliotian consensus in which Shelley had been unfairly 'transformed from one of the most praised and popular poets of the nineteenth century into the man on the dump of a Romantic tradition gone rancid with age', and in his first two books, Bloom hastened to the defence of Shelley and to that of the Romantic poets in general, boldly endorsing the importance and validity of the Romantic project, especially in the writings of Blake, Keats, Shelley and Wordsworth. The work of Abrams, Bloom, and Frye was instrumental in Romanticism recovering from its critical disesteem; as Frye wrote in 1963, 'The anti-Romantic movement, which in Britain and America followed the Hulme-Eliot-Pound broadsides of the early twenties, is now over and done with, and criticism has got its sense of literary tradition properly in focus again.'

For several decades Harold Bloom has seen Wordsworth and his preoc-cupation with poetic selfhood as the *fons et origo* of modern poetry, the instigator, as he put it in his 1968 essay 'The Internalization of Quest Romance', of 'a Copernican revolution in poetry' which had ensured 'the evanescence of any subject but subjectivity'. In *Agon* (1982), Bloom returned to the theme of Wordsworth's centrality in Western poetry in the last two hundred years in archetypical words:

> Poetry through Homer and Alexander Pope ... had a subject matter in the charac-ters and actions of men and women clearly distinct from the poet who observed them. [After that] the best poetry internalized its subject matter, particularly in the mode of Wordsworth after 1798. *Wordsworth had no true subject except his own subjective nature*, and very nearly all significant poetry since Wordsworth ... has repeated Wordsworth's inward turning.

In the 1970s, Bloom turned to theory. In *The Anxiety of Influence* (1973) and *A Map of Misreading* (1975), he argued that 'major' poets engage in a kind of Oedipal strife with their predecessors, creatively producing verse by fruitfully 'misreading' their elders. Bloom's notion of a 'strong' misreading is seen as fecund, as a creative misinterpretation which he calls 'poetic misprision'; thus Shelley's misprision of Wordsworth is a manoeuvre which allows the poet to escape an otherwise overpowering literary father figure. (After his theoretical and deconstructionist moments, Bloom went on his merry critical way, becoming nationally famous in the United States for the anti-egalitarian tenor of his *The Western Canon* (1994), a passionate and forcefully-argued defence of the notion of literary 'greatness'.)

Reception Theory

Bloom has been followed by other Romanticists working within a tradition of the study of influence – 'the burden of the past', in W. Jackson Bate's phrase. Whereas Bloom's critical terminology boils down in the end to the notion that many authors find their own voice by picking a fight, so to speak, with the literary tradition which shaped them, critics such as Lucy Newlyn have examined the way in which the poets of Romantic modernity reacted to the past and learned from it in a less adversarial manner than Bloom has it (though, as she has argued, 'ironically, any disagreement with Bloom can be read as yet further evidence of the anxiety of influence, which applies as much to criticism as to poetry'). Newlyn's *Paradise Lost and the Romantic Reader* (1993), for example, looked at the way in which the 'shaping spirit' of Milton fashioned the Romantic poets in a less argumentative manner than Bloom acknowledged. Newlyn has also worked on the related and increasingly critically important notion of how the Romantics were read and received and their relationships with their audiences. Her *Reading, Writing, and Romanticism: The Anxiety of Reception* (2003), its subtitle echoing Bloom, examines the way in which 'in high Romantic writers, the anxiety of reception manifested itself as a double attachment to the past and to genius'. Unlike *The Anxiety of Influence*, the book pays attention to women writers (Bloom was heavily criticised by feminist critics in the 1970s for the all-male nature of his poetic canon). In related manner, the work of Andrew Bennett, notably in *Romantic Poets and the Culture of Posterity* (1999), has addressed the manner in which Romantic poets 'resuscitate the work of dead poets by allusion, reference, imitation, plagiarism, pastiche, parody, repetition or "misreading"' (this last a reference to Bloom). As well as raising the poetic dead, Bennett examines the manner in which Wordsworth also confidently expected his poetic DNA, so to speak, to live on: 'Thus Wordsworth could declare in "Michael" that his poem is for "youthful Poets" who will constitute his "second self when I am gone".' Other important work on literary audience and readership in Romantic Studies, and on the relationship between a published work and the history of its contemporary reception, includes Jon P. Klancher's *The Making of English Literary Audiences, 1790–1832* (1987), Alan Richardson's *Literature, Education and Romanticism: Reading as Social Practice 1780–1832* (1994), and William St Clair's monumental *The Reading Nation in the Romantic Period* (2004).

Psychoanalysis

In *The Anxiety of Influence*, Harold Bloom summoned Freud from the shades in his attempt to understand how the family drama ('family romance' is

Bloom's term) of poetry works, and the way in which great verse is fashioned by 'an ego seeking to recover a primary narcissism from which it is withheld by its immediate predecessor'. Bloom was not alone in co-opting psychoanalytical theory to literary analysis of Romantic-era writing. Since the 1970s there have been a significant number of critics who would agree with Terry Castle's contention in *The Female Thermometer: Eighteenth-Century Culture and the Invention of the Uncanny* (1995) that 'psychoanalysis seems the most poignant critique of Romantic consciousness to date, and its richest and most perverse elaboration'. This is not to say that there was no post-Freudian literary criticism on Romanticism before this period. As we have seen, F. L. Lucas's renowned 1936 study was informed by Freud, and there were psychological accounts of the British Gothic novel in the 1930s by the Surrealist critics André Breton and David Gascoyne. There were also occasional readings of Romantic poems in psychoanalytical terms, such as the psychiatrist-critic D. W. Harding's 1941 account of Coleridge's 'Rime of the Ancient Mariner', published in the Leavis circle's journal *Scrutiny*, in which the Mariner's 're-experiencing his guilt and horror ... the perpetual penance of a man who can never forgive himself' is seen as being prompted by the poet's troubled 'relations with his mother in very early life'. However, these were exceptions, and in the last three decades there has been a decidedly larger number of psychoanalytical studies of Romanticism, in such works as Peter J. Manning's *Byron and his Fictions* (1978), in which, for instance, Byron's narrative of the biblical story of Cain's killing of his brother Abel is read as a displaced way of attacking 'patriarchal subordination'. Among the many contributions to the field that have followed are Mary Jacobus's tracing of Wordsworth's 'maternal sublime' in *Romanticism, Writing and Sexual Difference: Essays on The Prelude* (1989), Daniel P. Watkins's fusion of psychoanalysis, gender studies and Marxism in *Sexual Power in British Romantic Poetry* (1996), and Joel Faflak's *Romantic Psychoanalysis: The Burden of the Mystery* (2008), a book which sets out to demonstrate 'how Romanticism invents psychoanalysis in advance of Freud'.

Post-colonial Criticism

John Barrell's *The Infection of Thomas De Quincey. A Psychopathology of Imperialism* (1991) psychoanalyses the great essayist, arguing that his 'Orientalist' attitudes – and 'the demonised Far East' evident in the *Confessions of an English Opium Eater* – was in part a 'displacement' of his guilt about the death of his sister as a child and his fear of the London poor. Barrell's work was followed by a number of studies of British writers and the East informed by post-colonial theory, notably Nigel Leask's *British*

Romantic Writers and the East: Anxieties of Empire (1992), which looks at the work of Byron, De Quincey, Shelley and others, painting 'a dark picture ... of the unbreakable spell of the Other for our constitutional imperial culture and those people subjugated in its name', alongside a few moments – as in Shelley's *Prometheus Unbound* – where 'the relations of power and desire are actively and creatively re-thought against the grain of history'.

Other work in this area of Romantic studies includes *Romanticism and Colonialism: Writing and Empire, 1780–1830*, edited by Tim Fulford and Peter J. Kitson (1998), Alan Bewell's *Romanticism and Colonial Disease* (2003), and *Writing the Empire: Robert Southey and Romantic Colonialism* (2007) by Carol Bolton. Bewell's valuable study, to consider but one example of this post-colonial criticism, argues that 'The colonial world was a dark mirror in which Europeans read their own destinies.' Bewell addresses the way in which 'colonial experience was profoundly structured by disease, both as metaphor and as reality'. While imperialists such as De Quincey saw the Western body politic as potentially infected by the Orient, Bewell focuses on the way in which colonialism spread pandemic in colonised nations, with the infection both literal – in the pandemics of the late Georgian Empire – and also a profound metaphor for the ravaging force of colonisation.

Medical and Scientific Criticism

Bewell's *Romanticism and Colonial Disease* is both post-colonial theory and a study of Romantic-era medicine and science. Criticism dealing with these latter subjects has proliferated since the 1990s, from single author monographs such as Hermione de Almeida's *Romantic Medicine and John Keats* (1991) and Neil Vickers's *Coleridge and the Doctors* (2004), through to magisterial surveys such as Alan Richardson's *British Romanticism and the Science of the Mind* (2001) and Richard Holmes's *The Age of Wonder: How the Romantic Generation Discovered the Beauty and Terror of Science* (2008) (see 'Science and Medicine', above). There have also been a number of substantial scholarly editions (among them Tim Fulford's *Romanticism and Science, 1773–1833* (5 vols, 2002) and Neil Chambers's *The Scientific Correspondence of Sir Joseph Banks, 1765–1820* (6 vols, 2007)) and monographs. Sharon Ruston's *Shelley and Vitality* (2005), for instance, looks at P. B. Shelley's discussion of the very principle of life, while Clark Lawlor's *Consumption and Literature: The Making of the Romantic Disease* (2006) examines the literary figurations of the disease which did for Keats and which echoes through Romantic poetry and music, seeking to learn how tuberculosis, 'a horrible disease, came to be [seen as] glamorous and artistic'.

Gothic Studies and Psychological Criticism

In *The Female Thermometer*, Terry Castle's preoccupation is with the Romantic 'Uncanny', and this is indicative of the manner in which the host body of much of the most important psychological criticism on late eighteenth- and early nineteenth-century literature influenced by Freud – and to a rather lesser extent Jung and Lacan – has been the Gothic novel. 'Psychology dominates criticism of the Gothic', writes Robert Mighall in *A Geography of Victorian Gothic Fiction* (2003). Perhaps this is not surprising; Fred Botting, the author of the most notable book-length introduction to the genre, *Gothic* (1996), maintains that 'much Gothic writing' can be seen as 'prefiguring Freud'. As the leading modern British scholar of Gothic, David Punter, has written, 'Gothic has to do with the uncanny [and] the uncanny is one of the major sites on which the reinvestigation of Freud and the re-institution of psychoanalysis can take place.' This fact, alongside the feminist attention to women's Gothic writing and the critical attention to the representation of women in the genre, has reinvigorated Gothic studies since the late 1970s. As Robert Miles wrote, humorously but not inaccurately, in 2001, 'Over the last twenty years the Gothic has, Lazarus-like, lurched from its critical grave.'

The resurrection man – so to speak – in Miles's account and in the opinion of many contemporary students of Gothic – is Punter, the author of *The Literature of Terror: A History of Gothic Fictions from 1765 to the Present Day* (1980). According to Punter, 'Gothic fiction has proved a godsend to psychoanalytically-minded critics, and it is not hard to see why this is so. Gothic fiction deals intensively in symbolism, to the point of naivety.' This is 'a literature', writes Punter, 'whose key motifs are paranoia, manipulation and injustice, and whose central project is understanding the inexplicable, the taboo, the irrational'. Small wonder that Freud suits it. Nonetheless, Punter's 'psychologising' book offers an interesting fusion of both Freud and Marx, and does not lose sight of history in the manner of some critics of the Gothic (William Patrick Day's *In the Circles of Fear and Desire* (1985) baldly maintains that the Gothic entails a 'rejection of the very idea of history as something to be taken seriously'). *The Literature of Terror* views Gothic as deeply informed by the socio-political anxieties of the late eighteenth and early nineteenth centuries. Even its founding document, the carelessly-written novel *The Castle of Otranto* by Horace Walpole (1764), Punter maintains, is 'serious about history': 'whatever its shortcomings and infelicities, it does give evidence of an eighteenth-century view of feudalism and the aristocracy, and in doing so originates what was to become perhaps the most prevalent theme in Gothic fiction: the revisiting of the sins of the fathers upon their children'.

Punter's book informs many subsequent psychoanalytically-tinged studies of Gothic, from Rosemary Jackson's *Fantasy, the Literature of Subversion* (1981) and Botting's *Making Monstrous: Frankenstein, Criticism, Theory* (1991) through to Miles's *Gothic Writing, 1750–1820: A Genealogy* (1993) and Paulina Palmer's *Lesbian Gothic: Transgressive Fictions* (1999). The turn to history at the turn of the 1980s discussed below is also evident in Punter's work and beyond; history, theory and psychoanalysis are not always stand-alone disciplines.

Modern Critical Approaches II: From Historicism to Ecological Criticism

Historicist Accounts of Romanticism

The Romantic poets were politically-minded individuals who closely engaged with the great historical events which surrounded them, and – as we have seen – from its initial appearance their work was interpreted in political terms, with the Tory wits of the *Anti-Jacobin* attacking Coleridge and Southey and those of *Blackwood's* lambasting Hunt and Keats, both on the grounds of their supposedly dangerous radicalism. From the first, the Romantics were read and understood in political terms as well as in aesthetic ones. That said, in the Victorian age (as per William Howlitt's rhapsodical frenzy quoted above) and in the first half of the twentieth century there were those who tended to see them as sublimely unconcerned with history, their fine elevated minds dwelling on higher things. Stopford A. Brooke maintained in 1907, for example, that Keats had 'no vital interest in the present [and] the political movement of human thought', and Graham Hough wrote in 1949 that the poet 'was little concerned with politics and speculative thought'. Neither man meant these descriptions as slurs; after all, Hough elsewhere declared that the purpose of criticism in the university was to attend to matters 'primarily literary'. The chief business of a poet, in this line of argument, was to write aesthetically pleasing or innovative and complex verse rather than to pontificate about world affairs. Hough's point of view is typical of a mid-twentieth-century critical sense, best exemplified in the New Criticism's formalist tendency, to address a work of art as a self-sufficient object rather than to pay heed to the immediate cultural or historical contexts in which it was created.

There were a number of exceptions to this critical rule, of course. In *Keats* (1926), the most notable inter-war study of that poet, H. W. Garrod (1878–1960), wrote of 'Keats's early revolutionary sympathies, of his Huntian or Wordsworthian sympathies'. 'Keats', declares Garrod, 'is more the child of the Revolutionary Idea than we commonly suppose.' In the very same year the young Harvard professor Crane Brinton (1898–1968) published his still highly readable monograph *The Political Ideas of the English Romanticists* (1926), originally an Oxford D.Phil. thesis, which similarly reads the Romantics in explicitly historical terms. There was certainly political criticism before the New Historicism, in studies such as these, and in other important works such as David V. Erdman's groundbreaking *Blake, Prophet Against Empire: A Poet's Interpretation of the History of his Own Times* (1954), which attempts to wrest Blake from the mystics and art connoisseurs, and Carl Woodring's compendious and perceptive survey *Politics in English Romantic Poetry* (1970). John Barrell has produced a number of brilliant socio-historically charged studies of British Romantic-era culture since *The Idea of Landscape and the Sense of Place: An Approach to the Poetry of John Clare* (1972). The British Marxist historians and critics E. P. Thompson (a life-long admirer of Blake) and Raymond Williams paid detailed attention to the politics of Romanticism, and it might also be pointed out that M. H. Abrams himself maintained that the Romantic poets 'were all centrally political and social poets', in his important essay 'English Romanticism: The Spirit of the Age' (1963).

New Historicism

Though it would be tendentious to argue that critics of Romanticism in the first six decades of the last century were completely uninterested in both the politics of Romantic poetry and the historical contexts in which it was written, it is fair to say that from the late 1970s onwards there has been what has been described as a 'turn to history' within Romantic studies. 'The problem of Romanticism continues to dominate the other problems of historiography and literary criticism,' wrote Paul de Man in *The Rhetoric of Romanticism* (1983), and works such as Erdman and Woodring's were succeeded by a flood of historically motivated readings of the Romantics, with a generation of scholars arguing for the restoration of the socio-political contexts of Romantic thought against the kind of ahistorical attitudes exemplified in Graham Hough. The caricature of the Romantic poet as someone purely concerned with poetry and the creative imagination has been put under relentless question and the spirit of H. W. Garrod has triumphed over those of Hough and Brooke. The modern consensus that Keats was indeed deeply engaged with politics in both his life and his art is encapsulated in historically-informed books such as Marjorie Levinson's *Keats's Life of Allegory: The Origins of a Style* (1988), Nicholas Roe's edited collection *Keats and History* (1995) and the same author's monograph *John Keats and the Culture of Dissent* (1999).

Levinson, alongside Jerome. J. McGann, was one of the principal instigators of what has come to be known as the 'New Historicism' in Romantic Studies, a critical method which insists upon the necessity of studying literature within its historical and social contexts (this began in Renaissance studies from the 1970s onwards in the work of Stephen Greenblatt and his journal *Representations*). The best and clearest manifesto of New Historicism in Romantic Studies is Marjorie Levinson's, in her *Wordsworth's Great Period Poems* (1986):

> A new word is abroad these days in Wordsworth scholarship – 'historicist' – and the adjective carries distinctly heterodox overtones. What is thereby refused is an idealizing interpretive model associated with Harold Bloom, Geoffrey Hartman, Paul de Man, and even M. H. Abrams.

The Yale School, whether deconstructionist or Bloomian, and the traditional scholarship of Abrams are all dismissed as 'formalist' in this account, portrayed as being as ahistorical in their methodologies as the critical schools – New Criticism and the archetypal criticism of Frye – which they succeeded. Equally culpable is their 'idealising' interpretive manner. McGann's *The Romantic Ideology* (1985) argues forcefully that critics of high Romanticism had uncritically dealt with that literature to the point where it internalised the 'ideology' of Romanticism. The New Historicist charge is that criticism of Romanticism does not inspect it critically but has instead bought into its particular value system, a charge summed up in Clifford E. Siskin's book *The Historicity of Romantic Discourse* (1988): 'We have joined Wordsworth in taking the "mind of man" to be the "main haunt and region" of our "song".' Siskin's highly sceptical book, alongside Alan Liu's *Wordsworth. The Sense of History* (1989, which attends to the poet's 'denial of history') and David Simpson's *Wordsworth's Historical Imagination* (1987, on Wordsworth's 'displacement' of history), was part of a significant body of North American theoretically-inflected writing which succeeded and developed McGann's work. The critic, Siskin argued, should be sceptical of Romanticism and the siren-like temptations to fall into its arms, as the likes of Abrams and Bloom had done before (Don H. Bialostosky wrote wittily in his *Wordsworth, Dialogics, and the Practice of Criticism* (1992) that the New Historicism 'enrolls critics addicted to Romanticism in something like a Romanticists Anonymous', and imagines a putative gathering of these unfortunates, 'where they will hear over and over the "tale of [their] need to be cured" and recognize at each hearing the "ongoing power" of Romantic discourse').

There is little reverential about the New Historicist account of Romanticism. Instead of Harold Bloom's adoring attitude to Wordsworth, the Byronist McGann and his colleagues cast a somewhat withering eye at the poet, just as the great satirist had, to his poetic contemporary in the early nineteenth century. For Bloom, Wordsworth is the benign, founding figure of modern literature, but in New Historicist thought he is sometimes a rather villainous presence. There is undeniably something sermonical about this critical tendency, as in the manner in which Wordsworth is accused of political bad faith in Levinson's famous account of 'Tintern Abbey', where the poet is chided for his lack of attention to the presence of the rural poor in the landscape which prompted his celebration of the creative imagination.

In the wake of McGann's founding manifesto of the new method, *The Romantic Ideology*, Levinson writes in *Wordsworth's Great Period Poems* that 'a number of works published over the last three years position themselves as demystifications of Romanticist readings as well as of Romantic poems. They use history, or sociopolitical reconstruction, to resist the old control of Yale.' The plague on that house is also brought down on another, the tradition of orthodox political scholarship in the manner of Erdman's *Prophet Against Empire*, which, on the face of it, one might have expected the New Historicists to value:

> At the same time, historicist critique distinguishes its interests and method from *historical* scholarship ... the researches and argumentation of David Erdman, Carl Woodring and E. P. Thompson. ... They repudiate the empiricist, positivist concept of historical fact [and] focus on textual antinomy and erasure rather than manifest theme and achieved form.

'Positivist' accounts of Romanticism are faulted for focusing empirically on what the Romantics had to say rather than on the counter-intuitive manner of the New Historicism, with its preoccupation with matters 'erased' and left unsaid. This is a critical manner owing much to the French structural Marxism of Pierre Macherey (itself heavily indebted to that of Louis Althusser), in which, to borrow Terry Eagleton's summary in *Criticism and Ideology* (1976), 'in putting ideology to work, the text necessarily illuminates the absences, and begins to "make speak" the silences, of that ideology'. McGann traces the 'absences' within Romantic poetry, acts of socio-historical 'evasion'. In his well-known essay 'Keats and the Historical Method in Literary Criticism' (1979), Keats's volume *Lamia, Isabella, The Eve of St Agnes and Other Poems* (1820) is dismissed as a 'politically reactionary book' inasmuch as it attempts to evade and silence the turbulent history of post-Napoleonic England. Though illuminating on the timeless significance of nightingales, Grecian urns, the coming of autumn and so on, Keats's poetry fails to mention many important things which surrounded him as he composed it – 'This is the reflexive world of Romantic art, wherein all events are far removed from the Terror, King Ludd, Peterloo [and] the Six Acts.' McGann comments, astringently, that 'Failing such things, I do not see how we can reciprocate the transcendence of Romantic verse, or feel anything but shame when we read such poetry.'

Marilyn Butler and British Historical Criticism

In the year in which McGann's essay on Keats was published, a new form of English historicism began to emerge, in large part from Oxford. In her study of Thomas Love Peacock, which has the peerless title *Peacock Displayed* (1979), Marilyn Butler argued that 'General histories of English Romanticism have tended to seem dazzled by the brilliance of the theoreticians of that movement' (the position later developed theoretically in *The Romantic Ideology*). In her short but highly influential *Romantics, Rebels and Reactionaries* (1981), Butler, describing herself as an 'historian-critic', insisted on the need 'for studying Romantic literature against its historical background'. She anticipates the New Historicist call for a critical distance between critic and criticised in her account of Harold Bloom's *Visionary Company*: 'Like many other latter-day pronouncements on Romanticism, Bloom's work seems itself ultra-Romantic.' Being unduly wedded to particular concepts of the Romantic era which stress the sublime and the creative imagination limits, Butler argues, our sense of what was important and significant in late eighteenth- and early nineteenth-century literature: 'going out to look for "Romanticism" means selecting in advance one kind of answer'. For Butler, 'the historian-critic [should] inevitably [be] more sceptical than [Bloom, Abrams *et al.*] of theories which exalt the autonomy of art and the magus-role of the artist'. The Romantics have shaped the criticism by which they are received; Butler notes 'the high prestige of Coleridgean inwardness in modern times' which ensures that 'unwarily, the philosophical critic favours unduly authors of Coleridge's type'.

Instead of Coleridge and Wordsworth, Butler praises 'Shelley and Scott, those two historically-minded men of the Enlightenment'. Butler's work here and elsewhere offers hints and examples taken up by many later critics of the Romantics: in applying a sceptical eye to Wordsworth's primacy, attending to women novelists and poets, valuing the prose of Godwin, Hazlitt and Wollstonecraft as highly as the poetry of the age, valuing 'the author of *Waverley*', expanding the 'Romantic canon' in new and fascinating ways, endorsing the vigour of Romantic-era satire and suggesting that Robert Southey might have been more than a prosy buffoon. Though not everyone has agreed with every one of Butler's arguments, her call for a more thoroughgoing historical consciousness has resounded through criticism since, and her 1981 book remains a landmark in Romantic Studies.

In *Romantics, Rebels and Reactionaries*, instead of the idealising work of Bloom and others, Butler endorses critical 'empiricism, and in a methodology which gives weight both to the collection of evidence and to analysis as opposed to synthesis'. This historical method has co-existed with what Levinson proudly described as the anti-empiricism of the American New Historicism. Indeed, some have seen a transatlantic divide between historical criticism in the United States and the United Kingdom evident in the 1980s and 1990s. To venture a generalisation to which there are admittedly many exceptions, in the last three decades there has been a tendency in British historicist writing to work in the line of Erdman and Thompson rather than – with Levinson and McGann – to repudiate them (even now that the New Historicist controversies have cooled, there is arguably a greater attention to theoretically-informed work in American rather than in British criticism of Romanticism).

Perhaps the iconic figures here in this tradition are Jonathan Bate (see below) and Nicholas Roe, whose *Wordsworth and Coleridge: The Radical Years* (1988), though less sceptical of the Lake Poets than Butler's work, is no less historically minded. Roe argues for a positive political view of the most notable period of Wordsworth and Coleridge's poetry; against some critics of the poets, who argued that they retreated from politics into introspective self-obsession, Roe argues that their Jacobinism lasted until late into the 1790s. For Roe, 'there was no generalised pattern of retreat from politics into retirement' in the later part of that decade; the *Lyrical Ballads* were admirable and radical documents in their social progressiveness and benevolence. Similarly generous treatment is afforded Keats in *John Keats and the Culture of Dissent* (1999), in which – far from running away from historical reality as McGann has it – Roe argues that in such works as 'To Autumn' there is a discernible political agenda. The Yale critic Geoffrey H. Hartman had celebrated the poem's timeless resonance; McGann had attacked it for the very same reason. Nicholas Roe argues against both. Noting that in his 'contextual reading of "To Autumn" McGann coincides with Hartman's manifestly anti-historical understanding of the poem as "enchanted ground", a spellbound refuge from history', Roe maintains that 'maybe a less mysterious interpretation of history in [the poem] is possible'. He attempts to 'locate the impersonal voice of the poem in relation to contemporary discourses of political and social conflict'. 'To Autumn', far from a 'shameful' turn away from history, can be related to the recent events at St Peter's Field at the 'Peterloo' massacre. (Roe has been followed by other important British critical voices working within a historical frame of reference, such as Simon Bainbridge in *British Poetry and the Revolutionary and Napoleonic Wars: Visions of Conflict* (2003), Angela Keane's *Women Writers and the English Nation in the 1790s* (2000) and the much-published Tim Fulford, in books such as *Romantic Indians* (2006), alongside several others.)

'Green Romanticism'

Just as deconstruction prompted vigorous and often antipathetic debate in the early 1980s, so did the New Historicism in the late 1980s and early 1990s. Opponents of the school, if that is what one might call it, argued from two principal positions. Traditionalist critics such as Thomas McFarland attacked the New Historicists from a conviction that the every-day business of literary criticism was dissecting, engaging with, and analysing a body of literary work rather than inculcating revolution, wagging one's finger at sins of political omission or challenging gender stereotypes within society. In a series of engaging polemics, most notably in *William Wordsworth: Intensity and Achievement* (1992), McFarland attacked the scholarship and reading methods of McGann and Levinson. The other body of critics to engage with the New Historicism were 'empiricist' – to use Butler and Levison's word – historically-aware Romantic critics. The likes of Roe, while conceding the central importance of history within Romantic Studies, questioned the antipathetic portrayal of Wordsworth and Keats in the New Historicism and concentrated – as empiricists do – on what their texts had to say, however deeply hidden, rather than on their various lacunae and absences.

However, one of the strongest critiques was by the British critic Jonathan Bate, a rebuttal made from an ecological standpoint. Bate has initiated major critical developments in recent years within Romantic Studies in what has been labelled 'eco-criticism' and 'Green studies'. The groundbreaking book in this area of the Romantic field, so to speak, was his short but highly influential *Romantic Ecology: Wordsworth and the Environmental Tradition* (1991). Bate positioned himself against the New Historicism, then in its critical zenith, repudiating what he calls, accurately enough, the 'counter-intuitive' nature of New Historicist criticism in the manner of McGann and Levinson and arguing for the existence of what he calls a 'Green Romanticism'. In Bate's narrative of Romantic poetry, William Wordsworth is given pride of place. While he is heavily faulted in New Historicist criticism, matters are different in Bate's Romantic eco-land. *Romantic Ecology* is something of a polemic on behalf of Wordsworth against the 'bad faith' charge levelled by the brigades of New Historicism. Bate argues once more for a radical Wordsworth in his project of 'recuperating the Wordsworthian pastoral'. To Bate's mind, Wordsworth offers a 'radical', indeed a 'republican pastoral'.

Jonathan Bate subsequently wrote a biography of another great poet of nature in his life of John Clare and returned to eco-criticism in a later book, *The Song of the Earth* (2000), which declares that 'a new Geographism is replacing the New Historicism'. His *Romantic Ecology* was, meanwhile, succeeded by a series of books which engage with Romanticism and its ecological implications. Karl Kroeber (who had written a pioneering essay on Wordsworth and ecology as long ago as 1974) published his full-length study *Ecological Literary Criticism: Romantic Imagining and the Biology of Mind* in 1994, in which he argued that British Romanticism is 'proto-ecological'; its poets 'believed that humankind belonged in, could and should be at home within the world of natural processes'. Kroeber's work has been followed by – amongst others – Laurence Coupe's *The Green Studies Reader: From Romanticism to Ecocriticism* (2000), Kevin Hutchings's *Imagining Nature: Blake's Environmental Poetics* (2002), James C. McKusick's *Green Writing: Romanticism and Ecology* (2000) (which claims that Romantics were the 'first full-fledged ecological writers in the Western literary tradition') and Timothy Morton's *Ecology without Nature: Rethinking Environmental Aesthetics* (2007).

In 'Romanticism and Ecology', a special issue of *Romantic Praxis*, McKusick writes, in a discussion of the implications of the poetry of Erasmus Darwin (grandfather of the more famous Charles), that 'if humans are truly related to all living things, then all living things must be entitled to a share in the "natural rights" that will surely be vindicated in the progress of human liberation'. Related to ecological criticism is the matter of discussion of animal rights in Romantic Studies. Timothy Morton, who argues that 'Shelley was a proto-ecological thinker and poet', one 'interested in concrete nature; in animals, plants and what humans do to them, and with them', examined the poet's writings on diet and its context in contemporary vegetarian thought in *Shelley and the Revolution in Taste* (1994). Christine Kenyon-Jones, in *Kindred Brutes: Animals in Romantic-Period Writing* (2001), and David Perkins, in *Romanticism and Animal Rights* (2003), both examine the manner in which Romantic writers debated the rights of animals and how the notion of kindness to the 'brute creation' began to achieve wider currency in the period. Perkins argues that 'there was a close connection between the cultural world we call Romanticism with its ideals of sympathy, sentiment, and nature, and the tender attitudes expressed in writing about animals'. Ecological criticism continues to inform Romantic criticism in innovative ways.

Modern Critical Approaches III: Gender Criticism

Feminist Criticism

In his 1996 study *Sexual Power in British Romantic Poetry*, Daniel P. Watkins sets himself this task: to examine 'the Romantic constructions of gender in relation to the changing structures of historical, social and cultural authority in the Romantic period'. These words are emblematic of a critical approach which has become such an important part of Romantic studies since the 1980s. Gender studies – written by both men and women – has produced some of the most significant work in the field. From the feminist criticism of the 1970s which culminated in the publication of Sandra Gilbert and Susan Gubar's *The Madwoman in the Attic* (1979) onwards, critics have paid great attention to the sexual politics manifested within the canon of English literature. In Romantic Studies these enquiries have taken two principal hermeneutical forms. The first is the reinterpretation of the lives and works of the (male) Romantic poets in terms of gender analysis (as, for instance, Mary Jacobus's aforementioned *Romanticism, Writing and Sexual Difference: Essays on The Prelude* (1989)). The second is a form of literary archaeology, the scholarly and editorial labours which have led to the recovery and re-recognition of several once-famous and critically esteemed – but eventually forgotten – women poets of the Romantic period. This latter project has been accompanied by a critical willingness to identify a 'feminine Romanticism', in contradistinction to existing notions of male canonical Romanticism.

To begin with the first of these approaches, let us take, by way of an example, the case of John Keats, the 'Big Six' Romantic poet most frequently discussed in terms of gender, and someone who has been the subject of a great deal of feminist critical attention since the 1970s, when the poet and critic Adrienne Rich identified women's 'tremendous powers of intuitive identification and sympathy with other people' with Keatsian 'negative capability', and the novelist and critic Erica Jong declared that 'feminism *means* empathy, and empathy is akin to the quality Keats called "negative capability"'. Perhaps this is unsurprising; since its first appearance Keats's work has been read in terms of gender. Susan J. Wolfson writes in her essay 'Keats and Gender Criticism' (1998) that 'from his debut, Keats attracted, even courted, judgements in the language of gender' ('The favourable views of his work,' she notes, 'mostly from friends, gave an inadvertently feminizing emphasis to his stylistic beauties').

Some of these early gendered judgements, it might be said, were not meant flatteringly. William Hazlitt wrote of Keats shortly after the latter's death in 1821 that: 'I cannot help thinking that the fault of Mr Keats's poems was a deficiency in masculine energy of style.' Where Hazlitt chided, however, the second wave feminists of the next century – Rich and Jong – celebrated Keats's supposed 'femininity'. Their position has been developed by Philip Cox, who writes in *Gender, Genre, and the Romantic Poets: An Introduction* (1996) that Keats can 'be read as a poet who adopts a feminine subject position within his work in an attempt to challenge cultural constructions of masculinity'. It has also been qualified, by Anne K. Mellor, who writes in *Romanticism and Gender* (1993) that though 'the male Romantic Poet who has most often been characterised as "effeminate" is John Keats ... Keats subtly complicates the issue ... either by occupying the position of the woman in life or in discourse, or by blurring the distinction between genders, between masculine and femininity'.

Keats, Mellor declares, was capable both of 'ideological cross-dressing' in striking attitudes generally seen as 'feminine' and, indeed, of a belligerent form of masculine self-assertion (Susan Wolfson herself notes the 'array of gender forms' evident in Keats's work, 'and the contradictions between Keats's historical meaning, both as these varying positions reflect ideological divisions in his own age and as they are transmitted through his captivating example'). For Mellor, Keats at his best – as in the 'Ode to Psyche' – spans both male and female roles: 'In this ode, Keats triumphantly and climactically occupies the positions of both the male and the female lover: he has made love to, penetrated, received, and possessed his own Fancy, his own shadowy thought.' Daniel Watkins, who is quoted above, is sterner than his female colleagues on Keats, whose work, he argues, demonstrates the anxiety of 'the masculine subject construction under the pressure of an emergent bourgeois world'. Unlike Mellor's positive reading, Watkins sees the 'Ode to Psyche' as a poem which manifests a sexually aggressive and 'masculinist' – in the sense of oppressive to women – 'poetic strategy'.

Women's Writing

The second principal focus within gender-focused criticism of the Romantic era, instead of interrogating writing by men, examines its female-authored poetry – which had been neglected for many decades – and argues for its critical importance. Though she was by no means the first critic to write on women poets of the Romantic period, Anne K. Mellor, the author of *Romanticism and Gender* (1993), an impassioned critical manifesto on the importance of gender in Romantic studies, is exemplary of this critical tendency. Mellor's book is an important revisionist recasting of Romanticism which is reminiscent of the then recent New Historicist assault on existing pieties in the field. Mellor's opening critique, which rebukes the tenor of the vast majority of existing Romantic criticism, is similar in tone to the declaration of principle found in Marjorie Levinson's

Wordsworth's Great Period Poems (1986) quoted above (indeed, Mellor cites and criticises many of the same critical authorities):

> What difference does gender make to our understanding of British literary Romanticism? ... Whether we interpret British literary Romanticism as a commitment to imagination, vision and transcendence, as did Meyer Abrams, Harold Bloom and John Beer, or as a questioning, even systematic demystification, of the very possibility of a linguistically unmediated vision, as have Geoffrey Hartman, Paul de Man and a host of others, or as an ideology located in specific political and social events, as urged by Carl Woodring, Jerome McGann and the school of new historical Romanticists inspired by their work, or as a complex configuration derived from all of these recent critical approaches, we nonetheless have based our constructions of British Romanticism almost exclusively upon the writings and thought of six male poets (Wordsworth, Coleridge, Blake, Byron, Shelley and Keats).

Against the hegemony of the male poets, Mellor argues for the centrality and importance of what she calls 'women's literary Romanticism'. From the 'enormous body of female literary production' which appeared in Great Britain in the late eighteenth and early nineteenth centuries, she attends in particular to writers then 'unknown to current scholarship', such as the poets Letitia Elizabeth Landon, Anna Laetitia Barbauld and Mary Robinson. Her book is presented as one of the first fruits of a long-term critical project: 'It will require decades of research and hundreds of books before we fully grasp the complex intellectual and formal configurations of this terra incognita.'

'When we look at this female-authored literature', writes Mellor, 'we find a focus on very different issues from those which concerned the canonical male Romantic poets':

> Women writers of the Romantic period for the most part foreswore the concern of their male peers with the capacities of the creative imagination, with the limitations of language, with the possibility of transcendence or 'unity of being', with the development of an autonomous self, with political (as opposed to social) revolution, with the role of the creative writer as political leader or religious saviour. Instead women Romantic writers tend to celebrate, not the achievements of the imagination nor the overflow of powerful feelings but rather the workings of the rational mind, a mind relocated – in a gesture of revolutionary gender implications – in the female as well as the male body.

Mellor sees (sexual) difference in the two forms of Romantic poetry rather than similarity. Though there has been some recent critical attention to the task of identifying similarities between traditional Romanticism and women's poetry, for example in identifying Wordsworth's debt to Charlotte Smith, or Mary Robinson's relationship to Coleridge and to Wordsworth (Stuart Curran writes in 1993, for instance, that 'She was a principal creator of the records of the marginalized that are most commonly exemplified ... by the publication of Wordsworth and Coleridge's *Lyrical Ballads* in 1798. Her *Lyrical Tales* ... by its title indicates its rivalry'), it has to be said that in the first flush of enthusiasm for the women poets of the Romantic period, the general critical emphasis – such as that of Mellor – has stressed what is seen as the differences between 'male' and 'female' Romanticism. Curran, for instance, maintains that 'As men turned inward to reflect on and to imagine the nature of imaginative activity ... women turned in upon their essential sensibility.' He sees their work as manifesting two principal tendencies – 'an investment in quotidian [i.e. everyday, non-sublime, non-'Romantic'] tones and details and a portrayal of alienated sensibility'. Similarly, Andrew Ashfield, the editor of *Romantic Women Poets 1770–1838: An Anthology* (1995), declares that 'women's Romantic poetry develops along different lines to those of the major male Romantics, [becoming the] supreme vehicle for the expression of isolated dramatic thought in situations of loneliness before the landscape.' 'This sense of loneliness', he adds, was 'acute in [the] female experience' expressed in Romantic-era poetry.

Writing in 1996, Leon Litvack offers an explicitly politicised account of this sexual difference in terms which echo the Levinsonian critique of Wordsworth's unsound ideological position:

> An examination of Wordsworth's poetry demonstrates the extent to which masculine Romantic ideology was imbued with patriarchal rhetoric, radical politics, and the unquestioned authority of the subject. Feminine Romantic discourse, on the other hand, offered an alternative mode of expression based on the family politic.

Male Romanticism is 'patriarchal', implicitly authoritarian; 'feminine Romantic discourse' is more communal, less beholden to the Urizenic sublime. Interestingly, Litvack's notion – derived from Mellor – of a female poetics which mirrors the family unit is diametrically opposed to Ashfield's notion of feminine poetic isolation and Curran's hypothesis of 'alienation'. However, underpinning both viewpoints – and this area of Romantic gender studies in general – is the conviction, well-expressed by Tamsin Spargo in 1996, that a 'key issue for feminist critics [is] the way in which the privilege of male poets and of poetic traditions which privilege male views have worked to disadvantage their female counterparts'. In the twenty-first century, the voices of those 'counterparts' are being heard loudly and clearly once again.

Queer Studies

Though queer studies and feminist criticism are closely aligned within gender studies in general, it is undeniable that there has been rather less attention to Romanticism's relationship to lesbian and gay sexuality. Louis Crompton's pioneering *Byron and Greek Love: Homophobia in Nineteenth-Century England* (1985) examines Byron's homosexual side, beginning with a useful survey of the legal, social, political and religious nature of 'Georgian homophobia', and contrasting the state of affairs in Great Britain to the somewhat more liberal nature of attitudes in southern Europe – of which Byron took full advantage, of course. There is also work on the poet Blake's radical sexual politics, which are examined in *Blake and Homosexuality* (2000) by Christopher Z. Hobson ('his conceptualisation of homosexuality (female and male)', notes Hobson approvingly, 'is far in advance of most other contemporary thought').

The antipathetic attitudes of late Georgian culture to homosexuality is examined in a chapter on the Romantic era in Paul Hammond's *Love Between Men* (1996), which argues that 'it was almost impossible for writers to create public texts which gave unambiguous expression to homosexual desire'. That said, contemporary homosexuality was a love that dared to speak its symbol, if not its name, and it was possible to hint at gay desire, as in *The Monk* (1796) by Matthew Lewis (identified as homosexual in Byron's correspondence), in which the anti-hero Ambrosio contracts a passionate desire for a young noviciate (who, as a sop to contemporary conventional morality, is eventually revealed as a diabolical female). Perhaps unsurprisingly in a genre which includes amongst its pioneers Horace Walpole, William Beckford and Lewis, men who would all be seen as 'gay' in this day and age, much of the attention in queer theory in Romantic Studies has attended to that symbolic adventure playground, the Gothic tale (there is a useful introduction to the subject in George E. Haggerty's *Queer Gothic* (2006) which declares that 'Gothic fiction was the one semi-respectable genre that regularly explored sexual and social transgressions during the eighteenth and nineteenth' centuries and offers readings of novels by Lewis, Ann Radcliffe and C. R. Maturin, works with 'Gothic set-pieces that have as much to say about the history of sexuality as anything that emerged later from nineteenth-century sexologists'). Perhaps the key study here is *Between Men: English Literature and Male Homosexual Desire* (1985) by Eve Kosofsky Sedgwick (1950–2009), which argues that the Gothic has much to say 'about entirely unanswered questions about the constitution and social meaning of male homosexuality itself'. Building on Sedgwick's work and that of Terry Castle, notably in *The Female Thermometer* (1996) (see above), Paulina Palmer's *Lesbian Gothic: Transgressive Fictions* (1999) argues that '"Gothic" and "queer" share a common emphasis on transgressive acts and subjectivities.'

Epilogue: The Expansion of the Romantic Canon

A student arriving at an American or British university twenty or thirty years ago to read English, when setting out on a survey course on Romanticism generally came across a fairly narrow range of writers. Certainly he or she would have been most unlikely to have studied the women poets who have been the subject of so much critical attention in recent years, and indeed, would have encountered few women writers *per se*, with the possible exception of Dorothy Wordsworth, Jane Austen or Mary Shelley, the author of *Frankenstein* (and not much else, in the critical estimation of the day). The standard anthology of the time, Harold Bloom and Lionel Trilling's *Romantic Poetry and Prose* (Oxford University Press, 1973), did not include a single female poet, confining itself in terms of female composition only to the Grasmere Journals of Dorothy Wordsworth, and over 90 per cent of the poetry included was by the so-called 'Big Six' Romantic poets (it might also be pointed out that the range of male poets was also painfully small, with no space found for the likes of Leigh Hunt and Thomas Moore and very little even for John Clare).

On the other hand, someone arriving at the same university today and taking a Romanticism module would be more than likely to encounter several women – most probably Charlotte Smith, Mary Robinson, Felicia Hemans and Letitia Elizabeth Landon ('L.E.L.'). In the last two decades, as a result of the scholarly and editorial efforts of advocates of women's writing, the Romantic canon, once highly restricted and once almost exclusively male, has seen a process of expansion, with until recently forgotten – but in their time extremely successful and critically respected – female authors now generally seen as being an important part of that canon. Nowadays, the successors to Bloom and Trilling, the two most successful contemporary period anthologies – Duncan Wu's *Romanticism: An Anthology* (in three editions, 1994, 1998, 2006) and Anne K. Mellor and Richard E. Matlak's *British Literature 1780–1830* (1996, its revisionist credentials signified by the absence of the words 'Romanticism' or 'Romantic' in its title) – feature women's poetry and prose heavily.

This evolution of the Romantic canon into fascinating new shapes since the early 1980s is a direct consequence of the recent critical willingness to re-inspect the literature of the later eighteenth and earlier nineteenth centuries to see if it might afford riches beyond the treasures found in Bloom and Trilling. 'It is', writes Marilyn Butler of the late Georgian literary scene around the turn of the nineteenth century, 'a splendid and splendidly varied body of literature,' and since the publication of *Romantics, Rebels and Reactionaries* in 1981 the old Romantic mainstream (poetry by six male poets, novels by one or two 'lady' novelists, and the work of three essayists,

Hazlitt, Lamb and De Quincey) has received a strong new tributary in the form of the aforesaid Landon, Robinson, Smith *et al.* At the same time, some figures who had previously hovered in what might be called the margins of Romanticism have moved nearer to its putative centre – the extraordinary literary family of William Godwin, Mary Wollstonecraft and Mary Shelley most notably.

New critical directions have also emerged in Romantic criticism. We have begun to realise that there was more to Romantic-era drama than the closet dramas of Byron and Shelley – *Manfred* and *Prometheus Unbound* and the like – that there was no prohibition on writing satire after the death of Alexander Pope, and that the 'peasant poets' Burns and Clare were only the meringue peak of a wealth of labourer-class poets. The post-Butler, post-McGann, historically-informed critical writing which has accomplished these small miracles has been accompanied by textual scholarship in the appearance of many important scholarly editions of Romantic-era writers published since the 1980s. Butler complemented her work as an 'historian-critic' with important editions of her favoured authors, with these textual labours in turn serving to spread the word about their critical importance. In the context of Romantic Studies in the second decade of the twenty-first century, it now seems remarkable that there was no scholarly edition of the collected works of Mary Wollstonecraft until Marilyn Butler and Janet Todd's 7-volume edition of 1989, of Mary Shelley's novels until 1996 (8 vols, gen. eds Nora Crook and Pamela Clemit), or of the works of Maria Edgeworth (Butler again, 12 vols, 1999–2003). (These are all published in Pickering and Chatto's multi-volume scholarly editions designed for university libraries, entirely admirable – if highly expensive – collections; this press has also issued major new scholarly editions of William Godwin, Charlotte Smith, Mary Robinson, Thomas De Quincey, and Leigh Hunt.)

Editorial work such as this has both led and complemented scholarly enquiry. Collections of women's writing such as Roger Lonsdale's *Eighteenth-Century Women Poets: An Anthology* (1990), Andrew Ashfield's *Romantic Women Poets 1770–1838: An Anthology* (1995) and Paula Feldman's *British Women Poets of the Romantic Era: An Anthology* (1997) go hand-in-hand with the critical writings of the likes of Anne Mellor or Stuart Curran (indeed, both of these latter critics have done significant editorial work on Romantic-era verse – Mellor's Longman anthology with Matlak, and Curran's (two) editions of the writings of Charlotte Smith). In recent years dozens of relatively neglected Romantic-era plays and novels have also been re-published and reinterpreted in editions such as *The Broadview Anthology of Romantic Drama*, ed. Jeffrey N. Cox and Michael Gamer (2003). Broadview, a Canadian press, has also championed hitherto obscure Romantic-era novels, especially by women, in re-publishing Mary

Robinson's *Walsingham, or the Pupil of Nature* (2003), Charlotte Smith's *The Old Manor House* (2002), Lady Morgan's *The Missionary* (2002), and many others.

Given how relatively under-historicised the Romantic period has been in much twentieth-century criticism it is unsurprising that the new critical history has produced work on many hitherto neglected aspects of late Georgian print culture. Romantic-era criticism has considered the importance of literatures outwith the mainstream canonical poets, engaged with the popular-cultural and ephemeral, and has spoken of writers and genres renowned, controversial and infamous in their day but since forgotten. There are studies of women poets and novelists (Gary Kelly's *Women, Writing, and Revolution, 1790–1827* (1993) among many others (see 'Gender Criticism' above)), children's writers (James Holt McGavran's *Romanticism and Children's Literature in Nineteenth-Century England* (1991)), the drama (Gillian Russell's *Women, Sociability and Theatre in Georgian London* (2007)), anti-Jacobin poets and novelists (M. O. Grenby's *The Anti-Jacobin Novel: British Conservatism and the French Revolution* (2001)), hitherto obscure horror fictions (E. J. Clery's *The Rise of Supernatural Fiction, 1762–1800* (1995)), artisan ultra-Radicals (Kevin Gilmartin's *Print Politics: The Press and Radical Opposition in Early Nineteenth-Century England* (1996)), labourer-class poets not called John Clare (John Goodridge's *Rural Life in Eighteenth-Century English Poetry* (1995) and Anne Janowitz's *Lyric and Labour in the Romantic Tradition* (1998)), satirists and parodists (Gary Dyer's *British Satire and the Politics of Style, 1789–1832* (1997), and Steven E. Jones's *Satire and Romanticism* (2000)), minstrelsy and balladry (Maureen N. McLane's *Balladeering, Minstrelsy, and the Making of British Romantic Poetry* (2009)), letter-writers (Mary A. Favret's *Romantic Correspondence: Women, Politics and the Fiction of Letters* (1993)), advocates of kindness to the 'brute creation' (David Perkins's *Romanticism and Animal Rights* (2003)), pornographers (Iain McCalman's *Radical Underworld: Prophets, Revolutionaries, and Pornographers in London, 1795–1840* (1988)), millenarianists (Tim Fulford's *Romanticism and Millenarianism* (2002)), advertisement writers (John Strachan's *Advertising and Satirical Culture in the Romantic Period* (2007)), writing about science (Richard Holmes's *The Age of Wonder: How the Romantic Generation Discovered the Beauty and Terror of Science* (2008)), accounts of the interface between graphic and prose satire (Marcus Wood's *Radical Satire and Print Culture 1790–1822* (1992)), disability and Romanticism (Andrew Elfenbein's 'Byron and Disability' (2001), an attempt to 'start a dialogue about disability in Romanticism more generally'), religious enthusiasm (John Mee's *Romanticism, Enthusiasm and Regulation: Poetics and the Policing of Culture in the Romantic period* (2003)), and atheism (Martin Priestman, *Romantic Atheism: Poetry and Freethought,*

1780–1830 (1999)). Romantic period print culture is a literary well showing few signs of running dry.

Despite the recent re-historicising of our perception of the literature – in the widest sense – of the Romantic era and the scholarly archaeology which has challenged, problematised and expanded our sense of the nature of Romanticism and its canon in recent years, there is as yet no sign of over-population in that canon. That great Romanticist Harold Bloom, in his controversial defence of literary greatness *The Western Canon* (1994), declared that 'the Canon … has become a choice amongst texts struggling with one another for survival'. It remains to be seen which of the authors and texts to have received a renewed lease of life since the 1980s will prosper and 'survive' in ensuing years and it also remains to be seen what new shapes Romanticism and the Romantic canon will take in the future. One lesson the recent history of Romanticism has taught us, however, is that some of these shapes will be new and all of them will be interesting.

Further Reading

M. H. Abrams, 'English Romanticism: The Spirit of the Age', in Northrop Frye (ed.), *Romanticism Reconsidered: Selected Papers from the English Institute* (1963), 26–72.
M. H. Abrams, *Natural Supernaturalism* (1971).
Andrew Ashfield (ed.), *Romantic Women Poets 1770–1838: An Anthology* (1995).
Irving Babbitt, *Rousseau and Romanticism* (1919).
Simon Bainbridge, *British Poetry and the Revolutionary and Napoleonic Wars: Visions of Conflict* (2003).
John Barrell, *The Idea of Landscape and the Sense of Place: An Approach to the Poetry of John Clare* (1972).
John Barrell, *The Infection of Thomas De Quincey. A Psychopathology of Imperialism* (1991).
Jonathan Bate, *Romantic Ecology: Wordsworth and the Environmental Tradition* (1991).
Jonathan Bate, *The Song of the Earth* (2000).
Andrew Bennett, *Romantic Poets and the Culture of Posterity* (1999).
Alan Bewell, *Romanticism and Colonial Disease* (2003).
Don H. Bialostosky, *Wordsworth, Dialogics, and the Practice of Criticism* (1992).
Harold Bloom, *Shelley's Myth-Making* (1959).
Harold Bloom, *The Visionary Company* (1961).
Harold Bloom, *The Anxiety of Influence* (1973).
Harold Bloom, *A Map of Misreading* (1975).
Harold Bloom, *Agon* (1982).
Harold Bloom, *The Western Canon* (1994).
Carol Bolton, *Writing the Empire: Robert Southey and Romantic Colonialism* (2007).
Fred Botting, *Making Monstrous: Frankenstein, Criticism, Theory* (1991).
Fred Botting, *Gothic* (1996).
Crane Brinton, *The Political Ideas of the English Romanticists* (1926).
Cleanth Brooks, *The Well Wrought Urn* (1947).
Marilyn Butler, *Peacock Displayed* (1979).

Marilyn Butler, *Romantics, Rebels and Reactionaries* (1981).

Terry Castle, *The Female Thermometer: Eighteenth-Century Culture and the Invention of the Uncanny* (1996).

E. J. Clery, *The Rise of Supernatural Fiction, 1762–1800* (1995).

Laurence Coupe, *The Green Studies Reader: From Romanticism to Ecocriticism* (2000).

Jeffrey N. Cox and Michael Gamer (eds), *The Broadview Anthology of Romantic Drama* (2003).

Philip Cox, *Gender, Genre, and the Romantic Poets: An Introduction* (1996).

Louis Crompton, *Byron and Greek Love: Homophobia in Nineteenth-Century England* (1985).

Stuart Curran, 'Women Readers, Women Writers', in S. Curran (ed.), *The Cambridge Companion to British Romanticism* (1993), 177–95.

Gary Dyer, *British Satire and the Politics of Style, 1789–1832* (1997).

Terry Eagleton, *Criticism and Ideology* (1976).

Andrew Elfenbein, 'Editor's Introduction: Byron and Disability', *European Romantic Review*, 12 (2001), 247–8.

David V. Erdman, *Blake, Prophet against Empire: A Poet's Interpretations of the History of his Own Times* (1954).

Joel Faflak, *Romantic Psychoanalysis: The Burden of the Mystery* (2008).

Mary A. Favret, *Romantic Correspondence: Women, Politics and the Fiction of Letters* (1993).

Paula Feldman, *British Women Poets of the Romantic Era: An Anthology* (1997).

Northrop Frye, *Fearful Symmetry* (1947).

Northrop Frye, *Anatomy of Criticism* (1957).

Tim Fulford, *Romantic Indians* (2006).

Tim Fulford (ed.), *Romanticism and Millenarianism* (2002).

H. W. Garrod, *Keats* (1926).

Sandra M. Gilbert and Susan Gubar, *The Madwoman in the Attic: The Woman Writer and the Nineteenth-century Imagination* (1979).

Kevin Gilmartin, *Print Politics: The Press and Radical Opposition in Early Nineteenth-Century England* (1996).

John Goodridge, *Rural Life in Eighteenth-Century English Poetry* (1995).

M. O. Grenby, *The Anti-Jacobin Novel: British Conservatism and the French Revolution* (2001).

George Haggerty, *Queer Gothic* (2006).

Paul Hammond, *Love Between Men* (1996).

D. W. Harding, 'The Theme of "The Ancient Mariner"', *Scrutiny*, 9 (1941), 334–42 (reprinted in K. Coburn (ed.), *Coleridge: A Collection of Critical Essays* (1967), 51–64).

Geoffrey H. Hartman, *Wordsworth's Poetry 1787–1814* (1964).

Christopher Z. Hobson, *Blake and Homosexuality* (2000).

Richard Holmes, *The Age of Wonder: How the Romantic Generation Discovered the Beauty and Terror of Science* (2008).

William Howlitt, *Homes and Haunts of the Most Eminent British Poets* (1847).

Kevin Hutchings, *Imagining Nature: Blake's Environmental Poetics* (2002).

Mary Jacobus, *Romanticism, Writing and Sexual Difference: Essays on The Prelude* (1989).

Rosemary Jackson, *Fantasy, the Literature of Subversion* (1981).

Anne F. Janowitz, *Lyric and Labour in the Romantic Tradition* (1998).

Anne Janowitz, *Woman Romantic Poets: Anna Barbauld and Mary Robinson* (2004).

Steven E. Jones, *Satire and Romanticism* (2000).

302 Criticism: Approaches, Theory, Practice

Alan Richardson, *British Romanticism and the Science of the Mind* (2001).

Christopher Ricks, *Keats and Embarrassment* (1974).

Nicholas Roe, *Wordsworth and Coleridge: The Radical Years* (1988).

Nicholas Roe, *Keats and History* (1995).

Nicholas Roe, *John Keats and the Culture of Dissent* (1999).

'Romanticism and Ecology', special issue of *Romantic Praxis* (http://www.rc.umd.edu/praxis/ecology/toc.html)

Gillian Russell, *Women, Sociability and Theatre in Georgian London* (2007).

Sharon Ruston, *Shelley and Vitality* (2005).

Eve Kosofsky Sedgwick, *Between Men: English Literature and Male Homosocial Desire* (1985).

David Simpson, *Wordsworth's Historical Imagination* (1987).

Clifford Siskin, *The Historicity of Romantic Discourse* (1988).

William St Clair, *The Reading Nation in the Romantic Period* (2004).

John Strachan, *Advertising and Satirical Culture in the Romantic Period* (2007).

Helen Vendler, *The Odes of John Keats* (1983).

Neil Vickers, *Coleridge and the Doctors* (2004).

Daniel P. Watkins, *Sexual Power in British Romantic Poetry* (1996).

Susan J. Wolfson, 'Keats and Gender Criticism', in Robert M. Ryan and Ronald A. Sharp (eds), *The Persistence of Poetry: Bicentennial Essays on Keats* (1988), 88–97.

Susan J. Wolfson, *Formal Charges: The Shaping of British Romanticism* (1997).

Marcus Wood, *Radical Satire and Print Culture 1790–1822* (1992).

Carl Woodring, *Politics in English Romantic Poetry* (1970).

Duncan Wu (ed.), *Romanticism. An Anthology* (1994, 1998, 2006).

Chronology and Necrology

Chronology

1789
Storming of the Bastille; outbreak of the French Revolution.
Washington inaugurated as first President of the United States.
Dr Richard Price's 'Nunc Dimittis' sermon, the 'Discourse on the Love of Our Country'.
William Blake, *Songs of Innocence*.
Olaudah Equiano, *The Interesting Narrative of the Life of Olaudah Equiano ... The African. Written by Himself*

1790
William Wordsworth makes first visit to France.
Edmund Burke, *Reflections on the Revolution in France*.
Immanuel Kant, *The Critique of Judgement*.
Helen Maria Williams, *Letters from France* (1790–6).
Mary Wollstonecraft, *A Vindication of the Rights of Men*.

1791
Ann Radcliffe, *The Romance of the Forest*.
Founding of the United Irishmen in Belfast.
William Gifford, *The Baviad*.
Tom Paine, *Rights of Man, Part 1*.
William Gifford, *The Baviad*.

1792
Abolition of the French monarchy; proclamation of the Republic.
Girondins take power in France.
P. B. Shelley born.
Samuel Rogers, *The Pleasures of Memory*.
Mary Wollstonecraft, *Vindication of the Rights of Woman*.

Necrology

Wolfgang Amadeus Mozart (1756–91), composer (cause of death much disputed).

Sir Joshua Reynolds (1723–92), artist and President of the Royal Academy (liver disease).

Chronology

1793

Execution of Louis XVI (January) and Marie Antoinette (October)

France declares war on Great Britain.

Overthrow of the Girondins; Robespierre's Jacobins assume power in France.

French Terror Begins.

John Clare born.

Felicia Hemans born.

Blake, *America. A Prophecy*.

William Godwin, *Enquiry Concerning Political Justice*.

Mary Robinson, *Modern Manners*.

Charlotte Smith, *The Emigrants*.

1794

Execution of Robespierre and the end of the Terror.

London Treason Trials.

Blake, *Songs of Innocence and Experience*.

Godwin, *Caleb Williams*.

Radcliffe, *The Mysteries of Udolpho*.

1795

John Keats born.

Hannah More, *The Sorrows of Yamba, or, The Negro Woman's Lamentation*.

1796

Edward Jenner introduces vaccination.

Robert Bage, *Hermsprong*.

S. T. Coleridge, *Poems on Various Subjects*.

M. G. Lewis, *The Monk. A Romance*.

John Stedman, *Narrative of a Five Years' Expedition against the Revolted Negroes of Surinam*.

Wollstonecraft, *Letters Written During a Short Residence in Sweden, Norway and Denmark*.

Ann Yearsley, *The Rural Lyre*.

1797

Anti-Jacobin; or, Weekly Examiner (1797–8) established.

Mary Shelley born.

Radcliffe, *The Italian*.

Robinson, *Walsingham; or, The Pupil of Nature*.

Necrology

Marie Antoinette (1755–93), Queen of France (guillotined).

Fletcher Christian (1764–93), chief mutineer of the *Bounty* (disputed).

Louis XVI (1754–93), King of France (guillotined).

Maximilien Robespierre (1758–94), French Jacobin (guillotined).

Louis XVII (1785–95), King of France (died in prison of misuse and/or tuberculosis).

Robert Burns (1759–96), poet (rheumatic heart disease).

Edmund Burke (1729–97), statesman and aesthetic theorist (stomach, in his own account, 'irrecoverably ruin'd').

Horace Walpole (1717–97), antiquarian, letter-writer and first of the Gothic novelists (pneumonia).

Chronology

1797
Robert Southey, *Poems*.
William Wordsworth, *The Borderers*.
William Wilberforce, *A Practical View of the Prevailing Religious System of Professed Christians*.

1798
Nelson's fleet wins the Battle of the Nile.
Uprising of the United Irishmen.
Joanna Baillie, *A Series of Plays* (first series).
Godwin, *Memoirs of the Author of A Vindication of the Rights of Woman*.
Wollstonecraft, *The Wrongs of Woman; or, Maria*.
Wordsworth and Coleridge, *Lyrical Ballads with a Few Other Poems*.

1799
Napoleon appointed First Consul of France.
William and Dorothy Wordsworth move to Dove Cottage in Grasmere.
Godwin, *St Leon*.
More, *Strictures on the Modern System of Female Education*.

1800
Robert Bloomfield, *The Farmer's Boy*.
Maria Edgeworth, *Castle Rackrent*.
Robinson, *Lyrical Tales*.
Wordsworth and Coleridge, *Lyrical Ballads, with Other Poems* (the two-volume edition); this includes Wordsworth, 'Preface' to the *Lyrical Ballads*.

1801
Union of Great Britain and Ireland.
Fall of William Pitt.
Thomas Jefferson becomes President of the United States.
Southey, *Thalaba the Destroyer*.

1802
Birth of Letitia Elizabeth Landon.
Peace of Amiens between Great Britain and France.
Baillie, *A Series of Plays* (second series).

Necrology

Mary Wollstonecraft (1759–97), novelist and feminist philosopher (complications arising from childbirth).

Theodore Wolfe Tone (1763–98), Irish revolutionary (committed suicide while awaiting execution).

George Washington (1731–99), American Revolutionary and first President of the United States (raging throat infection and fever).

William Cowper (1732–1800), poet and Calvinist ('a worn-out constitution' according to his friend William Hayley).
Mary Robinson (1757 or 1758–1800), actress, mistress of the Prince of Wales, later poet and novelist (dropsy of the lung (pulmonary oedema)).

Robert Bage (1730–1801), 'Jacobin' novelist and manufacturer (unestablished).

Erasmus Darwin (1731–1802), scientist and poet (lung infection).

Chronology

Wordsworth and Coleridge, *Lyrical Ballads, with Pastoral and other Poems* (includes expanded version of 1800 'Preface').

1803
Robert Emmet's uprising in Dublin.
War between Britain and France recommences.
Mary Hays, *Female Biography*.

1804
Napoleon becomes Emperor of France.
Pitt becomes Tory Prime Minister once more.

1805
Battle of Trafalgar.
William Hazlitt, *An Essay on the Principles of Human Action*.
Godwin, *Fleetwood; or, The New Man of Feeling*.
Amelia Opie, *Adeline Mowbray; or, The Mother and Daughter*.
Sir Walter Scott, *The Lay of the Last Minstrel*.
Southey, *Madoc*.

1806
The 'Ministry of All the Talents' coalition ministry formed.
Charlotte Dacre, *Zofolya; or, The Moor*.
Thomas Moore, *Epistles, Odes and Other Poems*.
Sydney Owenson, *The Wild Irish Girl*.

1807
Abolition of the slave trade.
Lord Byron, *Hours of Idleness*.
Lady Anne Hamilton, *The Epics of the Ton*.
Charles and Mary Lamb, *Tales from Shakespear*.

Necrology

Robert Emmet (1778–1803), Irish revolutionary (executed).

William Gilpin (1724–1804), artist, aesthetic theorist and clergyman (unestablished).
Joseph Priestley (1733–1804), scientist, theologian and political theorist (unestablished).
Immanuel Kant (1724–1804), Prussian philosopher (suffered physical and mental decline for years before his death).

Horatio, Lord Nelson (1758–1805), admiral and war hero (battle wounds).
Friedrich Schiller (1759–1805), poet, philosopher and dramatist (tuberculosis).

Charles James Fox (1749–1806), Whig statesman and orator (dropsy of the abdomen and legs).
William Pitt the Younger (1759–1806), Prime Minister (overwork and drink).
Charlotte Smith (1749–1806), poet and novelist (suffered from gout, pleurisy and arthritis).

John Newton (1725–1807), evangelist, hymn writer and quondam slaver captain (not clearly established).

Chronology

1807
Charles Robert Maturin, *Fatal Revenge, or, The Family of Montorio.*
Southey, *Letters from England.*
Wilberforce, *A Letter on the Abolition of the Slave Trade.*
Wordsworth, *Poems in Two Volumes.*

1808
Beethoven composes his fifth symphony.
The Examiner founded.
Moore, *Irish Melodies*, first number.

1809
Battle of Corunna.
Birth of Charles Darwin.
Launch of *Quarterly Review.*
More, *Coelebs in Search of a Wife.*

1810
Coleridge gives lectures on Shakespeare.
Baillie, *The Family Legend.*
George Crabbe, *The Borough.*

1811
George, Prince of Wales, becomes Prince Regent.
Luddites begin industrial sabotage.
P. B. Shelley expelled from Oxford for proselytising for atheism.
Jane Austen, *Sense and Sensibility.*
Mary Brunton, *Self-Control.*
Mary Tighe, *Psyche, and Other Poems.*

1812
Lord Liverpool becomes Tory Prime Minister.
Byron, *Childe Harold*, canto 1.

1813
Leigh Hunt imprisoned for libelling the Prince Regent, later George IV.
Southey appointed Poet Laureate.
Austen, *Pride and Prejudice.*
Coleridge, *Remorse.*
Byron, *The Giaour. A Fragment of a Turkish Tale.*
James Hogg, *The Queen's Wake.*
P. B. Shelley, *Queen Mab.*

Necrology

Sir John Moore (1761–1809), lieutenant general in the Peninsular War (wounds sustained at Corunna).

Peter Beckford (*c.*1740–1811), fox-hunter and sports writer (unknown).

Spencer Perceval (1762–1812), Tory Prime Minister (murdered).

Sir William Erskine (1770–1813), lieutenant-general of the Duke of Wellington's army in the Peninsular War and lunatic (suicide).

Chronology

1814
Napoleon abdicates after the fall of Paris and is exiled to the island of Elba.
New Monthly Magazine established.
Austen, *Mansfield Park*.
Byron, *The Corsair*.
Scott, *Waverley; or, 'Tis Sixty Years Since*.
Wordsworth, *The Excursion*.

1815
Napoleon returns from exile in the so-called 'Hundred Days'.
Wellington and allies defeat Napoleon at the Battle of Waterloo.
Byron marries Annabella Milbanke.
Austen, *Emma*.
Byron, *Hebrew Melodies*.
Henry Hart Milman, *Fazio, A Tragedy*.
Scott, *Guy Mannering*.
Wordsworth, *Poems*.

1816
Riot at Spa Fields.
Byron leaves England for the final time.
Shelley marries Mary Wollstonecraft Godwin.
Byron, *Childe Harold*, canto III.
Coleridge, *Christabel; Kubla Khan: A Vision; The Pains of Sleep*.
Hogg, *The Poetic Mirror; or, The Living Bards of Britain*.
Leigh Hunt, *The Story of Rimini*.
Lady Caroline Lamb, *Glenarvon*.
Charles Robert Maturin, *Bertram; or, The Castle of St Aldobrand*.
P. B. Shelley, *Alastor; or, The Spirit of Solitude and Other Poems*.

1817
Founding of *Blackwood's Edinburgh Magazine*.
Austen, *Northanger Abbey* and *Persuasion*.
Byron, *Manfred*.
Coleridge, *Biographia Literaria; or, Biographical Sketches of my Literary Life and Opinions*.
Coleridge, *Sybilline Leaves*.
Hazlitt and Hunt, *The Round Table*.
Hazlitt, *Characters of Shakespear's Plays*.

Necrology

Joanna Southcott (1750–1814), prophet and religious maniac (ovarian dropsy).
Thomas Spence (1750–1814), satirist and luminary of the London Corresponding Society (bowel complaint).

Emma, Lady Hamilton (1765–1815), celebrity and mistress of Lord Nelson (probably liver disease).

Harriet Shelley (1795–1816), first wife of the poet (suicide).
R. B. Sheridan (1751–1816), dramatist and politician (health declined for several years before his demise).

Jane Austen (1775–1817), novelist (disputed; possibly Addison's disease (a hormonal condition) or Hodgkin's disease (a cancer of the blood)).
Princess Charlotte Augusta (1796–1817), estranged daughter of the Prince Regent, later George IV, and heir to the British crown (complications arising from childbirth).

Chronology

1817
John Keats, *Poems*.
Maturin, *Manuel*.
Mary and P. B. Shelley, *History of a Six Weeks' Tour through a Part of France, Switzerland, Germany and Holland*.
P. B. Shelley, *The Revolt of Islam*.

1818
'Z' (J. G. Lockhart) attacks Keats in *Blackwood's*.
Thomas Bowdler, *Family Shakespeare*.
Byron, *Beppo*.
Keats, *Endymion: A Poetic Romance*.
Moore, *The Fudge Family in Paris*.
Thomas Love Peacock, *Nightmare Abbey*.
Mary Shelley, *Frankenstein*.
Scott, *Rob Roy*.

1819
Birth of Princess Victoria.
'Peterloo' Massacre at Manchester.
Byron, *Don Juan* (1819–24).
William Hone, *The Political House that Jack Built*.
John Polidori, 'The Vampyre'.
Scott, *Ivanhoe*.
P. B. Shelley, *The Cenci. A Tragedy*.
Wordsworth, *Peter Bell. A Tale in Verse*.
John Hamilton Reynolds, *Peter Bell: A Lyrical Ballad*.
P. B. Shelley, *Peter Bell the Third*.

1820
The Cato Street Conspiracy.
John Clare, *Poems Descriptive of Rural Life and Scenery*.
Keats, *Lamia, Isabella, The Eve of St Agnes, and Other Poems*.
Maturin, *Melmoth the Wanderer*.
P. B. Shelley, *Prometheus Unbound*.

1821
Greek War of Independence begins.
Byron, *Sardanapalus, The Two Foscari, Cain*.
'Barry Cornwall' (B. W. Proctor), *Mirandola, A Tragedy*.
Pierce Egan, *Life in London*.
Hazlitt, *Table-Talk; or, Original Essays*.

Necrology

1818
Mary Brunton (1778–1818), novelist (complications arising from delivering a still-born child).

1819
John Wolcot ('Peter Pindar') (1738–1819), satirist (old age).

1820
George III (1738–1820), King of Great Britain (porphyria and general decrepitude).
Arthur Thistlewood (1774–1820), English revolutionary and leader of the Cato Street conspiracy (executed).

1821
Queen Caroline (1768–1821), estranged wife of George IV (probably stomach cancer, though poison according to some).
Napoleon Bonaparte (1769–1821), general and Emperor of France (probably stomach cancer, though poison according to some).

Chronology

P. B. Shelley, *Adonais. An Elegy on the Death of John Keats.*
Southey, *A Vision of Judgement.*

1822

Byron, *The Vision of Judgment.*
Thomas De Quincey, *Confessions of an English Opium Eater.*
P. B. Shelley, *Hellas.*
Wordsworth, *A Description of the Scenery of the Lakes in the North of England.*

1823

Charles Lamb, *Essays of Elia.*
William Hazlitt, *Liber Amoris; or, The New Pygmalion.*
Mary Shelley, *Valperga, or, The Life and Adventures of Castruccio, Prince of Lucca.*

1824

Hogg, *The Private Memoirs and Confessions of a Justified Sinner.*
Letitia Elizabeth Landon, *The Improvisatrice, and Other Poems.*
Scott, *Redgauntlet.*

1825

Stockton and Darlington railway opened.
Hazlitt, *The Spirit of the Age.*
Felicia Hemans, *The Forest Sanctuary, and Other Poems.*

1826

University College, London, founded.
Mary Shelley, *The Last Man.*

1827

Lord Liverpool resigns as Prime Minister; his successor George Canning dies after less than four months in office.
Clare, *Shepherd's Calendar.*

Necrology

John Keats (1795–1821), poet (consumption (tuberculosis)).
John Polidori (1795–1821), physician to Lord Byron and author of *The Vampyre* (suicide).
John Scott (1783–1821), editor of the *London Magazine* (killed in a duel with Jonathan Christie, friend of J. G. Lockhart of *Blackwood's Edinburgh Magazine*).

Viscount Castlereagh (1769–1822), politician (suicide).
P. B. Shelley (1792–1822), poet (drowning).

Robert Bloomfield (1766–1823), 'peasant poet' ('dying neglected', in the words of John Clare, and in poverty).
Ann Radcliffe (1764–1823), Gothic novelist (pneumonia).

Lord Byron (1788–1824), poet (fever).
The Reverend C. R. Maturin (1780–1824), Irish novelist and dramatist (unestablished).

Anna Laetitia Barbauld (1743–1825), poet and editor (asthma).
Henry Fuseli (1741–1825), painter and friend of William Blake (not clearly established).

William Gifford (1756–1826), satirist and editor of the *Anti-Jacobin* and the *Quarterly Review* (he retired from the *Quarterly Review* in 1824 on the grounds of failing health).

William Blake (1757–1827), poet and artist (described himself as suffering from 'shivering fit[s]' and 'ague' in his last days).

Chronology

1827
Hemans, *Records of Woman*.
Landon, *The Golden Violet, and Other Poems*.

1828
Wellington becomes Tory Prime Minister.

1829
Passing of Catholic Emancipation Act.

1830
Accession of William IV.
July Revolution in France.
Resignation of Wellington as Prime Minister.
Charles Grey, the Second Earl Grey, becomes Whig Prime Minister.
Hemans, *Songs of the Affections, with Other Poems*.

1831
Defeat of the first and second Reform Bills.
Darwin's voyage on HMS *Beagle* begins.
Mary Prince, *The History of Mary Prince, A West Indian Slave*.

1832
Passing of the Great Reform Act

Necrology

George Canning (1770–1827), satirist of the *Anti-Jacobin* and Prime Minister (suffered from gout and inflammation of the liver and lungs).

Lady Caroline Lamb (1785–1828), novelist and spurned mistress of Lord Byron (dropsy).

Sir Humphrey Davy (1778–1829), chemist, inventor and author (series of strokes).

George IV (1762–1830), King of Great Britain (suffered from gout, arteriosclerosis, and bladder inflammation).
William Hazlitt (1778–1830), critic, philosopher and essayist (probably cancer of the stomach).

William Roscoe (1753–1831), historian and patron of the arts (influenza).

Sir Walter Scott (1771–1832), novelist, antiquarian and poet (series of strokes).
Johann Wolfgang von Goethe (1749–1832), novelist, dramatist and poet (pneumonia and heart attack).

Index

Page numbers in *italics* denotes an illustration.

protest, political 18, 22–3, 85–91
  see also radicalism
Protestant Orange Order 53
psychoanalysis 280–1, 283
psychological criticism
  and Gothic novel 283–4
Pugin, Augustus 196
  Contrasts 196
Punter, David 203
  The Literature of Terror 283–4

Quarterly Review 64, 77, 230, 236, 237–8,
  240, 242, 246
queer studies 295–6
Quintuple Alliance 23

Radcliffe, Ann 177, 199, 200, 202, 223
  The Italian 177, 199, 202
  The Mysteries of Udolpho 199
  'On the Supernatural in Poetry' 202–3
  The Romance of the Forest 199, 201
radicalism 18, 22–3, 93, 215
  and the French Revolution 85–8
  post-Napoleonic 88–91
  see also 'Jacobin' novel
railways 30
Ramsay, Allan 189
Ransom, John Crowe 273
rationalism 133–4
Read, Herbert 270
'real language of men' 231, 264
reception theory 280
Reeve, Clara 201–2, 213
Reform Act (1832) 91
Regency, The 21, 55
  see also Prince Regent
Reid, Ian
  *Wordsworth and the Formation of English
    Studies* 269
Reid, William Hamilton 208
Reiss, Daniel 163
religion 92–102
reviews 235–8
Revolutionary Controversy 17–18, 236
Revolutionary Wars 16, 18, 18–20
Reynolds, Sir Joshua 133, 179, 227
  Discourses 179
Ricardo, David 49
Rich, Adrienne 292
Richards, I. A. 273, 275
  Coleridge on Imagination 273, 274
Richardson, Alan 280, 282
Richardson, Samuel 199, 212
  Clarissa 217
Richmond, Reverend Legh 114–15
  The Negro Servant 115–16
Ricks, Christopher 274
Roberts, Adam 167
Robespierre, Maximilien 16, 215
Robinson, Mary 2, 140–4, 218–20, 294–5
  Ainsi va le Monde 141
  Angelina 220
  and Della Cruscans 140–1

and fashion 62
and French Revolution 253–4
'The Gamester' 61–2
'The Haunted Beach' 142, 143
and the Lake Poets 142–4
A Letter to the Women of England 105,
  219
'A London Summer Morning' 141–2
Lyrical Tales 142, 295
Modern Manners 60, 253
Nobody 61
novels written by 219–20
'Ode to Della Crusca' 141
personal life and acting career 140–1,
  219
and politics 141–2
pseudonyms 141, 143, 253
Sappho and Phaon 141
and satire 253–4
'To the Poet Coleridge' 142, 143
Roe, Nicholas 157, 274, 285, 289
Rogers, Samuel 266
Romantic poets
  reception of and Victorian responses to
    263–9
Romanticism
  definition and features of 1–8
  expansion of canon 297–300
  historical definitions and
    conceptualisations of 8–14
  influence 1
  Modernism's critique 270–2
  plurality of 1
Rossini, Gioachino 80, 82
Rousseau, Jean-Jacques 15, 217
Ruskin, John 196
  Lectures on Art 5–6
Russell, Bertrand 146
Russell, Gillian 299
Russell, Lord John 26
Ruston, Sharon 282
Rutgers University 269

St Albans, Duchess of (Harriot Beauclerk)
  41
St Clair, William 280
Saintsbury, George 10
satire 67, 248–62, 298
  and *Anti-Jacobin* 256–7
  and Byron 249, 259–61
  on the Lake Poets 257–9
  political 250–2
  Romantic-era verse 248–50
  socio-political 25–6
  on women and by women 252–4
Schelling, Felix 10
Schlegel, August Wilhelm von 7
Schlegel, Friedrich von 7, 9
science 74–9
Scott, Geoffrey 10
Scott, John 245
Scott, Sir Walter 29, 81, 136, 161, 197, 202,
  214, 217, 220–2